Buddhist-Muslim Relations in a Theravada World

Iselin Frydenlund · Michael Jerryson
Editors

Buddhist-Muslim Relations in a Theravada World

Editors
Iselin Frydenlund
MF Norwegian School of Theology,
Religion and Society
Oslo, Norway

Michael Jerryson
Department of Philosophy
and Religious Studies
Youngstown State University
Youngstown, OH, USA

ISBN 978-981-32-9886-6   ISBN 978-981-32-9884-2   (eBook)
https://doi.org/10.1007/978-981-32-9884-2

© The Editor(s) (if applicable) and The Author(s), under exclusive license to Springer
Nature Singapore Pte Ltd. 2020
This work is subject to copyright. All rights are solely and exclusively licensed by the
Publisher, whether the whole or part of the material is concerned, specifically the rights
of translation, reprinting, reuse of illustrations, recitation, broadcasting, reproduction
on microfilms or in any other physical way, and transmission or information storage and
retrieval, electronic adaptation, computer software, or by similar or dissimilar methodology
now known or hereafter developed.
The use of general descriptive names, registered names, trademarks, service marks, etc. in this
publication does not imply, even in the absence of a specific statement, that such names are
exempt from the relevant protective laws and regulations and therefore free for general use.
The publisher, the authors and the editors are safe to assume that the advice and
information in this book are believed to be true and accurate at the date of publication.
Neither the publisher nor the authors or the editors give a warranty, expressed or implied,
with respect to the material contained herein or for any errors or omissions that may have
been made. The publisher remains neutral with regard to jurisdictional claims in published
maps and institutional affiliations.

Cover image: © Lewis Inman/Alamy Stock Photo

This Palgrave Macmillan imprint is published by the registered company Springer Nature
Singapore Pte Ltd.
The registered company address is: 152 Beach Road, #21-01/04 Gateway East, Singapore
189721, Singapore

Foreword

In a recent issue of *The New York Times Style Magazine,* there was an article about Myanmar. But rather than simply using the country as a backdrop to showcase haute couture, the thrust of the article—"What Happened Here"—was actually about the ethics of visiting the country formerly known as Burma.[1] In short, the author grappled with the historical and moral issues of visiting a country that had recently committed genocide. In addressing these questions, the author did not mince words about what had happened: Bamar and Rakhine Buddhists had burned, killed, raped and ethnically cleansed nearly a million Rohingya Muslims.

> In August 2017, Myanmar initiated a round of ethnic slaughter, mass gang rape and the burning and razing of hundreds of villages. Despite the installation of a nominally democratic government headed by the Nobel Peace Prize laureate Daw Aung San Suu Kyi the previous year, hundreds of thousands of Rohingya Muslims were driven from their homes by Myanmar's military forces and Buddhist mobs...[who] initiate[d] a massive genocidal campaign. Aung San Suu Kyi, who is the country's de facto leader but does not control the military, has been criticized for her inaction during the crisis and for her refusal to call it ethnic cleansing. That is Myanmar's truth, and everyone from the military to government officials has doggedly stuck to it.[2]

[1] Rafia Zakaria, "What Happened Here," *The New York Times Style Magazine* (May 19, 2019): 128–135.

[2] Zakaria, "What Happened Here," 131.

Sadly, however, it is not only the government and people of Myanmar who have their own "truth" about the history of Buddhist–Muslim interaction across Asia. Rather, all too often this complicated thousand-year history is reduced to the predictable stereotypes: Buddhists good, Muslims bad.

Indeed, as I have personally experienced, it is precisely this Manichean dichotomy that shapes the conventional understanding about the meeting of Buddhists and Muslims. Ten years ago, namely, I wrote a book about Buddhist–Muslim interaction on the Silk Road. And although the work was generally well received by the academic community—including winning three book awards—there were others who felt that the book made several grave historical mistakes. Or in other words, I was challenging stereotypes and thereby not telling the truth.

In particular, many refused to believe my historical argument that the Muslim assault on Nalanda monastery in the thirteenth century did not signal the end of the Dharma in India.[3] One exasperated online critic, for example, exclaimed, "next, we'll find out einstein himself was a devout muslim. Must be humiliating for a scholar to write such things only because Saudi money pays for his bills."[4] Someone else named "Jacques" similarly proclaimed, "Who pays this 'distinguished professor' to utter such stupidities. When the British got to India Buddhism had been wiped out for more than five centuries. It was barely surviving in Nepal." And "D. Rarest Pepe" fumed, "What a pile of tripe! Buddhism doesn't or hardly exists in India today. It exists in Burma and Thailand and is hanging on in Sri Lanka. There is only one reason why it has all but vanished from India and this author's denials won't change that fact. It's the same reason why it has vanished from Afghanistan."

But my historical re-evaluation of Nalanda's "destruction" and the larger history of Buddhist–Muslim interaction in South Asia was not the only issue with which readers took umbrage. Others focused on how I problematized the Taliban's destruction of the Bamiyan Buddhas.[5]

---

[3]Johan Elverskog, *Buddhism and Islam on the Silk Road* (Philadelphia: University of Pennsylvania Press, 2010), 1–3.

[4]All the comments in this paragraph are in response to an excerpt of my book published in *Tricycle: The Buddhist Review* ("When the Monks Met the Muslims," Spring 2018), which was part of a series of articles on the Rohingya crisis, https://tricycle.org/magazine/monks-met-muslims/, accessed April 11, 2018.

[5]An excellent study on the context and meaning of the Taliban's destruction of the Bamiyan Buddhas is Finbarr Barry Flood's "Between Cult and Culture: Bamiyan, Iconoclasm, and the Museum," *The Art Bulletin* 84, 4 (2002): 641–659.

This wanton act of destruction not only reenacted the story of Nalanda, but also reaffirmed all of our stereotypes. What better image could one have to encapsulate Buddhist-Muslim history than a group of fanatical Muslim militants senselessly mauling the peaceful and passive representations of the Buddha in the name of Islam? Which is invariably how it was presented in the international media. Little thought, however, was given to the possible historical contingencies shaping this event; much less the fact that the statues had till then somehow survived thirteen-hundred years of Muslim rule. This was another of those inconvenient facts that somehow muddied the story. It was perhaps better not to think about it since, if one did, it opened the door for the whole messy reality of history to come rushing in, and this could very well challenge, possibly even shatter, the conventional narrative that has been told these last one thousand years.[6]

Not everyone was willing to take such a nuanced historiographical approach, however.

Ramachandra B. Abhyankaron, for example, responded to this idea with the claim that "[p]erhaps Islam lacked the technology to destroy the Bamiyan Buddhas. The Taliban used modern tanks to destroy the Bamiyan Buddhas. The pyramids in Egypt also stand because Islam lacked the technology to destroy those."[7] An argument seconded by Rodney Hatch, who wrote, "Before the Taliban finished the job called for by Islam, the Bamiyan statues stood in body only. This was because there was no dynamite centuries ago when their faces were hacked off by zealots." And someone else with the moniker "MAn C." summed it all up with the pithy statement: "Buddhism meets Islam on the silk road = No more Buddhism on silk road." S/he then further expounded:

> the author asks 'how had the Bamiyan Buddha statues survived thirteen hundred years of Muslim rule?' simple answer–they did not have artillery strong enough to destroy them. The author conveniently ignores that thousands of buddhist temples were razed, millions of Buddhists killed/

---

[6]Elverskog, *Buddhism and Islam on the Silk Road*, 4.

[7]On the actual Muslim view of the pyramids, see Carl Ernst, "Admiring the Works of the Ancients: The Ellora Temples as Viewed by Indo-Muslim Authors," in *Beyond Turk and Hindu: Rethinking Religious Identities in Islamicate South Asia*, eds. David Gilmartin and Bruce B. Lawrence (Gainesville: University of Florida Press, 2000), 98–120.

viii   FOREWORD

converted, and the genocide committed against Buddhism eradicated their presence permanently. The author is desperately trying to spin fanciful tails [*sic*].[8]

Of course, on one level it is perhaps easy to dismiss these comments as the Islamophobic rantings of uneducated trolls.

But as with the case of Myanmar's "truths," by doing so, we too easily overlook and dismiss the powerful paradigms that underlie most people's view of Buddhist–Muslim interaction. Indeed, in the popular imagination there are probably no two traditions more different than Buddhism and Islam. One is synonymous with peace, tranquility and introspection, the other with violence, chaos and blind faith. One conjures up images of Himalayan hermitages and Japanese rock gardens, the other primitive and dirty villages with burqa-clad women. And while Buddhism is seen as modern, its teachings even in tune with the most cutting-edge science, Islam is backward, its teachings and punishments redolent of the Middle Ages. Yet as with the whole enterprise of orientalism and the construction of Islam as innately evil, this image of Buddhism as the perfect spirituality for the modern age is also a Western fantasy, or construction, of the nineteenth century.[9] And even though scholars have spent decades dismantling both of these popular misconceptualizations, they still sadly persist.

In fact, all too often the inordinately complicated thousand year history of these two religions interacting over the length and breadth of Asia—and their continuing interaction there today—is all too often boiled down into one image: Muslims destroying Buddhism, which for many is perfectly encapsulated in the story of Nalanda monastery; namely, the savagery was so great, it signaled the end of the Dharma in India. And this powerful story has been told countless times. Today it is ubiquitous, being found in everything from scholarly monographs to travel brochures. Indeed, by its sheer pervasiveness, this one episode has in many ways come to encapsulate and symbolize the entire

---

[8]These "reviews" can be found on Amazon, https://www.amazon.com/Buddhism-Islam-Silk-Road-Encounters/product-reviews/0812222598/, accessed April 7, 2018.

[9]On the origin of these stereotypes in the scholarship of the nineteenth century, see Tomoko Masuzawa, *The Invention of World Religions* (Chicago: University of Chicago Press, 2005), 121–146, 179–180.

Fig. 1 Mural in a Thai Buddhist monastery of "The ruin of Nalanta University which was destroyed by the Muslim militant in 1700 B.E." (Chiang Mai, 2010. Author photo)

thirteen-hundred-year history of Buddhist–Muslim interaction. And on account of this, whenever the topic of Buddhism and Islam is ever mentioned, it almost invariably revolves around the Muslim destruction of the Dharma (Fig. 1).[10]

Indeed, the story of Nalanda's destruction functions not only as a perfect synecdoche for the entirety of Buddhist–Muslim history, but also readily re-affirms all of our stereotypes.

---

[10]This is the common view in both popular and academic literature. See, for example, Lawrence Sutin, *All is Change: The Two Thousand-Year Journey of Buddhism to the West* (New York: Little, Brown and Company, 2006), 45–46; and Jerry H. Bentley, *Old World Encounters: Cross-Cultural Encounters and Exchanges in Pre-Modern Times* (New York: Oxford University Press, 1993), 131–133.

x   FOREWORD

It is therefore perhaps not surprising that many people pushed back when I challenged this comforting and conventional narrative. Yet, what is important to recognize is that I am far from the first person to unearth this truth. Rather, more than forty years ago, Marshall Hodgson made the same observation regarding the history of Nalanda monastery:

> The record of the massacre of one monastery in Bengal, combined with the inherited Christian conception of Muslims as the devotees of the sword has yielded the widely repeated statement that the Muslims violently "destroyed" Buddhism in India. Muslims were not friendly to it, but there is no evidence that they simply killed off all the Buddhists, or even all the monks. It will take much active revision before such assessments of the role of Islam, based largely on unexamined preconceptions, are eliminated even from educated mentalities.[11]

Yet, as pointed out by William Dalrymple in his review of Charles Allen's *The Buddha and the Sahibs*, such untruths—sadly and dangerously—still persist.

> What is perhaps especially valuable about *The Buddha and the Sahibs* is Allen's gentle reminder of exactly how and why Buddhism died out in the land of its birth. Every child in India knows that when the Muslims first came to India that they desecrated temples and smashed idols. But what is conveniently forgotten is that during the Hindu revival at the end of the first millennium AD, many Hindu rulers had behaved in a similar fashion to the Buddhists.
>
> It was because of this persecution, several centuries before the arrival of Islam that the philosophy of the Buddha, once a serious rival to Hinduism, virtually disappeared from India: Harsha Deva, a single Kashmiri raja, for example boasted that he had destroyed no less than 4000 Buddhist shrines. Another raja, Sasanka of Bengal, went to Bodh Gaya, sacked the monastery and cut down the tree of wisdom under which the Buddha had received enlightenment.
>
> According to Buddhist tradition, Sasanka's "body produced sores and his flesh quickly rotted off and after a short while he died." At a time when Islamaphobia is becoming endemic in both India and the west, and when a far-right Hindu government is doing its best to terrorise India's Muslim

---

[11]Marshall G. S. Hodgson, *The Venture of Islam, Volume 2: The Expansion of Islam in the Middle Periods* (Chicago, University of Chicago Press, 1977), 557.

minority, the story of how an earlier phase of militant Hinduism violently rooted out Indian Buddhism is an important and worrying precedent, and one that needs very badly to be told, and remembered.[12]

But as the comments quoted above regarding my own work readily attest—much less the recent re-election of Narendra Modi as India's prime minister—that has obviously not happened.

And what is remarkable to think about is that this distorted history even persists at a time when contrary to all our stereotypical assumptions Buddhists have actually carried out a genocide against Muslims. A fact so well known that it is even used to frame a fashion shoot in a high-end magazine! Yet even so, the stereotypes persist: Buddhists good, Muslims bad. Indeed, is it such "unexamined preconceptions" that explain the current global inaction about the genocide in Myanmar? Should we simply accept "Myanmar's truth"?

To begin to get to the truth of the matter, we clearly need a better understanding about the realities of Buddhist–Muslim interaction. We need scholarship that looks at these complicated realities truthfully, which is precisely what this book does. It offers us not only detail rich historical surveys of Buddhist–Muslim interaction in Myanmar, Thailand and Sri Lanka, but also four fascinating and nuanced anthropological studies of Buddhist–Muslim interaction in the contemporary Theravada world. And as such, this work offers us a range of new ways to think about the little understood dynamics of Buddhist–Muslim exchange across time and space. In short, this excellent collection of essays gives us new stories about Buddhist–Muslim interaction that are built on fact and wisdom, not fantasy and hatred, and thus offer us a possible way forward.

Dallas, US   Johan Elverskog

Johan Elverskog is Dedman Family Distinguished Professor and Chair of Religious Studies, at Southern Methodist University, US.

---

[12]William Dalrymple, "When Buddha Was Sacked," *The Guardian* (September 28, 2002), https://www.theguardian.com/books/2002/sep/28/featuresreviews.guardianreview, accessed April 3, 2018.

Acknowledgements

We would like to thank the Peace Research Institute Oslo (PRIO) and Norwegian Centre for Conflict Resolution (NOREF) who provided backing in the early phase of the project, through financial support to a seminar series held at PRIO in 2015 on Buddhism and conflict in contemporary Asia. Also, we would like to show our gratitude to the American Association for Asian Studies (AAS) for their financial support to a panel we organized called "Buddhist–Muslim Interactions in South and Southeast Asia," at the AAS Annual Conference in Seattle 2016. A special thanks to Georgia Kasamias for excellent editorial assistance. Finally, we would like to express our deepest gratitude to our universities, Youngstown State University, US, and MF Norwegian School of Theology, Religion and Society for their support throughout the process.

CONTENTS

**1 An Introduction: Buddhist–Muslim Relations
    in a Theravada World**   1
Iselin Frydenlund and Michael Jerryson

Part I   Historical Country Overviews

**2 Historical Threads of Buddhist–Muslim Relations
    in Sri Lanka**   25
Rohan Bastin and Premakumara de Silva

3 Buddhist–Muslim Interactions in Burma/Myanmar   63
Matthew J. Walton

4 Buddhist–Muslim Dynamics in Siam/Thailand   101
Raymond Scupin and Christopher M. Joll

Part II   Case Studies: Particular Moments of Interaction

**5 Sri Lanka's Anti-Muslim Movement and Muslim
    Responses: How Were They Gendered?**   139
Farzana Haniffa

xv

6 A Corpse Necessitates Disentangled Relationships: Boundary Transgression and Boundary-Making in a Buddhist-Muslim Village in Southern Thailand
Ryoko Nishii
169

7 The Role of Myth in Anti-Muslim Buddhist Nationalism in Myanmar
Nyi Nyi Kyaw
197

8 Arakanese Chittagong Became Mughal Islamabad: Buddhist–Muslim Relationship in Chittagong (Chottrogram), Bangladesh
D. Mitra Barua
227

Part III Concluding Thoughts

9 Buddhists, Muslims and the Construction of Difference
Michael Jerryson and Iselin Frydenlund
263

Index
299

Notes on Contributors

D. Mitra Barua is an Annette and Hugh Gragg postdoctoral fellow at Rice University's Chao Center for Asian Studies. He examines the contested history of the North Bay of Bengal region crisscrossed by three national boundaries: India, Bangladesh and Myanmar. With a focus on the Buddhist–Muslim relationship in the Chittagong-Rakhine area, he investigates how a linguistically diverse, culturally tolerant and religiously syncretic society has been plagued by ethno-religious bigotry, intolerance and violence. This investigation is an extension of Mitra's developing monograph tentatively entitled *Staging Bengali Buddhism: Chittagong Buddhists in Muslim Bangladesh, Hindu India and Buddhist Myanmar.*

Rohan Bastin teaches Anthropology at Deakin University in Australia. He has conducted research in Sri Lanka principally on religion and ethnic conflict since 1984 and worked various parts of the Eastern, North Western, Western and Southern Provinces of the island. He is the author of *The Domain of Constant Excess: Plural Worship at the Munnesvaram Temples in Sri Lanka* (Berghahn Books, 2002) and is currently writing a monograph on civil war with special reference to the Sri Lankan civil war while leading a research team of Australian and Sri Lankan researchers studying post-conflict religion and society.

Premakumara de Silva is a professor at the Department of Sociology, University of Colombo, Sri Lanka. His research interests include political use of religion and ritual, pilgrimage, nationalism, local democracy, youth culture, Indigenous study, grass-root development, Social Welfare

xvii

and globalization. He has published several books in English and local languages, including number of book chapters and over forty articles on his credit. His most recent work (2017) is a co-authored book chapter with Rohan Bastin "Military Tourism as a State-effect in the Sri Lankan civil war" In *Military Pilgrimage and Battlefield Tourism* (eds.) John Eade and Mario Katic. Currently, he is the Dean of the Faculty of Arts and an honorary research professor of Anthropology at Deakin University in Australia.

Iselin Frydenlund holds a Ph.D. in the History of Religions from the University of Oslo and is professor of Religious Studies and Director of MF CASR at MF Norwegian School of Theology, Religion and Society. She has published numerous articles, book chapters and policy reports on Buddhism, politics and violence in Sri Lanka and Myanmar. She has previously served as a senior researcher at the Peace Research Institute Oslo (PRIO) and is currently an advisor to the Norwegian Centre for Human Rights, University of Oslo. She has also been engaged in Buddhist dialogue work in Asia concerning religious minorities in Buddhist majority states.

Farzana Haniffa received her Ph.D. in Anthropology from Columbia University in 2007. Her research and activist interests since 1999 have concentrated on the social and political history of Muslim communities and on gender politics in Sri Lanka. She has published on Islamic reform movements, on minority involvement in electoral politics and the peace process, and the post-war mobilizing of anti-Muslim rhetoric. Haniffa's feminist writings have looked at women in the Islamic piety movement, militarization and masculinity among eastern Muslim communities, and more recently, the gendered nature of anti-Muslim sentiment. In 2016, Haniffa was appointed by the Prime Minister's Office to the Consultation Task Force on Reconciliation Mechanisms. In 2016, Haniffa was also a visiting research fellow at the Leibniz Zentrum Moderner Orient in Berlin. Haniffa serves on the Social Scientists' Association's management council and on the Director Boards of the Law and Society Trust and the Ibn Battuta Foundation.

Michael Jerryson is a professor of Religious Studies at Youngstown State University. His research interests pertain to religion and identity, particularly with regard to gender, race and class. He is the author of *Buddhist Fury: Religion and Violence in Southern Thailand* (2011), and he has co-edited *The Oxford Handbook of Religion and Violence* (2013) and *Buddhist Warfare* (2010). His latest publication is *If You Meet the Buddha on the Road: Buddhism, Politics, and Violence* (2018), and he is working on a forthcoming edited volume, tentatively entitled: *Religious Violence Today: Faith and Conflict in the Modern World.*

Christopher M. Joll is a New Zealand anthropologist whose primary ethnographic subjects since 2005 have been Thailand's Muslim minority. His first monograph, *Muslim Merit-Making in Thailand's Far-South* (Springer, 2011), was based on 10 years living and working among bilingual Malays. Since 2012, he has conducted fieldwork among Sufi orders (*tariqat*) scattered between Ayutthaya and the Malaysian border. In addition to religious, linguistic and visual anthropology, he also writes on how Malays in Thailand are adversely impacted by local language policies and linguistic discrimination. He is a Research Fellow, at the Muslim Studies Centre, Institute of Asian Studies, Chulalongkorn University, Research Associate, at the Religious Studies Program, Victoria University of Wellington, and Adjunct Professor, at National University of Malaysia's Institute of Ethnic Studies.

Nyi Nyi Kyaw is a postdoctoral research fellow at the Centre for Asian Legal Studies at the Faculty of Law at the National University of Singapore. His areas of interest are religion, nationalism, law, social movements, constitutionalism and human rights. His research on Myanmar has been published in the *Review of Faith & International Affairs, Journal of Immigrant & Refugee Studies.* He has also contributed to two edited volumes on Islam and citizenship on Myanmar.

Ryoko Nishii is a professor at Research Institute for Languages and Culture of Asia and Africa, Tokyo University of Foreign Studies. She is an anthropologist who has studied Buddhist–Muslim relationships in Southern Thailand for many years. Her recent works include *Ethnography of Affect* (Kyoto University Press, 2013 in Japanese), an edited book *Anthropology of Time* (Sekaishisosha, 2011 in Japanese), and "The Muslim community in Mae Sot: The transformation of the Da'wa Movement," in Shigeharu Tanabe's edited volume, *Communities of Potential Social Assemblages in Thailand and Beyond* (Chiang Mai: Silkworm Books, 2016).

Raymond Scupin is an emeritus professor of anthropology and international studies at Lindenwood University. He did ethnographic research on Muslims in Central Thailand in 1976–1977, 1994 and 2002. His research focused on the emergence of Islamic and ethnic revitalization movements that have influenced Muslims in Central Thailand. Aside from his publications based on his ethnographic research, he is the author of *Cultural Anthropology: A Global Perspective* (9th ed.) and edited *Race and Ethnicity: The United States and the World* (2nd ed.), *Religion and Culture: An Anthropological Focus* (2nd ed.) and *Peoples and Cultures of Asia*.

Matthew J. Walton is an assistant professor in Comparative Political Theory at the University of Toronto. From 2013 to 2018, he was the inaugural director of the Programme on Modern Burmese Studies at St Antony's College, University of Oxford. His research focuses on religion and politics in Southeast Asia, with a particular emphasis on Buddhism in Myanmar. He is the author of *Buddhism, Politics, and Political Thought in Myanmar* (CUP 2017).

List of Figures

Fig. 6.1	Thai-Malaysian border	171
Fig. 6.2	Distribution of Muslim and Buddhist household in a research village (1988)	172
Fig. 6.3	Cases of conversion	179
Fig. 9.1	Posters from U Wirathu's temple wall in Mandalay. Before elections in 2015 U Wirathu had supported Aung San Suu Kyi and NLD's call for democratic reform. However, during the 2015 elections he became her most ardent critic for her refusal to support the "race and religion laws" and claimed that she was becoming too Muslim-friendly (Photo: Iselin Frydenlund)	288

CHAPTER 1

An Introduction: Buddhist–Muslim Relations in a Theravada World

Iselin Frydenlund and Michael Jerryson

Is there an Islamic campaign to take over Sri Lanka and Myanmar? Did Muslims drive the Buddhists out of India? Have Buddhists and Muslims always had problems trying to live together? In recent years, these questions have emerged in both popular parlance and the news. Even though

---

By "Theravada", we refer to those traditions who today self-identify as "Theravada Buddhist"—as a particular type of Buddhism. We are well aware that the term has been used in different ways through history, particularly as a marker of a particular monastic lineage (among many early Buddhist schools and lineages). "Theravada Buddhism" as used today is thus a neologism denoting a variety of historically connected traditions. Theravada Buddhism has traditionally held a stronghold in Sri Lanka, Myanmar, Thailand, Laos, Cambodia and parts of Vietnam. This volume is confined to the Theravada majority states that have experienced the highest levels of Buddhist–Muslim contention in recent years, namely Sri Lanka, Myanmar and Thailand.

I. Frydenlund (✉)
MF Norwegian School of Theology, Religion and Society, Oslo, Norway

M. Jerryson
Department of Philosophy and Religious Studies,
Youngstown State University, Youngstown, OH, USA

© The Author(s) 2020
I. Frydenlund and M. Jerryson (eds.),
Buddhist-Muslim Relations in a Theravada World,
https://doi.org/10.1007/978-981-32-9884-2_1

Muslims represent numerically small minorities in Sri Lanka, Myanmar and Thailand, the Buddhist majority in these countries have expressed concern that a Muslim population increase will drive out the Buddhists. When Buddhists voice these concerns, they often point to a historical legacy of Islamification, carried out by various Muslim rulers that purportedly drove out the Buddhists from India. Even though scholars have questioned this interpretation of South Asian history the narrative not only persists,[1] but seems to take on new significance among Buddhist activist groups in the region.

The current public concern over Muslim–Buddhist relations in South and Southeast Asia take place in the wake of massive violence against Muslim minority communities in Buddhist majority states in the region. During these years, scholars and journalists raised questions about Buddhist–Muslim relations in the wake of anti-Muslim violence.[2] Certainly, threads of Buddhist anti-Muslim sentiments can be traced historically, but the scale of attacks on Muslim minorities is historically unprecedented. One example of this is the 2017 exodus of over 670,000 people from the Rohingya community in Myanmar. The Rohingya are a small Bengali-speaking Muslim community comprised of roughly 1.1 million people, who live on both sides of the Bangladeshi-Burmese border. The human rights violations against the Rohingya will stand in world history as a grotesque reminder of how adherents of a religion— Buddhism—justified ethnic cleansing and horrific acts of violence against an ethnic and religious minority community.

The recent pattern of religiously fueled conflicts in Sri Lanka, Myanmar and southern Thailand suggest that Buddhists and Muslims have irreconcilable differences. However, history shows that Muslims and Buddhists have lived together for centuries without violence, or even major instances of contestation. In fact, Muslim communities have a long

---

[1] The reasons for Buddhism's demise in India are multiple, the most important being monastic Buddhism's withdrawal from lay life and Buddhism's loss against Hindu devotional religiosity (*bhakti*). See Lars Fogelin, *An Archaeological History of Indian Buddhism* (New York: Oxford University Press, 2015).

[2] Matthew Walton and Susan Hayward, *Contesting Buddhist Narratives: Democratization, Nationalism, and Communal Violence in Myanmar, 71 Policy Studies* (Honolulu: East–West Center, 2014); Farzana Haniffa et al., *Where Have All the Neighbours Gone? Aluthgama Riots and Its Aftermath: A Fact Finding Mission to Aluthgama, Dharga Town, Valipanna and Beruwela* (Colombo: Law and Society Trust, 2014).

history in Buddhist majority states, representing ethnically, culturally and religiously complex—albeit small—populations.

Yet, Buddhist–Muslim relations in a Theravada Buddhist context have received surprisingly little academic attention. Surely, due to the prolonged military involvement, imposed martial law and the rise of Malay Muslim separatist movements over the last 14 years, Buddhist–Muslim relations in southern Thailand have received scholarly attention.[3] In addition to examining areas of conflict between Muslims and Buddhists, ethnographic work in this region has paid attention to coexistence and notions of civility in mixed Muslim–Buddhist villages in southern Thailand.[4] Furthermore, just beyond the borders of Thailand, there have been very informative ethnographic works on Buddhist–Muslim interactions in Malaysia.[5] Recently, and largely in response to the massive violence against Muslim minorities since 2012, scholars have started to address the research lacuna of Muslim–Buddhist relations (or even research on Muslim communities in their own right) in Myanmar[6] and in Sri Lanka.[7] These studies offer powerful insights into contemporary Muslim–Buddhist formations in particular regions. Yet, it would be fair to say that the academic community is only beginning to unpack the more than a thousand years of Muslim–Buddhist relations in Asia, and

[3] See for example, Michael Jerryson, *Buddhist Fury: Religion and Violence in Southern Thailand* (New York: Oxford University Press, 2011).

[4] See Ryoko Nishii, "Coexistence of Religions: Muslim and Buddhist Relationship on the West Coast of Southern Thailand," *Tai Culture: International Review on Tai Cultural Studies* 4, no. 1 (June 1999): 77–92; Alexander Horstmann, *Class, Culture, and Space: The Construction and Shaping of Communal Space in South Thailand* (Bielefeld: Transcript, 2002).

[5] See Irving Chan Johnson, *The Buddha on Mecca's Verandah: Encounters, Mobilities, and Histories Along the Malaysian-Thai Border* (Seattle: University of Washington Press, 2012); Mohamed Yusoff Ismail, *Buddhism and Ethnicity: Social Organization of a Buddhist Temple in Kelantan* (Singapore: Institute of Southeast Asian Studies, 1993); Jeffrey Samuels, "Forget Not Your Old Country: Absence, Identity, and Marginalization in the Practice and Development of Sri Lankan Buddhism in Malaysia," *South Asian Diaspora* 3, no. 1 (January 2011): 117–132.

[6] For instance, a recent analysis of Myanmar's Buddhist–Muslim interactions is Melissa Crouch's *Islam and the State in Myanmar: Muslim–Buddhist Relations and the Politics of Belonging* (New York: Oxford University Press, 2016).

[7] For Sri Lanka, see John Holt's edited volume *Buddhist Extremists and Muslim Minorities: Religious Conflict in Contemporary Sri Lanka* (New York: Oxford University Press, 2016).

that the academic study of Buddhist–Muslim encounters in South and Southeast Asia is in its infancy. While previous research offers specific glimpses into instances of Muslim–Buddhist interaction in particular contexts, few studies so far have been devoted to Muslim–Buddhist relations from a comparative regional perspective or on transnational webs across states.

AIMS OF THIS VOLUME

We conceived this edited volume in a response to this need. The aim of this book is to unravel the various dimensions of Muslim–Buddhist relations in Buddhist majority states in South and Southeast Asia. Collectively, the chapters provide an informed and scholarly response to contemporary Buddhist–Muslim interaction in Sri Lanka, Myanmar and Thailand. What brings the contributions of this volume together is that they take as their starting point Buddhist–Muslim encounters within the framework of Buddhist majority states. We have also included a chapter on Bangladesh as this case very specifically illustrates two important points of this book, namely the importance of shifting state formations for Buddhist–Muslim relations and the fluid nature of religious and national identities.

By bringing together experts on Myanmar, Sri Lanka, Thailand and Bangladesh, this volume seeks to bring country-specific knowledge into a broader discussion about Muslim–Buddhist interactions across the region. This is important, we believe, as religious identities are shaped differently in majority and minority contexts. Buddhist minority nationalism in Muslim majority Bangladesh takes on different qualities than majority Buddhist nationalisms in Buddhist majority states. Furthermore, majority–minority relations are not confined to state borders: Muslims are in majority in Bangladesh, but a minority in Thailand. Muslims in Bangladesh sympathize with the sufferings of the Rohingyas; simultaneously, Buddhist monks throughout the region focus on minority Buddhists in Muslim majority societies like Bangladesh, southern Thailand and Malaysia. Facilitated by social media, migration and new forms of political communities such as the Association of Southeast Asian Nations (ASEAN), there is a new regional concern about religious minorities and majorities across the region.

Thus, the aim of this volume is three-fold. First, by bringing together detailed knowledge on Muslim–Buddhist relations in three majority

Buddhist states we seek to provide a work that allows the identification of similarities and differences embedded in Buddhist–Muslim relations in nation-states that retain a preference for Buddhism. Second, by bringing in an explicit regional perspective in the study of Buddhist–Muslim relations we seek to identify regional and global factors that inform relations at local and state levels. Third, we employ analytical tools that are useful for further exploration into the study of Muslim–Buddhist relations. Here we wish to contribute to a broader understanding of religious encounters, both in terms of mix and exchange but also in terms of resistance, purification and differentiation. Also, we want to be clear that this volume is not concerned with Buddhist or Islamic normative sources for peace-building in the region,[8] but rather with contributing with fresh perspectives and nuanced understandings of complex interreligious dynamics.

The Historical Legacy of Muslim–Buddhist Relations

What, then, do we know about Buddhist–Muslim relations in the past? In the following, we will provide an overview over major historical developments that have shaped Buddhist–Muslim relations and that will place this volume in its broader historical context.

In his comprehensive historical account of the encounter between Islam and Buddhism on the Silk Road, Johan Elverskog shows the rich and complex history of Buddhist–Muslim encounters from Iran to China. These first meetings took place in the Sindh, Afghan and Iranian areas, as a result of Arab trade in the eighth century CE. Importantly, conversion of non-believers was not the primary aim of these expeditions as at this early stage only Arabs could become Muslims.[9] Moreover,

---

[8] In academia, there are also philosophical reflections on the two religions and their capabilities. Perry Schmidt-Leukel's edited volume, *Buddhism and Religious Diversity: Critical Concepts in Religious Studies* (2013), for example, abstract conceptual qualities of Islam and Buddhism to point to overlapping values.

[9] Non-Arab Muslims were called *malawi*. Under the Umayyad dynasty (661–750), *malawi* were not entitled to equal treatment with Arab Muslims. Preferential treatment of Arab Muslims came to be a source of contention since it violated the Quranic declaration of equality of all believers. Under the subsequent Abbasid dynasty (750–1258), distinctions between Arab and non-Arab Muslims were not stressed (Oxford Islamic Studies Online, "Malawi" http://www.oxfordislamicstudies.com/article/opr/t125/e1473, last accessed June 30, 2016).

most of northwest India was brought under Muslim control not by force, but through treaty,[10] and Buddhists were classified in relation to Zoroastrianism and thus given *dhimmi* status and subsequent protection and privilege within the emerging Muslim polities.[11] Important sources for such early instances of Buddhist–Muslim contact are texts produced along the Silk Road; Islamic authors produced studies on Buddhist thought and practices,[12] and the North Indian Buddhist text the *Kalacakra Tantra* (transmitted to Tibet in 1027) offers us one of the earliest Buddhist interpretations of Muslim beliefs and practices, including condemnation of circumcision and animal sacrifice.[13] Elverskog's work on the multiple Buddhist–Muslim encounters along the Silk Road shows in important ways the historical fluctuations of Buddhist–Muslim interaction and how they relate to wider political contexts and imperial policies. Such a perspective allows for a fine-grained analysis of contradictions and change, showing that imperial policies might entail an interplay between pluralistic approaches to religious diversity on the one hand and brutal suppression on the other.

Muslim–Buddhist Relations in Pre-colonial South and Southeast Asia

At the dawn of European colonialism, Southeast Asia encompassed some of the most diverse cultures in early modern history, marked by circulation of people, commodities, ideas and beliefs along the key trading routes, from the Eastern edge of the Mughal empire to the southern Chinese border.[14] Muslim rulers expanding into Asia did not reach the Buddhist polities of Burma, Siam or Lanka. As such, Muslim communities in these regions are not the heritage of Arab, Turkish or Persian expansionism, like in parts of the Indian subcontinent. Rather, through

---

[10] Elverskog, *Buddhism and Islam on the Silk Road*, 49.

[11] "Dhimmi" is the term for Non-Muslim under protection of Muslim law. Islamic rulers made a covenant of protection with the conquered "Peoples of the Book," which included Jews, Christians, Sabaeans and sometimes Zoroastrians and Hindus (Oxford Islamic Studies Online, "Dhimmi" http://www.oxfordislamicstudies.com/article/opr/t125/e536?_hi=1&_pos=1, last accessed October 27, 2019).

[12] Such as the Muslim geographer al-Yaqubi (died 897). His work *Tā'rīkh ibn Wāḍiḥ* is a comprehensive account of pre-Islamic and non-Islamic peoples, especially of their religion and literature.

[13] Elverskog, 98.

[14] Tara Alberts and D.R.M. Irving, *Intercultural Exchange in Southeast Asia: History and Society in the Early Modern World* (London: I.B. Tauris, 2013).

trade networks, Muslim communities formed an integral part of culturally diverse states. In the early modern period, Muslims across the region comprised of a great variety of ethnic and linguistic groups, including Persian Shias, Cham refugees from Cambodia, and Javanese, Chinese and Arab traders. Muslim trading communities settled in cosmopolitan port cities, and from there to the inlands.

The manner in which different state formations and ideologies across the region dealt with cultural difference obviously varied through time and space. Pre-colonial state formations in the region were very different from the modern states of Sri Lanka, Myanmar and Thailand. The most important pre-colonial state formation is what Stanley Tambiah defines as the "galactic state."[15] This entails an organic state formation based on concentric circles of power, which stresses hierarchical inclusion of cultural difference, rather than cultural homogenization and outer boundaries as the modern nation-state. Pre-colonial polities in the region were kingdoms, mostly ruled by a king who justified his rule with reference to Buddhism. In spite of its Buddhist legitimacy, these states organically included a variety of religious, cultural and linguistic groups. While the early modern kingdoms of Burma, Siam or Lanka were explicitly Buddhist, non-Buddhists were included through complex systems of occupational and ritual inclusion.

For example, in pre-colonial Sri Lanka, the geographically dispersed Muslim communities played a modest political role in the Buddhist polity, but were nonetheless important to Sinhala Buddhist kings, as Muslim traders' extensive international networks were useful for diplomacy and foreign policy purposes.[16] Exactly what this "Muslim" identity was, however, is harder to define, and which aspects of these identities that have come to the fore have depended upon the time-period. In a pre-colonial setting, they were conceptualized as a particular caste group outside of the Sinhala caste hierarchy; in terms of language and civilization, they have been regarded as Islamic Tamils. The Sinhala text called the *Dambadeni Asna* (see Bastin and de Silva this volume) tells of the importance of the Muslim traders to the thirteenth-century Dambadeniya

---

[15] Stanley J. Tambiah, "The Galactic Polity in Southeast Asia," *HAU: Journal of Ethnographic Theory* 3, no. 3 (2013): 503–534.

[16] Lorna Dewaraja, *The Muslims of Sri Lanka, 1000 Years of Ethnic Harmony 900–1915 AD* (Colombo: Lanka Islamic Foundation, 1994), 17.

kingdom, but also of how they were perceived by the Buddhist majority as a potential threat to the ideal Buddhist order.

In Burma/Myanmar too, Islam has a long historical presence as Arab and Persian traders and occupational specialists arrived prior to the establishment of the early Buddhist kingdom of Bagan (eleventh century).[17] Like in pre-colonial Sri Lanka, the early modern Buddhist kingdom of Mrauk-U in Rakhine in Western Myanmar had Muslim communities as an integral part of its societal structure, both as traders as well as soldiers for the Buddhist king. Even more, as pointed out by Michael Charney, through trade connections, the early Mrauk-U rulers became the "chief patrons of the Islamic culture in the region."[18]

These regions, which today are marked by the borders between modern Myanmar, Bangladesh and India, were in pre-modern times marked by shifting ruling empires. The Chittagong sea port in the Bay of Bengal became the epicenter for political rivalry between three medieval kingdoms of Hindu, Muslim and Buddhist orientation, respectively, which resulted in a remarkable atmosphere of religious tolerance in the region. For extended periods of time, Buddhist Arakanese ruled the Chittagong hill areas (in now Bangladesh), but eventually lost to the Mughals in 1666. The Mughals showed little understanding of Buddhism within the areas they controlled, or in neighboring Buddhist kingdoms such as Arakan or Bagan (in now Myanmar). For example, one text that came to have wide circulation in Mughal India is the early seventeenth-century Persian work *Rauzat ut-Tahirin*, which expresses pejorative views on Buddhists in neighboring kingdoms particularly for their eating habits and for being "backwards."[19] Also, certain Mughal historians depicted the Arakanese Buddhists (in Myanmar) as uncivilized "others," through which they justified their conquest of Arakanese-held territories in Chittagong (Barua, this volume).

While much focus recently has been paid to the Rohingya Muslims and shifting political landscapes in the Arakan-Chittagong regions, as Matthew Walton points out in this volume, the Muslim communities of Myanmar belong to multiple ethnic groups and have diverse stories

---

[17] Moshe Yegar, *The Muslims of Burma* (Wiesbaden: O. Harrassowitz, 1972).

[18] Michael Charney, "Rise of a Mainland Trading State," in *The Journal of Burma Studies* 3 (1998): 6.

[19] Muzaffar Alam and Sanjay Subrahmanyam, "Southeast Asia as Seen from Mughal India: Tahir Muhammad's 'Immaculate Garden' (Ca. 1600)," *Archipel* 70 (2005), 209–237.

of origin. With regard to Buddhist–Muslim relations, early modern Burmese polities seem to have negotiated between notions of Muslims as lucrative trading partners (for example, from Yunnan) and notions of aggressive expansions from the West (the Mughals).

The "galactic" organization of Thai kingdoms implied a high degree of provincial autonomy. In the Ayutthayan kingdoms (1351–1767), this meant a high degree of inter-ethnic and inter-religious conviviality. Even more, as discussed by Ray Scupin and Chris Joll in this volume, historical records show that Thai Buddhist kings generously supported Shia Muharram and other Muslim rites. Also, Thai chronicles indicate that Ayutthayan kings sought to integrate non-Buddhists within the Buddhist-dominated polity through the inclusion of non-Buddhists as seen in the pilgrimage to the Buddha's footprint at Saraburi.[20]

European Colonialism and the Rise of Modern Nationalism

Shifting state formations and trade networks have always had an enormous impact on Muslim–Buddhist interaction, the paramount example being European trade and subsequently colonial rule in Asia. With the advent of European colonialism, social orders changed. Until then, in Sri Lanka for example, Muslims had close relations to Tamil and Sinhala communities, but to Portuguese and Dutch rulers the Muslims posed a threat to imperial trade, and Sinhala kings offered fleeing Muslims protection.[21] Restrictions on Muslims were liberalized with subsequent British policies, but, the European colonial state's codification of ethnic and religious identities as a means of ruling colonial subjects implied that ethnic and religious categories altered their meaning, implying a new order of status and rank within the state.

---

[20]There are notable works that address the revival of Buddhism during the Ayutthaya period, such as Chris Baker and Pasuk Phongpaichit, *A History of Thailand* (Cambridge: Cambridge University Press, 2005), 19–21; Stanley J. Tambiah, *World Conqueror and World Renouncer: A Study of Buddhism and Polity in Thailand Against a Historical Background* (Cambridge: Cambridge University Press, 1976), 89–97. For a more recent account that focuses on religious diversity within the Buddhist polity, see John Smith, "The Pilgrimage to Saraburi and the Ayutthayan Political Community, 1610–1767" (Paper presented at Interrogating Buddhism and Nationalism Conference, Oxford University, 2018).

[21]Dennis McGilvary, "Islamic and Buddhist Impacts on the Shrine at Daftar Jailani, Sri Lanka," in *Islam, Sufism and Everyday Politics of Belonging in South Asia*, eds. Deepra Dandekar and Torsten Tschacher (New York: Routledge, 2017), 62–76.

British colonialism also had a deep impact on Buddhist–Muslim relations in Burma. In the transnational British colonial economy, workers were moved from India, including present-day Pakistan and Bangladesh, to other parts of the empire, resulting in a large population of Indian workers in colonial Burma. The Indian political and economic dominance during British rule eventually resulted in Burmese Buddhist resentment and a "colonial trauma," which help explain certain xenophobic tendencies in the Burmese Buddhist majority society in the post-colonial period (see Nyi Nyi Kyaw this volume). By comparison, although Sri Lanka also witnessed Sinhala-Muslim economic competition and minor anti-Muslim riots in 1915, in Burma the anti-Indian and anti-Muslim riots of the 1920s and 1930s were much more severe. Thailand, as is well known, was never under European colonial rule, but Thai kings embarked upon large modernization schemes of the state in the early twentieth century. This in turn radically transformed Muslim–Buddhist relations, particularly in the Malay sultanate of Patani (southern Thailand).

The rise of nationalism and the formation of the modern Sri Lankan, Burmese and Thai states again re-configured Muslim–Buddhist relations. As will be discussed in detail throughout this volume, anti-colonial resistance and eventually independence after World War 2, led to new ways of imagining the political community, based on Buddhism and majority ethnicity in ways that excluded non-Buddhist and ethnic minority communities. This affected not only the Buddhist majorities, but also the self-identification of minorities and subsequently majority–minority relations.

In Burma and Ceylon, British colonial constructions of difference and marginalization of the Buddhist majority population led to resistance and the growth of a plethora of religious and nationalist associations across both countries. Concerns for Buddhism, ethnicity/race and language resulted in what is often referred to as "Burmese Buddhist" or "Sinhala Buddhist" nationalism. In Thailand, the Siamese state exerted control over the periphery through the means of a modern bureaucratic state, but importantly, also through a new ethno-ideology that emphasized notions of race and culture.

However, for Buddhists in the Chittagong Hill tracts—in the far corner of Bangladesh, bordering India and Myanmar—the situation is reverse. They did not feel included in the new forms of majority nationalism expressed by the modern state to which they belonged. Neither

Pakistani nationalism based on Urdu language and Islam, nor the later Bangladeshi nationalism based on Bengali language and Islam, left much room for non-Muslim and non-Bengali identities, leaving ethnic minority Buddhists in Bangladesh largely excluded from the modern nationalist project.

Contemporary Issues

Looking at contemporary state formations, the three Buddhist majority states comprehensively analyzed in the first section of this book—Sri Lanka, Myanmar and Thailand—all share a form of Buddhist constitutionalism, that is, state protection of Buddhism enshrined in their respective constitutions.[22] All three constitutions balance between notions of privilege and equality, organized in a hierarchy of subordination with Buddhism at its top.[23] The role of Buddhism in post-colonial nation-building, and the historical legacy of state protection of Buddhism (as expressed in Theravada Buddhist political ideology across the region) have made protection of religious minorities a pertinent question within Buddhist-dominated states. Buddhist monks and interest groups play influential roles in elite politics, and Buddhist ideas and institutions figure prominently as topics of constitutional negotiation. From a religious minority perspective, Buddhist "rights" often seem to trump minority rights, while minority rights are depicted by Buddhist activists as a neo-colonial liberal enterprise to undermine Buddhism, or to allow for "Islamization." A similar tendency of exclusionary policies toward minorities is certainly noticeable in neighboring Bangladesh, which since the 1977 Constitution has a clear preference for Islam.

Theravada Buddhist states regulate religion in different ways, and what exactly Buddhist constitutionalism implies for Buddhist–Muslim relations is not given beyond indicating state preference for Buddhism. In some states, however, particular policies concerning religion and ethnicity are very obvious tools of governmentality. Nowhere is this

---

[22] Benjamin Schonthal, "Securing the Sasana Through Law: Buddhist Constitutionalism and Buddhist-Interest Litigation in Sri Lanka," *Modern Asian Studies* (2016): 1–43.

[23] For more on the notion of hierarchical subordination, see Iselin Frydenlund, "Particularist Goals Through Universalist Means: The Political Paradoxes of Buddhist Revivalism in Sri Lanka," in *Buddhism and the Political Process*, ed. Hiroko Kawanami (London: Palgrave Macmillan, 2016), 97–120.

clearer than in Myanmar, with its 1982 Citizenship Law and a list of 135 "national races", in which the state adopts religion and ethnicity as legal and policy categories as means of control over its subjects. Despite the categories' colonial origins, it is continued in the present-day, as expressed in the denial of citizenship to the Rohingya, or through adding foreign national identity to local Muslims in their National Identity Cards.

In Buddhist majority states concerns to protect the *sasana*, that is Buddhism in this world, are often played out in electoral politics. Buddhist moral authority is extremely important to the ways in which politics are formed.[24] In the Thai case, we see how Buddhist monks have integral roles in local and regional elections. Buddhist temples become major electoral battlegrounds for prospective candidates, and Thai political candidates convert religious prestige into political credit and votes.[25] Politicians need to be seen as *khon dee* (good persons), and this is achieved through Buddhist personas. In line with this, politicians do occasionally politicize Muslim–Buddhist relations for electoral purposes, as powerfully shown in the 2015 Myanmar elections when none of the leading parties filed a Muslim on their lists and a notable percentage of Muslim candidates were rejected by the Electoral Commission.[26]

Similar trajectories are found in Sri Lankan politics, in which the "protection of Buddhism" trope—often at the expense of non-Buddhist minorities—has been a useful tool for the mobilization of electoral masses that otherwise were difficult to rally around a single cause.[27] In a setting of electoral competition, so-called "religious outbidding" plays an important role, in which radical Buddhist groups compete to protect Buddhism the most. This in turn, has a negative impact on non-Buddhist minorities and their place within the polity.

[24] Matt Walton, *Buddhism, Politics and Political Thought in Myanmar* (Cambridge: Cambridge University Press, 2017).

[25] Daniel Arghiros, *Democracy, Development and Decentralization in Provincial Thailand* (Richmond, Surrey: Curzon Press, 2001), 149–150.

[26] European Union Election Observation Mission Myanmar, General Elections, 2015, "Preliminary Statement," November 10, 2015, http://eeas.europa.eu/archives/eueom/missions/2015/myanmar/index_en.htm, accessed March 29, 2016.

[27] James Manor, *The Expedient Utopian: Bandaranaike and Ceylon* (Cambridge: Cambridge University Press, 1989).

In recent years, gender, sexuality and reproduction have become focal points in Muslim–Buddhist contestation. While colonial Burma witnessed similar concerns for Buddhist female bodies, particularly in mixed marriages, the gendered imaginaries of contemporary Buddhist protectionism are even more powerful and radical, and distributed across local communities at a scale not witnessed before. Haniffa Farzana (this volume) powerfully illustrates this in her analysis of Sri Lanka's anti-Muslim movement, but also in the Muslim response.

By way of conclusion, we also need to ask ourselves what conditions Buddhist–Muslim relations in an era of global hyper-connectivity. Historians like to point out that globalization is not new, or as discussed above, that Muslim–Buddhist marriages were high on the agenda also during British colonial rule. That is all true. But it is also true that with increased mobility, migration and new technologies, new identity formations arise. Moving to our age of social media, it is clear that text and images transmitted through digital media has the potential of flaring up emotions and deepening divides across long distances and only within hours. For example, sentiments run high in Bangladesh in 2012 when thousands of angry Bangladeshi Muslims reacted to an inflammatory Facebook image of a Quran. They set fire to 10 Buddhist monasteries and 40 homes and injured over 20 local Buddhists in the process.[28]

Reflections on the Study of Buddhist–Muslim Relations

By presenting various examples of Buddhist–Muslim encounters across South and Southeast Asia, we do not intend to force similarities between the cases. Rather, the intent of such a comparative project is to shed light on similarities *and* differences across states and communities. Bruce Lincoln and Cristiano Grottanelli point to problems in strong comparisons that seek only establishing universal patterns, or hierarchical differences. They argue that instead of this, there is need for making "weak" comparisons that are "equally attentive to relations of similarity

---

[28] Associated Press, "Bangladeshi Muslims Burn 10 Buddhist Temples Over Facebook Photo," September 30, 2012, http://www.csmonitor.com/World/Latest-News-Wires/2012/0930/Bangladeshi-Muslims-burn-10-Buddhist-temples-over-Facebook-photo, accessed June 25, 2016.

and those of difference."[29] Therefore, in this volume, we will pay equal attention to local specificities as to broader patterns of similarities, for example, in relation to colonialism, modern state-formation processes or state policies of religion. Furthermore, we aim to paint a larger picture of Muslim–Buddhist interaction *across* the region and underscore that religious formations also need to be addressed beyond the confines of the state, for example, with regard to migration or transnational religious networks. Therefore, with this volume, we aim to show the importance of scale: from local, regional, state and global levels, seeking to identify points of interaction between these levels, or possible shifts over time in the importance of one level over another.

This volume pays specific attention to the ways in which state formations, state policies and the economy have powerful ways of redesigning Buddhist–Muslim interactions. In addition, it is important to pay attention to other cultural and social processes that shape Muslim–Buddhist relations. While the analytical focus is on factors at the macro level that in various ways condition religious identities, it is also important in a volume like this to provide some general reflections about "religious encounters." For instance, it is important to remember that daily life in these societies more often than not involves interaction across religious boundaries, e.g., through personal relations, intermarriage, systems of patronage, economic co-operation, shared urban spaces or shared experiences in education or at work. In lack of a better term, perhaps, when people of different religions live together, scholars often refer to this activity as "co-existence." But what does Buddhist–Muslim co-existence mean in urban Yangon, Dhaka or in rural Sri Lanka? Does it mean that they live in shared spaces, but keep interaction with defined religious "Others" to a minimum, or does it imply deeper structures or mechanisms of interaction, recognition or even boundary transgression? The case of southern Thailand discussed by Ryoko Nishii in this volume shows that in certain areas, the relationship between Buddhists and Muslims is surprisingly fluid, and that their exchanges impact both their communities and their sense of self-identity. But border areas might also imply marginalization and securitization as in the case of the Rohingyas,

---

[29] Bruce Lincoln with Cristiano Grottanelli, "Theses on Comparison," in *Gods and Demons, Priests and Scholars: Critical Explorations in the History of Religion* (Chicago: University of Chicago Press, 2012), 121–130.

or assimilation policies as in the case of the Buddhists in Chittagong Hill Tracts.

Thus, the study of Muslim–Buddhist encounters raise larger questions about group identities and the ways in which ethnic and religious boundaries are made and kept—what social anthropologists refer to as "boundary-making."[30] This perspective rejects a primordialist view on identity and offers a processual approach, investigating under what conditions group purity and exclusiveness are made into priorities, on how difference is produced and articulated, by whom and for what purpose. And finally, and equally important for our understanding of religious encounters, such a constructivist view on identities investigates under what conditions such differences are consciously transgressed or considered irrelevant.

Religious traditions are sustained, performed and articulated through the cultures in their locality; they are fluid and mutable systems, and in this way, it is no small surprise that the Buddhists and Muslims of South and Southeast Asia may have coterminous beliefs and practices. Surprisingly to many perhaps, there are numerous instances of hybridity and moments of transculturation between Buddhist and Muslim traditions. Transculturation refers to mutual influence, a two-way process in which different religious and cultural elements meet and new forms emerge. Importantly, such encounters are influenced by—and perhaps also expressions of—power asymmetries. Minorities might adopt more to the majority religion than the other way around. In the South and Southeast Asian contexts, we see this reflected in the ways in which Muslim communities have adopted Buddhist practices such as merit-making and the practice of *samadhi* meditation.[31]

Studying processes of cultural encounters, also begs the question about a culture's ability to absorb other elements, or what we may call the permeability of culture. One way to study the openness or closeness of a culture is to study processes whereby group boundaries are penetrated, for example conversion and mixed marriages, a point which leads

---

[30] Fredrik Barth, *Ethnic Groups and Boundaries: The Social Organization of Culture Difference* (Oslo: Universitetsforlaget, 1969).

[31] Chris Joll, "Making Sense of Thailand's 'Merit-Making' Muslims: Adoption and Adaption of the Indic in the Creation of Islamicate Southern Thailand," *Islam and Christian–Muslim Relations* 25, no. 3 (2014). Issue 3: Islam and Muslim-Buddhist and Muslim-Christian relations in Southeast Asia.

us directly to much of the current Muslim–Buddhist controversy in Sri Lanka and Myanmar. In southern Thailand, both Muslim and Buddhist communities show themselves to be hyper-flexible in this regard, while Muslim–Buddhist boundaries are built and kept to greater degrees than before in urban Sri Lanka or Myanmar. According to Buddhist nationalists, their own culture is marked by openness in terms of mixed marriage as well as conversion, but Islam, they argue, is marked by closed boundaries that do not allow for such flexibility. In Sri Lanka, a frequent accusation made by Sinhala nationalists against the Muslim community is that the Muslims keep to themselves and do not allow for cultural mix and exchange, and moreover, that Sinhalese and Muslim cultures are polar opposites. Myanmar's four "race and religion laws" passed in 2015 to counter "islamization" of Myanmar show that law can be used to restrict cultural permeability when this is considered to pose a threat to Buddhism and perceived ethnic purity.[32] Also, global Islamic movements' call for purity put pressure on more localized and inclusivist Sufi-traditions. Therefore, the ways in which cultural exchange is conceptualized is often a matter of politics. At times, cultural mix can be celebrated; at other occasions, calls for "authenticity," purification and homogenization are vociferous.

VOLUME OVERVIEW

This book contains a foreword by Johan Elverskog, an introduction, a conclusion and seven chapters divided into two sections. The first section provides a comprehensive historical review of three countries with a significant amount of Buddhist–Muslim interaction.

Viewing Muslim–Buddhist interaction in the context of shifting economic relations, Premakumara de Silva and Rohan Bastin examine the porous boundaries and shifting contexts of significance and antagonism of Buddhist–Muslim interaction in Sri Lanka. They make a strong call for viewing the island's ethno-religious communities not as fixed entities, and moreover, to consider them as practice-related entities largely defined by economic relations. Furthermore, de Silva and Bastin challenge local imaginaries that romanticize pre-colonial Buddhist–Muslim

---

[32] Iselin Frydenlund, "Religious Liberty for Whom? The Buddhist Politics of Religious Freedom During Myanmar's Transition to Democracy," *Nordic Journal of Human Rights* 35, no. 1 (2017): 55–73.

relations, reducing contemporary tensions and violence to the product of colonial divide-and-rule and externally imposed modernity. To think that way, they argue, would not only be historically inaccurate, "it would also amount to a denial of responsibility regarding the island's current ethnic predicaments."

Matthew Walton writes on the history of interaction between Buddhists and Muslims in Burma/Myanmar. He shows the complexity of the categorization process for various Muslim groups in the country and that such categorization attempts have differed over time. This variability makes it almost impossible to present consistent historical outlines of the numerous Muslim groups. Furthermore, Islam and Muslims in Myanmar presents a research lacunae, which makes our knowledge of Buddhist–Muslim interactions fragmented. A common thread in the story of Buddhist–Muslim interaction in Myanmar, Walton points out, is that those producing knowledge about Muslims—be it Burmese Buddhist chronicle writers or British civil servants—do so in a way that portray Muslims as "foreign" to the state and the ethnoreligious community. In their chapter on Thailand, Raymond Scupin and Chris Joll present portrayals of local contact, comfort and conflict between Buddhists and Muslims between Central and South Thailand. They argue there is a desperate need for fresh air in the analysis dynamics commonly—and erroneously—assumed as primarily an inter-religious issue.

The second section focuses on particular encounters between Buddhists and Muslims in South and Southeast Asia. Whereas the first section's articles looks at the larger history of interaction at a national level, the second section's articles provide thick descriptions to historically confined engagements.

Farzana Haniffa examines the intersections of ethnicity, Islam, Buddhism and gender in Sri Lanka after the end of the civil war in 2009, a period marked by Sinhala triumphalism and increased marginalization of the island's ethnic and religious minorities. She finds a male cultural ethos crossing ethno-religious alliances that see women as owned by the collective and defined by their reproductive capacity. Her chapter looks at the gendered elements of hate rhetoric and the complete male dominance in nationalist discourse.

Ryoko Nishii writes on Muslim and Buddhist interaction and co-existence in a specific area of southern Thailand, in which shared language, village identity and cultural ethos often are placed before religious difference. Furthermore, multiple conversions, particularly among female villagers, from Buddhism to Islam and from Islam to Buddhism—and back again—are frequent, challenging notions of fixed Muslim–Buddhist boundaries. Nishii points out that the principle that husband and wife must be of the same religion (and thus their children) is strongly associated with posthumous merit-making, not only for Buddhists, but for Muslims as well. Death rituals, then, become important mechanisms for boundary-maintenance between Buddhist and Muslim communities in her fieldwork village.

Nyi Nyi Kyaw turns to Myanmar and traces the development of anti-Muslim rhetoric and discourse. He raises the question to what extent there is historical continuity between the anti-Indian/Muslim campaigns of the colonial era and present-day anti-Muslim sentiments, and concludes that one persistent contribution to the vitriol is the problematic myth of deracination of Burmese Buddhist culture and people. This myth of deracination, Kyaw concludes, has re-emerged during Myanmar's political transition where identities are in flux.

In nearby Bangladesh, Mitra Barua looks at the Buddhist community in the Chittagong region, from early modern cosmopolitanism and tolerance to Mughal intolerance and demonization of Buddhist political others. He finds a discursive competition that addresses tensions between the Buddhist minority and the Muslim majority with use of the new term of "Bengali Buddhists," and the older derogatory term "Magh," stemming from Mughal anti-Buddhist and anti-Arakanese prejudice.

In the last chapter, Michael Jerryson and Iselin Frydenlund address the various historical ways in which Buddhists have constructed the "Other" in South and Southeast Asia. In linking their work to the contemporary period, Jerryson and Frydenlund trace a pattern of Buddhist constructions of "Muslim Otherness." Their chapter raises questions such as, is there something internal to Buddhism in the ways that the "Other" is constructed, or are such constructions external to Buddhism itself?

As mentioned at the onset of this introduction, the contemporary crises in southern Thailand, Myanmar and Sri Lanka can suggest to the casual observer that Buddhists and Muslims cannot co-exist peacefully. Collectively, these chapters seek to redress this limited view of history by providing a wider lens both regional and historically, in order to show a legacy of both harmonious interaction and conflict. The authors hope that the contents of this volume may serve as a platform for further exploration of the unfolding reconfigurations of Buddhist–Muslim relations.

References

Alberts, Tara, and D.R.M. Irving. *Intercultural Exchange in Southeast Asia: History and Society in the Early Modern World*. London: I.B. Tauris, 2013.

Arghiros, Daniel. *Democracy, Development and Decentralization in Provincial Thailand*. Richmond, Surrey: Curzon Press, 2001.

Associated Press. "Bangladeshi Muslims Burn 10 Buddhist Temples Over Facebook Photo." *The Christian Science Monitor*, September 30, 2017, http://www.csmonitor.com/World/Latest-News-Wires/2012/0930/Bangladeshi-Muslims-burn-10-Buddhist-temples-over-Facebook-photo.

Baker, Chris, and Pasuk Phongpaichit. *A History of Thailand*. Cambridge: Cambridge University Press, 2005.

Barth, Fredrik. *Ethnic Groups and Boundaries: The Social Organization of Culture Difference*. Oslo: Universitetsforlaget, 1969.

Bhabha, Homi. *The Location of Culture*. London: Routledge, 1994.

Burke, Peter. *Cultural Hybridity*. Cambridge: Polity Press, 2009.

Charney, Michael. "Rise of a Mainland Trading State." *The Journal of Burma Studies* 3 (1998).

Chia, Jack Meng-Tat. "Toward a Modern Indonesia Buddhism: The Buddhist Nationalism of Ashin Jinarakkhita." Paper presented at the Interrogating Buddhism and Nationalism Conference, Oxford University, 2018.

Crouch, Melissa, ed. *Islam and the State in Myanmar: Muslim–Buddhist Relations and the Politics of Belonging*. New York: Oxford University Press, 2016.

Dewaraja, Lorna. *The Muslims of Sri Lanka, 1000 Years of Ethnic Harmony 900–1915 AD*. Colombo: Lanka Islamic Foundation, 1994.

Elverskog, Johan. *Buddhism and Islam on the Silk Road*. Philadelphia: University of Pennsylvania Press, 2010.

Fogelin, Lars. *An Archaeological History of Indian Buddhism*. New York: Oxford University Press, 2015.

Frydenlund, Iselin. "Religious Liberty for Whom? The Buddhist Politics of Religious Freedom During Myanmar's Transition to Democracy." *Nordic Journal of Human Rights* 35, no. 1 (2017): 55–73.

———. "Particularist Goals Through Universalist Means: The Political Paradoxes of Buddhist Revivalism in Sri Lanka." In *Buddhism and the Political Process*, edited by Hiroko Kawanami, 97–120. London: Palgrave Macmillan, 2016.

Haniffa, Farzana, et al. *Where Have All the Neighbours Gone? Aluthgama Riots and Its Aftermath: A Fact Finding Mission to Aluthgama, Dharga Town, Valipanna and Beruwela*. Colombo: Law and Society Trust, 2014.

Holt, John, ed. *Buddhist Extremists and Muslim Minorities: Religious Conflict in Contemporary Sri Lanka*. New York: Oxford University Press, 2016.

Horstmann, Alexander. *Class, Culture, and Space: The Construction and Shaping of Communal Space in South Thailand.* Bielefeld: Transcript, 2002.

Hu, Minghui, and Johan Elverskog. *Cosmopolitanism in China, 1600–1950.* New York: Cambria Press, 2016.

Ismail, Mohamed Yusoff. *Buddhism and Ethnicity: Social Organization of a Buddhist Temple in Kelantan.* Singapore: Institute of Southeast Asian Studies, 1993.

Jerryson, Michael. *Buddhist Fury: Religion and Violence in Southern Thailand.* New York: Oxford University Press, 2011.

Johnson, Irving Chan. *The Buddha on Mecca's Verandah: Encounters, Mobilities, and Histories Along the Malaysian-Thai Border.* Seattle: University of Washington Press, 2012.

Keyes, Charles. *The Golden Peninsula: Culture and Adaptation in Mainland Southeast Asia.* Honolulu: University of Hawai'i Press, 1995.

Landon, Kenneth. *Siam in Transition.* New York: Greenwood Press, 1939.

Lincoln, Bruce, and Cristiano Grottanelli. "Theses on Comparison." In *Gods and Demons, Priests and Scholars: Critical Explorations in the History of Religion,* 121–130. Chicago: University of Chicago Press, 2012.

Manor, James. *The Expedient Utopian: Bandaranaike and Ceylon.* Cambridge: Cambridge University Press, 1989.

McGilvray, Dennis B. "Sri Lankan Muslims: Between Ethno-Nationalism and the Global Ummah." *Nations and Nationalism* 17, no. 1 (January 2011): 45–64. http://onlinelibrary.wiley.com/doi/10.1111/nana.2010.17.issue-1/issuetoc.

———. "Rethinking Muslim Identity in Sri Lanka." In *Buddhist Extremists and Muslim Minorities: Religious Conflict in Contemporary Sri Lanka,* edited by John Holt, 54–77. New York: Oxford University Press, 2016.

———. "Islamic and Buddhist Impacts on the Shrine at Daftar Jailani, Sri Lanka." In *Islam, Sufism and Everyday Politics of Belonging in South Asia,* edited by Deepra Dandekar and Torsten Tschacher, 62–76. New York: Routledge, 2017.

Nishii, Ryoko. "Coexistence of Religions: Muslim and Buddhist Relationship on the West Coast of Southern Thailand." *Tai Culture: International Review on Tai Cultural Studies* 4, no. 1 (June 1999): 77–92.

Schonthal, Benjamin. "Securing the Sasana Through Law: Buddhist Constitutionalism and Buddhist-Interest Litigation in Sri Lanka." *Modern Asian Studies,* First View (2016): 1–43. Available on CJO2016. https://doi.org/10.1017/s0026749x15000426.

Smith, John. "The Pilgrimage to Saraburi and the Ayutthayan Political Community, 1610–1767." Paper presented at the Interrogating Buddhism and Nationalism Conference, Oxford University, 2018.

Tambiah, Stanley J. "The Galactic Polity in Southeast Asia." *HAU: Journal of Ethnographic Theory* 3, no. 3 (2013): 503–534.

———. *World Conqueror and World Renouncer: A Study of Buddhism and Polity in Thailand Against a Historical Background*. Cambridge: Cambridge University Press, 1976.

Walton, Matthew, *Buddhism, Politics and Political Thought in Myanmar*. Cambridge: Cambridge University Press, 2017.

Walton, Matthew, and Susan Hayward, *Contesting Buddhist Narratives: Democratization, Nationalism, and Communal Violence in Myanmar, 71 Policy Studies*. Honolulu: East-West Center, 2014.

Yegar, Moshe. *The Muslims of Burma*. Wiesbaden: O. Harrassowitz, 1972.

PART I

Historical Country Overviews

CHAPTER 2

Historical Threads of Buddhist–Muslim Relations in Sri Lanka

Rohan Bastin and Premakumara de Silva

In 2008, Champika Ranawaka, a Buddhist nationalist politician and lay member of the clerical Jathika Hela Urumaya (Nationalist Heritage Party), delivered a public declaration. Quoted by the moderate journalist Tisaranee Gunasekara in her newspaper feature article aptly entitled "That Familiar Impasse," the lay spokesman of the Buddhist monks' political party declared as follows:

> The Sinhalese are the only organic race of Sri Lanka. Other communities are all visitors to the country, whose arrival was never challenged out of the compassion of Buddhists. But they must not take this compassion for granted. The Muslims are here because our kings let them trade here and the Tamils because they were allowed to take refuge when the Moguls

R. Bastin (✉)
Deakin University, Melbourne, VIC, Australia
e-mail: rohan.bastin@deakin.edu.au

P. de Silva
University of Colombo, Colombo, Sri Lanka

© The Author(s) 2020
I. Frydenlund and M. Jerryson (eds.),
Buddhist-Muslim Relations in a Theravada World,
https://doi.org/10.1007/978-981-32-9884-2_2

were invading them in India. What is happening today is pure ingratitude on the part of these visitors.[1]

Erstwhile member of the Sinhalese left-wing and sometimes extremist People's Revolutionary Front (JVP), Ranawaka is closely connected to the Sinhala Buddhist chauvinist groups that produced the Jathika Hela Urumaya (JHU) and from the 2000s onward more violent off-shoots such as the Bodu Bala Sena (Buddhist Power Force) and Sinhala Ravaya.[2] With records of antagonism toward Christians, lobbying for religious anti-conversion laws, and in more recent times violence against Muslims, these Buddhist nationalist groups seem intent on both religious and ethnic "cleansing" in a country where roughly 75% of the population is Sinhalese of whom roughly 90% are Buddhists.

Critically, Ranawaka's remarks about authentic ("organic") native hosts and foreign guests reveal the same kind of historical logic, albeit with an incendiary subtext, as historical works some by reputed scholars that depict a romantic pre-colonial time when tolerance prevailed, and ethnic relations were harmonious.[3] The notion of an "organic race" is, moreover, simply a thinly veiled reference to the equally absurd nationalist concept of *bhumiputra* (son of the soil). We stress that when we compare the likes of Ranawaka with historians, we are not suggesting that the historians subscribe to such pregnant language. Rather, we are suggesting that the extremists share with the historians the notion of a pristine Buddhist tolerance; a notion that is not only inaccurate but ideological and a means of denying responsibility for contemporary predicaments. This chapter contests the view, but only to understand better the nature of ethnic relations in Sri Lanka today and the kinds of trigger for intolerance and violence that have long existed. In doing so, we show that Ranawaka's depiction of Sri Lanka's principal minorities as ungrateful visitors remains an ongoing emergent possibility of an ideology with a long

---

[1] Champika Ranawaka quoted in Tisaranee Gunasekara's "That Familiar Impasse," *The Island*, 2008, http://www.island.lk/2008/10/19/features12.html, last accessed December 5, 2016.

[2] Roar of the Sinhalese; see Haniffa this volume; John C. Holt, *Buddhist Extremists and Muslim Minorities: Religious Conflict in Contemporary Sri Lanka* (New York: Oxford University Press, 2016).

[3] E.g., Lorna Dewaraja, *The Muslims of Sri Lanka: One Thousand Years of Ethnic Harmony* (Colombo: Lanka Islamic Foundation, 1994); Asiff Hussain, *Sarandib: An Ethnological Study of the Muslims of Sri Lanka* (Colombo: Neptune Publications, 2011).

history of varied intensity. Such an ideology must be revised if Sri Lanka is to move beyond that "familiar impasse" of ethno-religious antagonism. How history is imagined and taught is central to this. For that reason, the following chapter charts Sri Lankan history from the spread of Islam to the present.

TAMIL-SPEAKING MUSLIMS

Sri Lanka's Muslims speak Tamil, even in the areas of the country where Sinhala predominates as the vernacular and official language. This is interesting because it suggests that Tamil was the regional *lingua franca* particularly for trade and retained that role until relatively recently. Coupled with the use of Tamil by certain Sinhalese fishing communities and their relatively recent incorporation to the Sinhalese ethnic group, one develops the sense that Tamil was the language of the sea and with that of trade.[4]

Trading groups and guilds have long played a role in the mercantile history of the island. There is evidence of donations to Buddhist temples in Anuradhapura's Jetavana Stupa, which dates from the third century CE. This highlights the long-acknowledged role of religious institutions as nodal points articulating agriculture and commerce in state formation and reproduction.[5] From the Nanadesi traders of South India to the Añjuvaṇṇam of West Asia (or the Middle East from a Eurocentric perspective) different groups have converged on Sri Lanka for several centuries prior to the advent of Islam, with different Asian empires rising and falling in both the west and the south and associated geo-political shifts in the major urban trading centers in the region. The rise of Islam and with it the transformation of empires shifted these trading assemblages,

---

[4]R.L. Stirrat, *On the Beach: Fishermen, Fishwives, and Traders in Post-Colonial Lanka* (Delhi: Hindustan Publishing Corporation, 1988), 24.

[5]See, for example Max Weber, *The City*, trans. and ed. Don Martindale and Gertrud Neuwurth (New York: The Free Press, 1958). For the Indian Ocean see K.N. Chaudhuri, *Asia Before Europe: Economy and Civilisation of the Indian Ocean from the Rise of Islam to 1750* (Cambridge: Cambridge University Press, 1990); Susan Bayly, *Saints, Goddesses and Kings: Muslims and Christians in South Indian Society, 1700–1900* (Cambridge: Cambridge University Press, 1990).

28   R. BASTIN AND P. DE SILVA

intensified their importance and altered many aspects of spatio-temporal perspective, orientation and value.[6]

The expansion of the South Indian Chola Empire in the tenth and eleventh centuries CE is generally regarded in Sinhalese nationalist historiography as a principal element in the collapse of Sri Lanka's hydraulic (Buddhist) civilization and the southwest drift of political capitals away from Rājaraṭṭa ("Kings' Country," now the North Central Province). Certainly, the southwest drift occurred and certainly one of the later invading kings, the thirteenth-century Kalinga prince Māgha, was tyrannically anti-Buddhist.[7] Nevertheless, a different perspective is warranted. Instead of the imagined pillaging, anti-irrigation, and, worse, anti-Buddhist Tamil invaders, we and especially the creators of this historiography should consider the Chola Empire at its height as a sizeable trading empire throughout the Bay of Bengal extending rather than introducing South Indian social, cultural and politico-economic practices, including Hinduism and Buddhism into Southeast Asia and commanding a monumental temple architecture for deities that should not immediately be presumed to be anti-Buddhist.[8]

Semi-autonomous, local kingdoms in the empire were subject to its economy, which often challenged those local religious institutions in their existing political and economic linkages. The empire was unstable, but herein rested its power and its threat. From being a rice exporter, the island of Sri Lanka became an importer, which *inter alia* highlights that state patronage of some kind was necessary to preserve the otherwise fragile hydraulic civilization in the Rājaraṭṭa.[9] In their place, the spice

[6] Chaudhuri, *Asia Before Europe*, 28–41.

[7] Amaradasa Liyanagamage, *Society, State and Religion in Premodern Sri Lanka* (Colombo: Social Scientists' Association, 2008), 243–271.

[8] R.A.L.H. Gunawardana, "The People of the Lion: The Sinhala Identity and Ideology in History and Historiography," reprint, *Sri Lanka: History and the Roots of Conflict*, ed. Jonathan Spencer (London: Routledge, 1990); R.A.L.H. Gunawardana, *Historiography in a Time of Ethnic Conflict: Construction of the Past in Contemporary Sri Lanka* (Colombo: Social Scientists' Association, 1995).

[9] The nature of state formation and irrigated agriculture broadly known as the Wittfogel thesis, has long been debated by Sri Lankanists (R.A.L.H. Gunawardana, "Irrigation and Hydraulic Society in Early Medieval Ceylon," *Past and Present* 53, no. 1 (1971); E.R. Leach, "Hydraulic Society in Ceylon," *Past and Present* 15, no. 1 (1959); Michael Roberts, *Exploring Confrontation: Sri Lanka: Politics, Culture and History* (Chur, Switzerland: Harwood Academic Publishers, 1994), 73–88).

economies opened up to feature a growing number of Arab and other Indian trading communities and guilds as well as Chinese. The centers of power began to drift to the southwest as new players in regional trade appeared.

Whether the decline of the Rājaraṭṭa irrigated agriculture was caused by destructiveness, disinterest or a combination of the two in hand with amplifying ecological factors such as drought and malaria is a question that suggests greater complexity behind the southwest drift than what is commonly understood and taught in Sri Lankan schools simply as the result of Tamil invasion. The decline of the Rājaraṭṭa irrigated agriculture is an unrecognized complexity that powerfully informs the nature of relations between Buddhists and the other ethno-religious groups in the island in contemporary times. Founded upon a deep sense of Sinhala Buddhist identity—Ranawaka's "organic race" and previous ideologies of an "Aryan race"[10]—it is a parochial history that imagines the island as a beleaguered bastion of Buddhist civilization and not part of a politically, economically and ideologically busy region.

Seen in an alternative light, the Cholas did not simply destroy a Sinhala Buddhist hydraulic civilization. They changed its foci, its centers of power and its relevance in the regional economy. Instead of depicting a pristine and isolated Sinhala Buddhist civilization beset by maliciously invading heathens, Sri Lankan history should instead be framed by a sense of the vicissitudes of world systems in the *longue durée* of Indian Ocean commerce and civilization[11] producing historical dynamics rather than distinctive bounded periods[12] which themselves connote bounded identities. In a closely related way, the history of the island should be situated in the history of the region and in the recognition that bodies of water are barriers promoting a sense of confinement and isolation for the landlubber when, for the sailor, they enable commerce and interaction in both commodities and ideas utilizing appropriate currencies including

---

[10] Gunawardana, "The People of the Lion."

[11] Sunil S. Amrith, *Crossing the Bay of Bengal: The Furies of Nature and the Fortunes of Migrants* (Boston: Harvard University Press, 2013); Abdul Sheriff and Engseng Ho, eds., *The Indian Ocean: Oceanic Connections and the Creation of New Societies* (London: C. Hurst and Co., 2014).

[12] R.A.L.H. Gunawardana, *Periodization in Sri Lanka History: Some Reflections with Special Emphasis on the Development of the State* (Colombo: Social Scientists' Association, 2008).

30 R. BASTIN AND P. DE SILVA

kinship and alliance as much as money and valuables, temples as much as markets.

Language is also critical as part of the currency of exchange, not simply as an ethnic marker, which is a modern perspective, but as an assemblage that does not take identity as its goal, rather than the simple interactions of everyday life. Consider, for example, the role of Tamil that the Cholas employed as the regional commercial language. As one of a group of Sri Lankan historians actively rethinking the older and barrier-driven approaches K.S. Indrapala writes:

> The dominance of the Tamil mercantile communities in the maritime trade of south India and Sri Lanka sems [sic] to have led to the use of Tamil as the language of trade in this region in the twelfth century. Apart from the records of these traders being written in Tamil, even a royal proclamation by a Sri Lankan king, relating to overseas traders, is in Tamil. Parākaramabāhu I, the prosperity of whose reign depended to a considerable extent on overseas trade, issued a proclamation relating to merchandise from shipwrecks and this was inscribed in Tamil and set up at the northern port of Ūrātturai (known in modern times in English writings as Kayts). The proclamation refers specifically to traders who brought horses and elephants to the island. Clearly the horses were originating from West Asia and were in all probability brought by Muslim traders such as the Añjuvaṇṇam.[13]

Two points arise from this. First, we note that Parākaramabāhu I (1153–1186 CE) is one of the most highly revered Sinhala Buddhist kings in traditional Sri Lankan historical accounts. He is associated mainly with hydraulic civilization and not with the trade that Indrapala notes was key to his kingdom. Second, the Añjuvaṇṇam was a mercantile organization of traders from West Asia who were not only Muslim but likely to have professed other West Asian Abrahamic religions as well.[14] The ancient port of Kollam (Quilon) in Kerala and its connection to Syrian Christians around the same period suggests this.[15] More importantly, though, the Añjuvaṇṇam became a Tamil-using

---

[13] K. Indrapala, *The Evolution of an Ethnic Identity: The Tamils in Sri Lanka C. 300 BCE to C. 1200 CE* (Colombo: MV Publications, 2005), 273.

[14] Indrapala, *The Evolution of an Ethnic Identity*, 272.

[15] A. Sreedhara Menon, *Cultural Heritage of Kerala*, 2nd ed. (Madras: Viswanathan Printers, 1996), 18.

trading community that would later participate in the formation of the Tamil-speaking Muslim community of Sri Lanka today.

Occupying nearly all of the urban commercial centers in the island as well as a number of agricultural sites, including areas where Sinhala-speakers predominate, the nonetheless Tamil-speaking Sri Lankan Muslim community's origins are thus intimately connected to the maritime trade of the Indian Ocean. It is for this reason that they are Tamil-speaking, and while their numbers may well have included the absorption of exclusively Tamil-speaking populations, particularly through marriage, they are not as Ponnambalam Ramanathan contentiously asserted in 1885 ethnically Tamils who profess Islam. We return to this point below, because our historical account of enmity focuses especially on the period roughly from the 1880s to the 1920s.[16]

The Berber travel writer Ibn Battuta describes meeting the Jaffna king in Puttalam in the mid-fourteenth century and conversing with him in Persian. He then traveled to Śrī Pāda (Adam's Peak) with other Muslim pilgrims and visited the Hindu-Buddhist god Viṣṇu temple at Dondra.[17] Some 60 years later, the Chinese fleet commanded by Admiral Zheng He made its second visit to the island bringing a stele describing in Persian, Chinese and Tamil offerings to the same multi-religious sites. The choice of the three languages indicates their commercial relevance at the time with, notably, Persian not Arabic and Tamil not Sinhala. That the Jaffna king had also used Persian to communicate with Ibn Battuta suggests its importance as the trade language without in any way indicating that Sri Lanka's Muslims are any more Persian than they are Tamil. Nor does this evidence deny Arabic its prime location for Muslims as the language of the Prophet and the language of prayer.

[16] An early nationalist leader well regarded by Sinhalese and Tamils, Ramanathan made his case in the Legislative Council and subsequently published the work in the Royal Asiatic Society (Ceylon Branch) journal. The article is reprinted in *The Sri Lanka Reader*, edited by John Clifford Holt as well as I.L.M. Abdul Azeez's critique published in 1907 and McGilvray and Raheem's excellent historical survey of Muslim settlement first published in 2007.

[17] Battuta's description is partially reproduced in *The Sri Lanka Reader*. He describes the rituals practiced by Muslim pilgrims over the three days of their morning and evening visits to the sacred footprint as well as the offerings of gems, jewelry and gold (see also Premakumara de Silva, "Hindu and Muslim Connections to Sri Pada," *Religion in Context*, ed. Jayadeva Uyangoda (Colombo: Social Scientists' Association), 143).

Our commencing point for the consideration of Muslim communities in Sri Lanka must, therefore, be an acknowledgment of multiple influences over a long period. While we broadly agree with the assessment by McGilvray and Raheem[18] that Muslim impact was "Arabic in culture and mercantile in motivation," and note too their insistence that Sri Lankan and South Indian Muslims are not descended from the same groups who conquered North India, we also want to suggest that the label "Arabic" be used carefully on account of the multiple West Asian influences over several centuries of Indian Ocean trade where the dominant trade languages were Persian and Tamil and the Arabs included Christians and Jews as well as Muslims. It is this diversity, probably unremarkable at other times, that is actively suppressed in the modern period. In a related way, the kingdoms of this time are too readily defined ethnically. The Jaffna king who met Ibn Battuta in Puttalam was the king of the north. The Kotte kingdom centered on Colombo developed later, and the king whom Admiral Zheng met (and abducted), Vīra Alakeśvara, was linked to a South Indian trading family-corporation, the Alagakkōnāra.[19] To imagine a Sinhalese south and Tamil north is simply inaccurate. What is more accurate, though, is the acknowledgment that both kingdoms were more closely connected to Hindu-Buddhist state ideology than to Muslim, because this was a critical dimension of the North Indian conquest that did not occur in the south.

When Ramanathan made his contentious assertion of Tamil Muslim ethnicity in 1885, the storm clouds of ethno-religious antagonism were brewing in Sri Lanka in conjunction with religious revitalization movements and the democratization of the British colonial government. This led to (almost) universal suffrage in 1931 and independence in 1948.[20] Best documented of the revitalization movements are those of

[18] Dennis McGilvray and Mirak Raheem, "Origins of the Sri Lankan Muslims and Varieties of the Muslim Identity," reprint, *The Sri Lanka Reader: History, Culture, Politics*, ed. John Clifford Holt (Durham and London: Duke University Press, 2011), 410.

[19] De Silva, *A History of Sri Lanka*, 114.

[20] Determinations of citizenship eligibility excluded people of recent Indian arrival during the transition to self-rule thereby intensifying the insider/outsider debates and with them the growth of communalism. Sinhalese and Tamil politicians were complicit, as were the labor unions, in making these distinctions and thereby feeding the nationalist rhetoric (Nira Wickramasinghe, *Sri Lanka in the Modern Age: A History of Contested Identities* (London: Hurst and Company, 2006), 122).

the Buddhists particularly in their resistance to Christianity.[21] However, movements among all the island's religions were taking place including the Christian—established and new—and the Muslim with new groups of traders immigrating as well as new lines of communication being established. New groups led to new mosques and new expectations for communal coexistence.

Territoriality became increasingly contentious with a riot between Buddhists and Roman Catholics occurring in the inner part of Colombo in 1883 over religious festivals, processions and music.[22] This led to the implementation of legislation (the 1865 Police Ordinance) that would later have a bearing on the anti-Muslim riots of 1915.[23] In the Legislative Council in 1885 debates over the Council's representative nature were also developing along both caste and ethnic lines, even influencing later debates over women's suffrage (see below). This is why Ramanathan's remarks were so contentious and why they fed into the Muslim revitalization of Arabic genealogies going on at the time. These genealogies were being spurred by internal transformations in the Muslim community, associated with the more recently arrived trading groups, their competitive participation in certain markets and their construction of their own mosques.

The period is thus central to understanding contemporary Sinhala-Muslim antagonisms. In order to understand it better, we must first delineate a long-standing tension between agriculture and trade that informs relations between Buddhists and Muslims, and indicates that these relations are not to be grasped simplistically in terms of ethnic groups and boundaries, majorities and minorities. Rather, it should be understood in terms of concepts of identity emergent from forms of human practice. Our point is very simple: if Persian and Tamil were at one time the trade languages, Sinhala was the language of the land and the dynamics of ethnicity—antagonistic as well as accommodating—were

---

[21] Kitsiri Malalgoda, *Buddhism in Sinhalese Society, 1750–1900: A Study of Religious Revival and Change* (Berkeley, Los Angeles, and London: University of California Press, 1976).

[22] G.P.V. Somaratna, *Kotahena Riot 1883: A Religious Riot in Sri Lanka* (Colombo: Deepanee, 1991).

[23] Roberts, *Exploring Confrontation*, 149–181; Stanley J. Tambiah, *Leveling Crowds: Ethnonationalist Conflicts and Collective Violence in South Asia* (Berkeley, Los Angeles, and London: University of California Press, 1996), 48–56.

34 R. BASTIN AND P. DE SILVA

emergent properties of the material practices associated with commerce and agriculture.

ROBE AND PLOUGH ... AND TRADER

We return to the Cholas and the decline of the hydraulic civilization of the Rājaraṭṭa and suggest that the bias in Sinhala Buddhist nationalist historiography regarding the Cholas is not simply rooted in an ethnic antagonism that regards the Rājaraṭṭa as purely Sinhala and Buddhist and the Chola invaders as Tamil and Hindu. More radically, it describes the agrarian bias in Sinhala Buddhist historiography as this derives from Sri Lanka's long-standing tradition of historical chronicles written and preserved by monastic Buddhist monks who were maintained by an agrarian political system that we refer to as a polity in order to distinguish it from a modern bureaucratic state.[24] Where the state defines itself through its boundaries, the polity starts with the center and has more porous boundaries.[25]

This agrarian bias is an important point for understanding the nature of ethnic relations in Sri Lankan history, because it is a bias toward the perceived essence of the Sinhala Buddhist ethnicity and, concomitantly, toward what is perceived to be external or marginal to that ethnicity. The critical issue is the way in which the historical importance of trade is suppressed in the awareness of history and how this suppression of awareness itself relates to social and cultural identity. Put simply, at the heart of the "people of the lion" ("*sinha*") is, as Gunawardana[26] long argued, the agrarian hydraulic civilization that is also the heart of the Buddhist monastic traditions out of which the chronicles appeared.

As K.M. De Silva[27] notes in the revised edition of his magisterial *A History of Sri Lanka* (first published in 1981) external trade was of considerable importance to the kingdoms of Sri Lanka, albeit virtually absent from the chronicles (as well as the first edition of his book!). Absence

---

[24] Stanley J. Tambiah, *World Conqueror and World Renouncer: A Study of Buddhism and Polity in Thailand Against a Historical Background* (Cambridge: Cambridge University Press, 1976), 102–131.

[25] See also Stanley J. Tambiah, *Buddhism Betrayed? Religion, Politics, and Violence in Sri Lanka* (Chicago and London: University of Chicago Press, 1992), 150.

[26] Gunawardana, "The People of the Lion."

[27] De Silva, *A History of Sri Lanka*, 43.

does not, however, make for insignificance, especially in social ideologies where the margins of the polity were invested with special meaning. Sri Lanka's Muslims and more broadly the category of the "Demala" (Tamil but we suggest Tamil-speaker) were thus categories of outsider vis-à-vis the Sinhala Buddhist polity. That polity has long celebrated a special relationship of sovereignty as the order of the village, its irrigation tank and the Buddhist temple.[28] Just as the "Triple Gem" of Buddha, Dhamma and Sangha (crudely Lord Buddha, his teachings and the order of monks) establishes the ideal order of Buddhist polity and society, its localized expression is in the form of an agrarian village (*gama*) practicing wet rice cultivation fed by a village tank (*wewa*) and supporting its own Buddhist temple and resident monks (*vihāra*). Such an ideal community—the *Śāsana* as this describes both the institutions and the society of adherents[29]—is also Sinhala-speaking.

Thus, just as we can recognize the contingent nature of Persian and Tamil as the regional trade languages, we should also recognize the contingent nature of Sinhala as the language of the land for those kingdoms that professed Buddhism and patronized the Sangha. In doing so, we can recognize how ethnicity in Sri Lanka is a circumstantial and relational quality grounded in a distinction and tension between movable and immovable wealth.

Instead of commencing our analysis of ethnicity with the ethnic groups, we insist in short on commencing with the *relations* between groups based on their practices instead of their imagined essential identities. We are not saying that every paddy farmer in Sri Lanka is or was a Sinhala Buddhist or that every trader was a Tamil-speaking Muslim or Hindu, any more than we are saying that this is a feature throughout the ancient Hindu-Buddhist world. We are simply noting a well-known feature of the "galactic polities"[30] of South and Southeast Asia that the traders were typically members of ethno-religious minorities vis-à-vis the monarch and more especially his/her subjects spatially configured and territorialized in a *mandala*-like centric pattern. It is a relation that has led *inter alia* to less historical acknowledgment than what Indian Ocean

---

[28] R.A.L.H. Gunawardana, *Robe and Plough: Monasticism and Economic Interest in Early Medieval Sri Lanka* (Tucson: the University of Arizona Press, 1979).

[29] John Ross Carter, *On Understanding Buddhists: Essays on the Theravada Tradition in Sri Lanka* (Albany: State University of New York Press, 1993), 14–19.

[30] Tambiah, *World Conqueror and World Renouncer.*

commerce merits and, with that, to inadequate appreciation of the social dynamics of the region. We stress, though, that this is not simply the result of an Orientalist bias or even a terra-centric archaeology that builds its accounts out of stone to the neglect of more perishable artifacts like boats, but also of a bias in local ideologies and their regal histories suppressing the importance of trade and more importantly traders. Such bias was there in the work of the doyen of Sri Lankan academic history, K.M. De Silva, but subsequently corrected in 2005. That correction has, however, not yet permeated and may never permeate those nationalist ideologies that always start with the ethnic groups and read the old chronicles as factual accounts of all that was there rather than all that mattered in the eyes of the Buddhist monk authors.

CASTE AND ETHNICITY

Notwithstanding historical and regional variations, caste in Sinhalese society bears out this agrarian bias. Castes are occupation-based and formally endogamous entities that do not form a coherent system in the manner of the Indian phenomenon, because at the heart of Sinhalese caste is the concept of regal service (*rājakāriya*) whereby group access to land and agriculture is achieved through caste-specific labor obligations.[31] Every citizen-subject of the polity was thus a farmer, albeit with different occupational commitments to the polity that gave these subjects access to land; commitments that included maintaining the tanks as well as the temples that enjoyed land tenure through royal decree. To be Sinhalese was thus to belong to a caste and to have a practical relationship to land and its ultimate owner the sovereign ruling through local landed elite, as well as a relationship to Buddhism and its land-holding institutions that also tended to be under the same elite control. The numerically largest caste in such a system was, not surprisingly, the *goyigama* or cultivator caste with the dominant social distinction being that of a landowner and a landless laborer. It was from the *goyigama*, moreover, that the members of the *sangha* were drawn, albeit unevenly depending on the temple and its lands, which contributed toward the internal status differentiation of the caste as a whole including the existence of aristocratic sub-castes. Degrees of endogamy, post-marital residence,

---

[31] Patrick Peebles, *Social Change in Nineteenth Century Ceylon* (Colombo: Navrang in Association with Lake House Bookshop, 1995), 44–51.

polygamy and the property rights of women all varied according to this scale of relative landed wealth.[32]

Sovereignty was thus heavily connected to territory, a feature strongly evident, for example, in the Sinhalese system of personal names whereby the village name accompanies extended and immediate family names. This made every household head the lord of his or her domain in a nested series upon the apex of which sat the king as the chief protector of the Buddha *Śāsana*, which we reiterate describes the teachings and institutions of Buddhism as well as the community of citizens who supported those institutions.[33] Finally, the system of castes was not an unchanging element of the pre-colonial polity any more than the system of *rājakāriya* only ever identified regal service as caste-specific labor. Military service and capital works, for example, could meet service requirements, as could the production of trade commodities like cinnamon peeling become associated with people whose erstwhile occupation was weaving. Under European colonialism, *rājakāriya* was modified even further, being for example, banned and then reinstituted with new and loyal subaltern elite to implement it.[34]

Significantly, there was no trader caste in the Sinhalese caste system and traders thus remained the members of ethnic minorities even when the medieval drift of centers of power to the southwest of Sri Lanka took place in hand with the intensification of maritime trade and disruptions to the ideal agrarian order. With Arab and Persian, as well as Chinese and Indian merchants, the wealth of South India and Sri Lanka shifted from rice to spices in hand with the ongoing commerce in elephants, timber, arecanut, pearls, gems and coconut products. The thirteenth-century Dambadeniya Kingdom centered on the city of Kurunegala and included extensive trade networks running across the island to the many ports of the east and especially west coasts. Muslim traders featured prominently, but their marginality remained, as the following myth of the

---

[32] Gananath Obeyesekere, *Land Tenure in Village Ceylon* (Cambridge: Cambridge University Press, 1967); Nur Yalman, *Under the Bo Tree: Studies in Caste, Kinship, and Marriage in the Interior of Ceylon* (Berkeley and Los Angeles: University of California Press, 1967).

[33] Carter, *On Understanding Buddhists*.

[34] Peebles, *Social Change in Nineteenth Century Ceylon*, 48–51.

38   R. BASTIN AND P. DE SILVA

thirteenth-century king Wattimi Baṇḍāra (also known as Galē Baṇḍāra) attests.[35]

A Myth of a Trader Deity

According to the text *Dambadeni Asna*, Galē Baṇḍāra's father was King Bhuveneka Bahu I (1272–1284) and his mother, a Muslim. On account of this inappropriate union, the boy Ishmael was raised in secret by Muslims in their main trading base at Beruwala on the west coast.[36] The king subsequently had a legitimate heir by one of his wives and later died in tragic circumstances in a pattern that is repeated in several Sinhala Buddhist myths describing the origins of the class of deity to which Galē Baṇḍāra belongs. These are minor deities transformed or apotheosized from significant humans after their untimely deaths and are referred to as the *baṇḍāra* (guardian) deities.[37] Frequently, the local myth for such a *baṇḍāra* deity describes a king going to battle. The king instructs his wives that if he is victorious, a white flag would be waved while a black flag indicated defeat (and its dire consequences for the royal household).

Though he wins, the king's messenger drunkenly waves the wrong flag prompting the king's wives to commit suicide followed by the king when he learns of the disaster. The king then transforms into a *baṇḍāra* deity and the wives into forms of the pious Buddhist goddess Pattini.[38] Such a deity is more accurately a *baṇḍāra devata* (guardian deity-demon) capable of demonic destructiveness tempered into righteous violence through the mediation of the Pattini, but always unstable and occupying

[35] H.W. Codrington, *A Short History of Ceylon*, reprint of the 1929 original (New Delhi: Asian Educational Services, 1994), 77.

[36] Noting the presence of Arabs, Berbers and the ritual of whirling dances at Beruwela, Gunawardana ("Changing Patterns of Navigation") suggests a close connection between the island and the Mamluk Kingdom of Egypt (1250–1517 C.E.) whereby a permanent settlement of merchants was established at Beruwala between 1287 and 1293 or between 1302 and 1326.

[37] Bruce Kapferer, *The Feast of the Sorcerer: Practices of Consciousness and Power* (Chicago and London: University of Chicago Press, 1997), 32; Gananath Obeyesekere, *The Cult of the Goddess Pattini* (Chicago and London: University of Chicago Press, 1984), 69, 285–296.

[38] Rohan Bastin, *The Domain of Constant Excess: Plural Worship at the Munnesvaram Temples in Sri Lanka* (New York and Oxford: Berghahn Books, 2002), 150.

2   HISTORICAL THREADS OF BUDDHIST–MUSLIM RELATIONS IN SRI LANKA   39

the cusp between divine and demonic.[39] The Galē *Baṇḍāra* myth is a variant with the interesting twist of its extension to the king's illegitimate son Ishmael who claims the throne after his father's suicide by presenting a copperplate inscription as evidence of his ancestry.

Ishmael's rule then becomes harsh, as, obsessed with prophecy of a fortune hidden in the Kurunegala lake, he causes large numbers of his subjects to be put to death trying to find it. He is subsequently assassinated in a conspiracy of Buddhist monks and Sinhalese nobles, whereupon he becomes the deity-demon Galē Baṇḍāra a contemporary sorcery deity with both a Buddhist and a Muslim shrine by the shores of the lake. Strikingly, at the Muslim shrine, sorcery offerings take the form of small bags of pepper corns hung from the eaves of the building. With pepper having been one of the principal commercial items passing through the Dambadeniya capital, its use in sorcery is matched by the use of chilli in other sorcery shrines where the link between sorcery and trade is also very clear.[40] What the contemporary Sinhala Buddhist cosmology thus highlights is the persistent idea that trade is magically dangerous.

The Galē Baṇḍāra myth, its location in the Dambadeniya kingdom of the thirteenth century, a time of an intensifying spice economy, and its inclusion of Muslims in the story illustrate our broader point about the cosmology of trade and with that the relation of Muslims to the Sinhala Buddhist polity. For Galē Baṇḍāra is obsessed with wealth. In other words, he displays excessive attachment and lack of regard for his subjects. He thus reveals an ambivalence that is at the heart of the polity itself. The traders might thus be outsiders to the ideal agrarian Buddhist polity, but that does not mean they are excluded. Rather, it means that they and their commerce are hierarchically subordinated and, like the demonic in Sinhala Buddhism, considered dangerous especially when, in the logic of hierarchical reversal, they are understood to threaten the ideal order.[41] Ishmael the trader becomes the king, but in his greed (worldly attachment) never ceases to be a merchant and this causes his subjects to suffer. Put to death he becomes a deity-demon, a member of

[39] Kapferer, *The Feast of the Sorcerer*, 308–309.

[40] Kapferer, *The Feast of the Sorcerer*, 243.

[41] Bruce Kapferer, *Legends of People, Myths of State: Violence, Intolerance, and Political Culture in Sri Lanka and Australia* (Revised and updated edition, Oxford and New York: Berghahn Books, 2012), 106–107.

40 R. BASTIN AND P. DE SILVA

a specific class of deities in the Sinhala Buddhist pantheon who remain oriented toward worldly and thus human practices.[42]

In other *bandāra* myths, it is the suiciding king who becomes the deity-demon. Taniyavalla Baṇḍāra whose historical personage is discussed below, is an example of this; his deity-demon ambivalence expressed in conjunction with the bright and dark halves of the year. For Galē Baṇḍāra, however, we find a mythical variant where it is the son of the dead king and, moreover, a son whose actions in this world were demonic in the sense that they are marked by excessive attachment that causes human suffering. The Muslim Galē Baṇḍāra deity, the figure in the Muslim shrine at Kurunegala, is thus more exclusively demonic in relation to the Buddhist figure in the Buddhist shrine. In other words, the ambivalence is less between the bright and dark halves of the year as it is between the Buddhist and the Muslim forms of the deity-demon. The mythical variant thus reveals a distinct characterization of Islam vis-à-vis Buddhism in the cosmology, a cosmology that the *bandāra* deities reveal as being fed by historical circumstances. Such circumstances, moreover, are not exclusively Muslim, but can also be Tamil as well as indigenous Vedda, because all these categories in their own way can be associated with cosmically dangerous externality in respect to the Sinhala Buddhist polity.[43]

MUSLIM PIRATES IN THE KOTTE PERIOD

Due west of Kurunegala, Madampe is a small town near the coast. Its large irrigation tank enables agriculture to support a sizeable population while its location on a major road to the interior as well as access to the Chilaw lagoon and port of Chilaw placed it on an old trade route albeit as a Buddhist agricultural site. During the Kotte Period from the late fourteenth century until the Portuguese conquest from the mid-sixteenth century, Madampe was a local political center inhabited by junior members of the ruling dynasty. Its population includes a sizeable Muslim segment.

The seventeenth-century Sinhala-language *Rājāvaliya* chronicle describes the ruling prince of Madampe, Taniya Walla assisting his elder

---

[42] Kapferer, *The Feast of the Sorcerer*, 33; see also Obeyesekere *The Cult of the Goddess Pattini*, 285–296.

[43] Kapferer, *The Feast of the Sorcerer*, 308–310.

2 HISTORICAL THREADS OF BUDDHIST–MUSLIM RELATIONS IN SRI LANKA

brother Sakalakalā Walla to defeat a Muslim "pirate" at Chilaw some-time during the first years of the reign of King Dharma Parākramabāhu IX (1489–1513). Kadirāyana Mudaliyār and his fellow Moors from Kayalpattinam (or Korkai in Arabic) who had come to Chilaw to fish illegally for pearls were routed by the princes who smashed their boats, killed the leader and delivered the survivors to the king.[44] Like Ishmael/Galē Baṇḍāra, the Muslim "pirate" challenged Sinhala Buddhist sover-eignty. Other Muslim traders were less bold, paying tribute to Kotte and enjoying a virtual monopoly over the island's maritime trade from which the kingdom's rulers kept apart. Over the next century, though, this rela-tion was violently challenged by the Portuguese who first arrived in the region in 1498 and in Sri Lanka in 1506.

The *Rājāvaliya* reads in places as if it were written by a Buddhist while elsewhere it talks of a singular Christian divinity. Composed dur-ing the period of the rise of Portuguese Roman Catholicism in the Kotte kingdom, it appears that the depiction of Muslims in the *Rājāvaliya* is colored by the deep antagonism held by the Portuguese. With the recapture of the Iberian Peninsula a few years prior to the advent of the Portuguese in the commercially busy Indian Ocean, the strong feature of the new maritime empire was its anti-Muslim crusader spirit. To imagine, though, anti-Muslim intolerance as solely European Christian would be a conceit. Instead, the hybrid nature of a text like the *Rājāvaliya* sug-gests a resonance that the Portuguese empire amplified. This is why it is important to consider myths like that of Ishmael/Galē Baṇḍāra and Taniyavalla Baṇḍāra to recognize the tension that existed between the land-based kingdoms and their trade on the threshold of the European era.

WESTERN EUROPEAN CHRISTIANITY: INTOLERANCE AND THE STATE

Anti-Muslim Portuguese impact was, nevertheless, immense, disrupting both the Muslim Mappilla monopoly on overseas trade in the region as well as fundamental features of the traditional polities at the local level. When, for example, the Kotte King Vijayabāhu VI was deposed by his

---

[44] B. Gunasekara, ed., *Rājāvaliya or A Historical Narrative of Sinhalese Kings from Vijaya to Vimala Dharma Surya II* (Colombo: George J.A. Skeen Government Printer, 1900), 61–62.

three eldest sons in 1521, the kingdom was divided into three: a reduced Kotte, Sītavāka and Kandy. The kingdoms were quickly beset by war stemming in part from the growing Portuguese presence in Kotte, and their violently expanding and deliberately anti-Muslim control over maritime trade.[45] In 1526, the Portuguese forced the new Kotte king Bhuvanekabāhu VII (1521–1551) to evict all Muslims from Kotte's port Colombo. Sītavāka and Kandy benefitted from the decision which in turn heightened tensions.

This is the context in which we read the *Rājāvaliya* account of Vijayabāhu VI's death when his three eldest sons deposed him in 1521. Refusing to commit the act of regicide (notwithstanding the fact that their father had arranged their murders), the three sons eventually enlisted "a stranger, Salmá by name"[46] to murder the king. He was most likely a Muslim. The interesting point for our purposes is that the *Rājāvaliya* documents this and thus reiterates the broader sense of danger associated with Muslims and trade.[47]

Portuguese power was not consolidated in Kotte until the 1550s when the new and it turned out last king Dharmapala IX (1551–1597) converted to Christianity and flattened every non-Christian temple in his capital. Elsewhere on the littoral, moreover, Portuguese suzerainty was not fully established until the collapse of Sītavāka in the early 1590s. Thereupon, the destruction of temples and erection of churches in their place proceeded apace.[48] Accompanied by extensive religious conversion and resettlement of Tamil-speaking communities from the Fishery Coast of South India to the Sri Lankan west coast, as well as violent incidents and massacres of both Christian and Muslim coastal communities in the Straits of Mannar, Portuguese rule profoundly changed the social and

---

[45] Jorge Manuel Flores, "The Straits of Ceylon, 1524–1539: The Portuguese-Mappilla Struggle Over a Strategic Area," in *Sinners and Saints: The Successors of Vasco da Gama*, ed. Sanjay Subrahmanyam (Delhi: Oxford University Press, 1998); Alan Strathern, *Kingship and Conversion in Sixteenth-Century Sri Lanka: Portuguese Imperialism in a Buddhist Land* (Cambridge: Cambridge University Press, 2010), 21ff.

[46] Gunasekara, *Rājāvaliya*, 66.

[47] The idea reappears in accounts of the 1818 rebellion by Kandyan chiefs led by Keppitipola with the British attempting to spy on the rebels through a Muslim trader (Kumari Jayawardena, *Perpetual Ferment: Popular Revolts in Sri Lanka in the 18th and 19th Centuries* (Colombo: Social Scientists' Association, 2010), 76).

[48] C.R. De Silva, *The Portuguese in Ceylon, 1617–1638* (Colombo: H.W. Cave, 1972); Strathern, *Kingship and Conversion*.

cultural landscape especially through the promotion of religious intolerance with the traditional role played by temples in the articulation of commerce and agriculture being subverted by missionary zeal.[49] Such articulation had hitherto preserved the separation between trade and agriculture whereby the former was an ethno-religious minority affair vis-à-vis the Sinhala Buddhist polity. Under Portuguese rule, though, it begins to open up in the absence of temples as regulatory institutions.[50] The changing nature of caste relations, of *rājakāriya*, and the emergence of new castes hitherto outside the structure of the agrarian service economy and, with that, the Sinhala Buddhist social formation was linked to this changing politico-cosmological landscape. Portuguese land grants to individuals were also important. They grew in number under the Dutch who ousted the Portuguese in the 1650s and, dramatically so, under the British who ousted the Dutch in 1796 and conquered Kandy in 1815.

From the seventeeth century onward, therefore, the traditional temple and caste-based demarcation between commerce and agriculture erodes through the intensification of trade and the transformation of the traditional hubs of articulation. With this shift emerged a greater ambiguity in the nature of sovereignty, a greater sense of slippage between the political, the economic and the religious as these had once clustered around the institution of the Sinhala Buddhist village and feudal territory. We stress again that this is not, as Lorna Dewaraja[51] contends, the end of a millennium of ethnic harmony, for we think that the tales of Kadirāyana and his pirates of Kayalpattinam or Galē Baṇḍāra the Muslim Dambadeniya king would say otherwise. We would certainly agree, though, that the fanatical intolerance intensified under the Portuguese in hand with their imposition of their political (and economic) cosmology.

---

[49] The history of Portuguese rule in Sri Lanka is extensively documented with both contemporary documents such as Fernaõ De Queyroz, *The Temporal and Spiritual Conquest of Ceylon* in three volumes (New Delhi: Asian Educational Services, 1992) and the three-volume archive created by V. Perniola, *The Catholic Church in Sri Lanka: The Portuguese Period Volume I, 1505–1565; Volume 2, 1566–1619; and Volume 3, 1620–1658* (Dehiwala, Sri Lanka: Tisara Prakasakayo, 1989, 1991a, 1991b). Among the more recent histories, we note C.R. De Silva, *The Portuguese in Ceylon, 1617–1638*; Strathern *Kingship and Conversion*.

[50] This point is discussed at length by Bastin, *The Domain of Constant Excess* who highlights important features of temple festivals as well as aspects of the cosmology of trade.

[51] Dewaraja, "The Muslims of Sri Lanka."

As the Portuguese required any natives in their employ to be Catholics, the Dutch East India Company (VOC) also required its subalterns to join the Dutch Reformed Church.[52] The principal reward sought by these subalterns was land.[53] Land tenure in the Dutch maritime territories thus began to reveal an amalgam of outright individual ownership and the more traditional caste feudalism evident in the Kandyan kingdom and its organization of villages.[54] Even there, however, the system of tenure and strength of caste relations varied in intensity over time and across space as the system of *rājakāriya* was also the source of peasant mobilization for the defense of the kingdom from European conquest.[55] The question of being Sinhalese and being loyal to the independent Buddhist kingdom was, therefore, more than a matter of providing obligatory regal service according to one's caste. It was also a matter of military mobilization and proximity to the border.

The fall of Kandy in 1815 and suppression of rebellions in 1818 and 1848 led to the assertion of complete British control, which enabled extensive private land ownership, the growth of a plantation economy, and an influx of Tamil-speaking wage labor. The demand for food imports and the location of markets also changed, creating new commercial opportunities and sites for foreign traders including Tamil-speaking Hindu Chettiars and Indian Muslims. The latter were able to purchase agricultural land, albeit typically in marginal areas some of which would later rise to prominence through post-independence hydel schemes in the Eastern Province from the 1960s onward and aquaculture (prawn farming) in the North–West from the 1990s onward. The subaltern elite whose roots lay in the Portuguese and Dutch commercial economies and who had acquired land in the maritime areas expanded their plantation and other commercial interests while their Kandyan counterparts also profited from complicity in the colonial order. Now largely Anglican, the emerging bourgeoisie presided over local agricultural domains sponsoring temples where they would later worship when the subaltern elite's

---

[52] Peebles, *Social Change in Nineteenth Century Ceylon*, 97.

[53] Peebles, *Social Change in Nineteenth Century Ceylon*, 40ff.

[54] Nirmal Ranjith Dewasiri, *The Adaptable Peasant: Agrarian Society in Western Sri Lanka Under Dutch Rule, 1740–1800* (Leiden: Brill, 2008).

[55] Newton Gunasinghe, *Changing Socio-Economic Relations in the Kandyan Countryside* (Colombo: Social Scientists' Association, 1990).

official commitment to Christianity was relaxed and the process of conversion to Buddhism began.

For the Kandyans, though, no such conversion took place, because the British had protected Buddhism when they annexed the kingdom. The demise of the last regal dynasty in Kandy thus did not end the institution of a sovereign Buddhist polity. Rather, it transformed it into an empty throne of ritual spectacle subsequently patronized by the British[56] and, more importantly in the preservation of Buddhist temporalities.[57] The Buddhist sovereign order connecting the village to the tank and the temple thus became patronized by the developing modern bureaucratic state which oversaw the acquisition and transformation of land into plantations while a sense of traditional agrarian village remained through the inalienable sanctity accorded temple lands. In the maritime areas, though, many lands like this were created by bourgeois donation; the reason being both (new) Buddhist piety as well as the important role that temples played in capturing and controlling labor (essentially what caste relations are all about). The subaltern elite, its members often belonging to old aristocracy as well as the parvenu, became a new bourgeoisie whose wealth derived from the colonial economy while at the same time affecting the manners and customs of traditional Sinhala Buddhist landlords.[58] The village headman system through which the British governed also replicated and reactivated this seemingly traditional order.[59]

Our history is admittedly broad brush. What we want to stress is how the boundaries between agriculture and trade that fractured in the growing spice economy of the medieval southwest drift crumbled more dramatically through the age of plantations when land was almost

[56] H.L. Seneviratne, *Rituals of the Kandyan State* (Cambridge: Cambridge University Press, 1978).

[57] British engagement with the Kandy *Āsala Pärahara* festival is important here (Seneviratne, *Rituals of the Kandyan State*). The empty throne was taken to Britain and used at Windsor Castle until the 1930s when it was repatriated and became a prominent symbol of independence as restoration (Nira Wickramasinghe, "From Hybridity to Authenticity: The Biography of a Few Kandyan Things," in *The Hybrid Island: Culture Crossings and the Invention of Identity in Sri Lanka*, ed. Neluka Silva (Colombo: Social Scientists' Association, 2002)).

[58] Kumari Jayawardena, *Nobodies to Somebodies: The Rise of the Colonial Bourgeoisie in Sri Lanka* (New Delhi: Leftword Books, 2000).

[59] Gunasinghe, *Changing Socio-Economic Relations in the Kandyan Countryside*.

completely commoditized. Plantation capitalism swept the island into the industrial age promoting tea and rubber as well as Tamil-speaking immigrants, but securing religious temporalities from the market as an extension of the special status accorded to Buddhism in the Kandyan Convention. It also provoked religious revitalization and the active reproduction of traditional Buddhism as a landed and agrarian religion, now sponsored by the relatively recent *arrivistes* many converting to Buddhism from Anglicanism into which their ancestors had previously converted from the Dutch Reformed Church in order to participate in the VOC administration and, before that, Roman Catholicism to work for the Portuguese. In doing so, the *arrivistes* encountered antagonism from the Kandyan Sinhalese who had resisted European incursion and actively endorsed the principle that Buddhism in Sri Lanka and with it the "People of the Lion" were under constant threat from alien religions most notably European Christian, but also Tamil Hindu and, to a lesser extent, Tamil-speaking Islam.

PLANTATION CAPITALISM

Importantly, all of these religions were transforming in the circumstances of religious revival and immigration by new trading groups and clergies, missionaries and religious teachers, as well as new social classes emerging in the conditions of the expanding bureaucratic state, urban hubs and plantation economies. French and Italian Catholic priests, English and American Protestant missionary-educators, Indian and Malay Muslims all came to the island along with South Indian plantation laborers and Hindu and Muslim traders, settling in numbers in different parts of the island but especially the commercial and administrative centers that became marked by their ethno-religious diversity and, in the rapidly growing primate city of Colombo, by the relative dearth of Sinhala Buddhists.[60]

Immediately outside Colombo, though, the rubber plantations that have in more recent years given way to suburbia stood adjacent to Buddhist temples built during the nineteenth century and serviced by

[60] Rohan Bastin, "Recognising the Spatial and Territorial Nature of Religious Communities in Colombo, Sri Lanka," in *Religion and Urbanism: Reconceptualising Sustainable Cities for South Asia*, ed. Yamini Narayanan (London and New York: Routledge, 2016).

agricultural villages ostensibly in a pre-plantation economy guise through which a sense of the traditional polity was reproduced, albeit with a profound sense of threat occasioned by the nature of the plantations, immigrant labor and the vicissitudes of the world economy.[61] That sense of threat conveyed in its way awareness of the radical transformation plantation capitalism wrought upon the traditional separation between movable and immovable wealth, including now the important distinction between movable wage labor and immovable caste-based farm labor.

The impact of plantation capitalism on Sri Lanka was thus enormous as it brought new forms of commerce that, as Dewasiri[62] shows, threatened but did not destroy the traditional agrarian economy and society. It also created traffic in people many of them traders and many of these traders Muslims coming from different parts of Asia. Written in 1950, S.L. Mohamed's description quoted below highlights this diversity as well as its concentration in commercial hubs like the Colombo Pettah which is the site of the first four mosques listed:

> There are large numbers of Muslims who sojourn in this country; they are Moplas [Mappillas], Memons, Hambayas, Borahs, Pathans, etc. They have their Mosques, Institutions, Associations and Clubs. They have their racial differences. The Hambayas Mosque in 2nd Cross Street, the Borah Mosque at 4th Cross Street, the Memon Mosque at 3rd Cross Street, the Moplah Mosque at Wolfendahl, Ahmedi Mosque at Negombo, and the Hanafi Mosques at Kandy and Gampola bear testimony to their distinct identity, like the local Malay Mosque at Slave Island and the Moorish Mosques all over the Island.[63]

"Moorish" here refers to the Muslims of long-standing identified in the British census reports as "Ceylon Moors" as distinct from "Coast Moors" who were more recent arrivals in the island. It is an important distinction drawn by the British because it resonates with the distinction between Ceylon and Indian Tamils as insiders and outsiders. Moreover, it resonates with the other distinction the British employed between

---

[61] This information derives from field research conducted separately and together by the authors.

[62] Dewasiri, *The Adaptable Peasant.*

[63] S.L. Mohamed, "Who Are the Moors of Ceylon?" reprint, *The Sri Lanka Reader: History, Culture, Politics,* ed. John Clifford Holt (Durham and London: Duke University Press, 2011), 430.

48   R. BASTIN AND P. DE SILVA

"Up-Country" or Kandyan Sinhalese and "Low-Country Sinhalese", not as a distinction between immigrant and native, albeit with some measure of this, but as a distinction between Sinhalese whose beliefs and lifestyle were closer to tradition and the coastal dwellers who had likely been Christian converts, possibly from an erstwhile inferior caste, and possibly an erstwhile Tamil-speaker. As Roberts[64] puts it, the Kandyans were thus the "Noble Savages" of the colony in the eyes of the British as well as their own.[65] The sentiment radiated to the minorities albeit with the important difference for Muslim groups especially that an outsider status could also connote a purer religious tradition.

Colonial taxonomies served, of course, to divide and rule, but were intra-ethnic as much as ethnic and, more importantly, related to social mobility more than administrative classification. The commoditization of land and the associated rupture in traditional forms of land tenure and use, the growth of wage labor and labor migration, and the rise of new entrepreneurial groups fractured the traditional separation between trade as an outsider activity and agriculture as the Sinhalese activity. Put differently, the old opposition between agriculture and trade, between insider (Sinhala Buddhist) and outsider (Tamil-speaking), transmuted into a multi-faceted antagonism within and between ethnic groups precisely as the traditional opposition was ruptured by plantation capitalism and its associated demographic and geographical shifts. The extent of such antagonism varied according to location, modernizing impact and the nature of the community. Nevertheless, it was widely felt. It was also ephemeral, with the currency and strength of certain antagonisms waxing and waning and mutually enhancing as well as suppressing each other in a kind of dance that persists to the present.

Democratization has played a key role. Representative institutions such as the Ceylon Legislative Council (started in 1833 and expanded with elections in 1910 and 1920) and the Colombo Municipal Council (1865) were central to the sense of citizenship and suffrage they instilled.

---

[64] Michael Roberts, *Caste Conflict and Elite Formation: The Rise of a Karāva Elite in Sri Lanka, 1500–1931* (Cambridge: Cambridge University Press, 1982), 229.

[65] Consider, for example, the villain in Leonard Woolf's 1913 novel *The Village in the Jungle*, the trader and moneylender Fernando whom Woolf describes as an unscrupulous town man who could barely speak Sinhala. Apart from the main characters, however, the villagers in the novel do not behave nobly. Leonard Woolf, *The Village in the Jungle* with an Introduction by E.F.C. Ludowyk (New Delhi: Oxford University Press, 1981).

Around these state institutions, moreover, developed civil society institutions where the representative politics played out in microcosm and in imitation of the often color-barred British equivalents. The Chilaw Planters' Association was modeled on the European-only Planters' Association; the Orient Club followed the principles of British social and sporting clubs; Ananda and Nalanda Colleges emulated Royal, St. Thomas's and Trinity right down to rivalrous annual cricket and rugby matches. Replete with their office bearers, membership criteria and rituals (where alcohol often played a key role), these various institutions informed debates regarding the nature of the state and the politics of citizenship and representation as they represented the subaltern elite as well as other less-integrated communities such as the Muslim, which was, nonetheless, drawn into the staged and relatively peaceful transition to self-rule. The democratization process that would inform elections from the 1920s onward was thus composed of multiple apparatuses not simply organizing the economy but also the social and religious life of the population. With so much in common between the old agrarian state formations and the bureaucratic state formation of plantation capitalism, the process of colonization thrived on its local resonances, but did so unevenly in respect to certain groups like the Muslims. While the force of numbers was an obvious factor, majoritarianism was also heavily influenced by these resonances between institutions of power and the hegemonic culture of colonial rule.

It was in these circumstances that Ponnambalam Ramanathan would claim the Ceylon Moors as ethnically Tamil in 1885 in a speech to the Legislative Council subsequently published in the Royal Asiatic Society journal.[66] It was in these circumstances, too, that the British would legislate over religious noise control associated with territorializing religious processions. This was part of what had provoked the Catholic-Buddhist Kotahena riot of 1883, as well as the sanctity of several religious spaces, including Adam's Peak which became more exclusively reconfigured as a Buddhist sacred site—Śri Pāda—to the exclusion of the other religious

---

[66]Tamil Hindu revivalism and that community's extensive engagement in the colonial bureaucracy are well known. See Rohan Bastin, "The Authentic Inner Life: Complicity and Resistance in the Tamil Hindu Revival," in *Sri Lanka: Collective Identities Revisited, Volume 1*, ed. Michael Roberts (Colombo: Marga Institute, 1997).

minorities notably Muslim that had long worshipped there.[67] The traditional relation of landed and movable wealth was thus recreated in a new form asserting the territorial priority of Sinhala Buddhism as if it were an ancient right.

Ethnic politics at the height of the British colonial period was thus born of a complex assemblage of plantation capitalism and bureaucratic administration of both people and land, with considerable immigration by South Indian plantation labor and merchants as well as growing involvement in commerce by groups active in the Buddhist revival. The relationship between agriculture and trade, between immovable and movable wealth was thus severely compromised at both the economic and political levels generating a profound tension that transmuted into the tensions between insiders and outsiders, authentic and inauthentic natives as well as authentic and inauthentic foreigners. We stress again that this is not simply a transition from tolerance to intolerance, for the violent history of the Sri Lankan polity shows otherwise. Nevertheless, it is a history where intolerance intensified during the modern period as the Sri Lankan economy and society became more closely articulated with a rapidly developing world system and its associated religious revitalizations.

GRAIN RIOTS AND 1915

Dramatic price increases in imported rice in 1866 provoked riots in different parts of the island with Indian Tamil laborers participating with local Sinhalese in the attacks on Indian Chettiar and Muslim shops.[68] As John Rogers shows, the antagonism was thus not communal but more simply the sense that consumers were being forced to bear the vicissitudes of the market. Nonetheless, ethnic antagonism deepened. In Chilaw, Madampe and nearby towns in December 1897, rice-price rioting directly targeted Muslim traders, prompting the British to send a special police detachment for six months.[69] Roman Catholics who

---

[67] Premakumara de Silva, "Reordering of Postcolonial Sri Pāda Temple in Sri Lanka: Buddhism, State and Nationalism," *History and Sociology of South Asia* 7, no. 2 (2013): 155–176.

[68] John D. Rogers, *Crime, Justice and Society in Colonial Sri Lanka* (London: Curzon Press, 1987), 164f.

[69] Rogers, *Crime, Justice and Society in Colonial Sri Lanka*, 166.

predominate in Chilaw were as much involved as Sinhala Buddhists. The Assistant Government Agent wrote in his annual report that:

> ... even as late as a fortnight after the disturbances I found it necessary to have certain young Sinhalese charged with insulting the Mohammedans by drawing pigs and indecent pictures on the walls of the mosque.[70]

With word of incidents like the Chilaw Christmas grain riot spreading, the ethnic nature of the antagonism grew and fueled the deepening sense of ethno-religious nationalism. Wickremeratne[71] captures this in an excellent description of the efforts at that time by upwardly mobile Sinhalese who were also revivalist Buddhists to break the age-old Sinhalese disdain toward trade as an ignoble profession in hand with an encouragement to shun non-Sinhalese traders. Embracing Sinhalese entrepreneurialism thus became part of the nationalist struggle in hand with embracing the nation's most ancient and authentic religion, the revival of which was also a revival of the historiography of the chronicles in all their parochialism and fear of invasion.

The First World War provided a tangible threat, provoking grain price hikes and in 1915 the worst ethnic rioting targeting a single ethnic community—the Muslim.[72] Ostensibly, the riots started over a dispute in the town of Gampola regarding Muslim protests at the failure by Sinhala Buddhist drummers on a procession organized by monks to obey the law and fall silent as they passed a mosque. Other factors contributed to the anti-Muslim mood, including Britain's invasion of the Ottoman kingdom of Turkey in the same year and the commemoration of the centenary of the fall of Kandy. Nor was it simply any mosque and its community that provoked the riot by reacting to the drumming, but a relatively new Coast Moor mosque whose members were more actively involved in Wahhabist religious revitalization.[73]

---

[70] Assistant Government Agent, *Administration Reports* (Colombo: Government Printers, 1897), G.18.

[71] L.A. Wickremeratne, "Religion, Nationalism, and Social Change in Ceylon, 1865–1885," *Journal of the Royal Asiatic Society of Great Britain and Ireland* 101, no. 2 (1969): 123–150, reprint (Colombo: Studies in Society and Culture: Sri Lanka Past and Present, 1993).

[72] Roberts, *Exploring Confrontation*, 149–212.

[73] Tambiah, *Leveling Crowds*, 74.

52   R. BASTIN AND P. DE SILVA

Taken all together, these factors suggest that the violence could have taken a different anti-British path that actually sided with the Muslims. That it did not stems in part from the long-standing xenophobic antagonism already well-entrenched. It also derives, we suggest, from the nature of the Sinhalese bourgeoisie whose members were actively involved (and subsequently jailed). For as we have argued, they were a subaltern elite whose class location was not only steeped in the colonial plantation economy, but also reactivating aspects of the traditional social formation such as building new caste-oriented Buddhist temples while at the same time forming and joining Anglo-style social clubs. The elite thus tended more toward mimetic desire for power than to its critique. In doing so, they tended toward the reinvention of communalism, rather than its rejection.

Closed and Open Economies and Their Changing Global Articulations

Writing in 1969 on the role of *arriviste* entrepreneurs in late nineteenth-century Buddhist nationalism Wickremeratne reveals a portent of what the socialist coalition government of Sirimavo Bandaranaike set about with the closed economy between 1970 and 1977. Minimizing imports in hand with a strong export economy from the state-run plantation sector extended the already expanding civil service, extensive nationalization of service industries, and the welfare state to impose a modernist state with a focus on land reform.[74] While such policies had secular ideological roots and a politico-economic orientation, they preserved a sense of xenophobic skepticism about overseas trade as they resonated with segments of the Buddhist revitalization movements that advocated welfare and social reform. This did not translate into complete support for the closed economy, specifically its austerity measures and autocratic bureaucracy, and nor did it achieve a greater distribution of landed wealth. Not surprisingly, then, the Bandaranaike Government was resoundingly defeated in 1977. Nevertheless, the sentiment of Buddhist nationalism and the sanctity of the village, tank and temple were preserved along with deep suspicion about minorities as foreign agents. Most importantly, though, was the legacy of centralized government which the new leader J.R. Jayawardene converted into an executive

[74] Sirimal Abeyratne, *Economic Change and Political Conflict in Developing Countries with Special Reference to Sri Lanka* (Amsterdam: VU University Press, 1998), 83–87.

presidency.[75] In doing so, he also actively asserted a sense of connection between the present and the past, stressing, for example, the links between his hydel/irrigation scheme and the ancient Sinhala Buddhist hydraulic civilizations at the same time that he opened the economy to globalization and offered the US Navy access to Trincomalee Harbor.

Governmentality in modern Sri Lanka, socialist and otherwise, has thus rarely been disentangled from the vestiges and reactivations of the traditional Buddhist polity, notably the elite patronage of landowning social strata whose intense personal and ideological rivalries are so underscored by kinship connections as to be worthy of the label "feudal."[76] Fought out largely in the democratic sphere, these rivalries were increasingly resolved in relation and reaction to minorities. Thus we find the scurrilous story that President Jayawardene had a Muslim ancestor, from Madampe no less! But this was small beer compared to the mobilization against those minorities threatening state sovereignty. It was thus that the Sri Lankan Tamils, whose traditional homelands included Trincomalee, became the main target of communal violence when the Tamil separatist movement grew in the mid-1970s. With extensive foreign investment backing Jayawardene's pro-American policies but also challenging India's growing sense of regional hegemony, Sri Lanka experienced an economic boom and an escalating civil war with multiple international players. Amid and indeed because of the rapidly expanding petro-capitalism of the Persian (Arabian) Gulf and its growing markets in East Asia, Sri Lanka's geopolitical significance rose and, with that, its civil war with the Tamils intensified.

Seemingly suppressed by the larger and more consequential violence between the Sinhalese state and Tamil separatists, anti-Muslim sentiments nonetheless persisted with multiple instances of isolated violence that, unlike the violence against Tamils, never received the amplifying support from government or from other states in the region.[77] Middle

[75] Wickramasinghe, *Sri Lanka in the Modern Age*.

[76] Janice Jiggins, *Caste and Family in the Politics of the Sinhalese 1947–1976* (Colombo: K.V.G. De Silva & Sons, 1979), 82–84.

[77] Rohan Bastin, "Globalisation and Conflict," in *A History of Ethnic Conflict in Sri Lanka: Marga Monograph Series on Ethnic Reconciliation, No. 23*, eds. Michael Roberts, Godfrey Gunatilleke, and Devanesan Nesiah (Colombo: MARGA Institute, 2001). The paper recounts how a riot arose from the enthusiastic celebration by a few young Muslim men of a televised cricket match victory by Pakistan over Sri Lanka. The paper goes on to describe how aspects of this violence reveal caste and class dimensions not reducible to ethnicity.

East labor migration contributed to this through the remittances from itinerant labor, which also brought thousands of Sri Lankans into direct contact with Arab Muslim societies and Islamic states with varying degrees of fundamentalism and indifference to the welfare of guest workers. As the demand for unskilled labor diminished, moreover, the preference to employ Sri Lankan Muslims increased. Anti-Arab and anti-Muslim attitudes were thus fostered.

Spared from the anti-Tamil pogrom of July 1983, Muslims became a buffer against Tamil self-determination demands, especially in the Eastern Province where a larger Muslim population was settled.[78] Through state-promoted hostilities between Muslims and Tamils in the Eastern Province in 1985, these areas of Muslim settlement were reconfigured, prompting the eviction of Muslims from the north and northwest by the Tamil Tigers in 1989. Massacres of Muslims in the east followed quickly with the Tiger leader Velupillai Prabhakaran later apologizing for his approach, which is arguably the most critical strategic blunder he made during the 30-year war, because it ultimately cost him the control of the Eastern Province.[79]

The Eastern Province was indeed the "crucible of conflict" as McGilvray described it, because the Tamil Tigers never controlled it fully and this provided the Sri Lankan government with a major military advantage. The Muslim population was critical through its members' neutrality. As the war progressed, this neutrality enabled the Muslim-dominated areas of the Eastern Province to prosper, especially after the 2004 Tsunami that flattened the east coast, wiping out thousands of lives and properties, but also enabling rapid capital investment especially in the main Muslim areas to the south of Batticaloa. Since the end of the war, these areas have become major sites of tension between Muslims and Tamils.

---

[78] Dennis B. McGilvray, *Crucible of Conflict: Tamil and Muslim Society on the East Coast of Sri Lanka* (Durham and London: Duke University Press, 2008).

[79] We stress arguably. Others would claim the greatest mistake was losing India's support after assassinating Rajiv Gandhi, while some would note the boycott of the presidential election that enabled Mahinda Rajapaksa to win office and prosecute the war to its bloody conclusion in 2009. In our view, however, the loss of control over the east that stemmed from the alienation and mistreatment of Muslims was the major mistake. See Karthigesu Sivathamby, "The Sri Lanka Ethnic Crisis and Muslim Tamil Relationships: A Socio-Political Review," in *Facets of Ethnicity in Sri Lanka*, eds. Charles Abeysekera and Newton Gunasinghe (Colombo: Social Scientists' Association, 1987).

The role of Muslims in the recent Sri Lankan civil war has perhaps been underestimated, highlighting in its own way the continuing marginality Muslims experience in the ideologies of economy and society that have historically informed ethnic relations between Muslims and the Sinhala Buddhist traditional polity and modern state. It is, moreover, a factor whose neglect has been compounded by the triumphalism of the victorious Rajapaksa Government which claimed a monopoly over the military defeat of the Tigers in 2009 matched only by its indifference and more accurately quiet support for the new wave of anti-Muslim antagonism that swept the island in the aftermath of victory (see Haniffa this volume).

A striking feature of the aftermath that brings us back to the beginning of this chapter where we quote the monks' political party spokesman Champika Ranawaka and note his connections to the left-wing and sometimes extremist JVP, is that the Buddhist nationalist political parties such as the Jathika Hela Urumaya and Bodu Bala Sena have a membership that is deeply entangled in the kinds of social transformation depicted here. They are predominantly petty bourgeois and socially mobile, albeit struggling in the face of post-war wealth.

Over the *longue durée* we have associated such transformation with the tensions between trade and agriculture, movable and immovable wealth, linking them to the formation and re-formation of ethno-religious groups as well as castes and other fractures within these groups. In more recent times, these fractures relate to class and the growth of the petty-bourgeoisie whose opportunities since the late 1960s have been not so much limited as fluid and sometimes short-lived avenues for education, labor migration, professional employment (including in the military) and investment. Class in contemporary Sri Lanka is thus open to multiple forces of fracture and alliance and was heavily influenced by three decades of war. Aspirational social segments of the petty bourgeoisie are confronted by a Sangha that is predominantly still controlled by the landed and *goyigama* elite while they themselves draw support from traders and their own social strata. Their antagonism for Muslims is matched by their demands that the government makes Buddhism the state religion, an action that would potentially liberate Buddhism from its existing structures of elite control. Thus, while they appear to be only antagonistic toward Muslims, the petty bourgeois Sinhalese are also involved in populist struggles with the old elite. This is an important feature of Sri Lanka's long civil war that was largely elided and twisted by issues of ethnicity that are ultimately only part of the story.

CONCLUSION

In taking the perspective of the *longue durée*, we have argued in this chapter that the history of interaction between Buddhists and Muslims in Sri Lanka must be situated in a broader history of the Sinhala Buddhist polity. The relation between agriculture and trade, as these were valued and devalued respectively, in the ideologies of kingship and the perfect Buddhist society over time, must be examined as a powerful element in Sri Lankan history and ideology.

We stress that this ideology is not merely a timeless feature going back to the original kingdom and the first Arabic-speaking traders who came to the island well over a millennium ago. Indeed, what we argue here is that in modernity, the original separation between commerce and agriculture has been blurred in hand with the formations of ethnicity within a modern bureaucratic state. The state was founded on the commoditization of land and the organization of citizenship around new criteria of inclusion and exclusion acting both between ethnic groups (Sinhala-"Demala") and *within* ethnic groups (native-migrant, authentic-inauthentic). To stress, therefore, a history of ethnic relations as a simple history of tensions between bounded categories—ethnic groups—is to ignore these internal differences and, with that, to fall into the trap of imagining a pristine state of harmony corrupted by modernity. It is in this way that historians and other scholars reproduce the nationalist ideology instead of working actively to debunk it for the broader benefit of the country. Not all of them, of course. We have drawn upon some excellent work in writing this chapter, but we have done so with an acute awareness of what Tisaranee Gunasekara calls "that familiar impasse" of populist historiography.

Accordingly, our sense of both ethnicity and ethnic relations in Sri Lankan history is one where a principle of dynamic relations is paramount, especially as these relate to the Sinhala Buddhist polity and to Tamil-speaking minorities. To that end, we have stressed how Sri Lanka's Muslim communities are not a single community descended from Arabs or any other specific group. They are not Tamils simply because they speak Tamil any more than the Sinhalese are Sinhalese simply because they speak Sinhala. Instead, they reflect in their diversity the richness of the island's history in the commerce and associated movement and upheaval of Indian Ocean trade over the last couple of millennia. The starting point for accommodation must not, therefore, be the roots of Muslim ethnicity *but the fact* of Muslim ethnicity in all its historical richness.

Such historical richness is not, moreover, a history of harmonious coexistence between Buddhist kings and Arab traders ruptured by zealous Christians. It was, instead, a tumultuous history involving a developing ambivalence between the hydraulic agrarian polities and expanding commerce. This led to the economy of spices on the western littoral and new participants articulated in different ways. Sinhala Buddhist polities weakened and fragmented in these circumstances as the relevance of marshaled territory diminished. The Portuguese entered that environment in the sixteenth century and set about their decades-long struggle with the Muslim Mappillas and an associated spiritual and temporal conquest, which not only targeted Muslims as well as the Hindu-Buddhist institutions that had historically played such an important role in the articulation of agriculture and trade, but also established the distinction between the spiritual and the temporal that their successors, the Protestant Dutch would amplify.

In breaking-up the temples, the Portuguese also commoditized land. The Dutch and the British dramatically expanded the process developing an increasingly secular bureaucratic state to survey and trade the old agrarian political spaces with a degree of secular ignorance and Protestant bias regarding the rights and functions of religious institutions as well as an egalitarian orientation toward ethnicity as differences within a degree—identities of the same kind. In such conditions, where elements of the traditional polity such as the notion of a landowner being a petty king were also being reproduced, tensions and animosities were bound to intensify albeit both within and between ethnic groups. Bourgeois Sinhalese thus struggled with other bourgeois Sinhalese to be the better caste and the better Buddhist while the minorities reinvented their foreignness in different ways such as documenting their Arab genealogies. The result was a civil war where not only was ethnicity a factor, but more importantly the fractures internal to the ethnic groups have been critical. This is especially important, because the internal fractures continue to be unresolved other than through the spurious chimera of an ethnic antagonism that with the end of the war against Tamil separatists rediscovered and reinvented the war with Sri Lanka's Muslims. This new war is, however, not simply the majority identifying the next minority in line, but itself a product of the social fractures that the war and global situation engendered.

Certainly, since 2009 the violence against Muslims has grown. It takes different forms from opposing new mosques, protesting cattle slaughter and staging riots on the basis of rumors of violence and even the presence of foreign Muslim extremists radicalizing locals to commit acts of terrorism. In the bombing attacks on Easter Sunday 2019 when Roman Catholic churches were targeted across the Sinhala-Tamil divide along with luxury Colombo hotels, it looked like all the anti-Muslim fears were being proven correct. Indeed, for many people, the violence appeared to be so aligned with these worst fears as to have been staged. In place of any conjectures along those lines, we simply note their existence and, at the same time, note that the kind of history we have developed here, a history of shifting tensions and antagonisms over decades of civil war, is one that can readily grant credence to even the most extraordinary conspiracy theories. Intrinsic to this, however, and what we have argued at several points in this paper, is the importance of the cleavages *within* the ethnic groups as much as between them.

References

Amrith, Sunil S. *Crossing the Bay of Bengal: The Furies of Nature and the Fortunes of Migrants.* Boston: Harvard University Press, 2013.

Assistant Government Agent. *Administration Reports.* Colombo: Government Printers, 1897.

Bastin, Rohan. "The Authentic Inner Life: Complicity and Resistance in the Tamil Hindu Revival." In *Sri Lanka: Collective Identities Revisited, Volume 1,* edited by Michael Roberts. Colombo: MARGA Institute, 1997.

———. "Globalisation and Conflict." In *A History of Ethnic Conflict in Sri Lanka: Marga Monograph Series on Ethnic Reconciliation, No. 23,* edited by Michael Roberts, Godfrey Gunatilleke, and Devanesan Nesiah. Colombo: MARGA Institute, 2001.

———. *The Domain of Constant Excess: Plural Worship at the Munnesvaram Temples in Sri Lanka.* New York and Oxford: Berghahn Books, 2002.

Bayly, Susan. *Saints, Goddesses and Kings: Muslims and Christians in South Indian Society, 1700–1900.* Cambridge: Cambridge University Press, 1990.

Carter, John Ross. *On Understanding Buddhists: Essays on the Theravada Tradition in Sri Lanka.* Albany: State University of New York Press, 1993.

Chaudhuri, K.N. *Asia Before Europe: Economy and Civilisation of the Indian Ocean from the Rise of Islam to 1750.* Cambridge: Cambridge University Press, 1990.

Codrington, H.W. *A Short History of Ceylon.* Reprint of the 1929 Original. New Delhi: Asian Educational Services, 1994.

De Queyroz, Father Fernaõ. *The Temporal and Spiritual Conquest of Ceylon.* Translated by Father S.G. Perera. Three Volumes Reprinted 1992. New Delhi: Asian Educational Services, 1930.

De Silva, C.R. *The Portuguese in Ceylon, 1617–1638.* Colombo: H.W. Cave, 1972.

De Silva, K.M. *A History of Sri Lanka,* 2nd ed. Colombo: Vijitha Yapa, 2005.

de Silva, Premakumara. "Hindu and Muslim Connections to Śri Pāda." In *Religion in Context,* edited by Jayadeva Uyangoda. Colombo: Social Scientists' Association, 2007.

———. "Reordering of Postcolonial Sri Pāda Temple in Sri Lanka: Buddhism, State and Nationalism." *History and Sociology of South Asia* 7, no. 2 (2013): 155–176.

Dewaraja, Lorna. *The Muslims of Sri Lanka: One Thousand Years of Ethnic Harmony.* Colombo: Lanka Islamic Foundation, 1994.

Dewasiri, Nirmal Ranjith. *The Adaptable Peasant: Agrarian Society in Western Sri Lanka Under Dutch Rule, 1740–1800.* Leiden: Brill, 2008.

Flores, Jorge Manuel. "The Straits of Ceylon, 1524–1539: The Portuguese-Mappilla Struggle Over a Strategic Area." In *Sinners and Saints: The Successors of Vasco da Gama,* edited by Sanjay Subrahmanyam, 57–74. Delhi: Oxford University Press, 1998.

Geertz, Clifford. *Negara: The Theatre State in Nineteenth-Century Bali.* Princeton: Princeton University Press, 1980.

Gunasekara, B., ed. *Rājāvaliya or A Historical Narrative of Sinhalese Kings from Vijaya to Vimala Dharma Surya II.* Colombo: George J.A. Skeen Government Printer, 1900.

Gunasekara, Tisaranee. "That Familiar Impasse." *The Island,* 2008. http://www.island.lk/2008/10/19/features12.html. Last accessed December 5, 2016.

Gunasinghe, Newton. *Changing Socio-Economic Relations in the Kandyan Countryside.* Colombo: Social Scientists' Association, 1990.

———. "The Open-Economy and Its Impact on Ethnic Relations in Sri Lanka." In *Newton Gunasinghe: Selected Essays,* edited by Sasanka Perera, 176–196. Colombo: Social Scientists' Association, 1995.

Gunawardana, R.A.L.H. "Irrigation and Hydraulic Society in Early Medieval Ceylon." *Past and Present* 53, no. 1 (1971): 3–27.

———. *Robe and Plough: Monasticism and Economic Interest in Early Medieval Sri Lanka.* Tucson: the University of Arizona Press, 1979.

60   R. BASTIN AND P. DE SILVA

———. "Changing Patterns of Navigation in the Indian Ocean and Their Impact on Pre-colonial Sri Lanka." In *The Indian Ocean: Explorations in History, Commerce and Politics*, edited by Satish Chandra, 54–89. New Delhi: Sage, 1987.

———. "The People of the Lion: The Sinhala Identity and Ideology in History and Historiography." Reprint, *Sri Lanka: History and the Roots of Conflict*, edited by Jonathan Spencer, 45–86. London: Routledge, 1990.

———. *Historiography in a Time of Ethnic Conflict: Construction of the Past in Contemporary Sri Lanka.* Colombo: Social Scientists' Association, 1995.

———. *Periodization in Sri Lanka History: Some Reflections with Special Emphasis on the Development of the State.* Colombo: Social Scientists' Association, 2008.

Harees, Lukman. *Clouding the Crescent in Sri Lanka: A Documentary on the Hate Campaign Against the Sri Lankan Muslims.* Colombo: Addictive International, 2015.

Holt, John C. *Buddhist Extremists and Muslim Minorities: Religious Conflict in Contemporary Sri Lanka.* New York: Oxford University Press, 2016.

Hussain, Asiff. *Sarandib: An Ethnological Study of the Muslims of Sri Lanka.* Colombo: Neptune Publications, 2011.

Ibn Battuta. "The Observations of Ibn Battuta." *Ibn Battuta in the Maldives and Ceylon 1333–1334*, translated from the French of M.M. Defremery and Sanguinetti by Albert Gray (New Delhi: Asian Educational Services, 1996). Reprint, *The Sri Lanka Reader: History, Culture, Politics*, edited by John Clifford Holt, 111–118. Durham and London: Duke University Press, 2011.

Indrapala, K. *The Evolution of an Ethnic Identity: The Tamils in Sri Lanka C. 300 BCE to C. 1200 CE.* Colombo: MV Publications, 2005.

Jayawardena, Kumari. *Nobodies to Somebodies: The Rise of the Colonial Bourgeoisie in Sri Lanka.* New Delhi: Leftword Books, 2000.

———. *Perpetual Ferment: Popular Revolts in Sri Lanka in the 18th and 19th Centuries.* Colombo: Social Scientists' Association, 2010.

Jiggins, Janice. *Caste and Family in the Politics of the Sinhalese 1947–1976.* Colombo: K.V.G. De Silva & Sons, 1979.

Kapferer, Bruce. *The Feast of the Sorcerer: Practices of Consciousness and Power.* Chicago and London: University of Chicago Press, 1997.

———. *Legends of People, Myths of State: Violence, Intolerance, and Political Culture in Sri Lanka and Australia.* Revised and Updated Edition. Oxford and New York: Berghahn Books, 2012.

Leach, E.R. "Hydraulic Society in Ceylon." *Past and Present* 15, no. 1 (1959): 2–26.

Liyanagamage, Amaradasa. *Society, State and Religion in Premodern Sri Lanka.* Colombo: Social Scientists' Association, 2008.

Malalgoda, Kitsiri. *Buddhism in Sinhalese Society, 1750–1900: A Study of Religious Revival and Change.* Berkeley, Los Angeles, and London: University of California Press, 1976.

McGilvray, Dennis B. *Crucible of Conflict: Tamil and Muslim Society on the East Coast of Sri Lanka.* Durham and London: Duke University Press, 2008.

McGilvray, Dennis, and Mirak Raheem. "Origins of the Sri Lankan Muslims and Varieties of the Muslim Identity." Originally Published as Sections of the Chapter "History, Culture, and Geography: The Sources of Muslim Identity." In *Muslim Perspectives on the Sri Lankan Conflict* (Washington: East–West Center, 2007). Reprint, *The Sri Lanka Reader: History, Culture, Politics.* Edited by John Clifford Holt, 410–419. Durham and London: Duke University Press, 2011.

Menon, A. Sreedhara. *Cultural Heritage of Kerala.* 2nd ed. Madras: Viswanathan Printers, 1996.

Mohamed, S.L. "Who Are the Moors of Ceylon?" Colombo: Moors Direct Action Committee, 1950. Reprint, *The Sri Lanka Reader: History, Culture, Politics,* edited by John Clifford Holt, 429–434. Durham and London: Duke University Press, 2011.

Obeyesekere, Gananath. *Land Tenure in Village Ceylon.* Cambridge: Cambridge University Press, 1967.

———. *The Cult of the Goddess Pattini.* Chicago and London: University of Chicago Press, 1984.

Peebles, Patrick. *Social Change in Nineteenth Century Ceylon.* Colombo: Navrang in Association with Lake House Bookshop, 1995.

Perniola, V. *The Catholic Church in Sri Lanka: The Portuguese Period Volume I, 1505–1565.* Dehiwala, Sri Lanka: Tisara Prakasakayo, 1989.

———. *The Catholic Church in Sri Lanka: The Portuguese Period Volume II, 1566–1619.* Dehiwala, Sri Lanka: Tisara Prakasakayo, 1991a.

———. *The Catholic Church in Sri Lanka: The Portuguese Period Volume III, 1620–1658.* Dehiwala, Sri Lanka: Tisara Prakasakayo, 1991b.

Ramanathan, Ponnambalam. "The Ethnology of the 'Moors' of Ceylon." *Journal of the Ceylon Branch of the Royal Asiatic Society,* 1888. Reprint, *The Sri Lanka Reader: History, Culture, Politics,* edited by John Clifford Holt, 420–423. Durham and London: Duke University Press, 2011.

Roberts, Michael. *Caste Conflict and Elite Formation: The Rise of a Karāva Elite in Sri Lanka, 1500–1931.* Cambridge: Cambridge University Press, 1982.

———. *Exploring Confrontation: Sri Lanka: Politics, Culture and History.* Chur, Switzerland: Harwood Academic Publishers, 1994.

Rogers, John D. *Crime, Justice and Society in Colonial Sri Lanka.* London: Curzon Press, 1987.

Seneviratne, H.L. *Rituals of the Kandyan State.* Cambridge: Cambridge University Press, 1978.

62 R. BASTIN AND P. DE SILVA

Sheriff, Abdul, and Engseng Ho, eds. *The Indian Ocean: Oceanic Connections and the Creation of New Societies*. London: C. Hurst and Co., 2014.

Sivathamby, Karthigesu. "The Sri Lanka Ethnic Crisis and Muslim Tamil Relationships: A Socio-Political Review." In *Facets of Ethnicity in Sri Lanka*, edited by Charles Abeysekera and Newton Gunasinghe, 192–225. Colombo: Social Scientists' Association, 1987.

Somaratna, G.P.V. *Kotahena Riot 1883: A Religious Riot in Sri Lanka*. Colombo: Deepanee, 1991.

Stirrat, R.L. *On the Beach: Fishermen, Fishwives, and Traders in Post-Colonial Lanka*. Delhi: Hindustan Publishing Corporation, 1988.

Strathern, Alan. *Kingship and Conversion in Sixteenth-Century Sri Lanka: Portuguese Imperialism in a Buddhist Land*. Cambridge: Cambridge University Press, 2010.

Tambiah, Stanley J. *World Conqueror and World Renouncer: A Study of Buddhism and Polity in Thailand Against a Historical Background*. Cambridge: Cambridge University Press, 1976.

———. *Buddhism Betrayed? Religion, Politics, and Violence in Sri Lanka*. Chicago and London: University of Chicago Press, 1992.

———. *Leveling Crowds: Ethnonationalist Conflicts and Collective Violence in South Asia*. Berkeley, Los Angeles, and London: University of California Press, 1996.

Weber, Max. *From Max Weber: Essays in Sociology*, edited by H.H. Gerth and C. Wright Mills, London: Routledge, 1948.

———. *The City*. Translated and edited by Don Martindale and Gertrud Neuwirth. New York: The Free Press, 1958.

Wickramasinghe, Nira. "From Hybridity to Authenticity: The Biography of a Few Kandyan Things." In *The Hybrid Island: Culture Crossings and the Invention of Identity in Sri Lanka*, edited by Neluka Silva, 71–92. Colombo: Social Scientists' Association, 2002.

———. *Sri Lanka in the Modern Age: A History of Contested Identities*. London: Hurst and Company, 2006.

Wickremeratne, L.A. "Religion, Nationalism, and Social Change in Ceylon, 1865–1885." *Journal of the Royal Asiatic Society of Great Britain and Ireland* 101, no. 2 (1969): 123–150. Reprint in Colombo: Studies in Society and Culture: Sri Lanka Past and Present, 1993.

Woolf, Leonard. *The Village in the Jungle* with an Introduction by E.F.C. Ludowyk. New Delhi: Oxford University Press, 1981.

Yalman, Nur. *Under the Bo Tree: Studies in Caste, Kinship, and Marriage in the Interior of Ceylon*. Berkeley and Los Angeles: University of California Press, 1967.

CHAPTER 3

Buddhist–Muslim Interactions in Burma/Myanmar

Matthew J. Walton

Myanmar is commonly characterized as a Buddhist country but this simplistic assessment belies the fact that its religious and cultural diversity has been one of its most politically salient factors. Questions of Muslim–Buddhist encounters and dynamics have been particularly present in recent years, with an uptick in inter-religious tension, discrimination and violence not only in Myanmar, but in other parts of the Theravada Buddhist world. This chapter introduces two aspects that broadly characterize Muslim–Buddhist engagement in Myanmar, from a pre-colonial time up to the present.

First, due to the Buddhist demographic majority and a tradition of political rule and authority that has relied on Buddhist symbolism and legitimation for centuries, these encounters have been overwhelmingly unequal, with Buddhists consistently in the dominant or controlling position. This has tended to be the case even in the few situations where Buddhists have not also been a numerical majority. Second, even during periods where political authorities practiced policies of religious inclusion, allowing non-Buddhists to practice their religions or hold

---

M. J. Walton (✉)
University of Toronto, Toronto, ON, Canada

© The Author(s) 2020
I. Frydenlund and M. Jerryson (eds.),
Buddhist-Muslim Relations in a Theravada World,
https://doi.org/10.1007/978-981-32-9884-2_3

influential political, economic or societal positions, Muslims of virtually any background have consistently been portrayed and viewed as foreign in particular ways, and as standing outside either the polity or a more nebulously defined ethno-religious community.

The first section of this chapter provides a brief historical overview, followed by a consideration of various categorizations of Muslims in Burma, noting the challenging overlap with ethnic and national identities as well as contested notions of indigeneity.[1] It also describes some of the overarching dynamics of interactions between Buddhists and Muslims. The next section considers particular patterns and events that characterize Muslim–Buddhist engagement across four broad eras, pre-colonial, colonial, post-independence and military rule. The conclusion brings the chapter up to the present, reviewing some of the persistent dynamics that continue to define interactions between members of the two religious groups in Myanmar today.

MUSLIM AND BUDDHIST IDENTITIES AND PRACTICES IN MYANMAR

Buddhist chronicles date the arrival of Buddhism in present-day Myanmar back as far as the third century B.C.E., however, until at least the eleventh century, Buddhism likely existed alongside many other religious and cultural practices, and probably in varied and syncretic forms. Burmese sources date the establishment of Theravada Buddhism to King Anawrahta's capture of the ethnic Mon city of Thaton in 1057, and his conversion by a Mon monk named Shin Arahan.[2] Even after this point, Buddhism coexisted with the worship and propitiation of spirits and ancestors, even as it was increasingly institutionalized and championed by successive Burmese dynasties.

Accounts of trading activities of Muslims in what is now Myanmar date back to the ninth century, but the permanent population of Muslims remained relatively low until at least the sixteenth century, and concentrated in coastal and border regions. The Muslim population

---

[1] Because there is a significantly larger body of scholarly work on variations of practice, belief and identity among Buddhists, it is not dealt with in detail here, although I provide extensive references in the following section.

[2] Although this suggests that Theravada Buddhism was already relatively well-established among the Mon.

increased rapidly in the nineteenth century, alongside the expansion of British colonial rule in several stages. While much of the Indian Muslim population was driven out in the first half of the twentieth century, Muslims of diverse ethnicities remain a significant religious minority in contemporary Myanmar.

It remains difficult to state with confidence the religious demographics of Myanmar. Decades of repressive and secretive military rule in Burma/Myanmar have accustomed scholars and analysts to distrust official government statistics. Even the census that took place in April 2014, with technical assistance provided by the United Nations Population Fund (UNFPA) was roundly criticized for methodological reasons, as well as because at the last minute, the government controversially decided not to allow people to self-identify as Rohingya.[3] That census returned a figure of 1.15 million enumerated Muslims in the country, for a share of 2.3% of the population. Even when accounting for the estimated 1 million un-enumerated in Rakhine State (assumed to be mostly Rohingya, but now significantly lower since at least 750,000 have fled the state in response to two periods of violent repression in 2016 and 2017), the overall percentage of Muslims in Myanmar is just 4.3%.[4]

Perhaps somewhat ironically, although the vast majority of studies on religion in Myanmar focus on Buddhism, they have produced an uneven understanding of the country's majority religion.[5] The 2014 census listed Buddhists as almost 88% of the population, but this unitary figure mischaracterizes a religious field that is much more diverse than is commonly understood. In addition to recognizing variations in Buddhist belief and practice among different ethnic populations (all nominally Theravada Buddhists),[6] we should also attempt to disentangle

[3] International Crisis Group, "Counting the Costs: Myanmar's Problematic Census," *Asia Briefing*, Yangon/Brussels, 2014.

[4] Republic of the Union of Myanmar, *The 2014 Myanmar Population and Housing Census, the Union Report: Religion* (Ministry of Labour Department of Population, Immigration and Population, 2016).

[5] Works that engage with different aspects of Buddhism in Myanmar include King (1964), Sarkisyanz (1965), Smith (1965), Spiro (1967, 1982), Mendelson and Ferguson (1975), Brohm (1957), Schober (1989, 2011), Houtman (1999), Charney (2006), Jordt (2007), Carbine (2011), Braun (2013), Kawanami (2013), Turner (2014) and Walton (2016).

[6] There are officially 135 recognized ethnic groups in Myanmar, although this figure is arbitrary and disputed. The largest groups, apart from the majority Burmans are the Shan, Karen, Kachin, Rakhine, Mon, Wa, Chin and Karenni. These eight groups all have either

various magical practices and spirit propitiation rituals that remain common in Myanmar today, even among those who would identify primarily as "Buddhist." Probably the strongest statement on the latter sets of beliefs and practices comes from the anthropologist Bénédicte Brac de la Perrière, who has argued that scholarly constructions of "religion" in Myanmar un-self-consciously presume the pre-eminence of a privileged, doctrinal understanding of "Buddhism," reinforcing its hegemonic position but also stigmatizing important and widespread other practices as mere "tradition" or even "superstition."[7] Much scholarly work remains to be done in recognizing the non-doctrinal or non-textual components of religious practice (Buddhist or otherwise) in Myanmar.[8]

Because the ground of Buddhism in Myanmar has been relatively better-trod, this first section will focus more on describing the Muslim population in the country. Only a few studies have made Muslims in Burma their primary topic of investigation, most notably Moshe Yegar (1972), Jean Berlie (2008) and Melissa Crouch's (2016) edited volume.[9] We can expect this situation to begin to change, as more dissertations are being written on Myanmar's Muslims and access to many parts of the country

---

ethnically defined states or, in the case of the Wa, an ethnically defined special region. However, the members of these ethnic groups, while usually concentrated in the states that bear their name, are also spread out across the country, especially in urban centers. Additionally, mixed ethnic heritage is anecdotally quite common, although no empirical study of this has ever been done and the 2014 census did not adequately capture mixed identities. Burmans, Shan, Rakhines and Mon are all majority Buddhist groups. Kachin, Chin and Karenni are majority Christian groups. The Karen are likely majority Buddhist, although clear evidence is not available and Karen ethnic oppositional identity has been more closely aligned and identified with Christian leadership. The Wa practice Christianity, Buddhism and Animism.

[7] Bénédicte Brac de la Perrière, "An Overview of the Field of Religion in Burmese Studies," *Asian Ethnology* 68, no. 2 (2009): 202.

[8] Recent examples of scholarship on non-doctrinal, non-textual or non-majoritarian Buddhisms in Myanmar include Foxeus (2011) on millenialist groups, Tannenbaum (1995) on Shan Buddhist beliefs, a 2009 special issue of the journal *Contemporary Buddhism* on Shan Buddhism, and an edited volume (Brac de La Perrière et al. 2014) on *weikza* (Burmese wizards or supermen).

[9] Moshe Yegar, *The Muslims of Burma* (Wiesbaden: O. Harrassowitz, 1972); Jean A. Berlie, *The Burmanization of Myanmar's Muslims* (Bangkok: White Lotus Press, 2008); Melissa Crouch, ed., *Islam and the State in Myanmar: Muslim–Buddhist Relations and the Politics of Belonging* (New Delhi: Oxford University Press, 2016a).

has opened up considerably in the past decade, but this continues to be an under-studied population. One other point is in order, that has implications for perceptions of indigeneity; these concerns are possibly most pressing with regard to the Rohingya, but are relevant for nearly all Muslims in the country, given the second argument around which this chapter is organized. There is a valid concern that, quite apart from the empirical evidence related to a given group's arrival in Myanmar, the mere fact that Muslims are usually categorized and described with regard to their place of origin—whereas non-Muslim ethnic groups are rarely subjected to the same type of scrutiny (at least not with the underlying suggestion of non-indigeneity)—reflects a bias against Muslims that academic scholarship unwittingly contributes to. Every effort has been made in this chapter to avoid this impression, but I acknowledge here that an initial focus on describing different categories of Muslims might have that result.

Several scholars have put forward categorizations of Muslim groups in Myanmar; these overlap in certain ways and contradict each other in others. Jean Berlie's four groups (Indian origin, Arakan Muslims, Panthays and Burmese Muslims) are problematic in that none of the categories seem consistent with the ways in which Muslims in Myanmar today delineate their own heritage(s).[10] Andrew Selth's categorization draws on Yegar's earlier work in establishing a slightly different set of criteria, defined by period and circumstances of arrival just as much as place of origin.[11] Curtis Lambrecht offers yet another categorization, with six different groups.[12]

It is notable that neither of the first two authors creates a separate category for the Kaman, although both acknowledge their presence, almost exclusively in contemporary Rakhine State. Berlie seems to group them with other "Arakan Muslims," but especially in recent years some

---

[10] Berlie, *The Burmanization of Myanmar's Muslims*, 7ff.

[11] Andrew Selth, "Burma's Muslims and the War on Terror," *Studies in Conflict & Terrorism* 27, no. 2 (2004): 107–109.

[12] Curtis Lambrecht, "Burma (Myanmar)," in *Voices of Islam in Southeast Asia: A Contemporary Sourcebook*, eds. Greg Fealy and Virginia Hooker (Singapore: Institute of Southeast Asian Studies, 2006), 23–25.

Kaman have sought to distinguish themselves from the Rohingya in particular.[13] According to most sources, the Kaman have their origins as a select group of archers of a seventeenth-century Arakanese king.[14] The fact that these two scholarly and generally accepted categorizations do not specifically designate the only Muslim ethnic group officially recognized by the Myanmar government to be "indigenous" alerts us to the high degree of complexity and contestation with regard to categories of recognition and levels of distinction.

Muslims from Yunnan came to Burma in large numbers near the end of the thirteenth century, when a Mongol invasion overthrew the ruling Pagan dynasty.[15] But the origin of the contemporary Panthay population came from waves of migration in the latter half of the nineteenth century. The 1857 Panthay Rebellion in Western Yunnan birthed the Dali Sultanate, which expanded its power rapidly before being finally defeated by the Qing Empire in 1873. This resulted in a major exodus of Muslims into Burma, which forced the Burmese monarchy to balance between lucrative trade with Yunnan and good relations with the Qing.[16] The term Panthay could be a derivation of a Burmese word for "Muslim," and was used by the British to describe this community, from at least the 1870s, although it was never used by members of the group to describe themselves, nor frequently by Burmese.[17] Stephen Keck also notes the relatively good treatment Panthays have received at the hands of successive Burmese states, likely because "they did not carry any of the baggage of being part of India."[18]

[13] Nyi Nyi Kyaw, "Alienation, Discrimination, and Securitization: Legal Personhood and Cultural Personhood of Muslims in Myanmar," *The Review of Faith & International Affairs* 13, no. 4 (2015).

[14] Thant Myint-U, *The River of Lost Footsteps: A Personal History of Burma* (London: Faber and Faber, 2008), 83.

[15] Andrew D.W. Forbes, "The 'Panthay' (Yunnanese Chinese) Muslims of Burma," *Institute of Muslim Minority Affairs Journal* 7, no. 2 (1986): 385.

[16] David G. Atwill, *The Chinese Sultanate: Islam, Ethnicity, and the Panthay Rebellion in Southwest China, 1856–1873* (Stanford: Stanford University Press, 2005).

[17] Forbes, "The 'Panthay' (Yunnanese Chinese) Muslims of Burma," 388.

[18] Stephen Keck, "Reconstructing Trajectories of Islam in British Burma," in *Islam and the State in Myanmar: Muslim–Buddhist Relations and the Politics of Belonging*, ed. Melissa Crouch (New Delhi: Oxford University Press, 2016), 66.

Yegar asserts that the term "Zerbadee" was used from the late nineteenth century to refer to Burmese Muslims that had at least one Burmese parent.[19] Berlie's description is more confusing, sometimes referring to them as the progeny of "Indian Muslim men and Burmese Buddhist women," but also noting different perspectives as to the offensiveness of the term and the efforts of those called "Zerbadee" to differentiate themselves from various other groups of Muslims in Burma.[20]

One of only a few authors to explore the Indian Muslim community in Burma was Nalini Chakravarti.[21] Recognizing the contradictory impulses connected with this group, he demonstrated that it was their economic success that had both helped to develop the country (Rangoon and other urban areas were largely built with Indian capital) yet also displaced and disaffected the Burmese Buddhists (especially those that found themselves indebted to Chettiyar moneylenders in the Irrawaddy Delta area).[22]

Classifying the group commonly referred to as Rohingya is perhaps the most challenging task. Berlie concludes that "the ethnonym 'Arakan Muslims'...is better accepted by many members of this community than 'Rohingyas.' In the context of legal problems, however, it is often necessary to use 'Rohingya' to designate them."[23] That the Rohingya are (at some point in the past) of Bengali cultural heritage does not seem to be in dispute, nor is the fact that their language is related to (but noticeably distinct from) Bengali. Yet the current discourse in Myanmar that denigrates them as illegal Bengali immigrants necessitates caution in describing their heritage, as many seek to establish their presence in the country for generations, if not more explicit claims to indigeneity. Nick Cheesman[24] has documented the contradictory logic of the 1982 Citizenship Law and its subsequent implementation, which requires groups that want to be recognized as citizens to articulate their identities

---

[19] Yegar, *The Muslims of Burma*, 33.

[20] Berlie, *The Burmanization of Myanmar's Muslims*, 11–12.

[21] Nalini Ranjan Chakravarti, *The Indian Minority in Burma: The Rise and Decline of an Immigrant Community* (London: Oxford University Press, 1971).

[22] Adas (1974) details the socioeconomic dynamics of moneylending practices, displacement, indebtedness and discontent in the Irrawaddy Delta region.

[23] Berlie, *The Burmanization of Myanmar's Muslims*, 48.

[24] Nick Cheesman, "How in Myanmar 'National Races' Came to Surpass Citizenship and Exclude Rohingya," *Journal of Contemporary Asia* 47, no. 3 (2017).

70   M. J. WALTON

in terms of indigenous ethnicity rather than nationality, precisely the formulation that many groups in Myanmar find so threatening in the case of the Rohingya.

As laid out below, there is ample documentation of Muslims having resided in what is now Rakhine State for centuries. However, there is not necessarily clear evidence that equates the contemporary community that identifies as Rohingya with any of these groups, at least not within the colonial era and Western-produced texts usually relied on by scholars.[25] There is, on the other hand, evidence that this particular name began to be used more consistently and exclusively at the end of World War II, not only by Rohingyas, but also by Burmese government figures.[26] Michael Charney has critically analyzed the historical claims of both Rohingya and Buddhist Rakhine scholars, pointing out the ways in which a shared cultural space that was likely more syncretic in the past has become increasingly bifurcated, with each group making claims of indigeneity and occupation that necessarily exclude the other group. Instead, he argues provocatively that:

> The symbols and vocabulary of both the so-called "Muslim" rulership and "Buddhist" kingship in early modern Arakan did not signify religious identity. Rather these were rooted in high-status political and cultural models of rulership adopted by indigenous rulers who sought to enhance their image vis-a-vis indigenous elite families and foreign rulers.[27]

Today, it is virtually impossible to avoid the politicization of any writing on the Rohingya, as their humanitarian plight continues to be absolutely tragic and compelling. But, in acknowledging the relative lack of historical evidence for "Rohingya" presence in pre-colonial Arakan, it is necessary to insist on three points: The fact that the particular ethno-political label of Rohingya only coalesced in the middle of the twentieth century does not necessarily invalidate Rohingya claims to have

---

[25] There is a single reference to "Rooinga" in a 1799 report by the British doctor Francis Buchanan-Hamilton. Other than this, reports refer to "Moslems" or "Mahommedans" or a range of other descriptors and ethnonyms.

[26] Jacques Leider, "Rohingya: The Name, the Movement and the Quest for Identity," in *Nation Building in Myanmar* (Myanmar Egress, 2014).

[27] Michael Charney, "Where Jambudipa and Islamdom Converged: Religious Change and the Emergence of Buddhist Communalism in Early Modern Arakan (Fifteenth to Nineteenth Centuries)" (Unpublished PhD dissertation, University of Michigan, 1999).

resided in Arakan for generations. Furthermore, the fact that we can track the "creation" (or consolidation) of the Rohingya political identity from this period means that it is no less valid of an identity than the "Myanmar" national identity that the former military regime imposed (or re-established) in 1989. And finally, persistent emphasis on the geographical and cultural "origins" of the Rohingya is not matched by a similar inquiry into that of the Buddhist majority Rakhine, whose indigenous ethnic status in Myanmar is naturalized and taken for granted in most scholarship.

The challenge of writing in accurate, careful and productive ways about the Rohingya is exemplified in two recent books. Azeem Ibrahim's 2016 book, *The Rohingyas: Inside Myanmar's Hidden Genocide*, often relies on unsubstantiated claims, including those drawn from websites that hawk conspiracy theories without evidence.[28] More problematically, he makes the category error of "proving" the Rohingya's historical presence in contemporary Rakhine State by equating every colonial and pre-colonial mention of "Muslims" (or other variant names) with the Rohingya, again without evidence. By contrast, Anthony Ware and Costas Lautides' 2018 book, *Myanmar's 'Rohingya' Conflict*, goes to great lengths to assess Rohingya-produced and Rakhine-produced scholarship fairly and equally, demonstrating to readers the points of convergence as well as the many places where the groups' competing narratives appear to be incommensurable, without the blanket invalidation of certain voices or perspectives.[29] At the same time, those authors' use of Rohingya in scare quotes (implemented largely as a device to promote constructive dialogue and not automatically alienate Rakhine or other Burmese interlocutors) has its own problematic effects in contributing to the erasure of Rohingya as a legitimate and acknowledged identity.

While it should not be over-emphasized, the debate over genuinely "indigenous" Muslim groups has existed in Burma since at least the colonial period, including among Muslims themselves. This question was taken up by the Burma Moslem Society, founded in 1909 to advocate for "Burmese Muslim interests." A memorandum that the Society wrote in 1929 to the Simon Commission, which was investigating Indian

---

[28] Azeem Ibrahim, *The Rohingyas: Inside Myanmar's Hidden Genocide* (London: Hurst & Co., 2016).

[29] Anthony Ware and Costas Laoutides, *Myanmar's 'Rohingya' Conflict* (London: Hurst & Co., 2018).

independence and the future status of Burma, sought to establish "the Muslim community's ties with Burma since the days of the Kings," giving them the right to be considered as "true Burmese."[30] Over a decade later, after the resumption of British rule following the defeat of the Japanese in WWII, the prominent Muslim political figure U Pe Kin (whose brief biography is given further below) described the formation of the Bamar [Burma] Muslim Congress in December 1945 as having come about due in part to concern among "Myanmar Muslims" (as he described himself when writing in 1994) that they were being lumped in with "alien Muslims of Indian origin."[31] Fearful of being perceived as "*kalars*" (a term that at one time could have signified "foreigner" but had increasingly come to mean someone of Indian or Muslim origin, or someone with darker skin; its negative connotations are described in more detail below), he cited the fact that the medium of instruction in his village school was Urdu as evidence of "Indianisation of Myanmar Muslims, pure and simple" and claimed that "we were as much victims of Indian cultural invasion as Myanmar...itself was of their economic exploitation."[32]

These brief examples of categorization and contestation demonstrate that there is no agreed-upon framework among scholars, the Myanmar government or members of Muslim communities themselves for grouping Muslims in Myanmar. Melissa Crouch argues that Muslim identity in Myanmar can be configured "along a spectrum that at one end strives to accommodate the state through a 'Burmese Muslim' identity, and at the other end [contains] Muslims who retain their (non-Burman) ethnic identity and are therefore perceived as a challenge" to the state.[33] Of course, these questions of indigeneity, loyalty and belonging have been central in shaping the ways in which the majority Buddhist population has considered and engaged with Muslims in the country, especially in moments of crisis or transition. Several examples below demonstrate that, even when certain groups of Muslims were understood (by some) to be indigenous or meaningfully part of the national community, their

---

[30] Yegar, *The Muslims of Burma*, 58–59.

[31] Pe Kin [U], *Pinlon: An Inside Story* (Yangon, Myanmar: Ministry of Information, Government of the Union of Myanmar, 1994), 18.

[32] Pe Kin, *Pinlon: An Inside Story*, 18.

[33] Crouch, *Islam and the State in Myanmar*, 18.

acceptance was still contingent and tenuous, based more on particular circumstances and less on fundamental shifts in popular attitudes or government policy.

Like other colonial outposts, Burma preserved separate legal codes for Muslims in areas of personal law. While this system of "Mahomedan Law" in Burma (implemented through the Burma Laws Act of 1898) was largely based on that developed in India, Melissa Crouch argues that it is somewhat remarkable that it did not develop further codification in the colonial period, specifically through the creation of Islamic courts, which are common in other countries in Southeast Asia.[34] However, post-independence developments have not been studied in detail, particularly the effects of Muslims having been pushed out of public service since the military coup in 1962, resulting in an odd situation in which non-Muslim judges with no training in Islamic law decide cases for Muslims who access the courts in matters of personal law.[35] While Islamic personal law remains in effect in Myanmar, much more research is needed on this subject, as well as the broader question of legal interactions between Muslims and non-Muslims in Myanmar today. The ways in which Burmese people of all religious backgrounds have sought to avoid the official legal channels of the state is relatively well-documented.[36] Yet especially in an era where the government is promoting rule of law and encouraging people to access official justice mechanisms, this is a clear area of importance. Tagliacozzo is probably right in stating that, "While Muslims may enjoy the same protections and the same rights as other communities do on paper, the lived experience of many if not most Burmese Muslims has been wholly different than the official picture."[37]

[34] Melissa Crouch, "Myanmar's Muslim Mosaic and the Politics of Belonging," in *Islam and the State in Myanmar: Muslim–Buddhist Relations and the Politics of Belonging*, ed. Melissa Crouch (New Delhi: Oxford University Press, 2016b), 70–71.

[35] Crouch, "Myanmar's Muslim Mosaic and the Politics of Belonging," 88.

[36] See, for example, Nick Cheesman, *Opposing the Rule of Law: How Myanmar's Courts Make Law and Order* (Cambridge: Cambridge University Press, 2015a).

[37] Eric Tagliacozzo, "Burmese and Muslim: Islam and the Hajj in the Sangha State," in *Burmese Lives: Ordinary Life Stories Under the Burmese Regime*, eds. Wen-Chin Chang and Eric Tagliacozzo (New York: Oxford University Press, 2014), 103.

74 M. J. WALTON

The Language and Practices of Othering

In addressing the history of Buddhist–Muslim interactions in Burma/ Myanmar, it is also necessary—if challenging—to discuss the controversial and offensive term *kala* (also sometimes transliterated as *kalar*). There is no scholarly consensus on the term's etymological origins.[38] At one point, it may have applied to any perceived "foreigners" who arrived via oceanic trade routes, including people of South Asian and Arab origins. It also—for a time, at least—included lighter-skinned foreigners who arrived by sea, such as the *kala phyu* ("white *kala*") and *Ingaleik kala* ("English *kala*"), but has never been used to refer to foreigners arriving overland from China or Thailand, for example. Whatever its origins, the word seems to have been applied as an umbrella term since at least the early decades of the twentieth century to refer variously to people with darker skin, people of or appearing to be of South Asian descent, or Muslims.

In the present, the word is understood by many to be a slur, albeit one that remains prevalent in everyday conversation. While it may have originally been a descriptive term, it has been deployed in pejorative ways since at least the nineteenth century, and likely much earlier. Chie Ikeya explains the contradiction that sometimes accompanied the term in that, "*kala*, as it was disseminated in the Burmese media in the 1920s and 1930s, pigeonholed immigrants from the Indian subcontinent as uneducated, lower-class (or lower-caste) men and women, typically of skin color darker than that of Burmese people, when in fact many of those categorized as 'Indian' in Burma were relatively prosperous."[39] The Burmese writer Maung Zarni has provocatively argued that we ought to understand the term, in the contemporary context at least, as rhetorically equivalent to the word "n*gger." Complicating views on the subject is the fact that the term has not only become normalized in many people's

---

[38] The word's origins and the related debates are discussed in more detail in Renaud Egreteau's "Burmese Indians in Contemporary Burma: Heritage, Influence, and Perceptions Since 1988," *Asian Ethnicity* 12, no. 1 (2011): 46–48; Chakravarti's *The Indian Minority in Burma*, 11; W.S Desai's *India and Burma, a Study* (Bombay: Orient Longmans, 1954), 37–38; Robert Taylor's *Refighting Old Battles, Compounding Misconceptions: The Politics of Ethnicity in Myanmar Today. ISEAS Perspective* (Singapore: Institute of Southeast Asian Studies, 2015), 4.

[39] Chie Ikeya, *Refiguring Women, Colonialism, and Modernity in Burma, Southeast Asia-Politics, Meaning, Memory* (Honolulu: University of Hawai'i Press, 2011), 138.

speech (leading those who use it to insist that it is not offensive precisely because they intend no offense), it has also been deployed in what appear to be laudatory ways, such as referring to independence hero U (Abdul) Razak as *kala-gyi* (the "big/important *kala*").[40] In the context of Muslim–Buddhist interactions, the term further serves to mark anyone who might visually present as darker skinned or possessing phenotypical features that are superficially (if not entirely accurately) associated with people of South Asian origin as "foreign" and outside of a presumed religio-national community.[41]

Beyond the use of this particular term, Islam in Burma/Myanmar has often been either misunderstood by non-Muslims, or portrayed in generalized and inaccurate terms.[42] Thant Myint-U notes the presence of fanciful or mythical "received knowledge" regarding Islam and its place in the world among leaders of the Burman Konbaung dynasty (1752–1885), writing that, "it was also generally accepted that Buddhism had been displaced in north India, and the culprits were seen as Muslim invaders from the west as opposed to a Brahmanical revival or new Hindu faiths."[43] The result has been a persistent sense of Muslims not only as foreigners, but as an invading force from the west, much like the European colonizers. This was reflected in a comment made by Burma's penultimate king, Mindon, to a visiting British official: "Our race once reigned in all the countries you hold in India. Now the *kala* have come close up to us."[44] While King Mindon's notion of his "race" having previously ruled the subcontinent might not be an accurate representation of the historical record, it was an instance of the sense of being under (ethnic, racial, religious, national) siege that has continued to appear

[40]Yeni, "A Leader of Men," *Irrawaddy*, September 2007, http://www2.irrawaddy.com/article.php?art_id=8463&page=1.

[41]Also see the chapter in this volume by Frydenlund and Jerryson on Buddhist ways of Othering.

[42]Imtiyaz Yusuf laments the almost total absence of Muslim or Buddhist scholars in Southeast Asia who study each other's tradition, noting instead the continued reliance on misleading Orientalist or Christian-produced scholarship, or uninterrogated popular tropes. See Imtiyaz Yusuf, "Nationalist Ethnicities as Religious Identities: Islam, Buddhism, and Citizenship in Myanmar," *The American Journal of Islamic Social Sciences* 34, no. 4 (2017): 101–103.

[43]Thant Myint-U, *The Making of Modern Burma* (Cambridge: Cambridge University Press, 2001), 83.

[44]Thant Myint-U, *The River of Lost Footsteps*, 140.

regularly (albeit in diverse forms with different points of reference) in Myanmar up to the present day, reflected currently in claims (some of dubious authenticity) that a whole host of places around the world with Muslim majorities were once "Buddhist countries."

British classifying efforts continued and even reinforced the notion that Muslims were not meaningfully an indigenous part of Burma. Stephen Keck describes the British "tendency to view Islam in Burma as a transitory phenomenon," which appears to have influenced later generations of Burmese political and religious leaders and even scholars of the country as well.[45] Despite the long-standing presence of a diverse community of Muslims in Burma for centuries, they have often struggled to be seen as meaningfully native. This was in part because of the instrumental way in which they seem to have been treated by colonial authorities. As Eric Tagliacozzo explains, "The British protected Muslims in Burma by law, not out of philanthropy, but because they were seen to be useful to the colony's interests, particularly in the economic sphere."[46] And Keck explains the irony of the rapid increase in the Muslim population during the colonial period:

> These newly arrived Muslims hardly supplanted the Burmese Muslims, but their existence had a rather paradoxical effect: namely, despite the fact that there were now more Muslims in Burma, they seemingly came to be regarded as non-Burmese. That is, as more Indian Muslims came to Burma, their presence would help to ensure that Islam would inevitably be seen as something external to the traditions and cultures of Burma.[47]

Not all colonial figures (whether British or Burman) saw this as an inevitable outcome. Keck demonstrates that some Burmese, such as the scholar and writer Taw Sein Ko (of Chinese-Burman descent) believed that communal tensions and divisions could be overcome by facilitating integrative policies to bring together Buddhists, Hindus and Muslims in a national culture, as they imagined had been accomplished in India.[48]

---

[45] Stephen Keck, "The Making of an Invisible Minority: Muslims in Colonial Burma," in *Living on the Margins: Minorities and Borderlines in Cambodia and Southeast Asia*, ed. Peter J. Hammer (Siem Reap, Cambodia: Center for Khmer Studies, 2009), 221.

[46] Tagliacozzo, "Burmese and Muslim: Islam and the Hajj in the Sangha State," 103.

[47] Keck, "The Making of an Invisible Minority," 222.

[48] Keck, "Reconstructing Trajectories of Islam in British Burma," 44.

Keck makes clear that this perspective was likely reflective of a relatively distinctive "Rangoon worldview," but does still indicate that there were those who did not see Islam as utterly foreign to Burma or its future trajectory.

Another common negative trope that continues to circulate in the country and dates to at least the early twentieth century refers to religious and social restrictions placed upon Muslim women, both in Myanmar and in other countries. Ikeya cites an unflattering representation of Muslim women in a 1936 issue of the journal *Myanmar Alin*, where the author claims that Muslim women were "deprived of numerous privileges," "locked up at home to perform domestic duties," and were "not able to read religious texts, newspapers, or anything written in English."[49] Numerous contemporary accounts include references to non-Muslims' beliefs about common Islamic practices related to the treatment of women.[50] While some of these claims might have their origin in fact, they are certainly not universal truths regarding Muslims or Muslim women and are regularly embellished as they are shared and revitalized in different periods.

Still, despite recurring moments of repression by political authorities since the early decades of the twentieth century, Muslim social and religious organizations remain strong and visible, especially in large cities. In a 2011 article on the dynamics of "Indo-phobia" in Myanmar, Egreteau lists a range of "mosques, social trusts and funds, private libraries, [and] community-oriented hospitals" in Yangon, many of which have been in existence since the late nineteenth or early twentieth centuries.[51] Muslim political parties and organizations have been significantly weakened and marginalized by recent anti-Muslim public sentiment and the opportunity for Muslims to have a formal voice in Myanmar's political process has been virtually cut off by the decision of the two major parties (the National League for Democracy and the Union Solidarity and Development Party) not to run a single Muslim candidate in the November 2015 elections. But Muslims ran and won seats in the 2010 elections, representing both Muslim-oriented parties and some of the

---

[49] Ikeya, *Refiguring Women, Colonialism, and Modernity in Burma*, 139.

[50] See, for example, the interviews cited in Schissler, Walton and Phyu Phyu Thi (2015).

[51] Egreteau, "Burmese Indians in Contemporary Burma," 44–45.

78   M. J. WALTON

prominent national parties as well.[52] Furthermore, in addition to social, religious and political organizations, educational and advocacy groups remain strong, with Muslims of all ages and identities playing central roles in inter-faith and peace-building activities.

HISTORICAL OVERVIEW

The following four sections broadly outline some of the key dynamics and moments of Muslim–Buddhist interaction in Burma, roughly categorized in the pre-colonial, colonial, post-independence Parliamentary and military eras. This is a relatively standard periodization, but one that is appropriate here as it reflects some of the major changes in governance structure over time, which had particular effects on Muslims and the ways in which Muslims engaged with or were treated by the majority-Buddhist state and population.

Precolonial Period (Ninth Century–1826)

Muslim traders apparently first came to Burma in the ninth century, to coastal areas including Arakan.[53] One of the first accounts from Burmese sources is of two Muslim brothers who survived a shipwreck in the eleventh century, during the reign of King Anawratha (1044–1077).[54] Up to the thirteenth century, there were likely only scattered Muslim enclaves, with the population occasionally increasing through the capture of slaves in battle, as was common in the region.[55] But by the sixteenth century, there was a lively trade between coastal areas of Burma and cities in the Middle East, along the Bay of Bengal, and into island Southeast Asia, much of which was in the hands of Muslims. Their position would begin to recede as European traders took over much of the commerce

---

[52] Nicholas Farrelly, "Muslim Political Activity in Transitional Myanmar," in *Islam and the State in Myanmar: Muslim–Buddhist Relations and the Politics of Belonging*, ed. Melissa Crouch (New Delhi: Oxford University Press, 2016), 108–115.

[53] G.E. Harvey, *History of Burma: From the Earliest Times to 10 March 1824, the Beginning of the English Conquest* (London: Longmans, Green and Co., 1925), 10.

[54] Harvey, *History of Burma*, 24.

[55] Bryce Beemer, "The Creole City in Mainland Southeast Asia: Slave Gathering Warfare and Cultural Exchange in Burma, Thailand and Manipur, 18th–19th c." (PhD dissertation, University of Hawai'i at Manoa, 2013).

beginning from the late sixteenth century, but in Burma, Muslims apparently occasionally played roles as messengers between European trading companies and Burmese monarchs.[56]

By the eighteenth century, Buddhism having been well-established among Burmese kings for centuries, Muslims often faced severe restrictions, both from royal decrees and through boycotts by local authorities.[57] However, in terms of religious practice, Burmese kings were generally reported to be tolerant of non-Buddhists, if only to assist in the maintenance of order. Tagliacozzo even notes that King Mindon (ruled 1853–1878) sponsored a *waqf* house in Arabia as a way to support Burmese Muslims going on the Hajj.[58] One exception was King Bayinnaung (1550–1581), who forbade the slaughter of goats and fowl and also cattle during Eid festivals.[59] Another famous (and possibly apocryphal) tale of religious intolerance came during the reign of King Bodawpaya (1782–1819). Wondering about the religious zeal of Muslims, the king summoned a group of Muslims from Ava, the capital, and commanded them to eat pork. An account by an English observer notes that they all obeyed the king.[60] However, Yegar claims that the version that still circulates among Muslims in Myanmar is that they refused to eat and were executed, thus making them martyrs who demonstrated their faith even in the face of death.[61]

The Burmese historian Thant Myint-U relates that, as part of an increase in religious conservatism among the majority Buddhist population during the Konbaung dynasty, Muslims and Christians experienced persecution in the 1840s.[62] But, in addition to his odd tests of faith, King Bodawpaya also sought to support and learn more about Islam, for example, appointing a Sufi from Western India named Abhisha Husseini to be the religious head of Muslims in the country and ordering the translation of all of his works into Burmese.[63]

---

[56] Yegar, *The Muslims of Burma*, 9.

[57] Yegar, *The Muslims of Burma*, 6.

[58] Tagliacozzo, "Burmese and Muslim: Islam and the Hajj in the Sangha State," 85.

[59] Yegar, *The Muslims of Burma*, 10.

[60] Harvey, *History of Burma*, 276–277.

[61] Yegar, *The Muslims of Burma*, 12.

[62] Thant Myint-U, *The Making of Modern Burma*, 50.

[63] Thant Myint-U, *The Making of Modern Burma*, 51.

80 M. J. WALTON

Prominent Mandalay-based Muslims were regular visitors to the Burmese court in the nineteenth century; one of them, the banker Moola Ismail, served as revenue minister to King Thibaw (1878–1885), the last ruler of the Konbaung dynasty.[64] When Thibaw faced a revenue shortage, he created new commodity monopolies to bring in additional funds. Although this controversial policy was met with strong resistance and eventually dropped, smaller concessions remained, some of them going to Muslim businessmen. As a potential indicator of how these men were viewed, Thant Myint-U notes that they were usually referred to in Burmese sources under Burmese names.[65] Similarly, according to British accounts, the sizable Islamic community in Ava in the mid-nineteenth century was apparently well-integrated into the broader Burmese community, at least in terms of dress. The court had many Muslims in high positions, including the mayor of Ava and the governor of Pagan.[66] This general practice, of broad cultural assimilation in terms of language, culture and dress, was likely replicated across many parts of the country, although some groups remained distinct in their practices.[67]

Another view uniting Buddhists and Muslims from the late eighteenth century was hostility toward the British. Colonial accounts from this period up through the nineteenth-century report opposition from local Muslim traders, including "a fierce anti-British propaganda campaign claiming that the Indian experience proved that British trading would be followed inevitably by military conquest."[68] Muslim advisors were also apparently effective in spreading this animosity to generations of Burmese kings, in part through their influential positions in successive courts.

While most accounts of Burma's history focus primarily on the monarchs at the center of the country, in the case of Muslim–Buddhist interactions, it is worth looking in more detail at one of the most dynamic and impactful sites of interaction. The multi-cultural identity of Arakan (at one time a kingdom, now a constituent state of Myanmar) dates from at least the fifteenth century. After being displaced by an invading army of the Burmese kingdom of Ava in 1404, the Arakanese king Naramithla

[64] Thant Myint-U, *The Making of Modern Burma*, 164–165.

[65] Thant Myint-U, *The Making of Modern Burma*, 164–165.

[66] Thant Myint-U, *The River of Lost Footsteps*, 126.

[67] Yegar, *The Muslims of Burma*, 12.

[68] Yegar, *The Muslims of Burma*, 15.

spent the next few decades in Bengal, where he absorbed the influences of a sultanate there that had Turkish and Afghan origins. When he re-established his rule in Arakan in 1430, he created a "hybrid Buddhist-Islamic court," that supported both Bengali and Arakanese literatures and included kings who took Islamic titles along with their Pali-language Buddhist ones.[69] Over the next few centuries, the power and influence of the Arakanese dynasty would shift in relation to its Bengali and Burmese neighbors, in addition to vying with Portuguese and other Westerners attempting to establish a foothold in lucrative trade in the region. A more recognized border between Bengal (as part of British India) and Arakan would be established by the end of the eighteenth century, although this would again become more porous after the British began to establish colonial rule in parts of Burma in the early nineteenth century, merging conquered Burmese territories with Indian ones.[70]

Yegar emphasizes the ways in which Muslims tended to assimilate to Burmese culture wherever they settled. And he is keen to make clear that there was never a movement for mass conversion to Islam, not does any evidence exist of attempts at conversion by Muslim missionaries.[71] However, he, like most other analysts, marks the importance of British colonial rule in Burma as fundamentally changing the dynamics related to this religious minority through the "extensive flow of immigration from India" that followed the establishment of British rule in stages from 1826 to 1886.[72] But before turning to that era, it is important to note the relative paucity and narrowness of sources in existing scholarly work on Muslims and Islam in Burma prior to the colonial period. As mentioned above in relation to the Rohingya, most accounts still rely on presumably biased British sources (Stephen Keck has conducted the best analyses of British biases in encountering and studying Islam) or equally unreliable royal or religious chronicles. There would likely be similar biases in accounts written by Muslims in Burmese (or other languages), yet these sources are relatively unknown and have not yet been studied in detail by scholars.

---

[69] Thant Myint-U, *The River of Lost Footsteps*, 73–74.

[70] Thant Myint-U, *The Making of Modern Burma*, 17.

[71] Yegar, *The Muslims of Burma*, 26–27.

[72] Yegar, *The Muslims of Burma*, 27.

Colonial Period (1826–1948)

Colonial rule did indeed facilitate the mass movement of people from the Indian subcontinent to Burma, a period of immigration, development and displacement that has fueled anti-Indian and anti-Muslim sentiment in the country since at least the early twentieth century. There was a major influx of Muslims from India into Arakan after the region was annexed by the British in 1826. The first census carried out by British colonial authorities took place in 1871 and returned a figure of about 100,000 Muslims, with 60% of that number residing in what is now Rakhine State.[73] However, it should be noted that this census covered what was British Burma at the time, which only included Arakan, Tenasserim (now Tanintharyi) and other parts of lower Burma, including Rangoon. The Muslim population of Rangoon more than doubled between 1869 and 1874 (from 4425 to 11,671).[74] In just the last decade of the nineteenth century, the Muslim population of both Upper and Lower Burma grew by over 150,000, but this would pale in comparison to the turn of the twentieth century, which would see annual immigration rates increase from 250,000 per year all the way to 480,000 in 1927.

Stephen Keck notes that British colonial sources tended to view the presence of Muslims in Burma as evidence of "cosmopolitanism," an opening up and modernization of the country. However, while some saw this as a positive development, others worried about the negative effects, namely the perceived threat to traditional Burmese ways of life. British writing about Muslims thus had the effect of coding them as "other," in their attempts to delineate and protect those that they saw as the country's native inhabitants.[75] This effect was reinforced by the gradually adopted norm of seeing Burma as "populated by Burmans and a host of ethnic minorities, all of whom belonged to the land," which further established the religiously categorized Muslims as inescapably "foreign."[76] Many influential Burmese leaders also adopted this perspective, further complicating Muslim efforts to be seen as part of the emerging nation.

---

[73] Berlie, *The Burmanization of Myanmar's Muslims*, 2–3.

[74] Yegar, *The Muslims of Burma*, 31.

[75] Keck, "The Making of an Invisible Minority," 225–226.

[76] Keck, "The Making of an Invisible Minority," 230.

Religious differences, but also important potential axes of inter-religious cooperation were on full display during the debate over separation from India under British governance. Members of the India Statutory Commission visited Burma at the beginning of 1929 to hear testimony from relevant parties. Representatives of the Muslim League did not strongly oppose separation from India (probably unsurprising, given the economic interests many of its members had in coastal shipping enterprises) and other Muslim representatives argued against laws that discriminated in favor of Burman Buddhists and for religious quotas for government jobs and grants.[77] However, in certain respects—such as refuting derogatory British views on Burmese capacity for self-government—opinions were shared across religious boundaries.

The rise in immigration (both European and from various parts of British India) that accompanied colonial rule also brought concern regarding children of "mixed" marriages (*kabya* in Burmese). It is challenging to disentangle the racial, ethnic, religious and "national" components of what was probably most commonly expressed as anti-Indian sentiment. Chie Ikeya, in her study of women in the colonial period in Burma, argues that, while some were explicitly critical of "Burmese-Muslim marriages," in practice, antipathy towards those associated with India could capture a wide range of people, including Hindus and Christians from India.[78] While intermarriage in general "became a morally and culturally reprehensible practice in the twentieth century," women who married Europeans were generally seen as moving up socially (if still being unfaithful to their race), whereas those who married Indians (whether Muslim or any other religion) were seen as marrying below their station.[79]

The trope of deracination thus became a common part of public discourse in colonial Burma, especially in the 1920s and 1930s. Burmese women's groups associated with the General Council of Burmese Associations (GCBA) in the early 1920s came out strongly against Burmese-Muslim marriages and the resulting mixed-race progeny. In particular, Burmese women who married Muslims were said to be hurting themselves, their *a-myo* (race/people), and their cultural heritage and

---

[77] John F. Cady, *A History of Modern Burma* (Ithaca: Cornell University Press, 1958), 295.

[78] Ikeya, *Refiguring Women, Colonialism, and Modernity in Burma*, 122.

[79] Ikeya, *Refiguring Women, Colonialism, and Modernity in Burma*, 130.

84   M. J. WALTON

they were publicly blamed for conspiring to bring about the ruin of the Burmese race and the Buddhist religion. Anthropologist Ma Khin Mar Mar Kyi has shown that the nationalist hero and patron of the *Dobama Asiayone*, Thakin Kodaw Hmaing, was one of the most virulent critics of women in mixed marriages, portraying them in his popular and influential writings as materialistic and selfish and inclined to destroy patriotism.[80]

Burma's nationalist movement began to coalesce in the early 1930s, particularly around the *Dobama Asiayone* ("Our Burma" or "We Burmese" Association). Nyi Nyi Kyaw notes the organization's origins in Indophobia, as its first manifesto, issued on May 30, 1930, called for boycotting Indian shops.[81] However, *Dobama* attitudes towards Indians and Muslims were also more nuanced than this at times. While the initial impetus of *Dobama* activism was the May 1930 dock riots that took place primarily between Indians and Burmans, Burmese scholar Khin Yi argues that the group's 1930 manifesto analyzed the riots primarily through an economic lens and urged Burmans "not to hate the Indians but to love one another more."[82] This complexity was evident throughout the nationalist movement, where monks such as the iconic U Ottama criticized both the British and Indians who were seen as exploiting the country, but also "spoke in Hindustani frequently and urged the unity of the Muslims, Hindus and Buddhists."[83]

One of the most commonly referenced set of examples of Muslim–Buddhist interactions in colonial Burma was the riots that took place in 1930 and 1938. Scholarly understandings of these events have been evolving alongside more nuanced appraisals of the associated identity categories of race, religion and nationality.[84] Both were initially portrayed as "anti-Indian," with later characterizations noting that the 1938 riots had

[80] (Ma) Khin Mar Mar Kyi, "In Pursuit of Power: Political Power and Gender Relations in New Order Burma/Myanmar" (PhD dissertation, Australian National University, 2013).

[81] Nyi Nyi Kyaw, "Islamophobia in Buddhist Myanmar: The 969 Movement and Anti-Muslim Violence," in *Islam and the State in Myanmar: Muslim–Buddhist Relations and the Politics of Belonging*, ed. Melissa Crouch (New Delhi: Oxford University Press, 2016), 192.

[82] Khin Yi, *The Dobama Movement in Burma (1930–1938)* (Ithaca: Southeast Asia Program, Cornell University, 1988), 5.

[83] Donald Eugene Smith, *Religion and Politics in Burma* (Princeton: Princeton University Press, 1965), 97–98.

[84] See Saha (2013) for a brief investigation of the inherent "slippage" between categories of race and religion in Burma/Myanmar.

more of an anti-Muslim orientation. Keck has convincingly argued that the process of de-Indianization (the separation of Burma from British India in 1937) had particularly deleterious effects on Muslims in the country. In addition to the active expulsion of many Indians, the long-term effect was "distrust and antipathy in Myanmar towards many things that might be connected with India–especially British India."[85]

The 1938 riots were apparently triggered by the publication of a novel entitled *The Abode of a Nat*, written by Htin Baw, but significantly, including as an appendix anti-Buddhist statements written by a Muslim author Maung Shwe Hpi that were part of a book that had been originally published (to little fanfare) in 1931. Word quickly spread and many newspapers contained statements from leading monks condemning Maung Shwe Hpi's writing. The *New Light of Burma* newspaper issued a call for a boycott of Muslim shops and sporadic attacks on Muslims started to occur.[86] Muslim groups attempted to make clear that they were not connected to its publication and that it did not reflect the views of Muslims in Burma, but fury among the Buddhist public, inflamed by monks, increased.

This public vitriol came to a head at a meeting convened by the General Council of the *Thathana Mamaka* Young Sangha's Association of Rangoon, a group that was particularly active in religious and nationalist issues in the 1930s (and would later morph into the *Yahan Byo Ahpwe*, or Young Monks' Association). On July 26, 1938, thousands of people gathered at the Shwedagon Pagoda to hear monks and others denounce Muslims, especially focusing on the Buddhist-Muslim marriage question.[87] A smaller contingent from the rally began to march to a Muslim part of the city, assaulting Muslims and others deemed to be of Indian descent, triggering violence that lasted for several days and spread outside of Rangoon. The official report from the colonial authorities stated that hundreds were killed.

There are, however, different perspectives on the factors that triggered this sentiment in the first half of the twentieth century. Challenging the common assumptions that anti-Indian and anti-Muslim sentiment were

[85] Keck, "Reconstructing Trajectories of Islam in British Burma," 40.

[86] Yegar, *The Muslims of Burma*, 36.

[87] Michael Mendelson and John P. Ferguson, *Sangha and State in Burma: A Study of Monastic Sectarianism and Leadership (Symbol, Myth, and Ritual)* (Ithaca: Cornell University Press, 1975), 211–212.

primarily generated by economic disenfranchisement (real or perceived), Nile Green uses a critical reading of an Urdu language text about colonial Burma to argue that contestation in the area of "religious economy" produced and expanded antagonism as well, especially as the colonial moment constituted a rapid pluralization of the religious sphere in Burma. As he states, "the colonisation of Burma saw the replacement of a religious economy dominated by a state/Theravada establishment with a new 'liberal' dispensation in which Christianity, Islam and Hinduism could, in principle, compete with Buddhism on equal terms."[88] Indeed, while economic concerns have always been a vehicle through which Buddhists in Burma/Myanmar have worried about the continued support and perpetuation of the Buddhist religious community, the idea that Buddhism requires official support from political authorities continues to motivate critics of equal treatment of religions in the country today.

By contrast, many scholars have noted the moment of inter-religious possibility that occurred after the war, during the late 1940s and early 1950s, "when a broad coalition of nationalist political forces was constructed under the umbrella of the Anti-Fascist People's Freedom League."[89] U Pe Kin, who was a member of the Bamar Muslim Conference (BMC), remembered the August 16, 1945 "Naythuyein Conference" convened by the Anti-Fascist People's Freedom League (AFPFL) as a "meeting of politicians and elders from various walks of life and communities—Buddhists, Muslims, Christians and Hindus."[90] The Burma Muslim Conference grew particularly close to the AFPFL in the second half of the 1940s as the predominantly Burman Buddhist leaders of the AFPFL appreciated the emphasis that BMC leaders put on loyalty to Burma. Yegar states that "One of the very first activities of the Congress was to explain to all the Muslims, and especially to the Indian Muslims, the inescapable fact that only one possibility existed for them and that was to demonstrate their unreserved loyalty to Burma alone."[91]

Of several notable Muslims deeply involved in Burma's independence struggle, two are worth describing in more detail. U Pe Kin was one of

[88] Nile Green, "Buddhism, Islam and the Religious Economy of Colonial Burma," *Journal of Southeast Asian Studies* 46, no. 2 (2015): 180.

[89] Robert Taylor, "Do States Make Nations? The Politics of Identity in Myanmar Revisited," *South East Asia Research* 13, no. 3 (2005): 276.

[90] Pe Kin, *Pinlon: An Inside Story*, 16.

[91] Yegar, *The Muslims of Burma*, 75.

the most influential Muslims in Myanmar's national politics in the 1940s. He was a major figure in the AFPFL, one of the people who made the historic Panglong Conference possible, and a diplomat for many years in post-independence Burma. Although he was born in what is now Mandalay Division, his family moved to Taunggyi in what was then the Shan States when he was a teenager. His familiarity with people in ethnic minority areas of different religious backgrounds was apparently one of the reasons why General Aung San asked him to be a mediator between the AFPFL and the Shan State Freedom League prior to the Panglong Conference in 1947.[92]

U Abdul Razak was not only a leader in the AFPFL, but also widely influential in the field of education, serving as Minister of Education and National Planning in the late 1940s. He was a leader of the Bamar Muslim Conference at a time when some Muslims in Burma saw value in the example of Pakistan separating to establish a Muslim state, yet spoke out strongly against this perspective, remaining dedicated to the AFPFL's efforts to achieve independence together.[93] Tragically, he was also one of seven prominent leaders (along with General Aung San) assassinated on July 19, 1947, only months before Burma was to achieve independence.

Once again, the dynamics in Arakan were somewhat distinct from those in other parts of the country. Yegar describes the conflict in the west of Burma during WWII as being initiated by Arakanese Buddhists during the period of British withdrawal, although as might be expected, there are different views on this question and available evidence is scarce. In southern Arakan State, where Buddhists were the majority, Muslim villages were attacked and inhabitants massacred. When word spread north to Muslim majority areas, via refugees fleeing the killings, Muslims responded in kind to Buddhist villages in the north, prompting a similar exodus and further solidifying the separation between the two communities.[94] Yegar states that some Muslims cooperated with the Japanese when they invaded Arakan in 1942 but turned back to the British in 1945 and were granted a "Muslim National Area."[95] A slightly different

---

[92] Pe Kin, *Pinlon: An Inside Story*, 7.

[93] Yeni, 2007.

[94] Yegar, *The Muslims of Burma*, 95.

[95] Yegar, *The Muslims of Burma*, 96.

interpretation comes from Huke, who mentions Rohingya's loyalty to the British during 1942–1945 as a major factor in the initial Buddhist attacks on Muslims.[96] Regardless of the initial dynamics of aggression, after independence, as the AFPFL started to try to re-settle populations displaced by war, tensions flared again, with some newly formed Muslim organizations seeking annexation to what was then officially known as The Province of East Bengal of the Dominion of Pakistan.

Post-independence Parliamentary Period (1948–1962)

Burma's independence in January 1948 was marred by the emergence of civil conflict on several planes. Communist factions rebelled both before and after independence and some of the ethnic rebellions that took place in the late 1940s and again in the early 1960s were linked to minority Christian identities (though they were never expressed as explicitly religious rebellions). The one religiously oriented civil conflict in Myanmar's early years of independence was the secessionist Mujahid movement. Following the creation of the Mujahid Party in 1947, this revolutionary movement sought to annex parts of Arakan to what would become East Pakistan. Understandably, this upset the new government, although apparently, Muhammad Ali Jinnah, who founded Pakistan in August 1947, had told General Aung San that he did not support this policy.[97] The seccessionists were successful in early years, controlling significant parts of northern Arakan by early 1949, but were gradually pushed out by government offensives, including "Operation Monsoon" in 1954, which effectively ended their rebellion.[98]

It is important to note that this brief revolutionary movement is not well-understood and has been mis-represented as a propaganda tool in contemporary Buddhist–Muslim relations. Yegar describes those who participated as "Arakanese Muslims" but says that the Rohingya did not support annexation to Pakistan and some even requested arms from U Nu to fight the Mujahid rebellion.[99] However, at least some of the rebels claimed to be fighting for recognition of the Rohingya as "indigenous

---

[96] Cited in Berlie, *The Burmanization of Myanmar's Muslims*, 51.

[97] Yegar, *The Muslims of Burma*, 97.

[98] Berlie, *The Burmanization of Myanmar's Muslims*, 57–58.

[99] Yegar, *The Muslims of Burma*, 97.

sons of Arakan, descendants of Muslim settlers of hundreds of years ago."[100] While the details might be muddy, the violence and suffering on both sides—Buddhist and Muslim—were real and continue to influence perceptions today.

Similarly, the tensions that stemmed from pre-independence conflicts persisted through the parliamentary period, and Rohingyas and other Muslims in Arakan campaigned against the U Nu government's announced intention in 1960 to create a separate Arakan State, or at least asked that Muslim-majority areas in northern Arakan not be included in it.[101] Others sought to carve out special recognition and were granted this on May 1961, when the Mayu Frontier Administration was created, encompassing an area along the border with Bangladesh, whose population is today largely Rohingya. While this region did not enjoy full autonomy, it was excluded from Arakan State when the state was created at the beginning of 1962 and maintained its separate status for several years, even after the military coup of March 1962.

Returning to electoral politics in the capital, a split within the Yangon-based Muslim community occurred in the early days of independence, when newly appointed Prime Minister U Nu asked the BMC to resign from the AFPFL because it was a religious organization. In response, BMC President U Khin Maung Lat (who had stepped into the leadership role after U Razak was assassinated) ended the Congress' religious activities, so that it could remain in the political alliance. Members upset with this change formed the rival Burma Muslim League, which became much more outspoken in its criticism of government policy and ongoing discrimination against Muslims.[102] Despite these tensions—and the continued growth of pro-Buddhist and anti-Muslim groups such as the All Burma Young Monks Association, or *Yahanphyu Aphwe*[103]—some inclusive practices such as institutionalized state support for Muslims on the Hajj continued for a time after independence, with the state assisting four or five hundred people per year in traveling for pilgrimage purposes.[104]

---

[100] Yegar, *The Muslims of Burma*.

[101] Yegar, *The Muslims of Burma*, 103.

[102] Yegar, *The Muslims of Burma*, 76–77.

[103] Smith, *Religion and Politics in Burma*, 189.

[104] Tagliacozzo, "Burmese and Muslim: Islam and the Hajj in the Sangha State," 85.

One of the most divisive issues of Burma's brief parliamentary period was the establishment of Buddhism as the state religion. While there had been advocates of this from before independence, the 1947 Constitution did not provide for a state religion, apparently in large part due to Aung San's insistence that this would damage national unity.[105] The issue returned to broader public consideration after Prime Minister U Nu convened the Sixth Buddhist Council in Burma from 1954 to 1956, assuring monks at the closing ceremony that his government wanted to make Buddhism the state religion.[106] At the same time, U Nu also seemed to want to ensure that implementing this policy would be done sensitively with regard to religious minorities.[107] After a political split in U Nu's ruling AFPFL in 1958, his faction campaigned on a promise of making Buddhism the state religion, although it is difficult to know how much U Nu supported it personally and how much he felt political pressure to push the policy. This undetermined position allowed prominent Muslim party members such as U Raschid to campaign for the party in the election yet oppose the legislation when it was ultimately proposed in Parliament.[108]

The State Religion Acts proposal was unsurprisingly strongly opposed by most non-Buddhist groups and also a sizable number of Buddhists. U Raschid's Burma Muslim Organization was joined by the Ulama Association, the Muslim Central Fund Trust, the Arakanese Muslim Association, the All Burma Muslim Students' Union and the Islamic Religious Affairs Council in campaigning against it. The latter group argued that it would effectively create two classes of citizens, where in practice non-Buddhists would face discrimination in many different areas, despite the existence of general constitutional protections.[109] Criticism also came in mid-1961 from the National Religious Minorities Alliance which linked the question of a state religion with the persistent question of federalism, that had been percolating since independence and would eventually be one of several triggering causes for the military coup in 1962.[110] Interestingly, one Burmese Muslim organization that

[105] Smith, *Religion and Politics in Burma*, 230.

[106] Mendelson et al., *Sangha and State in Burma*, 348.

[107] Smith, *Religion and Politics in Burma*, 233.

[108] Smith, *Religion and Politics in Burma*, 237–238.

[109] Smith, *Religion and Politics in Burma*, 248.

[110] Mendelson et al., *Sangha and State in Burma*, 350.

did support the legislation was the All Burma Moulvi Association, which "took the position that a state with a religion was preferable to a state without religion" (although Smith points out the essentially pragmatic nature of this stance).[111]

When the amendment (the third to Burma's Constitution at the time) was passed on August 26, 1961, U Nu followed almost immediately by proposing a fourth amendment, that would protect the rights of religious minorities. U Raschid again influenced this piece of legislation by inserting a clause that "prohibited minors in school from being taught any other religion than their own without written consent from parent or guardian."[112] Unsurprisingly, many monastic organizations immediately objected and began to organize protests. They also conducted more militant activities, such as occupying a partially built mosque in a suburb of Rangoon in October 1961 and leading riots in November in which two mosques were destroyed and five people were killed.[113]

Public debate and conflict over these two amendments was relatively short-lived, as on March 2, 1962, General Ne Win again took over the government, this time without U Nu's consent, initiating a coup that would establish military-led or military-influenced government in Burma for the next five decades.

Military Rule and After (1962–Present)

Ne Win's coup brought the Burma Socialist Programme Party to power and removed most opportunities for citizen participation in government. While that was true across the population, Muslims were particularly affected, being largely excluded from many aspects of public life, as well as from the military and government.[114] There have been exceptions to this, such as the visible presence of Muslim-owned construction companies in Yangon, and these have fueled contemporary narratives of Islamic economic dominance and exploitation of Buddhists that have wide circulation yet no supporting evidence. The monk-supported boycott campaign against Muslim-owned businesses in 2013 (most closely

---

[111] Smith, *Religion and Politics in Burma*, 247.

[112] Mendelson et al., *Sangha and State in Burma*, 352.

[113] Mendelson et al., *Sangha and State in Burma*, 353.

[114] Human Rights Watch, "Crackdown on Burmese Muslims," *Human Rights Watch*, 2002, https://www.hrw.org/legacy/backgrounder/asia/burma-bck4.htm.

92   M. J. WALTON

associated with the then-popular 969 Movement and the firebrand monk U Wirathu) has been the most visible moment of backlash, but protests have also taken place sporadically against the Minister and Ministry of Religious Affairs and Culture, with both being accused (by Buddhists) of being biased against Buddhism.

Sporadic but serious violence against Muslims has continued up to the present, often connected with broader political events or dynamics. Although in many places across the country, Muslims marched together with Buddhists and others in protesting military rule in 1988, in parts of central Burma and Shan State there were attacks on Muslims. Attacks led by Buddhist monks took place in Mandalay in 1997 and spread to other locations. In 2001, violence against Muslims took place in several cities in central Myanmar, with mosques particularly targeted for destruction, in apparent retaliation against the Taliban's destruction of the Bamiyan Buddha statues in Afghanistan.[115] There have been consistent claims that these attacks have been supported by or coordinated by military or military-allied groups or individuals, but concrete evidence for these claims is lacking. However, what does seem to be the case is that authorities have tolerated much of the violence, creating a "permissive environment" that persisted at least throughout the tenure of the USDP government.

Rohingyas in Rakhine State have been the targets of particularly brutal military campaigns of violence and expulsion. Andrew Selth, an authority on Myanmar's military, documents 13 operations between 1948 and 2004 in which the military targeted Rohingyas.[116] One of the most destructive and impactful took place in 1977–1978, with the *Naga-Min* ("Dragon King") operation, which was part of a wider census and documentation project across the country, but in Rakhine State was ostensibly targeting Rohingya insurgents. Authorities used mass arrests and violence against the broader population, resulting in an exodus of an estimated 200,000–250,000 people to Bangladesh.[117] Another similar campaign in 1991 included land confiscation, forced labor and arbitrary taxation and generated another 250,000 refugees over the Bangladesh border.[118] Over this same period, moments of violence or sustained

[115] Human Rights Watch, "Crackdown on Burmese Muslims."

[116] Selth, "Burma's Muslims and the War on Terror," 111–112.

[117] Kei Nemoto, "The Rohingya Issue: A Thorny Obstacle Between Burma (Myanmar) and Bangladesh," Unpublished Paper (2013), 5.

[118] International Crisis Group, "Counting the Costs," 5.

repressive policies by Bangladeshi authorities against the Rohingya have resulted in migratory moves back to parts of Burma and there have also been negotiated repatriations, most notably in 1992.[119]

The 1974 Constitution, written and promulgated under military rule, provided for freedom of religion, without direct reference to Buddhism. This would change in the 2008 Constitution, which declares the same freedom of religious belief and practice, but also noted the "special position" of Buddhism, as the religion professed by the majority of the population. Iselin Frydenlund argues that this clause, along with other complementary laws and policies, creates a situation in which Buddhism is de facto the state religion in Myanmar.[120]

Another impactful yet poorly understood political moment during military rule was the passage of the 1982 citizenship law, which many people refer to as having taken away Rohingya's citizenship. In fact, as Nick Cheesman has deftly shown, the law was a re-organization of citizenship along ethnic lines that did not retroactively strip any-one of citizenship, but rather was subsequently applied (almost a dec-ade later) through a re-registration process implemented by the ruling military government that had the effect of taking away citizenship from Rohingyas who did not have a place in an increasingly "ethnicized" cit-izenship regime.[121] The question of Rohingya citizenship remains one of the thorniest political challenges in Myanmar (apart from the other humanitarian aspects of the violence in Rakhine State), not only because of public perceptions of the Rohingyas' foreign-ness, but also because of perceived threats of demands for autonomy, that are not meaningfully present in the current discourse but are possibilities under the country's 2008 Constitution.

Concerns regarding deracination have also continued to surface in recent decades. Nyi Nyi Kyaw cites a series of fourteen articles entitled "We fear deracination!" that were published in the government news-paper *Working People's Daily* in 1989. These reviewed previous eras,

---

[119] Selth, "Burma's Muslims and the War on Terror," 12.

[120] Iselin Frydenlund, "Religious Liberty for Whom? The Buddhist Politics of Religious Freedom During Myanmar's Transition to Democracy," *Nordic Journal of Human Rights* 35, no. 1 (2017): 61.

[121] Nick Cheesman, "Problems with Facts About Rohingya Statelessness," *E-International Relations*, December 8, 2015b, http://www.e-ir.info/2015/12/08/problems-with-facts-about-rohingya-statelessness/, accessed May 25, 2017.

connecting immigration and citizenship to changing legal environments in the country, thus "invigorating the colonial-era myth of deracination."[122] These fears have animated the current violence against Muslims in Myanmar as well, connected to a sense of existential threat regarding both the Burmese/Myanmar nation and Buddhism.[123]

CONCLUSION

This chapter has painted a broad-brush stroke picture of the history of Muslim–Buddhist interaction in Burma/Myanmar, in an attempt to cover some of the existing scholarship and perspectives and to identify some broad dynamics that have been consistent throughout several different historical periods and into the present. Since 2012, fears regarding violence, discrimination or expulsion have animated interest in the topic, yet the tentative and conditional presence of Muslims within Myanmar's political and social life has remained a persistent feature. At the same time, Muslims in many places across the country are accepted as neighbors, co-workers and community members in unproblematic ways in terms of daily life, an aspect that should not be forgotten in the face of vocal assertions of Islamophobia or long-standing and deep-seated suspicions of Islam on the part of Buddhists. Muslims continue to be marginalized and victimized in contemporary Myanmar, with some groups having more access to pathways of national inclusion than others. And even where Muslims have been integrated with majority Buddhist populations, or live unproblematically within these communities, they are threatened by a dominant and persistent narrative of foreign-ness that leaves them vulnerable and always potentially outside of the national community. While inter-faith projects in the country have sought, in recent years, to articulate a discourse of inclusion in a religiously plural context, this is a nascent conversation in Myanmar, and the ground of Buddhist–Muslim interactions—especially those that are mediated through political, religious or military authorities—will continue to be unequal, at best tolerant of particular moments of inclusion rather than broader cultural change.

[122] Nyi Nyi Kyaw, "Islamophobia in Buddhist Myanmar," 194, and this volume.

[123] See Matthew Walton and Susan Hayward, *Contesting Buddhist Narratives: Democratization, Nationalism, and Communal Violence in Myanmar* (Honolulu: East West Center, 2014); Kyaw San Wai, "Myanmar's Religious Violence: A Buddhist 'Siege Mentality' at Work," *RSIS Commentaries*, 2014.

REFERENCES

Adas, Michael. *The Burma Delta: Economic Development and Social Change on an Asian Rice Frontier, 1852–1941.* Madison: University of Wisconsin Press, 1974.

Atwill, David G. *The Chinese Sultanate: Islam, Ethnicity, and the Panthay Rebellion in Southwest China, 1856–1873.* Stanford: Stanford University Press, 2005.

Beemer, Bryce. "The Creole City in Mainland Southeast Asia: Slave Gathering Warfare and Cultural Exchange in Burma, Thailand and Manipur, 18th–19th c." PhD dissertation, University of Hawai'i at Manoa, 2013.

Berlie, Jean A. *The Burmanization of Myanmar's Muslims.* Bangkok: White Lotus Press, 2008.

Brac de la Perrière, Bénédicte. "An Overview of the Field of Religion in Burmese Studies." *Asian Ethnology* 68, no. 2 (2009): 185–210.

Brac de la Perrière, Bénédicte, Guillaume Rozenberg, and Alicia Marie Turner. *Champions of Buddhism: Weikza Cults in Contemporary Burma.* Singapore: NUS Press, 2014.

Braun, Erik. *The Birth of Insight: Meditation, Modern Buddhism, and the Burmese Monk Ledi Sayadaw, Buddhism and Modernity.* Chicago: The University of Chicago Press, 2013.

Brohm, John. "Burmese Religion and the Burmese Religious Revival." Unpublished PhD dissertation, Cornell University, 1957.

Cady, John F. *A History of Modern Burma.* Ithaca: Cornell University Press, 1958.

Carbine, Jason A. *Sons of the Buddha: Continuities and Ruptures in a Burmese Monastic Tradition.* Berlin: Walter de Gruyter, 2011.

Chakravarti, Nalini Ranjan. *The Indian Minority in Burma: The Rise and Decline of an Immigrant Community.* London: Oxford University Press, 1971.

Charney, Michael W. "Where Jambudipa and Islamdom Converged: Religious Change and the Emergence of Buddhist Communalism in Early Modern Arakan (Fifteenth to Nineteenth Centuries)." Unpublished PhD dissertation, University of Michigan, 1999.

———. *Powerful Learning: Buddhist Literati and the Throne in Burma's Last Dynasty, 1752–1885.* Ann Arbor: University of Michigan Center for South and Southeast Asian Studies, 2006.

Cheesman, Nick. *Opposing the Rule of Law: How Myanmar's Courts Make Law and Order.* Cambridge: Cambridge University Press, 2015a.

———. "Problems with Facts About Rohingya Statelessness." *E-International Relations,* December 8, 2015b. http://www.e-ir.info/2015/12/08/problems-with-facts-about-rohingya-statelessness/. Accessed May 25, 2017.

————. "How in Myanmar 'National Races' Came to Surpass Citizenship and Exclude Rohingya." *Journal of Contemporary Asia* 47, no. 3 (2017): 461–483.

Crouch, Melissa, ed. *Islam and the State in Myanmar: Muslim–Buddhist Relations and the Politics of Belonging*. New Delhi: Oxford University Press, 2016a.

————. "Myanmar's Muslim Mosaic and the Politics of Belonging." In *Islam and the State in Myanmar: Muslim–Buddhist Relations and the Politics of Belonging*, edited by Melissa Crouch, 9–35. New Delhi: Oxford University Press, 2016b.

————. "Personal Law and Colonial Legacy: State-Religion Relations and Islamic Law in Myanmar." In *Islam and the State in Myanmar: Muslim–Buddhist Relations and the Politics of Belonging*, edited by Melissa Crouch, 69–95. New Delhi: Oxford University Press, 2016c.

Desai, Walter Sagdun. *India and Burma, a Study*. Bombay: Orient Longmans, 1954.

Egreteau, Renaud. "Burmese Indians in Contemporary Burma: Heritage, Influence, and Perceptions Since 1988." *Asian Ethnicity* 12, no. 1 (2011): 33–54.

Farrelly, Nicholas. "Muslim Political Activity in Transitional Myanmar." In *Islam and the State in Myanmar: Muslim–Buddhist Relations and the Politics of Belonging*, edited by Melissa Crouch, 99–126. New Delhi: Oxford University Press, 2016.

Forbes, Andrew D.W. "The 'Panthay' (Yunnanese Chinese) Muslims of Burma." *Institute of Muslim Minority Affairs Journal* 7, no. 2 (1986): 384–394.

Foxeus, Niklas. "The Buddhist World Emperor's Mission: Millenarian Buddhism in Postcolonial Burma." PhD dissertation, Stockholm University, 2011.

Frydenlund, Iselin. "Religious Liberty for Whom? The Buddhist Politics of Religious Freedom During Myanmar's Transition to Democracy." *Nordic Journal of Human Rights* 35, no. 1 (2017): 55–73.

Green, Nile. "Buddhism, Islam and the Religious Economy of Colonial Burma." *Journal of Southeast Asian Studies* 46, no. 2 (2015): 175–204.

Harvey, G.E. *History of Burma: From the Earliest Times to 10 March 1824, the Beginning of the English Conquest*. London: Longmans, Green and Co., 1925.

Houtman, Gustaaf. *Mental Culture in Burmese Crisis Politics: Aung San Suu Kyi and the National League for Democracy*. Tokyo: Institute for the Study of Languages and Cultures of Asia and Africa, Tokyo University of Foreign Studies, 1999.

Human Rights Watch. "Crackdown on Burmese Muslims." *Human Rights Watch*, 2002. https://www.hrw.org/legacy/backgrounder/asia/burma-bck4.htm.

Ibrahim, Azeem. *The Rohingyas: Inside Myanmar's Hidden Genocide*. London: Hurst & Co., 2016.

Ikeya, Chie. *Refiguring Women, Colonialism, and Modernity in Burma, Southeast Asia-Politics, Meaning, Memory.* Honolulu: University of Hawai'i Press, 2011.

International Crisis Group. "The Dark Side of Transition: Violence Against Muslims in Myanmar." *Asia Report,* 2013. https://www.crisisgroup.org/asia/south-east-asia/myanmar/dark-side-transition-violence-against-muslims-myanmar.

———. "Counting the Costs: Myanmar's Problematic Census." *Asia Briefing,* 2014. https://www.crisisgroup.org/asia/south-east-asia/myanmar/counting-costs-myanmar-s-problematic-census.

Jordt, Ingrid. *Burma's Mass Lay Meditation Movement: Buddhism and the Cultural Construction of Power.* Athens: Ohio University Press, 2007.

Kawanami, Hiroko. *Renunciation and Empowerment of Buddhist Nuns in Myanmar-Burma: Building a Community of Female Faithful.* Boston: Brill, 2013.

Keck, Stephen. "The Making of an Invisible Minority: Muslims in Colonial Burma." In *Living on the Margins: Minorities and Borderlines in Cambodia and Southeast Asia,* edited by Peter J. Hammer, 221–234. Siem Reap, Cambodia: Center for Khmer Studies, 2009.

———. "Reconstructing Trajectories of Islam in British Burma." In *Islam and the State in Myanmar: Muslim–Buddhist Relations and the Politics of Belonging,* edited by Melissa Crouch, 39–68. New Delhi: Oxford University Press, 2016.

(Ma) Khin Mar Mar Kyi. "In Pursuit of Power: Political Power and Gender Relations in New Order Burma/Myanmar." PhD dissertation, Australian National University, 2013.

Khin Yi. *The Dobama Movement in Burma (1930–1938).* Ithaca: Southeast Asia Program, Cornell University, 1988.

King, Winston L. *A Thousand Lives Away: Buddhism in Contemporary Burma.* Oxford: Bruno Cassirer, 1964.

Kyaw San Wai. "Myanmar's Religious Violence: A Buddhist 'Siege Mentality' at Work." *RSIS Commentaries,* February 20, 2014. http://www.rsis.edu.sg/publications/Perspective/RSIS0372014.pdf?utm_source=getresponse&utm_medium=email&utm_campaign=rsis_publications&utm_content=RSIS+Commentary+037/2014+Myanmar%E2%80%99s+Religious+Violence:+A+Buddhist+%E2%80%98Siege+Mentality%E2%80%9D+a.

Lambrecht, Curtis. "Burma (Myanmar)." In *Voices of Islam in Southeast Asia: A Contemporary Sourcebook,* edited by Greg Fealy and Virginia Hooker, 23–30. Singapore: Institute of Southeast Asian Studies, 2006.

Leider, Jacques. "Rohingya: The Name, the Movement and the Quest for Identity." In *Nation Building in Myanmar.* Yangon: Myanmar Egress, 2014.

Mendelson, E. Michael, and John P. Ferguson. *Sangha and State in Burma: A Study of Monastic Sectarianism and Leadership (Symbol, Myth, and Ritual).* Ithaca: Cornell University Press, 1975.

Nemoto, Kei. "The Rohingya Issue: A Thorny Obstacle Between Burma (Myanmar) and Bangladesh." Unpublished Paper, 2013.

Nyi Nyi Kyaw. "Alienation, Discrimination, and Securitization: Legal Personhood and Cultural Personhood of Muslims in Myanmar." *The Review of Faith & International Affairs* 13, no. 4 (2015): 50–59.

———. "Islamophobia in Buddhist Myanmar: The 969 Movement and Anti-Muslim Violence." In *Islam and the State in Myanmar: Muslim–Buddhist Relations and the Politics of Belonging*, edited by Melissa Crouch, 183–210. New Delhi: Oxford University Press, 2016.

Pe Kin [U]. *Pinlon: An Inside Story*. Yangon, Myanmar: Ministry of Information, Government of the Union of Myanmar, 1994.

Republic of the Union of Myanmar. *The 2014 Myanmar Population and Housing Census, the Union Report: Religion*. Naypyidaw: Ministry of Labour Department of Population, Immigration and Population, 2016.

Saha, Jonathan. "Anti-Islamic Abuse in Burma and Britain, the Colonial Past and Present." *Colonising Animals*, June 7, 2013. https://colonizinganimals.blog/2013/06/07/anti-islamic-abuse-in-burma-and-britain-the-colonial-past-and-present/.

Sarkisyanz, Manuel. *Buddhist Backgrounds of the Burmese Revolution*. The Hague: Martinus Nijhoff, 1965.

Schissler, Matt, Matthew J. Walton, and Phyu Phyu Thi. "Threat and Virtuous Defence: Listening to Narratives of Religious Conflict in Six Myanmar Cities." *Myanmar Media and Society Project, Working Paper* 1, no. 1 (2015).

Schober, Juliane. "Paths to Enlightenment: Theravada Buddhism in Upper Burma." Unpublished PhD dissertation, University of Illinois at Champagne-Urbana, 1989.

———. *Modern Buddhist Conjunctures in Myanmar: Cultural Narratives, Colonial Legacies, and Civil Society*. Honolulu: University of Hawai'i Press, 2011.

Selth, Andrew. "Burma's Muslims and the War on Terror." *Studies in Conflict & Terrorism* 27, no. 2 (2004): 107–126.

Smith, Donald Eugene. *Religion and Politics in Burma*. Princeton: Princeton University Press, 1965.

Spiro, Melford E. *Burmese Supernaturalism: A Study in the Explanation and Reduction of Suffering, Prentice-Hall College Anthropology Series*. Englewood Cliffs: Prentice-Hall, 1967.

———. *Buddhism and Society: A Great Tradition and Its Burmese Vicissitudes*. 2nd ed. Berkeley: University of California Press, 1982.

Tagliacozzo, Eric. "Burmese and Muslim: Islam and the Hajj in the Sangha State." In *Burmese Lives: Ordinary Life Stories Under the Burmese Regime*, edited by Wen-Chin Chang and Eric Tagliacozzo, 83–106. New York: Oxford University Press, 2014.

Tannenbaum, Nicola Beth. *Who Can Compete Against the World? Power-Protection and Buddhism in Shan Worldview, Monograph and Occasional Paper Series, No. 51*. Ann Arbor, MI: Association for Asian Studies, 1995.

Taylor, Robert. "Do States Make Nations? The Politics of Identity in Myanmar Revisited." *South East Asia Research* 13, no. 3 (2005): 261–286.

———. *Refighting Old Battles, Compounding Misconceptions: The Politics of Ethnicity in Myanmar Today. ISEAS Perspective*. Singapore: Institute of Southeast Asian Studies, 2015.

Thant Myint-U. *The Making of Modern Burma*. Cambridge: Cambridge University Press, 2001.

———. *The River of Lost Footsteps: A Personal History of Burma*. London: Faber and Faber, 2008.

Turner, Alicia Marie. *Saving Buddhism: The Impermanence of Religion in Colonial Burma, Southeast Asia-Politics, Meaning, Memory*. Honolulu: University of Hawai'i Press, 2014.

Walton, Matthew. *Buddhism, Politics and Political Thought in Myanmar*. Cambridge: Cambridge University Press, 2016.

Walton, Matthew, and Susan Hayward. *Contesting Buddhist Narratives: Democratization, Nationalism, and Communal Violence in Myanmar*. Honolulu: East West Center, 2014.

Ware, Anthony, and Costas Laoutides. *Myanmar's 'Rohingya' Conflict*. London: C. Hurst & Co., 2018.

Yegar, Moshe. *The Muslims of Burma*. Wiesbaden: O. Harrassowitz, 1972.

Yeni. "A Leader of Men." *Irrawaddy*, September 2007. http://www2.irrawaddy.com/article.php?art_id=8463&page=1.

Yusuf, Imtiyaz. "Nationalist Ethnicities as Religious Identities: Islam, Buddhism, and Citizenship in Myanmar." *The American Journal of Islamic Social Sciences* 34, no. 4 (2017): 100–119.

CHAPTER 4

Buddhist–Muslim Dynamics in Siam/Thailand

Raymond Scupin and Christopher M. Joll

Much has been written about the dynamics between Muslims and Thailand's Buddhist dominant majority. However, existing literature examining the nature of Buddhist–Muslim dynamics in Thailand leaves much to unpack. Thailand's approximately four million Muslims, who comprise the country's largest religious minority, accounting for approximately 5.8% of its 69 million citizens, reside primarily—though not exclusively—in the country's southern provinces of Pattani, Yala, and Narathiwat. Historically, these southern provinces, along with the northern provinces of Malaysia to their south, belonged to an Islamic sultanate, the Kingdom of Patani. Thai rule over the Patani was established in 1909 (when then-Siam annexed the sultanate), since which time,

R. Scupin
Lindenwood University, Saint Charles, MO, USA
e-mail: RScupin@lindenwood.edu

C. M. Joll (✉)
Muslim Studies Centre, Institute of Asian Studies,
Chulalongkorn University, Bangkok, Thailand

Religious Studies Program, Victoria University of Wellington,
Wellington, New Zealand

© The Author(s) 2020
I. Frydenlund and M. Jerryson (eds.),
Buddhist-Muslim Relations in a Theravada World,
https://doi.org/10.1007/978-981-32-9884-2_4

Thailand's Muslims have faced forced "Thaification" and cultural assimilation at the hands of Thai political leadership. By the mid-twentieth century, resistance to such efforts culminated in a separatist movement in Southern Thailand that in 2004 developed into an armed insurgency.

In this chapter, we move beyond Thailand's southern provinces and analyses of the region's southern separatist movement to present portrayals of local contact, harmony, and conflict between Thailand's Buddhists and Muslims across central, north, and south Thailand. There is a desperate need for fresh air to be breathed into the analysis of the nature of the dynamics and conflict between Thailand's Buddhists and Muslims, which is commonly—though erroneously—reduced to primarily an issue of religious conflict. Although the Buddhist–Muslim conflicts cannot be reduced to religious conflict, we suggest that these communities have elicited more extreme essentialist constructions of one another that have produced tensions in the current period.

This chapter begins with an overview of the contact between Muslims and Buddhists in Thailand. We assert that in Thailand, both Muslim and Buddhist populations are more linguistically and ethnically diverse than is usually assumed and as a result, ethnic minorities have been negatively affected by the motivation of political and religious elites to maintain relatively homogeneous communities of subjects. Drawing on the late Stanley Tambiah's work, we describe how the Thai polity expanded and how the elite tried to produce a uniformity of ethnic and religious identity within this diverse linguistic and multicultural environment. We will describe how Islam has adopted and adapted Indic-Brahministic and Buddhist influences in the Thai/Malay Peninsula as well as in north and central Thailand.[1] We discuss the diverse origins and contributions of Muslims in central and north Thailand from the Ayutthayan to the Bangkok period that often have been overlooked. This chapter will also review the endeavors by Siamese and Thai Buddhist elites to manage the ethnic and religious diversity of their subjects. Finally, the chapter will examine the current tensions between Muslims and Buddhists in

---

[1] See Christopher M. Joll, "Making Sense of Thailand's 'Merit-Making' Muslims: Adoption and Adaption of the Indic in the Creation of Islamicate Southern Thailand," *Islam and Christian–Muslim Relations* 25, no. 3 (2014): 303–320; Raymond Scupin, "Popular Islam in Thailand," in *The Muslims in Thailand, Volume 1, Historical and Cultural Studies*, ed. Andrew D.W. Forbes (Bihar: Centre for South East Asian Studies, 1988c), 31–46.

4 BUDDHIST–MUSLIM DYNAMICS IN SIAM/THAILAND   103

Thailand and some of the conditions and reasons that have led to these new developments.

Buddhist–Muslim Interactions Past and Present

The large Buddhist kingdoms of Thailand (formerly Siam)[2] were initially formed by the migration of the Tai (language group) peoples from southern China into Southeast Asia, beginning in the seventh century. Over a period of several centuries, Tai migrants moved into the Chao Phraya river basin, met, and married members of the native Mon, Khmer, and other ethnic groups. Through their encounters with the Mons and Khmer kingdoms, the Tai people became familiar with Hindu and Buddhist traditions. Eventually, as the Tai speaking peoples outnumbered other ethnic groups. They developed the first large kingdoms in the region and adopted the religious tradition of Theravada Buddhism and its Pali texts,[3] which had spread to the region by Sinhalese *bhikkhu* (monks) and was practiced by the Mon for many centuries.[4]

Muslims make up about one-third of the population in the southern region of Thailand or 85% of the three southern provinces of Pattani, Yala, and Narathiwat. Approximately two million Muslims live in these southern provinces. These provinces were once a part of the ethnically Malay, Islamic sultanate of Patani, which lay between the Malayan sultanates to the south and the power centers of the Siamese in the north. As will be discussed below, this Patani region was incorporated into the

---

[2] The name Siam was adopted to refer to the region at its broadest, under the Chakri dynasty, where the kingdom of Siam included the geographic region of Thailand, along with parts of Laos, Cambodia, and Malaysia. In 1939, the name Siam name was changed to Thailand by the nationalist General Phibulsongkhram (1938–1944) to incorporate the notion of a Thai nationality and "race."

[3] Theravada, literally meaning "school of the elder monks" in Pali—a language native to the Indian subcontinent, in which the earliest literature on Buddhism appears—is a branch of Buddhism that focuses on the Buddha's teachings preserved in the Pali canon, the only complete Buddhist canon that survives in a classical Indic language.

[4] Charles F. Keyes, *Thailand: Buddhist Kingdom as Modern Nation-State* (Boulder and London: Westview Press, 1987), 15–16; Stanley Tambiah, *World Conqueror and World Renouncer: A Study of Buddhism and Polity in Thailand Against a Historical Background* (Cambridge: Cambridge University Press, 1976), 73–199; Raymond Scupin, "Mainland Southeast Asia," in *Peoples and Cultures of Asia*, ed. Raymond Scupin (Upper Saddle River, NJ: Prentice Hall Press, 2006b), 335–383.

104 R. SCUPIN AND C. M. JOLL

Siamese state in the early twentieth century. The majority of the Muslims in south Thailand are bilingual, speaking both Thai and Malay. The Malay Muslims in the region identify themselves as *ore nayu* (a contacted version of Melayu in the local dialect referred to as Patani Malay), and they refer to the Thai Buddhists as *ore siye* (the Siamese people). In contemporary times, Thai Buddhists use the ethnic category *khaek* and/or *Musalayam* to describe Malay Muslims,[5] which is perceived as a pejorative term by the native Muslims in the south.

In central Thailand, the population of Muslims is approximately 670,000 and there are about 40,000 Muslim residents in north and northeast Thailand.[6] In central and north Thailand, both voluntary and involuntary migrants and sometimes refer to themselves as Thai Muslims or *Thai Isalam*, though their religious and ethnic backgrounds are very diverse. Historically, while the Muslims of south Thailand lived in a region imbued with a Malay-Indonesian Islamic political and religious cultural ethos, the Muslims of central and north Thailand have been influenced by the political-religious culture of the Theravada Buddhist traditions. However, because of the administrative practices and policies of the Thai state during the course of the twentieth century, all Muslims

---

[5] There has been a considerable amount of literature regarding the term *khaek* as used by the Thai people to refer to Muslims (Scupin, "Muslim Accommodation in Thai Society," Journal of Islamic Studies 9, no. 2 (1998), 229–258; Jerryson, *Buddhist Fury: Religion and Violence in Southern Thailand* (Oxford University Press, 2011), 151–155; Jory, "From Melayu Patani to Thai Muslim: The Spectre of Ethnic Identity in Southern Thailand," *South East Asia Research* 15, no. 2 (2007), 225–279). The term *khaek* has a quasi-racial, phenotypical or biological notion as well as an ethnic or religious reference. Traditionally, the Thai used the phrase *khon* (person) *khaek* to refer to international guests or strangers, especially the South Asian or Arab migrants or those with brown skin, as well as in respect to religion for the Malay Muslims and other Muslims in Thailand. Generally, the phrase *khon khaek* is used to classify those who are not Thai or *Chon Chat Thai*. Although originally *khaek* did not have a pejorative connotation, it has become a negative and offensive racialistic term for Muslims, especially for those southern Malay-speaking Muslims in south Thailand.

[6] We would like to thank Chaiwat Meesanthan in the Center for Southeast Asian Studies at Thammasat University for providing us with estimated current population numbers for Muslims in central and northern Thailand. Chaiwat completed a Ph.D. in 2017 at the University of Malaya with an ethnographic study of Malay Muslims in Bangkok and central Thailand, *Minoriti Melayu di Bangkok dan Kawasan Sekitarnya: Antara Survival dan Kejayaan* (Malay Minority in Bangkok and its Surrounding Areas: Between Survival and Success).

in Thailand have been largely affected by the dominant Buddhist political and religious culture.

THE THAI STATE AND ITS EXPANSION

In order to examine Buddhist–Muslim relations, we will begin with the political evolutionary approach used by the late Stanley Tambiah to discuss the development of the state and ethnic interactions in Thailand. Tambiah used the metaphors of the "galactic and radial polities" to describe the historical expansion of the Thai state. The galactic polity, a variant of Max Weber's patrimonial bureaucracy, is applied to the Sukhothai (1282–1350) and Ayutthayan (1351–1767) kingdoms. According to Tambiah, in the galactic polity, the king directly controls the population and resources in a central geographical location, while the outlying provinces essentially remain autonomous replications of the center. In the galactic phase of state development of these early kingdoms, inter-ethnic relations are not dramatically transformed. Tambiah refers to the Thai state that emerged with the establishment of the Chakri dynasty and Rama I during the Rattanakosin era (1782–1932), based in Bangkok as a radial polity. The radial polity is a state that has a capital center that attempts to exert direct political control over other provinces through its governmental agents. During the Rattanakosin or Bangkok period, the Thai kingdom became a full-fledged patrimonial bureaucratic state that expanded throughout the north, northeast, west, and southern frontiers and directly controlled peripheral provinces in which inter-ethnic relations were radically transformed.

Indic and Buddhist Influences in South Thailand

Prior to the spread of Islam in the Thai/Malay peninsula there were Indic-Brahministic-Buddhist kingdoms where Sanskrit had been adopted.[7] Islam was introduced to Southeast Asia via commercial interactions as Muslim traders traversed trade routes between Southeast Asia and regions farther east, including China, during the first several centuries of the common era, spreading to significant parts of the region by

---

[7] Michael F. Laffan, "Southeast Asia, History and Culture," in *Medieval Islamic Civilization: An Encyclopedia (Vol. 1: A-K)*, ed. Josef W. Meri (New York: Routledge, 2006), 767.

the twelfth century. First propagated along immediate trade routes, Islam grew in port villages, attracting Muslims from across the Far East while also converting local elites. As these communities grew, Islam spread from port cities to the interior, encountering local spiritual beliefs and practices—including Buddhism and Hinduism—which were practiced alongside Islam. Muslim states began to grow in size and economic and political prominence, leading to the founding of the Islamic sultanate (*Kerajaan*) of Patani around the start of the fourteenth century.

Far from operating in isolation, Islamic and Indic-Brahminist-Buddhist influences and practices interacted and co-mingled within local populations. Assertions regarding the overlapping influences in Southeast Asia are based on both linguistic and archeological evidence. Advances in proto-historic archaeology reveal the presence of Indic influence in the portion of the Thai/Malay Peninsula that corresponds to southern Thailand. The Patani *Kerajaan* located as it was between the Thai Ayutthaya kingdom of central Thailand and the Malay Malacca sultanate of central Malaysia, was unique among Malay states. In the Malay sultanates, Islam normally replaced the Hindu–Buddhist influences; however, in Patani, Islam and Buddhism interacted with each other in a harmonious way. As a result, Islam demonstrated some Buddhist influences. However, Francis Bradley, who has recounted—in often harrowing detail—the five decades of war that Bangkok waged against the Malay *Kerajaan* of Patani from 1786 through "massacre, slave-raiding, environmental warfare, and the expulsion of refugees,"[8] which brought an end to traditional cooperative state relations.[9]

[8]Joll, "Thailand's Muslim Kaleidoscope Between Central Plains and Far-South: Fresh Perspectives from the Sufi Margins" (2016), 317–358; Francis Bradley, "Siam's Conquest of Patani and the End of Mandala Relations, 1786–1838," in *The Ghosts of the Past in Southern Thailand: Essays on the History and Historiography of Patani*, ed. Patrick Jory (Singapore: National University of Singapore Press, 2012), 149–160. The dates of Siamese campaigns in south Thailand are 1785–1786, 1789–1791, 1808, 1831–1832, and 1838.

[9]Francis Bradley, *Forging Islamic Power and Place: The Legacy of Shaykh Da'ud bin 'Abd Allah al-Fatani in Mecca and Southeast Asia* (Honolulu: University of Hawaii Press, 2015), 39–62, 150.

Muslims in Central Thailand During the Ayutthaya Period (1351–1767)

Port cities located between the Patani and Ayutthaya kingdoms were sites of material, cultural, and ideological exchange, and the ships that visited arrived from both the east and the west. Before the rise of Ayutthaya, the first proto-Siamese state to emerge in the Chao Phraya basin in the late thirteenth century was Sukhothai. The most important document from this period is an inscription attributed to King Ramkhamhaeng. This is dated 1292 and contains the "Persianate" term "bazaar."[10] Ayutthaya became an important center for Persian Muslims, which explains the Persians references to it as the "new city" *Shahr-i Nau* (Pr. *Shahr'un-nuwi*),[11] although Christoph Marcinkowski regards *Shahr-e Nav* (Pr. The city of boats and canals) as its correct form.[12] By the sixteenth century, the kingdom of Ayutthaya, with a population of about 300,000—larger than that of London at that time—was a cosmopolitan and ethnically diverse center.

According to historical documents, Buddhist royal rulers were generally tolerant and even supportive of Muslim religious rites during the Ayutthayan period. For example, several mosques were established at royal expense, and King Narai (Ramathibodi III) contributed lavishly towards the Muharram and other Muslim rites.[13] There was, however, a split between official policy and practice regarding the proselytization of Islam in Thailand. According to an edict from the mid-seventeenth century, anyone allowing themselves or their kin to be converted to a foreign religion would be considered an enemy to the state. They could be imprisoned, have their property confiscated, or have other punitive

---

[10] Raymond Scupin, "The Socio-Economics Status of Muslims in Central and North Thailand," *Journal of Muslim Minority Affairs* 4, no. 2 (1981), 164.

[11] Christopher John Baker, "Ayutthaya Rising: From Land or Sea?" *Journal of Southeast Asian Studies* 34, no. 1 (2003), 45–46.

[12] Christoph Marcinkowski, *Persians and Shi'ites in Thailand: From the Ayutthaya Period to the Present*, Volume 15, *Nalanda-Sriwijaya Centre Working Paper* (Singapore: Nalanda-Sriwijaya Centre, 2014), 3.

[13] Simon de la Loubere, *The Kingdom of Siam* (Oxford: Oxford University Press, 1969), 112; Nicholas Gervaise, *The Natural and Political History of the Kingdom of Siam A.D. 1688* (Bangkok: Siam Observer Press, 1928), 95; Muhammad Ibn Ibrahim, *The Ship of Sulaiman*, trans. John O'Kane, Persian Heritage Series No. 11 (London: Routledge and Kegan Paul, 1972), 77.

108 R. SCUPIN AND C. M. JOLL

measures taken towards them. Yet, for some time during the Ayutthayan period, Thais who did convert to Islam were exempted from corvée labor.[14] And as Muhammad Ibrahim observed on his sojourn throughout the kingdom, there was some success in the spread of Shia doctrine among the Thai. The most famous Persian immigrant to Ayutthaya during this period was Shaykh Ahmad Qomi (1543–1631).[15]

The Siamese court granted permission to construct a mosque graveyard, and homes in the part of Ayutthaya known as *Ban Khaek Kuti Chao Sen*.[16] Tomé Pires mentioned in his *Suma Oriental* "Moors" and "Turks" having settled in Ayutthaya, this Siamese entrepôt.[17] In 1685, Chevalier de Chaumont observed that the Malays were "quite numerous" but that "most of them are slaves." Makassaris and "many people of the Island of Java" also had an established presence.[18] Cham Muslim refugees from Cambodia regions also came to settle in Ayutthaya. Three Cham brothers had arrived at the court of King Narai in the seventeenth century. Later, following an offensive against Cambodia on the part of the Vietnamese in 1758, many Cham refugees migrated to Ayutthaya to become part of its military. In general during the Ayutthaya period

[14] de la Loubere, *The Kingdom of Siam*, 112.

[15] The Persian leaders Shayk Ahmad and his brother Muhammad Sa-id, and their descendants laid the foundations of the Bunnag family, a politically prominent family of Thai life for over three centuries (Wyatt 1974, 154–155; Rabibhadana 1969, 213; Scupin 1980a, 62–64; Bajunid 1980, 4). Shayk Ahmad and the Persian leaders in Ayutthaya were responsible for establishing the Chularajmontri (Thai) or *Shayk al Islām* that has remained as the central religious authority for the Muslim population today. Despite its Shia heritage, it has become a non-sectarian Muslim position (Yusuf 1998, 277–298). The former Commander-in-Chief or the Royal Thai Army (2005–2007) General Sonthi Boonyaratglin is a Muslim descendant of Shayk Ahmad. In 2006 Sonthi led the military coup against the Thaksin Shiniwatra government. Shayk Ahmad and the Shia Muslims built the Ta'kiayokin mosque in Ayutthaya. Later Rama IV renamed the mosque Takiayokin Rajamisjinja Siam. The mosque is 392 years old. There is also an ornate tomb for Shayk Ahmad in Ayutthaya. Another mosque in Ayutthaya known as Kudi Chaufaa is over 300 years old (Pitsuwan, *Muslim Worship Sites in Thailand* (2001), 16).

[16] *Sen* is a corruption of *Hussein*, an important personality in Shia Islam.

[17] Tomé Pires, *The 'Suma Oriental' of Tomé Pires: An Account of the East, from the Red Sea to China*, trans. Armando Cortesão, 2 vols. (London: Hakluyt Society, 1990), 92, 104.

[18] Michael Smithies, *Descriptions of Old Siam, Oxford in Asia Paperbacks* (Kuala Lumpur: Oxford University Press, 1995), 42; Davisakd Puaksom, "The Pursuit of Java: Thai Panji Stories, Melayu Lingua Franca, and the Question of Translation" (PhD dissertation, Southeast Asian Studies Department, National University of Singapore, 2008), 89.

Buddhist–Muslim relationships appeared to be very cooperative and harmonious. Ayutthaya's cosmopolitan credentials are well known and widely cited by Thais actively advocating for the establishment of a more inclusive society.

Managing the Radial Polity

National cultures are composed not only of cultural institutions, but of narratives, symbols, and representations. As such, a national culture is also a *discourse*, a means of constructing meanings that influences and organizes both actions and conceptions of identity with an affective dimension. As a means of managing the radial polity and establishing direct bureaucratic control over various locales and regions, the Siamese state developed an ethnoideology that had a decisive influence on Buddhist–Muslim relations. Despite the actual ethnic diversity within the country, Siamese nationalist leaders and state officials promoted a uniform ethnic collective identity based on notions of race, culture, and on what has been referred to as the "Three Pillars." Various Siamese monarchs promoted the Three Pillars of national and ethnic identity for the country. The Three Pillars of this Thai collective identity are the "nation" (*chat*), "religion" (*sasana*), and "monarchy" (*phramahaksat*). This Siamese political and cultural code represented a symbol of a unified ethnic and religious identity that was formulated to mediate the actual ethnic ambiguities and contradictions within the country.

The first pillar, *chat* (derived from the Sanskrit-Hindi *jati*, which translates roughly as "caste"), was used by the Siamese majority to refer to birth, race, lineage, and origin. It also had the connotations of biology, birth, lineage, and descent, which made it somewhat equivalent to the early European concept of race. In linguistic usage, *chon chat Thai* was used to refer to the Thai race/nation/culture. This quasi-racial term of identity became the basis of ethnonationalism in Thailand and was also used to promote government policies that affected ethnic relations. The second pillar, *sasana*, religion, was synonymous with Theravada Buddhism, which is still practiced by the vast majority of the population in Thailand. The third pillar, *phramahakasat*, is an honorific term for "king" or "monarch" and embodies the vertical or hierarchical symbolic relationship between the ruler and the people in Siamese society. These three pillars were cultivated as the basis of ethnic and national identity within Siamese society.

110   R. SCUPIN AND C. M. JOLL

Later developments in Thai history provoked extreme nationalistic policies that were based on notions of "race" drawn from European and Japanese sources. Under the rule of General Phibul Songkhram (1938–1944), ultra-nationalist policies and dictatorial rule emerged that had a dramatic influence on Thai interethnic and interreligious relations for generations. In particular, Luang Wichit Wathakan, who was director general of the department of fine arts during the years 1932–1941, drew on racist and fascist ideas from Europe and Japan to promote nationalism in Thailand. During World War II, he became minister of foreign affairs. Wichit Wathakan, has been compared to Hermann Goebbels of Germany and he became the major propaganda minister in Thailand. He provided a conceptual framework sanctioned by the state to create a racial and nationalistic identity for the Thai people.[19]

Wichit Wathakan propagated the idea that the Thai were a heroic and martial "race." The Thai "race" was differentiated from that of Chinese, Indian, European, or American peoples. There were specific behaviors and cultural conventions assumed to be associated with the Thai "race." Thai culture and race (*Thai rathaniyom*) and a cultural policy based on "cultural rules" (*kot wattanatham*) were publicized and propagated through the educational system and media. The polysemic symbols of nationality, royalty, religion, and the advertising industries helped produce a modern Thai identity or Thainess (*kwam pen thai*) that has had major consequences for ethnic and religious minorities in Thailand, including Muslims.[20] Michael Connors emphasizes that Thainess is an ethnoideology that tolerates subordinate identities but accepts no *equals.*

[19] Scott Barmè, *Luang Wichit Wathakan and the Creation of a Thai Identity* (Singapore: Institute of Southeast Asian Studies, 1993), 1–186.

[20] Michael Connors has argued that the simplistic ethnonationalist ideological complex of three pillars of Thai identity have been weakened by new developments in nationalist and international discourse, with novel local sources of cultural diversity producing a new Thainess for a global age (2005, 523–551). Yet, a more primordial Thai identity based on royalist narratives and Buddhist notions continues to be promoted. In his political analyses, Duncan McCargo describes Thailand's nation-building elites as committed to the suppression of "all notions of ethnic difference," a "quietly repressive process" that led to the widespread concealment, denial, or downplaying of ethnic origins (2011, 836; Joll 2016, 317–358).

Muslims in South Thailand Since the Bangkok Period

Following the incorporation of the Patani region by the Thai state in 1909, the government aggressively began an attempt at controlling and assimilating the Malay Muslim population through the appointment of Thai Buddhist bureaucrats throughout southern Malay regions. In addition, Thai authorities began to interfere directly with the religious practices of the Muslims in the South. Bangkok authorities attempted to assume all legal matters under Thai law. Thai Buddhist officials established control and monitored the Muslim legal code, structured by the *Shari'ah* and *adat* (Malay custom), and administered by the local *qadi* (Muslim judge).

During the 1930s—the period following the establishment of a democratic regime in Thailand following the bloodless coup of 1932—the Bangkok-based government promoted education as the means of integrating this region into the Thai nation. This created a dilemma for the Malay Muslims in the south because the Thai educational system was based on Buddhist values and was intimately associated with a curriculum developed by the Buddhist *sangha*—and the language of education was Thai. Therefore, to become involved in the Thai educational process necessitated a rejection of one's language and religion, the primordial basis of ethnic identity for these Malay Muslims. To resolve this dilemma, the *ulama*, the local Muslim religious leaders and the source of political legitimacy, played a prominent role in mobilizing political support around Islamic religious and cultural symbols.

As Thai compulsory education spread into the southern provinces, the Islamic schools or *pondoks* were encouraged to modify the Islamic curriculum to include an emphasis on the three sacred pillars of the Thai state. The *pondoks* were the Islamic schools that were parallel to the Buddhist temple (*wat*) in providing the basic enculturation of individuals within the wider society. *Pondoks* were sacred centers within the Malay Muslim villages of the southern Thai region and became the preeminent symbols of Malay Muslim Islamic ideals and identity. The traditional curriculum of the *pondok* was based on the classical model of the *madrasah*, the educational institutions of the Islamic world. *Tok khru* (derived from the term *guru*), or Muslim teachers, were trained in the Islamic sciences, and many possessed a knowledge of classical Arabic and Jawi (Malay with Arabic script). They taught recitation of the Qur'an, exegesis of religious texts, the traditions of the Prophet, theology, logic, history, mysticism, and Islamic law and jurisprudence. The purpose of the *pondoks* was primarily religious and was tied to Islamic rituals, celebration of Muslim holidays and life cycle events. The *pondoks* produced the religious leaders, *ulama* and *tok khru* that officiated in Islamic jurisprudence procedures, ritual celebrations, and religious instruction. The Thai government continued to appoint central Thai Buddhists who were unable to speak Malay as the bureaucratic officials in these southern provinces. These officials promoted Buddhist or secular policies that resulted in negative attitudes and misconceptions between the Muslims and Thai Buddhists. In response, the *ulama*, the local Muslim religious leaders and the source of political legitimacy, played a prominent role in mobilizing political support around Islamic religious and cultural symbols.[21]

By the late 1930s, with the downfall of democratic politics and the resurgence of the military faction in the Thai state led by the extreme nationalist Prime Minister, Phibun Songkram, who emulated the state policies of fascist Germany, Italy, and Japan, Malay Muslim aspirations were devastated. However, after World War II, the Thai state began once again to liberalize and pluralize its policies toward its southern provinces by establishing governmental machinery to manage the Malay leadership and draw the *ulama* into the official bureaucratic network. Through legislation known as the Patronage Act of 1945, the *ulama*, the mosque councils, and the madrasas were centralized under the authority of the *Shaikh al-Islam* or *Chularajamontri* and articulated into the Thai bureaucracy through the Ministry of Interior. The *Chularajamontri* would advise the monarchy and be considered the spiritual leader of the Muslims in Thailand. The office was to be a counterpart to the *Sangharaja* (the supreme patriarch) of the Buddhist religious hierarchy. The patronage act also directed the government to develop Islamic educational institutions for Muslim children with an appropriate Islamic curriculum.

---

[21] Surin Pitsuwan, *Islam and Malay Nationalism: A Study of Malay Muslims in Southern Thailand* (Bangkok: ThaiKhadai Research Institute, 1985, 175–207); Pitsuwan, "The Lotus and the Crescent: Clashes of Religious Symbolism in Southern Thailand," in *Ethnic Conflict in Buddhist Societies: Sri Lanka, Thailand, and Burma*, eds. K.M. de Silva, P. Duke, E. Goldberg, and N. Katz (1988), 187–201; Ladd M. Thomas, "Bureaucratic Attitudes and Behavior as Obstacles to Political Integration of Thai Muslims," *Southeast Asia: An International Quarterly* 3, no. 1 (1974), 544–566; Hasan Madmarn, "Pondoks and Change in South Thailand," in *Aspects of Development: Education and Political Integration for Muslims in Thailand and Malaysia*, ed. Raymond Scupin (Selangor, Malaysia: Institute of Malay Language, Literature, 1989), 47–92.

In conjunction with this, an Islamic college was to be established in Thailand with king's scholarships for pilgrimages to Mecca. The *ulama* were to be integrated into the state bureaucracy through Islamic provincial committees set up by the minister of interior. One surreptitious clause of the act allowed the minister to appoint and dismiss *ulama* in order to insure loyalty and to subvert irredentism. Unfortunately, because of deep suspicions of Malay Muslims toward Thai authorities, the patronage act became a divisive issue in southern Thailand, splitting Malay Muslims between "loyalists" and "separatists."

A number of Islamic-based factions emerged during the 1960s and 1970s in south Thailand reflecting a diversity of political views became engaged in activist irredentist activities. One early separatist group, the National Liberation Front of Patani, the LFRP, desired the reestablishment of Patani in its former glory, with a raja or sultan at its head. Later, one of the most influential irredentist organizations in South Thailand, the Patani United Liberation Organization (PULO) emerged in the late 1960s and was the most well known and most effective guerrilla organization and separatist movement in the Patani region. PULO was devoted to preserving "Malayness" and the Islamic way of life in south Thailand. It had several levels of organization, with its headquarters in Mecca, Saudi Arabia. PULO also maintained a regional headquarters in Kelantan, where it coordinated its guerrilla operations. In Thailand itself, the military organization of PULO was well armed and had received financial support in the past from Libya and Syria.

Although there have been sporadic skirmishes in the recent past, throughout the 1980s and 1990s, the Malay Muslim communities of the Patani region had largely turned away from the extremist separatist movements such as PULO and LFRP. However, in 2004, a new chapter of violent resistance to Bangkok, led by the Barisan Revolusi Nasional (National Revolutionary Front) (BRN) and an older, loosely organized coalition known as Barison Revolusi Nasional-Coordinate (BRN-C) began in the southern provinces.[22] On January 4, 2004, over a hundred Muslim insurgents raided an arms depot of the 4th Army Engineers in Narathiwat province. As diversionary moves, they also torched 20 public schools, burned rubber tires, and planted fake explosives in neighboring Yala province. Shortly thereafter, a number of Buddhist monks were

---

[22] Duncan McCargo, *Tearing Apart the Land: Islam and Legitimacy in Southern Thailand* (Ithaca, NY: Cornell University Press, 2008), 168–174.

attacked and killed. Sporadic violence has continued for the past 16 years in southern Thailand. Since 2004, there have been over 6500 deaths of both Buddhists and Muslims in this southern insurgency in Thailand.

As a result of these developments, the prime minister at the time, Thaksin Shinawatra, called for curfews and the closing of schools in south Thailand. Since 2004, an aggressive campaign of Thai Buddhist nationalism and militarization has exacerbated Buddhist–Muslim relations in south Thailand. Between 2004 and 2007 sixteen Buddhist *wats* (temples) were attacked. As a consequence, a village defense volunteer system (*Or Ror* Bor) sponsored by Queen Sirikit, and a number of paramilitary organizations have also emerged in south Thailand. The Thai government has sponsored the militarization of various Buddhist temples in the southern provinces in order to quell the ethnic and religious violence.

Muslims in Central Thailand After the Bangkok Period

Because of historical and cultural conditions, the experience of Muslims in central Thailand has been much different than that of their Muslim affiliates to the south. Historically, the Muslims of the central corridor of Thailand have migrated, either voluntarily or involuntarily, into these regions, bringing distinctive ethnic, social, and religious conventions with them. Thus, these Muslim communities are much more ethnically heterogeneous than the Muslim communities of the South. Unlike their Islamic brethren to the south, these Muslims are ethnic minorities residing in the centers of predominantly Thai Buddhist cultural environment. This has influenced Buddhist–Muslim interactive relationships in central Thailand.

Various communities of Muslims in central Thailand, including Persians, Chams, South Asians, and Indonesians, all of which have a long history that extends back into the Ayutthaya period, settled in Bangkok. A number of the families related to the Persian Shia Muslims of Ayutthaya settled near Khlong Bangkok-Noi and Khlong Bangkok-Yai in Thonburi,[23] just across the Chao Phraya River from Bangkok. The descendants of these Persian Muslims, who settled amidst other Muslims and Buddhists, represent the oldest element of the Muslim

---

[23]Though historically Thonburi was a separate city and a previous site of the Thai capital, as of 1971, it was incorporated into the Bangkok metropolitan area.

community in Bangkok. Muslims from India and present-day Pakistan and Bangladesh have also settled in the Bangkok area. These Muslim migrants came from variant linguistic and geographical areas of the subcontinent. Gujarati and Bengali speakers came from North India, Madrasis from South India, and others from the Malabar coast. The Pathans, who were Pashto speakers, made up the majority of Muslims from present-day Pakistan or Afghanistan. The majority of the Indian Muslims who settled in the Bangkok area were Gujarati speakers from North India. Gujaratis are well known for their mercantile orientation and have been instrumental in establishing overseas Indian communities throughout Southeast Asia.

As we described above, the Cham Muslims had settled in Ayutthaya and played a military role. As a result of their loyalty in serving the Thai military King Rama I gave the Cham a tract of land in Bangkok known as Ban Krua. Ban Krua is situated on the *Saen Saab Khlong* (Saen Saab Canal) and currently has a population of about 5000. In 1994, the Cham Muslims established an Islamic school for their children near the Central Mosque known as Jami-ul-Khariya. Indonesian Muslims, including Makassares and Javanese Muslims also migrated to the Ayutthaya kingdom and later settled in Bangkok. Other Indonesian Muslims migrated to Bangkok during the nineteenth century. There was no mass migration of Indonesians to Thailand in any particular era; they tended to come as individual traders and established small businesses related to the Thai-Indonesian trade in cloth, batik products, or molasses. Another channel for immigrant Indonesians coming to Bangkok came with the visit of Rama V (Chulalongkorn) to Java and other parts of Indonesia in the 1870s. Impressed with their agricultural and gardening techniques, he invited some Javanese gardeners to Thailand to manage the royal gardens and teach nursery and gardening methods under his patronage. A location was provided for them along Khlong Saen Saeb in Bangkok. The various ethnic groups who are descendants of these Indonesian Muslims have a population of about 5000 people.

Descendants of Malay Muslims in Central Thailand

By far the largest group of Muslims in Bangkok and central Thailand, approximately 90% or about 600,000, are descendants of Malay peoples from the southern provinces of Thailand and parts of Malaysia. Their presence in Bangkok and surrounding areas resulted from the

116 R. SCUPIN AND C. M. JOLL

implementation of the vassalage network between Thailand and the Malay states. Most of central Thailand's Muslim population are descendants of these Malay war slaves (Th. *chalei*),[24] brought there during the five decades of war with Kedah and Patani. This practice caused frequent and sizable population movements, which explain the forms of Thai/Malay bilingualism found in some communities in Bangkok and central Thailand. Like the majority of the other Muslims of Southeast Asia, these descendants of the Malays residing in Bangkok are orthodox Sunnis of the school of Shafii. Innumerable mosques have been constructed along the canals in these and 70% were built by the Malays and their descendants.

Since the late 1970s and 1980s, many Muslims have migrated to Bangkok from the Middle East. Initially, some came as tourists but eventually decided to remain for business, trade, or religious purposes. As bilateral trade between Thailand and the Middle East increased, especially during the 1980s, a number of Muslims from Lebanon, Yemen, Egypt, and other Arab areas arrived in Bangkok. Middle Eastern restaurants and hotels developed to provide for Muslim Arab visitors and residents. One area of Bangkok has become known as the Arab quarter and is sometimes referred to as mini-Beirut of the East. The population of the Arabs and their descendants is about 1000 people. Arabic calligraphy, Arabian music, coffee-houses, belly-dancing, and other signs of Arabic culture became recognizable in this evolving cosmopolitan city of Bangkok.[25]

Muslims of North Thailand

Muslim communities were also established in north Thailand. Many of the Muslims in north Thailand came from the Islamicized portion of China. Most authorities refer to them as Chinese "Haw," *Cin-Ho*, or *Hui*. Most of the Chinese Muslims in Thailand originate from the southwestern part of Yunnan. Historically, this ethnic group operated

---

[24] *Chalei* is a Khmer term referring to "war captives used as laborers." Although low in Siamese society at the time, they were higher than ordinary slaves (Th. *that*), who could neither own land nor purchase their freedom.

[25] Chaiwat Satha-Anand, "Bangkok Muslims and the Tourist Trade," in *The Muslim Private Sector in Southeast Asia*, ed. Mohamed Ariff (Singapore: Institute of Southeast Asian Studies, 1991), 89–121.

an expansive trading network between the Shan states, China, and north Thailand. After the nineteenth century, the Chinese Muslims began to establish themselves as permanent residents in north and northeast Thailand. Then as a consequence of the Chinese revolution, in the 1950s another wave of Yunnanese refugees fled into northern Thailand, many settling in Chiang Mai province. Another group of Muslims that settled in north Thailand are the descendants of South Asian Muslims who came from Calcutta during the second half of the nineteenth century. Later, after 1947, with Indian independence and partition, there was a continuous flow of migrants from East Pakistan (now Bangladesh) who first settled in Burma and gradually moved into northern Thailand and Chiang Mai city. These Chiang Mai quarters and cities in northeast Thailand also received a Pathan (Pashtun) Muslim populace who either migrated directly from their homes in Pakistan and Afghanistan or via Myanmar.

Thai Muslim Identity in Central and North Thailand

Although Thai has become the first language and native language of most Muslims in central and north Thailand, some of these Muslims are bilingual, speaking their native Malay or Mandarin languages also. Through the education system and intermarriage between these Muslims and other Thais, traditional primordial ethnic differences among these early Muslim settlers have been, to some extent, partially weakened. A number of the Muslim migrants married Thai females, who then converted to Islam. An aphorism often heard in these Muslim communities is that the children of these mixed marriages would adhere to the dress, manners, and language of their Thai mothers, but to the religion of their Muslim fathers. Like many of the descendants of the Chinese immigrants in Thailand, many of these Muslims appear to preserve their ethnic identity on an individual basis rather than that of a communal basis.[26]

Muslims in central and north Thailand are sometimes referred to by Thai Buddhists as *khaek Isalam* or *khaek Musalam*.[27] In most of

[26]Thongchai Winichakul, "The Changing Landscape of the Past: New Histories in Thailand Since 1973," *Journal of Southeast Asian Studies* 26 (1995): 116.

[27]While Scupin was doing ethnographic research in 1976–1977 on Muslims in central Thailand, he was teaching at Ramkhamhaeng University, located in a Muslim area near the Saen Saab canal. He often found that young Thai Buddhist students would jokingly refer to their Muslim friends as *khaek* in conversations with them and there would be no negative reaction, instead just a smile or laugh.

the English discussions of these Muslims, including in the Thai academic and government literature, they are referred to as Thai Muslims. Historically, despite some mutual misunderstandings between Buddhists and Muslims, there appeared to be no aggressive anti-Muslim hostility in central, north, or northeast Thailand up until recently. Consequently, there was a good deal of structural assimilation that occurred among these Muslims in their accommodation to residing in a Thai Buddhist environment. Although the Muslim communities in these Buddhist regions are identifiable by their needs for an Islamic-based *halal* diet and mosques, they tend to participate in most of the same institutions as their Thai Buddhist neighbors. For example, many Buddhists attend the *tham bun* or *kinbun* or other communal rituals of Muslims and are eagerly welcomed into these practices. And, many Muslims attended the *tham bun* rituals or *kinbun* activities of the Thai Buddhists in Bangkok and central Thailand.

Islamic Reform in Thailand

One of the developments that has influenced both the ethnoreligious identity and the political aspects of Muslim communities in both the southern as well as the central and north regions of Thailand is the emergence of various Islamic movements. These Islamic movements have had consequences for Buddhist–Muslim relations in Thailand, as well as for their group identities. One of the movements was based on the modernist or reformist ideals of the early twentieth century, which emerged in the Middle East and spread throughout the Islamic world in Southeast Asia coincided with the global impact of Western capitalism, colonialism, and what is sometimes referred to as modernization, including increases in print journalism and improvements in literacy, especially in the urban centers. This Islamic reformist movement emerged among some members of the educated urban residents within the Muslim communities in Thailand.[28]

The Islamic reformists or *Salafists* attempted to "purify" the form of Islam that existed within the Muslim communities of Thailand. They criticized what they perceived as the syncretistic beliefs and practices of the popular forms of Islam that were influenced by Thai spirit beliefs and

[28] Scupin, "Islamic Reformism in Thailand" (1980b), 1–10.

Buddhist conceptions. During the early twentieth century, the reformist influence came to south Thailand primarily through Haji Sulong, who received his early education in Kampung Sungei, Pattani and then in Mecca. He was exposed to the reformist ideas circulating within the Middle East. When Haji Sulong returned to Patani, he became well-known for his reformist and *Salafist* outlook and had a tremendous influence on the Muslim communities. He was instrumental in reforming much of the curriculum within the *pondoks* in south Thailand. In 1954, Haji Sulong disappeared under mysterious circumstances, and this event has helped engender Muslim political activism in south Thailand.

Another Islamic movement known as *Tablighi Jamaat*, an Indian Muslim missionary group founded in 1927 that emphasized non-political *Salafist* activities including rigid norms regarding diet and dress. The reformist activities of *Tablighi Jamaat* in south Thailand have been described by German anthropologist Alexander Horstmann.[29] *Tablighi Jamaat* has also had an influence on some of the Muslim communities of Bangkok including Ban Krua, and the Hui communities of north Thailand. A more recent form of Islamic reformism has developed in the southern province of Yala under the leadership of the charismatic Ismail Lutfi Japakiya, rector of the Yala Islamic University. Born in Mecca, his family brought him to Thailand when he was six years old. Lutfi learned Arabic and Islam through his father, who had taught in Mecca. His father was a *tok guru* in a private *pondok* in Pattani province. Provided with a scholarship to Madinah University in Saudi Arabia, Lutfi completed a B.A., M.A., and Ph.D. in Islamic Studies. Returning to Thailand, he founded the Yala Islamic University. Although sometimes described as a "Wahhabist," Joseph Liow analyzed Lutfi's corpus of writings carefully to demonstrate that he is not a fundamentalist, Wahhabist, or radical-militant Muslim, but rather a reformist Muslim.[30]

---

[29] Alexander Horstmann, "The Inculturation of a Transnational Islamic Missionary Movement: Tablighi Jamaat al Dawa and Muslim Society in Southern Thailand," *Sojourn: Journal of Social Issues in Southeast Asia* 22, no. 1 (2007), 107–130.

[30] Liow, *Islam, Education, and Reform in Southern Thailand: Tradition and Transformation* (ISEAS, 2009), 88–95.

Dakwah (Dawah)

More recently, since the emergence of Islamic resurgence movements in the Middle East and elsewhere, some Muslims in Thailand have participated in contemporary Islamic movements similar to those that have influenced Malaysia and Indonesia. The major sources of the new Islamic movements stem from what has been referred to as the *dakwah* religious trends that have been growing in Thailand. The *dakwah* movement represents multiple strands of recent Islamic discourse within Thai society and is an extended continuation of the earlier reformist, or *islah* revivalist tendencies. Connections between Muslims in Thailand and the Middle East led many of the Muslim women involved in the *dakwah* or *salafi* activities to adopt Middle Eastern dress, including the *hijab*, and for some, the *niqab* or veil.[31] Despite these ethnoreligious markers of identity, however, some of the *dakwah* leadership has called for a Muslim–Buddhist dialogue and cooperation to help bring about mutual understanding and social and economic improvement throughout Thailand.

Tariqa (Sufism)

One additional Islamic development that has influenced the Muslims of Thailand is what is broadly known as the *tariqa* movement, based on the traditional Sufi mystical practices. Joll has conducted recent multi-sited ethnographic research on the Sufi orders (*tariqa*, pl., *turuq*, sg.) and their beliefs and practices among Muslims in south and central Thailand.[32] He did fieldwork on the *tariqa* practices in Ayutthaya, Bangkok, Narathiwat, Songkhla, Satun, Krabi, Phuket, Pattani, Yala, Kota Baru, and Mae Sot in Thailand, as well as in Kelantan in Malaysia. In south Thailand, the Ahmadiyyah-Idrisiyyah *tariqa* founded in Meccain the eighteenth century has spread at the expense of the more traditional Shattariyyah order, while in central Thailand, the Qadriyyah

---

[31] In a recent illuminating Ph.D. thesis "Gender Piety of Muslim Women in Thailand" (Faculty of Philosophy and History, University in Frankfurt am Main, 2016), ethnographer Amporn Marddent, who describes herself as an assimilated Thai of Malay descent, studied the women involved in the Islamic reformist movements, *dakwah*, and *salafi* activities in Bangkok and in south Thailand.

[32] Joll, "Revisiting Ethnic and Religious Factors in Thailand's Southern Discomfort" (2015), 91–113.

turuq associated with South India has been most prevalent in Ayutthayan and Bangkok Muslim communities. Another *turuq*, the Shazuliyya, was brought in 1929 by an Arab from Hijaz who was actively proselytizing along the Saen Saab Khlong in eastern Bangkok. Although the population numbers are small, the Sufi *tariqa* have had an influence on many of the traditional rituals and prayers in Muslim mosques throughout Thailand.

Buddhist Movements in Thailand

Similar modern economic, social, and political conditions that gave rise to Islamic movements were also prevalent for stimulating various Theravada Buddhist movements in Thailand. These movements within Buddhist communities have definitive similarities with the Islamic movements. European contacts with Thailand led to the earliest Buddhist reform movements. Theravada Buddhist reforms were initiated by King Mongkut (Rama IV; 1851–1868) in an attempt to bring Thai Buddhism in line with the newly introduced Western scientific ideas and to encourage a critical stance towards popular or folk elements within Theravada Buddhism Mongkut founded the Thammayut Buddhist monastic order as an institution to promote these reforms.[33] Thai Buddhist reforms of Mongkut were continued with the emergence of new class alignments in Thailand following the extension of capitalist and industrial developments. An emerging middle class opposed to the Thai economic, political, royalist, and religious elite began to offer new interpretations of Theravada Buddhism, providing for further rationalization of religious sources. With exposure to democratic and secular trends emanating from globalization, the Buddhist reformists began to reject metaphysical and supernatural doctrines that were based on post-canonical textual sources. During the 1960s and 1970s, Bhikkhu Buddhadasa, through his sermons and writings of the 1960s and 1970s drawn from the *dhamma*, recommended a new political and ethical focus for Theravada Buddhism. He strived to blend the moral aspects of the Theravada tradition with civic virtue and the public good. Buddhadasa's sermons and teachings were particularly influential with young urban Thai intellectuals, who were disillusioned with the ethical import of global capitalism and

---

[33] Keyes, "Buddhist Politics and Their Revolutionary Origins in Thailand" (1989): 121–142.

122   R. SCUPIN AND C. M. JOLL

excessive consumerism, individualism, and political expediency.[34] Since the 1980s, some of the educated middle class have been drawn to the *Santi Asoke* and *Dhammakai* sect. The *Santi Asoke* movement encouraged an inner-worldly ethic or "*Dhammic* action," which provides a blueprint for a new social and political order in Thailand. They advocated an austere ascetic lifestyle including strict vegetarianism and back-to-basics morality.[35] The *Dhammakai* movement emerged during the late 1960s at several universities in Thailand. This movement began to use the media, especially television, and has been compared to American TV evangelism.

Muslim Ethnicity and Essentialism in Thailand

In a widely cited essay, ethnographer Mattison Mines introduced the concept of Muslim ethnicity.[36] He indicated that as Islamization increased among the Muslim Tamils in rural Tamilnadu, their religious traditions became more intertwined with their ethnicity. In assessing the political conditions of south Thailand, Imtiyaz Yusuf refers to the "ethnification" of religion and uses the term "ethnoreligious" to focus on how religion blends with ethnicity for the Malay Muslims of south Thailand.[37] He discusses how the global Islamic movements including *salafi* and Wahhabi influences in south Thailand have created a clash between the ethnoreligious identities of Malay Muslims versus Thai Buddhists. Linguistic scholar Seni Mudmarn from south Thailand argues that the ethnonym "Malay Muslim" represents the inseparability of Islam with Malay ethnicity.[38] It appears that both Muslims and Buddhists in Thailand essentialize one another's ethnoreligious identities very easily. In south Thailand, Malay ethnicity and the Islamic (whether *salafist*

---

[34] Swearer, ed. and trans., *Toward the Truth* by Buddhadasa (Westminster Press, 1971), 1–189.

[35] Swearer, "Fundamentalistic Movements in Theravada Buddhism" (1991), 628–690.

[36] Mattison Mines, "Islamisation and Muslim Ethnicity in South India," *Man* 10, no. 3 (1975), 404–419.

[37] Yusuf, *Faces of Islam in Southern Thailand* (2007), 1–25.

[38] Seni Mudmarn, "Social Science Research in Thailand: The Muslim Minority," in *Muslim Social Science in ASEAN*, ed. Omar Farouk Bajunid (Kuala Lumpur: Yayasan Perataran Ilumu, 1994), 32; Joll, *Muslim Merit-Making in Thailand's Far-South* (2011), 69.

or *dakwah*) have become entwined in the morass of political struggles with the Thai Buddhists.

Norwegian anthropologist Thomas Hylland Eriksen, writing about the epistemological status of ethnicity, says,

> It is widely held, by social scientists as well as by lay people that the members of human groups have an 'innate' propensity to distinguish insiders and outsiders, to delineate social boundaries and to develop stereotypes about the 'other' in order to sustain and justify these boundaries. If this is indeed the case, ethnicity can be conceived of as being nearly as universal a characteristic of humanity as gender and age.[39]

For a number of decades, anthropological debates about ethnicity were divided between primordialists and instrumentalists or constructivists. Although both approaches to ethnicity have their own partisans, most contemporary anthropologists tend to agree with Stanley Tambiah's suggestion that ethnic identity is a combination of the "semantics of primordial claims" and "the pragmatics of calculated choices" in the contexts of political-economic competition among differing interest groups.[40] Many anthropologists and other scholars believed that ethnic and nationalist identities would become less essentialist, more flexible, situational, more hybrid, and less clunky as modernity developed. Yet, despite the widespread deconstruction of ethnic and nationalist identities by anthropologists and other scholars, essentialist identities have become more prevalent and powerful throughout the world. Essentialism is the tendency to treat members of certain categories like "ethnicities," "nationalities," or "religious groups" as though they have an underlying nature that governs the observable characteristics of their membership in that category. An ethnic, national, or religious group is essentialized when either members of the group or outsiders assume that the group's members share some internal property or essence that is supposedly inherited and that creates the behaviors typical of that group. As groups are essentialized, individuals make inferences about how the people in those groups think and behave. It appears that these essentialization processes

---

[39] Eriksen, Thomas Hylland, "The Epistemological Status of the Concept of Ethnicity," *Anthropological Notebooks* (Czech Republic), (2019), 1.

[40] Tambiah, "Ethnic Conflict in the World Today" (1989), 336.

are universal and transnational and have provided the foundations for in-group and out-group conflict.[41]

By the mid-1970s, although a great degree of structural and cultural assimilation had affected the Muslims in Bangkok and central and north Thailand, there were some tendencies toward more primordial and essentialized ethnoreligious expression and assertiveness. For example, ethnoreligious expression was explicit and observable within the context of Islamic activities during the celebration of holidays such as *Mawlid al-Nabi-*(the birthday of the prophet).[42] Ethnic groups such as the Pathans or Indonesians set up booths to serve their own foods and participate to assert their unique ethnoreligious identities. Also, with the spread of a global Islamic awakening in the 1970s and with the emergence of the Iranian revolution, many young Shia Muslims from Thailand were taking scholarships to get educated in Qum, the center of Shia religious scholarship in Iran.[43] There were even a small number of young Sunni Muslims in Thailand who were converting to the Shia tradition as a means of affirming their Islamic identity.

In the 1990s, Cham Muslim ethnoreligious identity was mobilized in a form of political protest against the Thai government. The Bangkok authorities wanted to develop a new highway system which would destroy the traditional Cham neighborhood of Ban Krua. Demonstrations mobilized many Muslims, and the Cham began to assert their ethnoreligious ties. In some senses, the Cham Muslim community represented a model of a moral community, standing together against the forces of globalization, corporate capitalism, vested interests, and corrupt government-inspired development.[44] Many other Muslims throughout Thailand were mobilized and joined the demonstrations to help support the Chams in their political and ethnoreligious struggle.

---

[41] Jerryson, *Buddhist Fury*, 143; Scupin, "Anthropology, Conflict, and International Relations" (2017), 163; Hirschfeld, *Race in the Making* (1996), 25; Gelman, *The Essential Child* (2003), 5.

[42] Imtiyaz Yusuf, "Celebrating Muhammad's Birthday in Buddha's Land: Managing Religious Relations Through Religious Festival," in *Religion, Public Policy and Social Transformation in Southeast Asia, Religion, Gender, and Identity*, Volume 2, ed. Dicky Sofjan (Jakarta: Indonesian Consortium for Religious Studies, 2016), 130–161.

[43] Scupin, "Muslim Accommodation in Thai Society," 256; Liow, *Islam, Education, and Reform in Southern Thailand*, 146.

[44] Scupin, "Cham Muslims in Thailand: A Model of a Moral Community" (2000), 453–464.

In a general survey of Muslims in Thailand in 2001, the French sociologist Michel Gilquin, observed that "in the universities and some districts, one can find men sporting a skullcap and trying hard to grow a beard. This is a recent phenomenon. If the visitor had come ten years or so earlier, he would not have seen skullcaps. Thai Islam is now more visible in the capital." He continued, pondering whether this phenomenon signaled "a return to a stricter observance of the faith by the younger generation in the face of increasingly aggressive modernisation" or whether it simply represented "a way of emphasizing its difference by external symbols."[45]

Recent Enhanced Essentialism Among Buddhists and Muslims

In our discussion above, we have identified some of the recent circumstances that have resulted in more essentialist ethnic and religious identities among both Buddhists and Muslims in Thailand. The resurgence of both Islamic and Buddhist movements since the 1970s has heightened the significance of ethnic and religious identity for these populations. In addition, the insurgency in south Thailand since, 2004 pitting Buddhists and Muslims against each other, in violent confrontations has certainly given rise to increases in essentialist characterizations and more Islamophobic reactions among the Buddhists. Although we cannot posit any ideal utopian harmony between Buddhists and Muslims at any stage of Thai history, as we have seen there were, at times, more cosmopolitan and pluralistic tendencies in the past. In contrast, recent historical and political developments have engendered more essentialist ethnoreligious identities that have been heightened and sensationalized in the Thai media.

Within the context of these trends in essentialization of ethnoreligious identities, Duncan McCargo has argued that the Thai state has encouraged a more restrictive and orthodox form of Theravada Buddhism as a means of reinforcing ethnic and religious homogeneity and repressing difference. In two essays published in 2009, McCargo criticizes Charles Keyes and Donald Swearer's emphases on how Buddhism has created

---

[45] Michel Gilquin, *The Muslims of Thailand*, trans. M. Smithies (Chiang Mai: Silkworm, 2005), 5.

126 R. SCUPIN AND C. M. JOLL

a more civil and democratic process in Thailand.[46] He suggests that Keyes and Swearer romanticize Thai Buddhism as having created a more pluralistic and civil order for religious freedom in Thailand. McCargo discusses a Buddhist sermon of an unidentified monk on a widely circulated DVD entitled *Muslim Kluen Phut* (Muslims Swallow Buddhists), heightening fears and Islamophobia. He also describes a book, *Dangers for Buddhism in Thailand*, by the prominent conservative Buddhist intellectual monk Prayudh Payutto, which discusses how Christians and Muslims encourage religious intolerance and describes the aggression of Christianity and Islam compared to the peaceful and civil traditions of Buddhism. Prayudh Payutto argues that only Buddhism can maintain religious freedom in Thailand and serve as the legitimate source of Thai national identity. McCargo indicates that these nationalist forms of Buddhism have been engaging Thai Buddhists since the insurgency in south Thailand. However, he also cites a chapter by Buddhist scholar Suwanna Satha-Anand, who had noted a "shrinking space" for tolerance in Thai Buddhism prior to the 2004 insurgency.[47]

Keyes responded to McCargo's criticism by noting that in his own analyses of Thai Buddhism, he distinguishes establishment Buddhism, militant Buddhism, and nationalist Buddhism from the more civil forms of Buddhism that are in competition with one another in Thailand.[48] When considering whether the inextricable connection between the Thai state and Buddhism has engendered more repressive or more tolerant and civil trends regarding non-Buddhist traditions, it would appear

---

[46] McCargo, "Thai Buddhists and the Southern Conflict" (2009a), 1–10; McCargo, "The Politics of Buddhist Identity in Thailand's Deep South" (2009b), 11–32; Charles Keyes, "Buddhist Politics and Their Revolutionary Origins in Thailand" (1989), 121–142; Donald Swearer, *The Buddhist World of Southeast Asia*. Second edition (2010), 1–320.

[47] Suwanna Satha-Anand, "Buddhist Pluralism and Religious Tolerance in Democratizing Thailand," in *Philosophy, Democracy and Education*, ed. Philip Cam (Seoul: The Korean National Commission for UNESCO, 2003), 193–213.

[48] Charles Keyes, "Theravada Buddhism and Buddhist Nationalism: Sri Lanka, Myanmar, Cambodia, and Thailand," *The Review of Faith & International Affairs* 14, no. 4 (2016), 41–52. In an illuminating essay entitled "Muslim 'Others' in Buddhist Thailand," Keyes traces a racial stereotype used to demonize *khaek* and the Malay Muslims of south Thailand to premodern sources and an image in a nineteenth-century mural painting in Wat Matchimawat in Songkhla depicting evil and violent beings associated with *Māra* who are attacking the Buddha. Charles Keyes, "Muslim 'Others' in Buddhist Thailand," *Thammasat Review* (Bangkok) 13 ([2008] 2009): 19–43.

that both McCargo and Keyes' views represent both types of tendencies within the very diverse Thai political milieu.[49] There are both conservative voices that contend and compete with more liberal and civil expressions regarding how religion and politics are interwoven. For example, in the 1990s, there were conservative Buddhist organizations that advocated that Theravada Buddhism become the national and official religion of Thailand. They tended to claim that followers of Theravada Buddhism are the sole, authentic representatives of a "single, homogeneous, authentic Thai people." Yet, the Thai constitution, developed in 1997 and approved by the late King Bhumiphol, expanded the interpretation of the pillar of *sasana* to refer to non-Buddhist religious traditions. The 1997 constitution did require that the King had to be a Theravada Buddhist, and in actuality and in practice, the Theravada Buddhist tradition is the default official state religion in Thailand, as noted in our discussion about how the Three Pillars had been implemented for centuries. Further evidence for the promotion of religious pluralism is reflected by how the royal family has served as a patron for various Islamic activities such as the Quranic *tajwid* chanting contests and Christian events based in Bangkok.

Following the bloodless coup d'état in September of 2006, the military overthrew the Thaksin government and repealed the 1997 constitution. In the constitution of 2007, minority religions were still offered protection, rights, and support. Section 37 of the 2007 constitution states, "A person shall enjoy full liberty to profess religion, religious sect or creed, and observe religious precept or exercise a form of worship in accordance with his or her belief; provided that it is not contrary to his or her civic duties, public order or good morals." "Civic duties" in Thai is *na thi khong phonlamuang*, which roughly translates to English as "duties of the citizens."

In the wake of the most recent coup in 2014, Prime Minister Prayut Chan-o-cha, the commander in chief of the Royal Thai Army, dissolved the government including the senate, declared martial law, and

---

[49] Both McCargo and Keyes refer to the Thai Buddhist monk Phra Paisal Visalo, who is a peace activist who wants to encourage Buddhist-Muslim dialogue and who served on the National Reconciliation Commission (NRC) to investigate the south Thailand conflict and make recommendations to resolve the insurgency. McCargo regards him as a minor influence in Thai politics, while Keyes views him as the ideal in Buddhist civil and peaceful relations in Thailand.

announced plans for a new codified constitution. The new codified constitution was developed in 2017 and was approved by the new King, Maha Vajiralongkorn (Rama X). In the 2017 constitution, Article 31 states,

> A person shall enjoy full liberty to profess a religion, and enjoy the liberty to exercise or practice a form of worship in accordance with his or her religious principles, provided that it shall not be adverse to the duties of the Thai people; neither shall it endanger the safety of the State, nor shall it be contrary to public order or good morals.

The wording in Article 31 uses the phrase "duties of the Thai people," which translates into Thai as *Puang chon chao thai*. This phrase translates into English as "the whole Thai people," which includes all Thais, regardless of ethnic or religious identities or sub-identities.[50] Thus, this is not the same meaning as *chon chat Thai*, which was used as an ethnic and religious, quasi-racial identity promoted by Phibun and other Thai royalty and officials in the nationalist project of earlier times. Yet, many Muslims objected to the notion in Article 31 that freedom of religion was conditional on adherents not undermining "the safety of the State," which was construed as a slur on their loyalty.

In addition, Article 67 in the 2017 constitution says that the State should support and protect Buddhism and other religions. However, Article 67 also emphasizes that the State should promote and support education and dissemination of *dhammic* principles of Theravada Buddhism and have measures to prevent Buddhism from being undermined in any form. This special clause to protect Buddhism has also created controversy for some Muslims who view this as state-sponsored religious chauvinism.[51] Thus, although the constitutions of 1997, 2007, and 2017 have promoted both freedom of religion and increased tolerance for non-Buddhist religious traditions, there appears to be an inclination for state-sponsored Theravada Buddhism.

A recent development during the March 24, 2019 elections appears as an ominous trend in Buddhist–Muslim dynamics. A new political

---

[50] Thongchai Winichakul helped confirm these translations of the Thai constitutions into English for us (personal communication, January 14, 2018).

[51] McCargo, Alexander, and Desatova, "Ordering Peace: Thailand's 2016 Constitutional Referendum" (2017), 86–87.

party known as the Pandin Dharma Party emerged to contest a seat in parliament in the March elections. A member of the party, clothing and cosmetics model, Sirima "Grace" Sarakul, contested the seat. The Pandin Dharma (translates as "Land of Buddhist Teaching") Party members claim that there is a considerable threat from the Muslim minority to Theravada Buddhism. They maintain that Thai secular authorities are promoting the interests of the Muslim minority who harass Buddhist monks and endanger the religion of the majority. The leader of the Pandin Dharma Party is a former Buddhist monk, Korn Medee, who asserts that the government favors other religions over Buddhism. Although some Buddhists have questioned the authenticity of Pandin Dharma adherents as "real Buddhists," this development is a concern for those who want to support civic and religious pluralism in Thailand.[52]

Ethnicity and religion have always been highly significant in marking and determining identity, solidarity, and political organization within and between states. However, the global expansion of capitalism and globalization have tended to accelerate the trends in the essentialization and assertiveness of ethnic and religious identities in Thailand. The religious tradition of Islam is perceived by the leaders of reform and *Salafist* movements as being undermined by these new capitalist-based, non-communal, individualistic, and anarchic conceptions of obligations and responsibilities. New cultural conceptions of individual autonomy conjoined with market consumerism compete with traditional notions of communal moral obligations along with the perceived attendant destruction of the Muslim (and Buddhist) communities. As the ethnic and religious movement in the Ban Krua Muslim community in the 1990s highlighted, ruthless economic liberalization and neoliberal capitalism left many people materially insecure and unmoored. Communal ties were discouraged in order to produce a mobile work force and economic development in these neighborhoods. These Muslims wanted to restore and cultivate cultures of community, care, and small-scale democracy.

Anthropologist and global theorist Jonathan Friedman notes that as hybridization emerges among cosmopolitan elites, an equivalent tendency towards rootedness and primordialism, to boundary-making, and

---

[52]Wongcha-um, Panu, "'Buddhism Under Threat' Thai Election Gives Platform to Radicals," *Reuters World News*, March 6, 2019, https://www.reuters.com/article/us-thailand-election-buddhism/buddhism-under-threat-thai-election-gives-platform-to-radicals-idUSKCN1QO0E1?utm.

130 R. SCUPIN AND C. M. JOLL

increasing Balkanization develops among locals.[53] A recent work by anthropologist Akbar Ahmed describes similar processes.[54] He compares numerous tribal and peripheral Muslim societies throughout the world, including the Muslims in south Thailand, and demonstrates how both state repression and globalization are contributing to current ethnic and religious assertiveness. Ahmed indicates that as these Muslims recognize that globalization is not incidental to their lives but is rather a recognizable transformation in their everyday circumstances, they draw on reconstructions of ethnic identity and religious fundamentalism as a means of restoring power over their lives. The reconstruction and reinvigoration of their ethnic and religious identities give these people a sense of greater control in what appears to be a "runaway" and destructive world. Fundamentalist or more *Salafist* religious movements articulate the uncertainties and distress brought about by expanding globalization and loss of control over local realities. These disruptive local and global conditions result in alienation for many of the young people from their ethnic, tribal, and communal ties. This destabilization of communal identity provides a context for the recruitment of some of these young people in these peripheral communities into political dissent and violent activities such as the Muslim insurgency in south Thailand.[55]

CONCLUDING COMMENTS

Buddhist–Muslim dynamics in Thailand confront clouded (and wishful) thinking by state-makers and scholars, who have long perpetuated the fallacy of an ethnically, linguistically, and religiously homogenous Siam (before the 1930s) and Thailand (after it). This chapter has placed the

[53] Jonathan Friedman, "Global Crises, the Struggle for Cultural Identity and Intellectual Porkbarreling: Cosmopolitans Versus Locals, Ethnics and Nationals in an Era of De-Hegemonisation," in *Debating Cultural Hybridity: Multi-Cultural Identities and the Politics of Anti-Racism*, eds. Pnina Werbner and Tariq Modood (London: Zed Books, 1997), 70–89.

[54] Akbar Ahmed, *The Thistle and the Drone: How America's War on Terror Became a Global War on Tribal Islam* (Washington, DC: Brookings Institution Press, 2013), 91–92.

[55] Another trend accompanying global capitalism in Thailand is secularization. Generally, global industrializing trends are conjoined with rationalistic-scientific modes of inquiry, and the separation of religiosity from other institutions within society. These scientific, secular ideals and rationalistic values and institutions tend to dislocate primordial ties whether based upon ethnic or religious communities.

range of interactions between Buddhists and Muslim in central, north, and south Thailand in their wider cultural and historical context. In what is now south Thailand, there has been a long history of interaction between Indic-Buddhist and Islamic influences. Muslim communities have contributed to the prosperity and security in central and north Thailand in the past and present. In all of these areas, one can discern some degree of cosmopolitanism and harmony between Buddhists and Muslims. Following the development of various Islamic and Buddhist movements, many Muslims and Buddhists have incorporated more essentialist views of their own ethnic and religious identities as well as the identities of each other. The recent insurgency in south Thailand has tended to accelerate more primordial and essentialist ethnoreligious identities within these populations. Most historical, sociological, and anthropological data tends to confirm that as different ethnic and religious groups interact with one another in efforts that involve collective strategies and goals, essentialist perceptions and primordial identities soften. It remains to be seen whether this will be the future for ethnoreligious identities and pluralism for Buddhists and Muslims in Thailand.

REFERENCES

Ahmed, Akbar. *The Thistle and the Drone: How America's War on Terror Became a Global War on Tribal Islam*. Washington, DC: Brookings Institution Press, 2013.

Allen, J. "History, Archaeology, and the Question of Foreign Control in Early Historic-Period Peninsular Malaysia." *International Journal of Historical Archaeology* 2, no. 4 (1998): 261–289.

Bajunid, Omar Farouk. "Shaykh Ahmad: Muslims in the Kingdom of Ayutthaya." *JEBAT* 10 (1980): 206–214.

Baker, Christopher John. "Ayutthaya Rising: From Land or Sea?" *Journal of Southeast Asian Studies* 34, no. 1 (2003): 41–62. https://doi.org/10.1017/s0022463403000031.

Baker, Christopher John, and Phongpaichit Pasuk. *A History of Thailand*. New York: Cambridge University Press, 2014.

Barmè, Scott. *Luang Wichit Wathakan and the Creation of a Thai Identity*. Singapore: Institute of Southeast Asian Studies, 1993.

Bougas, Wayne A. "Surau Aur: Patani's Oldest Mosque?" *Archipel* 43 (1992): 89–112.

Bradley, Francis R. "Siam's Conquest of Patani and the End of Mandala Relations, 1786–1838." In *The Ghosts of the Past in Southern Thailand: Essays* on the *History and Historiography of Patani*, edited by Patrick Jory, 149–160. Singapore: National University of Singapore Press, 2012.

Connors, Michael Kelly. "Ministering Culture: Hegemony and the Politics of Culture and Identity in Thailand." *Critical Asian Studies* 37, no. 4 (2005): 523–551.

Crawfurd, John. *History of the Indian Archipelago, Containing an Account of the Manners, Arts, Languages, Religions of Its Inhabitants.* Edinburgh: Constable, 1820.

de la Loubere, Simon. *The Kingdom of Siam.* Oxford: Oxford University Press, 1969.

Eriksen, Thomas Hylland. "The Epistemological Status of the Concept of Ethnicity." *Anthropological Notebooks* (Czech Republic), (2019): 1.

Friedman, Jonathan. *Cultural Identity and Global Process.* London: Sage, 1994.

———. "Global Crises, the Struggle for Cultural Identity and Intellectual Porkbarreling: Cosmopolitans Versus Locals, Ethnics and Nationals in an Era of De-Hegemonisation." In *Debating Cultural Hybridity: Multi-Cultural Identities and the Politics of Anti-Racism*, edited by Pnina Werbner and Tariq Modood, 70–89. London: Zed Books, 1997.

Gelman, Susan A. *The Essential Child: Origins of Essentialism in Everyday Thought.* Oxford: Oxford University Press, 2003.

Gervaise, Nicholas. *The Natural and Political History of the Kingdom of Siam A.D. 1688.* Bangkok: Siam Observer Press, 1928.

Gilquin, Michel. *The Muslims of Thailand.* Translated by M. Smithies. Chiang Mai: Silkworm, 2005.

Hirschfeld, Lawrence A. *Race in the Making: Cognition, Culture, and the Child's Construction of Human Kinds.* Cambridge, MA: MIT Press, 1996.

Horstmann, Alexander. "The Inculturation of a Transnational Islamic Missionary Movement: Tablighi Jamaat al Dawa and Muslim Society in Southern Thailand." *Sojourn: Journal of Social Issues in Southeast Asia* 22, no. 1 (2007): 107–130.

Ibrahim, Muhammad Ibn. *The Ship of Sulaiman.* Translated by John O'Kane. Persian Heritage Series No. 11. London: Routledge and Kegan Paul, 1972.

Jerryson, Michael K. *Buddhist Fury: Religion and Violence in Southern Thailand.* Oxford, New York: Oxford University Press, 2011.

Joll, Christopher Mark. *Muslim Merit-Making in Thailand's Far-South*, Vol. 4 of *Muslims in Global Societies*, edited by Gabriele Marranci and Bryan S. Turner. Dordrecht: Springer, 2011.

———. "Making Sense of Thailand's 'Merit-Making' Muslims: Adoption and Adaption of the Indic in the Creation of Islamicate Southern Thailand." *Islam and Christian–Muslim Relations* 25, no. 3 (2014): 303–320.

―――. "Revisiting Ethnic and Religious Factors in Thailand's Southern Discomfort." In *The Politics of Scholarship and Trans-border Engagement in Mainland Southeast Asia: A Festschrift in Honor of Ajarn Chayan Vaddhanaphuti*, edited by Oscar Salemink, 91–113. Chiang Mai: Silkworm Books, 2015.

―――. "Thailand's Muslim Kaleidoscope Between Central Plains and Far-South: Fresh Perspectives from the Sufi Margins." In *Ethnic and Religious Identities and Integration in Southeast Asia*, edited by Volker Grabowsky and Keat Gin Ooi. Chiang Mai: Silkworm, 2016.

Jory, Patrick. "From Melayu Patani to Thai Muslim: The Spectre of Ethnic Identity in Southern Thailand." *South East Asia Research* 15, no. 2 (2007): 225–279.

Keyes, Charles, F. *Thailand: Buddhist Kingdom as Modern Nation-State*. Boulder and London: Westview Press, 1987.

―――. "Buddhist Politics and Their Revolutionary Origins in Thailand." *International Political Science Review* 10, no. 2 (1989): 121–142.

―――. "Muslim 'Others' in Buddhist Thailand." *Thammasat Review* (Bangkok) 13 ([2008] 2009): 19–43.

―――. "Theravada Buddhism and Buddhist Nationalism: Sri Lanka, Myanmar, Cambodia, and Thailand." *The Review of Faith & International Affairs* 14, no. 4 (2016): 41–52.

Laffan, Michael F. "Southeast Asia, History and Culture." In *Medieval Islamic Civilization: An Encyclopedia (Vol. 1: A-K)*, edited by Josef W. Meri, 765–767. New York: Routledge, 2006.

Liow, Joseph Chinyong. *Islam, Education, and Reform in Southern Thailand: Tradition and Transformation*. Singapore: ISEAS, 2009.

Madmarn, Hasan. "Pondoks and Change in South Thailand." In *Aspects of Development: Education and Political Integration for Muslims in Thailand and Malaysia*, edited by Raymond Scupin, 47–92. Selangor, Malaysia: Institute of Malay Language, Literature, 1989.

Marcinkowski, Christoph. *Persians and Shi'ites in Thailand: From the Ayutthaya Period to the Present*. Vol. 15, *Nalanda-Sriwijaya Centre Working Paper*. Singapore: Nalanda-Sriwijaya Centre, 2014.

Marddent, Amporn. "Gender Piety of Muslim Women in Thailand." PhD dissertation, Faculty of Philosophy and History, University in Frankfurt am Main, 2016.

McCargo, Duncan J. *Tearing Apart the Land: Islam and Legitimacy in Southern Thailand*. Ithaca, NY: Cornell University Press, 2008.

―――. "Thai Buddhists and the Southern Conflict." *Journal of Southeast Asian Studies* 40, no. 1 (2009a): 1–10.

―――. "The Politics of Buddhist Identity in Thailand's Deep South: The Demise of Civil Religion?" *Journal of Southeast Asian Studies* 40, no. 1 (2009b): 11–32.

————. "Informal Citizens: Graduated Citizenship in Southern Thailand." *Ethnic and Racial Studies* 34 (2011): 833–849.

McCargo, Duncan J., Saowanee T. Alexander, and Petra Desatova. "Ordering Peace: Thailand's 2016 Constitutional Referendum." *Contemporary Southeast Asia* 39, no. 1 (2017): 65–95.

Mines, Mattison. "Islamisation and Muslim Ethnicity in South India." *Man* 10, no. 3 (1975): 404–419.

Mudmarn, Seni. "Social Science Research in Thailand: The Muslim Minority." In *Muslim Social Science in ASEAN*, edited by Omar Farouk Bajunid, 21–41. Kuala Lumpur: Yayasan Perataran Ilumu, 1994.

Pires, Tomé. *The 'Suma Oriental' of Tomé Pires: An Account of the East, from the Red Sea to China.* Translated by Armando Cortesão. 2 vols. London: Hakluyt Society, 1990.

Pitsuwan, Surin. *Islam and Malay Nationalism: A Study of Malay Muslims in Southern Thailand.* Bangkok: Thai Khadai Research Institute, 1985.

————. "The Lotus and the Crescent: Clashes of Religious Symbolism in Southern Thailand." In *Ethnic Conflict in Buddhist Societies: Sri Lanka, Thailand, and Burma*, edited by K.M. de Silva, P. Duke, E. Goldberg, and N. Katz, 187–201. Boulder, CO: Westview Press, 1988.

————. *Muslim Worship Sites in Thailand.* Bangkok: Ministry of Foreign Affairs, 2001.

Rabibhadana, Akin. *The Organization of Thai Society in the Early Bangkok Period 1782–1873.* Interim Report Series No. 12. Data Paper No. 74. Southeast Asia Program. Ithaca: Cornell University Press, 1969.

Satha-Anand, Chaiwat. "Bangkok Muslims and the Tourist Trade." In *The Muslim Private Sector in Southeast Asia*, edited by Mohamed Ariff, 89–121. Singapore: Institute of Southeast Asian Studies, 1991.

Satha-Anand, Suwanna. "Religious Movements in Contemporary Thailand: Buddhist Struggles for Modern Relevance." *Asian Survey* 30, no. 4 (1990): 395–408.

————. "Buddhist Pluralism and Religious Tolerance in Democratizing Thailand." In *Philosophy, Democracy and Education*, edited by Philip Cam, 193–213. Seoul: The Korean National Commission for UNESCO, 2003.

Scupin, Raymond. "Islam in Thailand Before the Bangkok Period." *Journal of the Siam Society* 68, no. 1 (1980a): 55–71.

————. "Islamic Reformism in Thailand." *Journal of the Siam Society* 68, no. 2 (1980b): 1–10.

————. "The Socio-Economics Status of Muslims in Central and North Thailand." *Journal of Muslim Minority Affairs* 4, no. 2 (1981): 162–189.

————. "Popular Islam in Thailand." In *The Muslims in Thailand.* Vol. 1, *Historical and Cultural Studies*, edited by Andrew D.W. Forbes, 31–46. Bihar: Centre for South East Asian Studies, 1988.

———. "Muslim Accommodation in Thai Society." *Journal of Islamic Studies* 9, no. 2 (1998): 229–258.

———. "Cham Muslims in Thailand: A Model of a Moral Community." In *Islamic Studies in ASEAN: Presentations of an International Seminar*, edited by Isma-ae Alee, Hasan Madmarn, Imtiyaz Yusuf, Yusof Talek, Arin Sa-idi, Muhammad Roflee Waehama, and Ibrahim Narongraksaket, 453–464. College of Islamic Studies, Prince of Songkhla University, Pattani, Thailand, 2000.

———. "Mainland Southeast Asia." In *Peoples and Cultures of Asia*, edited by Raymond Scupin, 335–383. Upper Saddle River, NJ: Prentice Hall Press, 2006.

———. "Anthropology, Conflict, and International Relations." In *Beyond Disciplinary Boundaries: Advancing the Study of International Relations*, edited by Steve Yetiv and Patrick James, 153–188. New York: Palgrave Macmillan Press, 2017.

Smithies, Michael. *Descriptions of Old Siam, Oxford in Asia Paperbacks*. Kuala Lumpur: Oxford University Press, 1995.

Swearer, Donald, ed. *Towards the Truth* by Buddhadasa. Translated by Donald Swearer. Philadelphia: The Westminster Press, 1971.

———. "Fundamentalistic Movements in Theravada Buddhism." In *Fundamentalisms Observed*, edited by Martin E. Marty and Scott Appleby, 628–690. Chicago: University of Chicago Press, 1991.

———. *The Buddhist World of Southeast Asia*. 2nd edn. Albany, NY: SUNY Press, 2010.

Tambiah, Stanley. *World Conqueror and World Renouncer: A Study of Buddhismand Polity in Thailand Against a Historical Background*. Cambridge: Cambridge University Press, 1976.

———. "Ethnic Conflict in the World Today." *American Ethnologist* 16, no. 2 (1989): 335–349.

Winichakul, Thongchai. "The Changing Landscape of the Past: New Histories in Thailand since 1973." *Journal of Southeast Asian Studies* 26 (1995): 99–120.

Wyatt, David. "A Persian Mission to Siam in the Reign of King Narai." *Journal of the Siam Society* 62, no. 1 (1974): 151–157.

Yusuf, Imtiyaz. "Islam and Democracy in Thailand: Reforming the Office of Chularajamontri/Shaikh al-Islam." *Journal of Islamic Studies* (Published by Oxford Centre for Islamic Studies) 9, no. 2 (July 1998): 277–298.

———. *Faces of Islam in Southern Thailand*. Policy Studies 7. Washington, DC: East–West Center Washington, 2007.

———. Celebrating Muhammad's Birthday in Buddha's Land: Managing Religious Relations Through Religious Festival." In *Religion, Public Policy and Social Transformation in Southeast Asia. Religion, Gender, and Identity*. Vol. 2, edited by Dicky Sofjan, 130–161. Jakarta: Indonesian Consortium for Religious Studies, 2016.

PART II

Case Studies: Particular Moments of Interaction

CHAPTER 5

Sri Lanka's Anti-Muslim Movement and Muslim Responses: How Were They Gendered?

Farzana Haniffa

Sri Lanka today is a country that has lived through a debilitating war fought between a Sinhala identified state and a rebel group claiming to be fighting for a Tamil homeland in the northern and eastern provinces. The rebels, the Liberation Tigers of Tamil Eelam (LTTE) were defeated at a great human cost in the northern District of Mulaitiwu in May 2009. In 2019, the country remains in the throes of a long drawn out transition process that is yet to come to terms with its fractious past. This paper outlines one element of this difficult transition period: the emergence of the post-war anti-Muslim movement. In describing the work of this movement the chapter will argue that the movement utilized a gendered rhetoric enabled by the militaristic and masculinized actions of the regime in the immediate post-war context. The paper will argue further that elements of this rhetoric were also reflected in the response to the movement by Muslim interlocutors as well.

The regime in power in 2009 claimed responsibility for the war victory, and consolidated its political power through touting its battlefield

F. Haniffa (✉)
University of Colombo, Colombo, Sri Lanka

© The Author(s) 2020
I. Frydenlund and M. Jerryson (eds.),
Buddhist-Muslim Relations in a Theravada World,
https://doi.org/10.1007/978-981-32-9884-2_5

139

successes. The public was mobilized on a victorious Sinhala supremacist platform that paid scant regard to the enormous human cost of the war victory or its debilitating effect on the people of the northern and eastern provinces, members of the armed forces and civilians targeted all over the country. The regime also encouraged rampant anti-minority sentiment that saw the war victory as teaching the recalcitrant minority Tamils a lesson. In the aftermath of the war anti-minority sentiment also took the form of Monks groups organizing against Muslims.[1]

The Bodu Bala Sena (BBS), the army of Buddhist Power, an organization comprising mostly of nationalist monks, began a sustained anti-Muslim campaign in post-war Sri Lanka. The movement accused Muslims of engaging in a conspiracy to increase their numbers, decrease the Sinhala population and become the country's majority community. In addition, Muslim dress practices, consumption of halal meat, and provision of halal certification service for local businesses, were found fault with. Additionally, Muslims were accused of hatching a violent Jihad conspiracy to take over the country from the Sinhalese.

This chapter argues that the BBS attacks against Muslims in the immediate post-war era were a profoundly gendered onslaught that targeted minority Muslims, but also propagated very particular and specific ideas about maleness and femaleness through their anti-Muslim rhetoric. The Muslim response was similarly gendered and drew on a set of ideas about masculinity and femininity that resonated with those of the Sinhala supremacists. This chapter will look at the gendered elements of the hate rhetoric, the gendered nature of the response that such rhetoric garnered, and how gender issues informed the ethico-political questions preoccupying activists responding to the problem.

Context and Background

The BBS consisted of a group of Buddhist monks, some of whom have been active in nationalistic agitations for years, and registered itself as an organization in May 2012.[2] From the time of its registration onwards the group engaged in an anti-Muslim campaign through social media, press conferences, prime time television coverage, and by virtue of

---

[1] An earlier version of this chapter entitled "Fecund Mullahs and Gonibillas: The gendered nature of anti-Muslim rhetoric" appeared in the *Southasianist* of December 2015.

[2] It has one public lay member—the CEO Dilantha Withanage.

massive rallies in various parts of the Island. The General Secretary of the organization, the monk, Ven. Galebodathe Gnanasara, once claimed that they have the best network in the country given their many temples all over the island and the number of times their monks engage with the laity, in the temple, and at alms-givings of different sorts (Sunday school, etc.).[3]

The BBS used the temple network extensively and became extremely popular in the immediate post-war years. The anti-Muslim movement resonated with the Sinhala public all over the country. When they enjoyed their greatest popularity in 2013 and 2014,[4] their movement succeeded in getting the halal label suspended from local grocery shelves.[5] While there was some opposition from certain members of the Sinhala intelligentsia and from some monks, the dissenting voices were muted.[6] The movement received extensive media coverage and for a limited time, the media seemed to collude to exclude perspectives that critiqued the BBS position.[7] The ideology enjoyed widespread support among a large number of Sinhalese of different social classes.

The movement also received the tacit support of the government.[8] The spewing of anti-Muslim rhetoric, the sporadic violent events throughout the Sinhala speaking areas of the country, and ultimately the orchestrated anti-Muslim violence of June 2014 occurred without

[3] Bodu Bala Sena press conference November 19, 2012, available at https://www.youtube.com/watch?v=CeJY0WkDVXU.

[4] Anti Muslim sentiment has been mobilized periodically in Sri Lanka by various forces. For an examination of one of the first instances of anti-Muslim mobilization in the post-war context see Heslop's exploration of the case of the Dambulla mosque (2014).

[5] F. Haniffa, "Merit Economies in Neoliberal Times: Halal Troubles in Contemporary Sri Lanka," in *Religion and the Morality of Markets*, eds. D. Rudnyckyj and F. Osella (Cambridge: Cambridge University Press, forthcoming).

[6] A fellow activist and myself circulated a petition asking that there be greater opposition against the phenomenon. The statement signed by 63 civil society organisations was published on February 15, 2013. However, the Human Rights NGOs were rather slow to realize or engage with the threat in any significant way. They became mobilized after the violence of June 2014 in Aluthgama. See statement at http://groundviews.org/2013/02/15/civil-society-organisations-condemn-anti-muslim-rhetoric-and-attacks-in-sri-lanka/.

[7] The Jamiathul Ulema found it difficult to publish articles outlining their perspective when the BBS was attacking their fee levying halal certification service (Personal Communication).

[8] Haniffa, 2016.

substantial comment or criticism by the regime in power.[9] There was little or no state action taken against the perpetrators. In fact in the attack against the Muslim owned Fashion Bug clothing store and warehouse in Pepiliyana, (March 2013) the Inspector General of Police chose not to press charges against the identified perpetrators.[10]

Mahinda Rajapaksa was defeated in the presidential elections of January 2015 and the mood in the country changed. And for a period— at least a year—public anti-Muslim rhetoric was muted. The successor Sirisena—Wickremasinghe regime's open criticism of anti-minority sentiment and their stated commitment to reconciliation helped ease Muslim fears as well. While the Ven. Gnanasara continued to be active, the media coverage that he received virtually disappeared in the immediate aftermath of the regime change. But in mid-2016, the Ven. Gnanasara was again briefly in the limelight signaling that there was still significant support for the anti-Muslim ideas. Today Muslims continue to be anxious and to organize in response to the anti-Muslim movement. The court cases against those perpetrating anti-Muslim violence have not progressed to date under the current regime.

This chapter references developments in the immediate post-war period where anti Muslim movements were permitted to flourish under the Rajapaksa regime.

WOMEN AND THE BODU BALA SENA

In this section, I draw attention to the deteriorating gender relations under the Rajapaksa regime and argue that the BBS rhetoric was reflected and was in fact enabled by the manner in which gender roles were understood by a militarized and militaristic regime.

The anxieties spawned by the end of the war were dealt with in various ways in the immediate post-war moment. The assertion of Sinhala supremacy simultaneously celebrated a combative masculinity emblematized by the figure of the Ven. Gnanasara using a raised fist and obscene language when faulting Muslims. Together with the celebration of the military victory, a combative masculinity was celebrated everywhere. In their choice of names the BBS and similar groups—Bodu Bala Sena,

---

[9] For more detail on the 2014 violence, please see "Where Have all the Neighbours Gone? Aluthgama Riots and its Aftermath," Law and Society Trust 2015.

[10] Haniffa, 2016.

Ravana Balakaya (The Ravana Brigade, they later called themselves Ravana Balaya or the Power of Ravana) are all modeled on an understanding that there continue to be wars to be fought on multiple fronts. The BBS in its invocations calls on young Sinhalese to become armies and police forces in order to save their nation from armed Muslim jihadists.

This loud and violent maleness also manifested itself in terms of an entitlement to demand a certain form of quiescence from women. This entitlement to speak for and about women manifested itself in a variety of ways among the BBS monks as will be illustrated in the body of the paper. However, it was also present in state policy and in the rhetoric of the regime's minister of women's affairs, a male. Under the Rajapaksa regime state rhetoric and policies about women mirrored the narrowing of the definition of women's roles. Sinhala women, for instance, were required to safeguard the nation from becoming minoritized through reproducing the necessary number of Sinhala citizens. Those refusing their function as vessels of procreation, were considered to be traitors to the nation.

The anxieties of post-war Sri Lanka, were articulated in gendered ways that draw from a long history of such gendered rhetoric and policy. The nationalist demand that women function as the symbolic repositories of the nation's cultural content has been well documented in different political contexts in the Global south. The nationalist preoccupation with Sri Lankan women, where they were considered primarily in relation to their reproductive function, where they were compelled to reproduce as part of their duty toward the preservation of their nation too are tropes that have been identified and critiqued in feminist literature, at different historical moments in Sri Lanka.[11]

Therefore this particular post-war instance where misogyny against Sinhala women and the violently sexualized othering of the Muslims— both men and women—are articulated freely in public, draws from

---

[11] See M. De Alwis, "Moral Mothers and Stalwart Sons: Reading Binaries in Times of War," in *The Women and War Reader*, eds. L.A Lorentzen and Jennifer Turpin (New York: New York University Press, 1998); N. De Mel, *Women and the Nation's Narrative: Gender and Nationalism in 20th Century Sri Lanka* (Lanham: Rowman and Littlefield, 2002); S. Maunaguru, "Gendering Tamil Nationalism: The Construction of 'Woman' in Projects of Protest and Control," in *Unmaking the Nation: The Politics of Identity and History in Modern Sri Lanka*, eds. P. Jeganathan and Q. Ismail (1995).

existing discourses and practices. The state and nationalist ideologues have long framed women's roles in overly narrow and limiting ways. However, as Kodikara has pointed out, the manner in which this rhetoric manifested itself and was reflected in policy in the post-2009 moment was also a rolling back of important policy developments that feminists had worked for.[12] According to Kodikara government policy on female migrant workers, on women's reproductive health and on legislation regarding gender-based violence, were all negatively impacted during the Rajapaksa regime.

Kodikara documents the manner in which, during that time, teenage pregnancies, high school drop out rates and childhood drug use was attributed to mothers leaving the country as domestic workers. President Rajapaksa also committed to overturning hard-won domestic violence legislation on the basis that it was leading to a higher divorce rate. The above two examples reflect the manner in which the rhetoric of the regime naturalized women's caregiving roles and normalized violence within marriages. Concrete actions taken by the regime that reflected this narrowing of space for women included controlling women's mobility for work overseas through administrative strictures, beauty culture training for female LTTE cadres, and prohibiting non-state agencies from working on reproductive health issues.[13]

MUSLIMS AS A MINORITIZED OTHER IN SRI LANKA

Muslims, worshippers of one of the four world religions represented in Sri Lanka are currently just 9% of the country's population and trace their origins to pre Islamic Arab merchants who traded with the island. Muslims are primarily a Tamil speaking group that are located in pockets throughout the country.[14] The social and economic consequences

---

[12] C. Kodikara, "Good Women and Bad Women of the Post-War Nation," *Groundviews*, May 22, 2014, http://groundviews.org/2014/05/22/good-women-and-bad-women-of-the-post-war-nation/.

[13] Kodikara, "Good Women and Bad Women."

[14] While Muslims had long featured as a despised "other" in the rhetoric of Sinhala Buddhist ideologues, the public articulation of this idea and mobilizing the public in opposition to Muslims was what was new in the post-war era (see Anagarika Dharmapala, *Return to Righteousness* [Colombo: Government Press, Ceylon, 1965], and de Silva and Bastin, this volume).

of anti-Tamil violence throughout the country that culminated in the pogrom of 1983 and the escalation of the war in the north and east after 1983 changed Sri Lanka's demographics. Significant outmigration of Tamils, increasing racism against all minorities, and the preoccupation with pious practice among Muslims were some developments during the years of the war.

These developments have sometimes been understood as caused by wartime preoccupations. The Muslim community in Sri Lanka also transformed itself during the years of the war. Reformist groups propagating stricter forms of Muslim religious practice flourished in Sri Lanka in those years. The Tabligh Jamaa't, the Jmaati Islami, Tauheed Jamaat across the country and Salafi influenced middle-class groups in Colombo dominated the scene of transformation and brought about enormous changes. One of the consequences of these changes was rendering the women's headscarf ubiquitous and proliferating the *abhaya* and *niqab* in Sri Lankan public spaces.

Another factor relevant to the understanding of Muslims in Sri Lanka is the manner in which Muslims were affected by the sustained minoritization[15] of all non-Sinhala Buddhists by the state in the aftermath of independence from the British. The later militarization of the state that saw the military defeat of the Tamil rebellion in the north as the country's primary political problem also minoritized the Muslims in particular ways. Finally with the anti-Muslim violence of the LTTE. Muslims' wartime minoritization took on a specific focus with the emergence of an openly ethnic Muslim political party from the war-affected the eastern province. Prior to the escalation of the conflict in the 1980s the Muslim political elite's engagement with successive Sinhala majority governments were influenced by good personal relations and membership and leadership roles in the national political parties.[16] During the war however,

---

[15] I use the term minoritization to mean the social political and economic steps taken by regimes in power to hierarchically order the different ethnic groups in the country and tailor citizenship entitlements in keeping with their ethnic identification. The Sinhala Only act of 1956, the doing away with constitutional provisions in the 1972 Republican constitution that guaranteed minority rights, and the institutionalization of Buddhism as the state religion are the most well known of these.

[16] Haniffa, 2012.

146 F. HANIFFA

Muslims of the north and east were victims of violence and the southern elite were unable to either appreciate or articulate their grievances.[17]

The Sri Lanka Muslim Congress (SLMC) emerged as a political party with a significant northern and eastern Muslim constituency in 1984.[18] The electoral reforms of the 1980s and the shift to proportional representation from a first-past-the-post system enabled national level success for smaller political parties. The SLMC therefore were able to successfully contest and win sizeable victories during its early years. The SLMC won 4 seats in the general elections of 1989 and 7 in 1994.[19] Popular Sinhala perceptions regarding the Muslims, however, shifted with the success of the SLMC in national politics. The anti-Muslim sentiment prevalent within nascent Sinhala nationalism—in the speeches of Buddhist ideologue Anagarika Dharmapala for instance—was mobilized against Muslims during the war. And more intensely in the post-war period.[20]

MUSLIMS AND COMMERCE

Throughout Sri Lanka, Muslims are known as a trading community greatly skilled in commerce. Almost all peripheral towns have small businesses—food, textile, hardware, and other retail commerce—run by Muslims and there are certain wholesale markets in Colombo that have a Muslim preponderance. The Southern Muslims are widely viewed as traders or businesspeople and the elite often represents themselves as such.[21] Muslim-owned businesses are also a visible presence in the Sri Lankan economy. These range from the large apparel exporting Brandix group and the plantation company Akbar brothers to retail clothing chains like Fashion Bug, No Limit, and Hameedias.

[17] M. Ashraff, "The Muslim Community and the Peace Accord," *Indo Sri Lanka Peace Accord, 29th July 1987, Comments, Reflections*, Special Issue of *Logos* 26 (1987): 48–76; Haniffa, 2011.

[18] Thaheer, 2017.

[19] Thaheer, 2017.

[20] See for instance the reference to Dharmapala in the article by Anonymous entitled, "The political economy of prejudice: Islam Muslims and Sinhala Buddhist nationalism today- some reflections." http://groundviews.org/2013/03/20/the-political-economy-of-prejudice-islam-muslims-and-sinhala-buddhist-nationalism-in-sri-lanka-today-some-reflections/.

[21] Ismail, 2014, Maunaguru, 1995.

There are high-end Jewelry Houses like Sifani, Colombo Jewellery Stores and Zam Gems that are also Muslim owned. While the 2 million strong Muslim population in the country includes many middle class professionals, agriculturalists in the east, north, and a large urban and rural underclass Muslims continue to be stereotyped as a trading community.[22] The anti-Muslim sentiment propagated by the Buddhist monks groups also specifically targeted Muslim businesses and called for their boycott. Muslim owned clothing chains, for instance, were accused of participating in a conspiracy to render Sinhala women barren through placing chemicals in women's underwear. In small rural communities, these boycotts were successful and in the months where the anti-Muslim sentiment was at its peak, we received news that many businesses were on the verge of closing down.[23]

There is much that can be said of the economic dimension of the anti-Muslim sentiment. In early 2013, halal certification carried out by the All Ceylon Jamiathul Ulema (council of theologians) became a contentious issue. The Jamiatul Ulema was accused of raising money for Jihad through providing the certification service. Monks calling for the banning of halal claimed that non-Muslims should not be compelled to buy halal labeled goods because they will be paying for the certification as well. When it was pointed out that the amount was negligible, it was stated that no one should be paying "*the thambiya*" (derogatory term for Muslims) even 5 cents.

As I have argued elsewhere[24] although the anti-Muslim movement had widespread support the fact that it is the Sinhala working class that became mobilized to do violence in the name of Sinhalaness needs to be interrogated. Further, the destruction during the violence in Aluthgama in 2014 for instance, was targeted very strategically at the destruction of Muslim property and businesses. The question as to what extent ethnic tensions are mobilized to achieve political and economic ends has always been a salient one in Sri Lanka.[25] This chapter, however, will concentrate on gendered dimensions of the hate rhetoric.

---

[22] Ismail, 2014.

[23] I have described the manner in which BBS monks spoke of Muslims in food outlets spitting in food served to non Muslims in order to discourage Sinhala patronage of Muslim establishments (see Haniffa, 2017).

[24] Haniffa, 2017.

[25] Also see de Silva and Bastin, this volume.

The BBS Hate Rhetoric on Muslims

The sexually predatory and aggressive Muslim male, and the Muslim women dressed in black *hijab*, *abhaya* and *niqab* were two main figures of the BBS hate rhetoric. The BBS and its allies were preoccupied with the "increase" in the Muslim population, and the rate at which Muslims were procreating, and the fact that there are Sinhala women marrying Muslim men and converting to Islam. At the same time, they attacked the black dress of Muslim women—specifically the *niqab* or face covering that they have often termed "*gonibilla*." The *gonibilla* is a Sinhala "monster" figure used to scare children. The term translates loosely to "sack monster" and was once associated with a monster who supposedly carried off children in his sack. It later expanded in meaning due to its use to name informants during the northern and southern insurgencies. Men (generally) wearing a gunny sack or a "goni" over their heads with holes to see with, were asked to inspect lines of prisoners and pick out those who were against the government, or against the rebels as the case may be.

Those identified were invariably shot or disappeared. The *gonibillas* doing such identifying in the south were usually people of the village, sometimes kin, who utilized the mood of the times to sort out many private grievances as well. The term *gonibilla* used in relation to Muslim women wearing the *abhaya* and *niqab* references a semantic content regarding childhood fears as well as notions of mistrust and betrayal by those among whom one lived, and a fearful not too far away political past. Muslims who embrace the *niqab*, however, are not self-conscious about the nature of the self-othering practice that they are participating in, and until the emergence of the hate rhetoric were unaware of the manner in which the *niqab* may invoke the *gonibilla*. The fact that they have no frame of reference through which to realize its import is telling of the gulf that exists between communities. The *niqab* is meaningful for those I interviewed—especially female members of the Tabligh Jamma'at—in terms of the *hijab* prescriptions that they have internalized as required practice for Muslim women. The piety groups' emphasis on transforming community, and their mobilizing a majority of Muslims as agents of such transformation have meant that the frames of reference through which Muslims think of community rarely include religious Others, their politics or their histories. Within this frame of reference, the social presence of Sinhala Others that perceive Muslims only as personifying the *gonibilla* has relevance only as an oppressive, racist anti-minority threat. The fact that they emerge out of Sinhala Buddhists own deeply felt fears and anxieties is rarely noted.

BBS monks, in referencing the "gonibillia" dress of the Muslim women at a large public meeting mobilized ideas of male sexual prowess as a means to hold its audience's attention. The following is an excerpt from a monk's speech at a BBS rally in the early days of the organization when its message seemed to take over the country's imagination and its popularity was ascending. In a mass rally held in the town of Kandy in March 2013, the BBS monk, Ven. Dr. Madegoda Abhayatissa, Senior Lecturer at the University of Sri Jayawardenapura, Viharadhipathi of the Pepiliyana Sunethra Devi Mahaprivena invoked women's dress. He said,

> You know, now with regards to their dress, I was telling the reverend Gnanasara that he should not be talking about women's clothing. But then, who knows who is behind that head covering? What kind of criminal might be hiding there? Lets say, I get into this garb? Who will know who is inside? Socks on the feet, gloves covering the arms, and they walk everywhere. Is this the Araabi? (Me Araabiyada?) Also how dangerous is this? Even I can go into a mosque like that, I can even go into the women's prayer room and you know what I can do? I can, I can, (monk grins) I am not going to say it. (Monk sniggers)[26]

The monk in his innuendo suggests that if he were to wear Muslim religious dress—the black *abhaya* with the *niqab*—he would be able to enter female spaces and commit sexual violence against Muslim women gathered there. Not only is the monk's rhetoric against the Vinaya, there is a defiling of the sanctity of the prayer room in the monk's suggested actions, and Muslim women are erased as agents and reduced to objects that can be abused without significant consequences.

On a public podium in the town of Kandy that day in February 2013, in front of that particular crowd (of thousands) the monk could casually reference sexual violence as a way of illustrating his point about the Muslim. I argue that the monk's rhetoric is directed at a male audience who will understand what is being said, suggested or proposed. The female audience is rendered so invisible as to be completely irrelevant to the monk's statement.

---

[26] Available on youtube at https://www.youtube.com/watch?v=inZa_HEbD8Q.

One reading could be that the reference was to violence against Muslim women, and therefore Sinhala women would not identify with this "other." I contend, however, that this illustrates the casual manner in which sexual violence was publicly referenced in Sri Lanka during the Rajapaksa years, and further the impunity for perpetrators of such violence. Arguably, the militaristic masculinity that was acceptable during that time endorsed such sexual violence, or at least, speech invoking such violence.[27] The monk's words, addressing men in a context where both men and women are present erases the presence of Sinhala women. The absence of the humanity of Muslims—male and female, and Buddhist women in the monk's rhetoric is perhaps the clearest illustration of ethnic and gender relations in Sri Lanka as propagated by the BBS and endorsed by the regime during the immediate post-war era.[28]

Further, the specificity of the critique of the *niqab* in this context is important. The critique emerges from a nationalism laced with misogyny and should not be conflated with discourses that claim to be feminist that also see the *niqab* as problematic. For the monk what is of importance is that the *niqab* invokes "Araabiya," and that the practice is not local.[29]

---

[27] Two examples of the manner in which male entitlement to commit sexual violence or harass women was talked about it post war Sri Lanka are interesting to note. S.B. Dissanayake, minister of higher education in the Rajapaksa cabinet speaking about former president Chandrika Curamatunge's role in getting Maitrhipala Sirisena to contest the presidential elections of 2015 stated on national television that the former president should be thrown on the ground stripped naked and made to run down the streets. http://www.adaderana.lk/news/29060/sb-should-apologize-from-all-sri-lankan-women-rosy-Another instance was the case of the "Wariyapola girl." There was a significant public outcry against one young women in Wariyapola for repeatedly slapping a youth who was harassing her. She was caught on camera and was later arrested by the Police after a complaint by the youth. The incident received widespread coverage and made national news. She was vilified for her act of slapping the youth who was "just fooling around" (*usulu visulu kirima*).

[28] The BBS drew greater male participation to its meetings than women. However with its concentrated propagation across several social media platforms—their website facebook, and youtube for instance—the rhetoric reached a much wider audience of both men and women.

[29] Other interlocutors have also made this same critique—for instance, Mrs. Jezima Ismail educationist and activist stalwart of the Muslim community criticizing the *hijab* during its early introduction, often stated that the practice is middle-eastern and therefore alien to the south Asian context that has had its own modes of covering. See also McGilvray and Raheem (2007) and Haniffa (2005a) on the evolution of the *hijab* and Muslim women's dress in Sri Lanka.

The monk's argument against the dress practice was due to its putative strangeness and "difference" within the Sri Lankan context.

The monk's rhetoric renders both women and minorities silent and irrelevant other than as subjects of Buddhist masculine address. The Muslims about whom much was being said in the hate rhetoric had no means of intervening and their perspective was absent for all intents and purposes. There was no participation of Muslims in these public conversations *about* Muslims throughout Sinhala speaking Sri Lanka over a period of two years. While there were a few token TV debates (see below) between Sinhala speaking Muslims and BBS monks, they were framed in ways that the Muslim perspective was either lost or further marginalized.[30]

The Ven. Madegoda Abhayatissa's anti-Muslim rhetoric was laced with sexual violence and misogyny irrespective of the fact that women were members of the audience and are known to be great lay patrons (*dayakas*) of Buddhist temples. There is no awareness that women might be disturbed at the suggestion of sexual violence, or that Sinhala women may feel some solidarity with Muslim women, or that Sinhala women might take exception to the monk virtually normalizing a crime against women. The Ven. Madegoda Abhayatissa's sniggering reference to sexually abusing Muslim women in prayer rooms assumed an audience of men (for whom sexual violence was not a crime of great consequence) where women were irrelevant as interlocutors.

ANXIETIES REGARDING THE MINORITIZATION OF THE MAJORITY

The preoccupation with numbers has informed much of Sri Lanka's engagement with democracy. The Sinhala claim to greater entitlements in Sri Lanka under modern conditions depends on the fact of numbers and is based mainly on the Sinhala "community" called into being as a political majority.[31] The ethical basis for Sinhala nationalist claims against the Tamils for instance, is the claim of number: in a democracy the majority rules.[32] As Uyangoda describes it and as Devasiri has recently

---

[30] There were a few exceptions. YA TV coverage over TNL station and one conversation with Ven. Gnanasara on the Derana TV station are noteworthy.

[31] J. Uyangoda, *Questions of Sri Lanka's Minority Rights* (Colombo: International Center for Ethnic Studies, 2001); Ananda Abeysekara, 2002.

[32] Uyangoda, *Questions of Sri Lanka's Minority Rights*.

152 F. HANIFFA

explored further, Democracy by definition is understood as being about the supremacy of the majority. Minorities claiming rights therefore goes against the majority's right to rule as they please. The Sinhalese Buddhists populace, therefore recognizes the significance of being less than the majority. Therefore the mobilizing potential of the idea that the Sinhalese would no longer be a majority is substantial.

The following two posts from the now deactivated Sorry.com Facebook page are illustrative of the attempt to mobilize Sinhala anxiety regarding numbers. The first carries a picture of the Ven. Aggamaha Panditha Athipoojya Dawuldena Gnanissara, the Mahanayaka of the Amarapura sect. It also features a hand holding a noose. The text attributed to the Ven. monk reads: "during the time of the Portuguese[33] the Sinhala Buddhist population of this country was 98%. Today the percentage has dropped to 60% and in 2040 the population will drop to 40%."[34] The next line references a government campaign from the 1980s that encouraged family planning. The line, referencing the government program's slogan reads. "A small family is golden they said. The politicians must take responsibility for this." At the end of the slide it states— "*Punchi Pavula Raththaran, Kaapu Lanuwa Istharam.*" The small family is golden they said—how skillfully were we misled![35]

The text in the next visual states that there are 12,000 jihadists trained in the east of the island, and that there is a global conspiracy to make Sri Lanka a Muslim land by 2040. The visual carries an image of the national identity card with a *niqab* clad woman's face on it. The two slides bring together two sets of anxieties: the Sinhalese being duped into turning themselves into a minority, and the Muslims—armed jihadists, waiting to take over through violence if necessary—the majority status in 2040. The face of the *niqab* clad woman "the *gonibilla*" is important. It is the Muslim woman, but as stated earlier it is also the scary figure of Sinhala children's stories and the despicable and dangerous figure that points out

---

[33] The Portuguese arrived in Sri Lanka in 1505 and stayed until they were ousted by the Dutch some 150 years later.

[34] It should be noted here that the Mahanayaka of the Amarapura Nikaya was the first senior Buddhist Monk to express his regret regarding the violence against Muslims in Aluthgama in 2014. See The Colombo Telegraph of June 17, 2014. https://www.colombotelegraph.com/index.php/mahanayake-asserts-unity/.

[35] The rough translation is mine. The Punchi Pavula Raththaran campaign was a population control initiative from the 1960s.

"traitors" to be killed off during the *Bhishana samaya* or the Time of Terror of 1988–1989. The rhetorical othering of the Muslims through the *gonibilla* figure is specific to the Sri Lankan context, and is emblematic of the intensity of the Sinhala anxiety caused by this particular brand of otherness.

The monks groups' rhetoric mobilizing anxieties regarding the minoritization of the Sinhalese was well worked out.[36] The Ven. Madegoda Abhayatissa stated that, of the Sinhala Buddhist population, a majority is over the age of 40 and no longer able to bear children. Of the remainder, another half is men. Of the group of women of childbearing age, a significant percentage has been "persuaded by NGOs" to engage in permanent birth control and therefore cannot have any more children. The remainder constitutes just one million Sinhala Buddhist women, out of a total population of twenty million, who are capable of having children, he said. At the present rate of population increase, if they even have three children each (which most will not) it will not be possible to replace the aging population. Therefore, a large section of the current Sinhala Buddhist population will be dead by 2040 and will not be replaced and thereby, the Sinhala Buddhists will lose their majority status in the country. The monk emphasized the need for young people to save Sinhalaness through having children. There is a clear coordination of information within the various fora where the hate rhetoric appears and naming the year 2040 as the moment of change remains constant.[37]

The Ven. Madegoda Abhayatissa Thero proceeded to describe how Muslims were different from the Sinhalese. In doing so the thero felt the need to sexualize Muslim women and reference Muslim fecundity. Muslims have many more than three children, he said. In Muslim households, the grandmother, the granddaughter and the mother, the monk stated, are all pregnant at the same time. He stated further "If you see a Muslim woman she will have one child in the hand one in the stomach, and a whole line of them following her."[38] Abhayatissa thero was referencing a popular trope among BBS monks.

---

[36] The following is drawn mainly from the presentation made by Ven. Madegoda Abhayatissa Thero at the BBS Kandy meeting on March 17, 2013. https://www.youtube.com/watch?v=inZa_HEbD8Q.

[37] Haniffa, 2016.

[38] Ven. Madegoda Abhayatissa Thero at the BBS Kandy meeting on March 17, 2013.

154   F. HANIFFA

The fecundity of the Muslim family is referred to in derogatory terms by the monks on a regular basis.[39]

The large and visible Muslim groups sometimes traveling together, eating in the middle class contexts of restaurants and cafes, are understood as oversized "nuclear families" whose numbers will contribute toward them taking over from the Sinhalese as the majority. Muslim othering routinely involves invoking the sexually predatory Muslim male and the rampant sexuality of both male and female Muslims. References to the fecundity of Muslim women—that they are constantly pregnant, that age is no barrier to Muslim women's pregnancy—is a reference to the hypersexuality, of all Muslims. In invoking a preoccupation with sex where even grandmothers are pregnant, there is a referencing of an absence of restraint and decorum on the part of Muslims in contrast to the Buddhist middle path.

The Facebook pages and monk's rhetoric against the No Limit and later Fashion Bug, clothing stores known to be owned by Muslims, were also a reference to Muslim predatory sexuality. In this invocation of predatory Muslims there is an erasure of Sinhala women "victims" agency. For instance, one Facebook post, calling for Sinhalese to not patronize Muslim owned clothing stores, referred to cameras being fixed in women's changing rooms. The post said "dear women, please be careful." (*kanthavanipraveshamvanna*) the next line read "share for the sake of your mother, sister, female friend, or girl friend."

The post is addressed to men to protect their women from Muslim predators. In the BBS Kandy meeting of March 2013, the Rev. Gnanasara read out names of Sinhala women who had worked at Muslim owned clothing stores, converted to Islam and married Muslim men. The Ven. Gnanasara shouted with reference to the clothing chains "can we let them create harems like this?" And concluded by saying "hereafter we will not send our daughters to work there. We will only send our sons!" Here the venerable Gnanasara is stating that Sinhala women cannot be permitted to make choices about sexual partners outside of

---

[39] See for instance the manner in which the Ven. Gnanasara listing Muslims' abilities at an interview on the TV channel Young Asia Television available at http://modernvdo.com/UVJiTHNEemZ4bHMz. He states that Muslims ability in trade and in "making children" (*Muslimayadaruwohadannadakshay*) should be valorized as an asset to the country. Also see the comment on Muslim fecundity by the chief monk of the Deegavapi temple quoted in Emannuel (2015).

5 SRI LANKA'S ANTI-MUSLIM MOVEMENT AND MUSLIM RESPONSES ...   155

the Sinhala Buddhist community. By saying that Sinhala women are the victims of the predatory sexuality of Muslim men the monk is also saying that Sinhala women have no agency of their own. Another comment worth making is that according to the monk's rhetoric only male Sinhalese will hitherto be "permitted" to be employed by Muslims. There is no complete rejection of the possibility of employment under Muslim entrepreneurs.[40]

THE MUSLIM RESPONSE

The Muslim elite response to the BBS positions—especially on the *niqab*—constituted a gendered discourse similar to that of the Buddhist monks. Mansur Dahlan a community spokesperson, a member of the advisory board of the All Ceylon Jamiathul Ulema (ACJU), on an interview with the local YA TV, also invoked the same *Punchi Pawula Raththaran* government initiative when discussing population.[41] He stated to the interviewer, "the falling Sinhala numbers is not the problem of the Muslims. Look at the number of abortion clinics that are opening up," he said. "Muslim women don't patronize those, they are mainly used by Sinhala women. If an incentive was offered to the Sinhala women to have more children rather than offer an incentive for birth control, then this problem can be solved." Population control has long been part of state policy. Even to date, doctors routinely provide family planning advice and the choice of permanent contraceptives to women after their third pregnancy. Dahlan too then echoes the monks

---

[40] In the case of Hindutva in India the sexualization of the Muslim other is a trope that has received much comment. In this case too there is a fear of Muslim sexuality and fecundity articulated as that of a minority overtaking the majority (see K. Menon, *Everyday Nationalism: Women of the Hindu Right in India* [Philadelphia: University of Pennsylvania Press, 2012]; T. Sarkar, "Semiotics of Terror: Muslim Children and Women in Hindu Rashtra," *Economic and Political Weekly* 37, no. 28 [July 2002]). Sarkar writing in the aftermath of anti Muslim violence in Gujarat where there was targeted rape and killing of Muslim women and children describes the mentality behind the violence as cultivated by an ideology of revenge for past wrongs and an obsession about viral male and fertile female Muslim bodies (see Sarkar, "Semiotics of Terror," 2874). The violence against Muslims in Sri Lanka is in no way comparable to India. But given the allegations of sexual violence against Tamil women during and after the conflict, and the BBS's call for allegiance with the BJP, such violence continues to be within the realm of the possible.

[41] *Muslimhalalanyagamikayantaharamda?* https://vimeo.com/59737224. Featured on TNL TV channel on February 21, 2013.

156 F. HANIFFA

and reproduces the prevailing stereotypes regarding Muslim fecundity. Muslim women perform their reproductive role satisfactorily, according to Dahlan. The solution to the monks' perceived problem lies in getting Sinhala women to perform as efficiently.[42]

The patriarchal notions regarding women's dress that prevailed among the Muslim elite was laid bare during this time. An email was circulated in the form of two graphics.[43] I was forwarded these as examples of an excellent response to the threats posed to the *niqab*. One was entitled *Why is my niqab your problem?* Done with a combination of Sinhala and English text, the graphic featured visuals of a *niqab* clad Muslim woman with a speech bubble indicating that what was represented in the graphic was her perspective. The graphic, done in the form of a poster stated that many religions prescribed a form of modest dress for women. A visual below that depicted a group of smiling women with different sorts of head coverings categorized as Christian-catholic, Orthodox Jewish, and Muslim. The visual was followed by text stating that both Buddhism and ancient Sinhala texts urge women to be modest. Then, an unnamed Sinhala literary source is quoted about how a woman should cover her body, not smile too broadly, and not leave the house without permission from her mate. The *niqab* clad woman's speech bubble states: "why then is my dress that is so modest considered to be alien to our culture? Is it not the types of dress below that are unsuitable for our culture?" The next illustration contains a line of women in tight pants, short skirts, midriff baring outfits and low cut tops. The text underneath reads: "Then why is my niqab a problem for you?"

The second poster/leaflet referred explicitly to sexual violence. Invoking the high incidences of sexual violence in the country—with a citation from a women's group's March 8 message—it stated,

---

[42] Dahlan was claiming to speak for two million Muslims. And a gyneacologist writing to the Ravaya newspaper in fact claimed that Muslim choices of reproductive technologies often were similar to those of others of their class background.

[43] This email was forwarded to me by a female feminist mentor, and a Muslim friend and colleague with whom I had done much work on the anti Muslim sentiment. I have since then found it featured on the following website http://jaffnamuslim.siteblogs. net/2014/12/06/why-my-niqab-is-your-problem/. The post is dated December 6, 2014. (Only the first poster, the second that invokes sexual violence is not shown.)

5 SRI LANKA'S ANTI-MUSLIM MOVEMENT AND MUSLIM RESPONSES ...

For sure the blame for these incidents should be placed entirely at the hands of the perpetrator. However, women who incited these men by walking around half-naked should also bare some amount of responsibility. In the same way as we lock our windows and bolt our doors against thieves and criminals in the night, in the same way that drivers wear helmets and put on seat belts, women too when they wear modest clothing receive a measure of protection. That is why every religion calls upon women to wear modest (*sheelachara*) dress.

Next to the text, there is a visual entitled "a simple theory"—there are two photographs—one of a lollipop with a wrapper on and one with the wrapper off. In the first, there is a fly moving away from the sweet. In the second the lollipop is covered with flies!

The next illustration further endorses the idea of the lecherous male. There is a woman in a bikini and sunglasses walking; she is being followed by a man with his pants down revealing his buttocks. There is a woman who is walking in the opposite direction dressed in the *niqab* to whom the man pays no attention. The speech bubble over the woman in the bikini says "I am minding my own business, why is he following me?" The *niqab* clad women looks on as she walks away and states— "thank goodness I was saved by my clothing!"[44]

The *Hijabi*'s speech bubble at the bottom of the page states in Sinhala-

---

[44] This particular graphic is culled from one that was in circulation internationally on facebook and a variety of other websites. The original features only the two women— one clad in *niqab* and the other in a bikini and sunglasses. In the original the bikini clad woman's speech bubble states—"only the eyes are shown, everything else is covered -how oppressed!" And the *niqab* clad woman states—"only the eyes are covered, everything else is shown, how oppressed!" http://www.democraticunderground.com/10026022609. A version of this graphic with an explanation that reflects much that I have laid out in this paper appears in the All Ceylon Jamiathul Ulema website on page 15 of their Sinhala Language Publication entitled *Anthavaadi Islaamiya Andum Palandum* (Extremist Muslim Dress and Adornments.) This publication was one a set that were done that were responding directly to the Sinhala Buddhist hate speech. The set was entitled *Saamaya saha Sanhindiyawa Vetha Yomuvu Sanwaada* (Discourses towards Peace and Reconciliation), available at http://acju.lk/si/published/item/1032-samaaja-sanwaada, accessed February 13, 2019.

> We are not casting aspersions on anyone's choice of dress. Every woman has the right to dress the way she wants. In the same way, don't we too have the right to dress in our religious dress in order to ensure our security? Why is my niqab your problem?

The two graphics subscribe to an understanding of women's roles and social worth that is similar to the monk's discourse, but also reflects a widely held justification among Muslims in South Asia and elsewhere for Muslim women's veiling practices. The first graphic extolling the virtues of Muslim women's dress, reworks the age-old trope of asking women to practice modest dress or be subjected to a predatory male gaze and the inevitability of sexual violence. The second graphic is explicit in making a connection between sexual violence and dress. It is also produced from an imagination that cannot comprehend solidarity among women. The possibility that the Muslim woman might be incensed enough by the prospect of sexual violence against a fellow human being to intervene to stop such violence is not permitted by the visual.

While the poster depicts women's bodies only as objects of male desire, the graphic also depicts men as flies—unclean and polluting, and unable to control themselves in the presence of a woman's body if not for the concealing and obstructing barriers of clothing. The normalization of sexual violence through the depiction of males as predatory and out of control and similar to vermin (flies) goes to further regularize violent and criminal male sexual behavior as an everyday occurrence that women are responsible for guarding against.

These two graphics were on email during the height of the circulation of anti-Muslim sentiment and the extent to which it received wider coverage is not clear. It most probably had a life on social media as well. I have also more recently come across social media photographs of the lollipop with and without the wrapper appearing in Billboards in the Middle East. These are generally advertisements favoring veiling practices for women. I use it here since it referenced a perspective that I periodically encountered among groups of Muslim men who were responding to the crisis.[45]

---

[45] Anti BBS monk—Watarakke Vijitha thero speaking at a meeting of the Upcountry Muslim Council—extolled the virtues of Islamic clothing for women as the most modest and most civilized dress for women—(*vinitha, sanwara*) since it covers a woman completely. The statement is available on a youtube video made by Knowledge Box and uploaded on August 24, 2013. https://www.youtube.com/watch?v=JbV3QUaWlLQ.

And that these graphics in particular had little to do with women's experiences was born out almost immediately afterwards. At a women's meeting that was organized by the Secretariat for Muslims in August 2013, we discussed these graphics. And the immediate response of the participating women—many of whom wore the *hijab* and some who wore the *niqab*—was that they wear the *hijab*, *niqab* or any form of Muslim dress not to protect themselves from predatory males, but because they believe it to be a direct request of Allah that appears in the *Qur'an*.[46]

Gender relations within the Muslim community were inevitably inflected by Muslims' minority consciousness. Maintaining segregated male and female spaces and performing the hierarchy of male-female relations among Muslims were important and were impacted by the non-endorsement, dismissal, and demonization of Muslim masculinity in a multi-religious and plural Sri Lankan public sphere. Maintaining strict gender hierarchies in the homes of middle class Muslims that I worked with, then, was important. While for some this performance was meaningful in one set of social interactions with little relevance in many others, for many it was performative in that it spawned greater restrictions for women regarding dress choice, freedom of movement, access to education, and strictures to practice their religion in particular ways.[47]

Interestingly this performance also spawns a sensibility among many Sri Lankan Muslim men regarding the place and role of women that was not widely shared by women. The following excerpt from veteran Muslim journalist Latheef Farook's article "Does Hijab prevent social development." In the Daily News of Monday, May 11, 2015 is

---

[46] During interviews a decade ago middle class Muslim women were less shy about stating that they covered in order to ensure that men were not tempted by women's beauty (see Farzana Haniffa, "Ethnic Conflict, Post-colonial Nation Building and Militarization," in *Militarising State Society and Culture in Asia: Critical Perspectives*, ed. J. Uyangoda [Hong Kong: ARENA, 2005a]). Leila Ahmad claims that there is no direct injunction in the Quran regarding veiling. The practice was prevalent during the time of the prophet Muhammad in many parts of the world including Arabia and was probably an elite practice. Within the young Muslim community veiling and seclusion became a norm only for the prophet's wives. In the Hadith or the practices of the prophet, the use of the phrase "she took to the veil" to indicate that "she became the wife of the prophet" suggests that even after Muhammad's death the practice was not common among Muslims. Today, however, this reading of the practice is less fashionable. Many prefer to understand the verse regarding the khimer as referencing women already wearing a head covering.

[47] Judith Butler, *Gender Trouble: Feminism and the Subversion of Identity* (London: Routledge, 1990).

160   F. HANIFFA

instructive in this regard. In this article, Farook defends *hijab* wearing women against their critics. Farook states that those who are "impressed with modern civilization" claim that "Hijab is an obstacle that prevents women from progressing in the spheres of personal and social development." Farook states that such people

> wish that women became an item to be traded in the market of immorality. They want to rid women of their chastity and bashfulness, and wish that their thinking and objectives becomes Westernized. Their desire is that women become experts in singing, dancing and acting. In short, they want the Muslim woman to be devoid of faith, belief, purity, morals and chastity.[48]

Farook claims that such sentiments are "westernized" and goes on to catalogue statistics in "western" countries on high rates of sexual violence, marital infidelity, and birth of illegitimate children. These are offered as "proof" of what happens in a context where the *hijab* and therefore "faith, belief, purity, morals and chastity" are rejected by society. The article concludes by advising Muslim women to "rejoice with their hijab….knowing that the good end is for the righteous." Farook's mobilization of dated notions of "western decadence" and Muslim women's purity went largely unchallenged.

Farook's article is an articulation of the purity discourse about Muslim women within which many Sri Lankan (middle class) Muslim women remain trapped. This discourse effectively limits the manner in which Muslim women can themselves speak about their position in the world. It is from within such a limited discourse that the opposition to the BBS's position on Muslim women's dress was also articulated.

Let me end this section with one other example of the gendered and sexualized nature of this discourse about *hijab*. I was forwarded an email by a male friend which many told me later was circulated widely via many of Colombo's old boys networks that share images that might be termed soft porn. The photos were paparazzi shots of a voluptuous young woman—obviously wealthy—and well dressed in revealing and flattering clothing. She was shown entering and leaving various venues accompanied by a retinue and in one shot waving to a photographer. She was

---

[48] Lateef Farouk, "Does Hijab Prevent Social Development," *Daily News*, May 11, 2015.

uniformly attired in low cut or strappy short dresses and high heels. After a series of images of this young woman the final slide states.

> Halal certified.
> Who is she?
> Princess Reem Al Waleed bin Talal of Saudi Arabia.
> No Burqa for her!!
> ... If she was in a Burqa, you would not have received this ... Be thankful for small mercies!

The middle class men consuming images of this young woman's body via social media were calling attention to Muslim hypocrisy by presenting the Saudi princess' non-*hijab* clad body as an "uncovered" Muslim female body. They were also asserting their own right to look at women's bodies for pleasure and celebrate the media's circulation of images of scantily clad and sexualized women thinly disguised as icons of female wealth and success. I draw attention to this set of images to illustrate once again the prevailing sexist and sexualized mainstream middle class culture in Sri Lanka which also drew from and participated in the anti-Muslim sentiment in circulation at that time.

So What?

I have argued so far, that the militarism that pervaded Sri Lanka's social and political worlds in the aftermath of the May 2009 end of the war against the LTTE influenced post-war nationalism and brought about a recalibration of gender orders within the country. I am arguing further that the Sinhala supremacist nationalist hate rhetoric against Muslims drew from and was formed by this discourse of militarism and for the purposes of this paper I have illustrated the gendered nature of the thus influenced rhetoric. I have also demonstrated the striking similarity between the BBS assertions and the Muslim response—both representing communal sensibilities that saw women as owned by the collective and defined by their sexuality and reproductive capacity.

I want to end with some speculation regarding what this means for women's solidarity and women organizing. As I have indicated in the analyses of both the Buddhist and Muslim rhetoric in relation to anti-Muslim sentiment, both have little space for entertaining ideas of women's solidarity.

162   F. HANIFFA

The stereotypes regarding women that are mobilized by both Muslim and Buddhist sets of representations and by representatives of the state celebrate archaic, obsolete and outmoded ideals about women and speak to the structural maintenance of gender hierarchies in what many Sri Lankans self identify as the south Asian country with the greatest freedom for women.

Women in the garment sector, the plantations and those who work as migrant labor form the base of the Sri Lankan economy. Women also have leadership positions in many professions and professional bodies, and the country's (male) diplomats often boast of having the world's first-ever woman prime minister and later, a woman president. Women constitute a majority of university-educated youth.[49] Every professional category in the country includes women and Sri Lanka boasts of the second highest ranking for the region in the Global Gender Gap index (at 79 out of 142, ten rankings behind Bangladesh who are ranked at 68).[50]

Several years into the emergence and spread of organized anti-Muslim sentiment in the country, there has been no substantive coming together of a strong women's voice in either the critique of the Bodu Bala Sena rhetoric or to question the very reductive response from Muslim interlocutors. Those who have looked at the issue with even a partially gendered lens have done so in ethnically specific terms. Chulani Kodikara's excellent piece calls attention to the BBS making statements about Sinhala women's fertility, and Qadri Ismail has pointed out the many problems that arise in instances where Muslim men police the actions of Muslim women.[51]

[49] In the 2012–2013 academic year alone out of total of 24198 admitted to the universities 14853 were women. From Sri Lanka University Statistics available at http://www.ugc.ac.lk/downloads/statistics/stat_2013/chapter2.pdf.

[50] As many have pointed out, however, the political participation of women remains abysmal at less than 5% in parliament and even lower in local government. This brings down Sri Lank as ranking in these indexes. The story about how women's lack of representation in parliament leads to but also stems from the prevalence of such gender stereotypes, and the manner in which it indexes a structural problem in the Sri Lankan society remains to be written.

[51] Ismail's intervention is problematic in that he attributes women's dress only to male policing and renders any choice that women may exercise in practicing Islamic dress absent. His analysis does not reference the immense literature on women's dress transformation either in Sri Lanka or elsewhere and speaks to a very problematic and reductive putatively ethical position on gender relations in Muslim communities embraced by many academics in Sri Lanka.

Neither calls attention to the fact that the BBS and the Muslim male discourse reflect derogatory ideas regarding women in general and are not specific to Sinhala or Muslim women alone.

Another issue that haunts the lack of feminist organizing around the BBS despite its very clearly gendered rhetoric is most active Sri Lankan feminists' (including those that identify as Muslim) mistrust of the *hijab*. Since the 1980s Muslim women's practice of the *hijab* has become institutionalized in the country. *Hijabs* are distributed by the state as part of the Muslim government school uniform. However, many "progressive" women's activists are skeptical regarding the "choice" that informs Muslim women's adoption of the dress and the difference from other women that Muslim women are thereby asserting.[52] While the *hijab* and *niqab* have both been practices that became common in the 1980s the *niqab* is arguably more prevalent today with many *niqab* clad women pursuing university education and public roles while maintaining their face cover.

The transformation of dress practices came with a movement and a project to transform the Muslim community toward stricter and more formalized religious practices. In many instances, women took the lead in propagating the practices among their "sisters." My own work has looked at one such women organizations, the Al Muslimaath, that led to many middle class Muslim families' transformations during the early days of the movements.[53] There has been no appreciation of the gendered impact of Muslims minoritized social and political existence and Muslim women seemingly differing to male authority are seen as "oppressed" with no room given for agency in making decisions regarding either their dress practices or their relationship with piety. They are especially not seen as participating in a different form of (minority) community. Saba Mahmood argues for an understanding of agency not exclusive to a liberal notion of personhood or indeed of "freedom." Unfortunately, feminist activism in Sri Lanka continues to inhabit this struggle. It is of course further exacerbated by dated male notions regarding women's roles (as described so far in the paper).

---

[52] Haniffa, 2005b; Mahmood, 2005; Farzana Haniffa, "Believing Women: Piety and Power Amongst Muslim Women in Contemporary Sri Lanka," *Islamic Reformism in South Asia* 42, no. 2 (2008): 347–375, *Modern Asian Studies*.

[53] Haniffa, 2011.

The piety movement-led transformation experienced by Sri Lankan Muslims during the conflict years has not been effectively communicated to ethnic and religious others and many stereotypes abound. Not just in terms of women's participation in the movement but the entire community's thirty-plus-year-old transformation is not well understood by either the scholarship or the progressive activist community. One of my feminist friends once told me that "the BBS are ok with the traditional Muslims. They are only against the fundamentalists." This feminist activist's remark invoking both problematic terms "traditional Muslim" and "fundamentalist" are part of a larger vocabulary shared by local civil society that includes the uncritical use of the term "radicalization." Such terms underscore the manner in which local discourses "know" the reality of Muslims in Sri Lanka—nearly two million strong—a large number of whom have committed to the self-transformation promised by the Islamic piety movement. The *hijab*-clad woman personifies this transformed Muslim community known through the above terms—radicalized, fundamentalist and so on. Additionally, evidence of community violence against Muslim women perceived to be transgressing moral codes that emerge from time to time from remote and war-affected areas of the country contribute to the idea of the backward Muslim.[54] The failure of Sri Lanka's "progressive" community including feminists, has been their inability to perceive these Muslim women's concerns and address them collectively.[55]

Under the Rajapaksas the latent racism and misogyny within Sri Lankan society found unprecedented public endorsement by Sinhala society's icons of authority—the sangha and the political leaders. This leadership claimed to speak about both women and minorities without letting representatives of either group on the podium. The minority Muslim (male) response has been to seek common cause with the monk's rhetoric through endorsing the monks' positions on women. The result is a complete erasure of women's perspectives.

[54] Haniffa, 2016.

[55] There have been local non-Muslim activists who have engaged with Muslim communities and participated in programs seeking to address Muslim concerns during the years when the BBS was at its most active. However, they have been in the minority and much of the work of documentation, engagement with the state and human rights activism has been carried out by Muslim activists. The issue of Muslim women has come up rarely other than in the ways outlined in this paper.

Women's speech in the public sphere—where women articulate political moral or ethical positions common to all—remains absented by this discourse. The complete dominance of nationalist public discourse by men with the assumption that they speak for all has silenced women institutionally and politically. Unfortunately, however, the Sri Lankan feminist movement that includes women of all ethnicities identifying with different religious faiths has not succeeded to date in finding a position from which it can critique the convergence of these misogynist discourses.

REFERENCES

Abeysekara, Ananda. *Colors of the Robe: Religion, Identity, and Difference.* Columbia: University of South Carolina Press, 2002.

Ashraff, Mohamed. "The Muslim Community and the Peace Accord." *Indo Sri Lanka Peace Accord, 29 July 1987, Comments, Reflections,* Special Issue of *Logos* 26 (1987): 48–76.

Bachetta, Paola. "Hindu Nationalist Women as Ideologues: The Sangh, the Samiti and Differential Concepts of the Hindu Nation." In *Communalising Women's Sexuality in South Asia,* edited by Kumari Jayawardena and Malathi De Alwis. Colombo: Social Scientists Association, 2004.

Butler, Judith. *Gender Trouble: Feminism and the Subversion of Identity.* London: Routledge, 1990.

De Alwis, Malathi. "Moral Mothers and Stalwart Sons: Reading Binaries in Times of War." In *The Women and War Reader,* edited by Lois Ann Lorentzen and Jennifer Turpin. New York: New York University Press, 1998.

De Mel, Neloufer. *Women and the Nation's Narrative: Gender and Nationalism in 20th Century Sri Lanka.* Lanham: Rowman and Littlefield, 2002.

Devasiri, Nirmal Ranjith. *Demalage Prashnaya: An Analytical Critique of the Sinhala Buddhist Nationalist Discourse on the Political Aspirations of Tamil People in Sri Lanka.* Colombo: Lakuna publishers, 2015.

Dharmapala, Anagarika. *Return to Righteousness.* Colombo: Government Press, Ceylon, 1965.

Enloe, Cynthia. *The Curious Feminist: Searching for Women in a New Age of Empire.* Berkeley: University of California Press, 2004.

Farouk, Lateef. "Does Hijab Prevent Social Development." *Daily News,* May 11, 2015.

Haniffa, Farzana. "Ethnic Conflict, Post-colonial Nation Building and Militarization." In *Militarising State Society and Culture in Asia: Critical Perspectives,* edited by J. Uyangoda. Hong Kong: ARENA, 2005a.

———. "Under Cover: Reflections on the Practice of *Hijab* Among Urban Muslim Women in Sri Lanka." In *Gender, Society and Change*. Colombo: Center for Women's Research, 2005b.

———. "Piety as Politics Amongst Muslim Women in Contemporary Sri Lanka." *Modern Asian Studies* 42, no. 2 (2008): 347–375.

———. *Three Attempts at Peace in Sri Lanka: A Critical Muslim Perspective Journal of Peacebuilding & Development* 6, no. 1 (2011): 49–62.

———. "Conflicted Solidarities? Muslims and the Constitution-making Process of 1970–72." In *The Sri Lankan Republic at Forty: Reflections on Constitutional History, Theory and Practice*, edited by Asanga Welikala. Colombo: Centre for Policy Alternatives, 2012.

———. "Who Gave These Fellows This Strength? Muslims and the Bodu Bala Sena in Post-war Sri Lanka." In *Sri Lanka: The Struggle for Peace in the Aftermath of War*, edited by Amarnath Amarasingham and Daniel Bass. London: Hurst, 2016.

———. "Merit Economies in Neoliberal Times: Halal Troubles in Contemporary Sri Lanka." In *Religion and the Morality of Markets*, edited by Daromir Rudnyckyj and Fillippo Osella. Cambridge: Cambridge University Press, 2017.

Heslop, Luke. "On Sacred Ground: The Political Performance of Religious Responsibility." *Contemporary South Asia* 22, no. 1 (2014): 21–36.

Ismail, Qadri. "On Not Knowing One's Place," 2014. ices.lk/wp-content/uploads/2014/.../On-Not-Knowing-One's-Place-Quadri-Ismail.pdf. Accessed March 19, 2018.

Kodikara, C. "Good Women and Bad Women of the Post-War Nation." *Groundviews*, May 22, 2014. http://groundviews.org/2014/05/22/good-women-and-bad-women-of-the-post-war-nation/.

Mahmood, Saba. *Politics of Piety: The Islamic Revival and the Feminist Subject*. Princeton: Princeton University Press, 2005.

Maunaguru, S. "Gendering Tamil Nationalism: The Construction of 'Woman' in Projects of Protest and Control." In *Unmaking the Nation: The Politics of Identity and History in Modern Sri Lanka*, edited by P. Jeganathan and Q. Ismail. Colombo: Social Scientists' Association, 1995.

Menon, K. *Everyday Nationalism: Women of the Hindu Right in India*. Philadelphia: University of Pennsylvania Press, 2012.

McGilvray, Dennis, and Raheem, Mirak. "Muslim Perspectives on the Sri Lankan Conflict". *Policy Studies* 41, (2007): 1–86.

Rajasingham-Senenayake, D. "Sri Lanka: Transformation in Legitimate Violence and Civil Military Relations." In *Coercion and Governance: The Declining Political Role of the Military in South Asia*, edited by Muthiah Alagappa. California: Stanford University Press, 2001.

Sarkar, Tanika. "Semiotics of Terror: Muslim Children and Women in Hindu Rashtra." *Economic and Political Weekly* 37, no. 28 (July 2002): 2872–2876.

Seneviratne, H.L. *The Work of Kings: The New Buddhism in Sri Lanka.* Chicago: University of Chicago Press, 1999.

———. "Buddhist Monks and Ethnic Politics: A War Zone in an Island Paradise." *Anthropology Today* 17, no. 2 (2001): 15–21.

Tambiah, Stanley J. *Buddhism Betrayed: Religion Politics and Violence in Sri Lanka.* Chicago: University of Chicago Press, 1992.

Thaheer, Minna. "Sri Lanka Muslim Congress: Politics of a Minority Ethnic Party." In *Formation of Muslim Ethnic Party in Contemporary Politics*, edited by Jayadeva Uyangoda and Amita Shastri. London: Oxford University Press, 2017.

Tillekeratne, Asanga. "The Role of Buddhist Monks in Resolving the Conflict." In *Buddhism Conflict and Violence in Modern Sri Lanka*, edited by Mahinda Deegalle. London: Routledge, 2006.

Uyangoda, Jayadeva. *Questions of Sri Lanka's Minority Rights.* Colombo: International Center for Ethnic Studies, 2001.

CHAPTER 6

A Corpse Necessitates Disentangled Relationships: Boundary Transgression and Boundary-Making in a Buddhist-Muslim Village in Southern Thailand

Ryoko Nishii

The primarily Theravada Buddhist area of mainland Southeast Asia (including Myanmar, Thailand, Laos, and Cambodia) and the primarily Sunni Islamic area of Insular Southeast Asia (including Malaysia, Indonesia, and Brunei) meet in Southern Thailand. As such, this border area provides many settings in which Muslims and Buddhists interact in everyday life.

According to Thai government statistics, Muslims account for 4.6% of Thailand's population. The remaining 94.6% are almost all Buddhists.[1] Concentrated in the four border provinces on the Malay Peninsula, two-thirds of Thai Muslims live in the south of Thailand. Here Muslims comprise 60–80% of the total population of each one of the four

[1] National Statistics Office, 2014.

R. Nishii (✉)
Research Institute for Languages and Cultures of Asia and Africa,
Tokyo University of Foreign Studies, Tokyo, Japan
e-mail: rnishii@aa.tufs.ac.jp

© The Author(s) 2020
I. Frydenlund and M. Jerryson (eds.),
Buddhist-Muslim Relations in a Theravada World,
https://doi.org/10.1007/978-981-32-9884-2_6

169

provinces. Tending to view Muslims as a minority group whose members speak a different language and possess a different culture, most studies of Muslims in Thailand have focused on the political problem of national integration in these four provinces. On the ground, however, it is clear that Muslims in Southern Thailand do not form a single coherent group. Two broad groupings can be distinguished. One is composed of Malay-speaking Muslims on the east coast, in Pattani, Narathiwat, and Yala provinces, where Islamic political movements are most active. The other comprises Thai-speaking Muslims who mainly live in Satun province on the west coast, where I studied, and in part of Songkhla on the east coast. In Satun, political problems involving Muslims are rare. The Thai government holds up Muslims who live in Satun as the model example of how Islam and Buddhism should co-exist.[2] In contrast to the unrest that has been brewing in Southern Thailand since 2004, violence in Satun remains rare.

This chapter will discuss Muslim–Buddhist relations in a village on the west coast in which the population is divided almost equally between Muslims and Buddhists who speak the same southern Thai dialect[3] (Figs. 6.1 and 6.2).

One salient feature of Muslim–Buddhist relations in this area is an extraordinarily high rate of intermarriage between Muslims and Buddhists. In my initial research, I found that 20% of marriages in the

---

[2] The upsurge of violence in Southern Thailand on the eastern coast began in January 2004 and has continued to date: 3500 died from January 2004 to June 2009: (*The Nation*, 5 June 2009); reported deaths to 2014, over 6000. Even so, no violence has been reported in Satun since 2004. Satun's distinctiveness has a historical background (Pitsuwan 1985; Satha-Anand 1987; Suwannathat-Pian 1988; Bajunid 1999). While Pattani was an Islamic kingdom, Satun is in a peripheral location, far from Kedah to the South. However, the term "four border provinces," used officially and in the press, does not distinguish Satun from the other three provinces of Pattani, Narathiwat and Yala. Since 2004, some media and academics have used the term "three southern provinces," excluding Satun when referring to southern Thailand's problem areas (Satha-Anand 1987; Saleh 2009; Hassarungsee et al., 2008). A NRC (National Reconciliation Committee, appointed by Prime Minister Thaksin in March 2005) report issued in June 2006 also referred to 3 instead of 4 provinces (NRC 2006). In June 2004, Deputy Prime Minister Chavalit proposed the creation of Maha Nakhon Pattani (Pattani Metropolis), which would extend to include Yala and Narathiwat, but not Satun (Funston 2009).

[3] My first fieldwork was conducted over 16 months between 1987 and 1988. Three subsequent two-month visits to the same village followed in 1989, 1991 and 1994. I re-visited several times for a short period from 1995 to 2019. Ethnographies are in my 2001 publication.

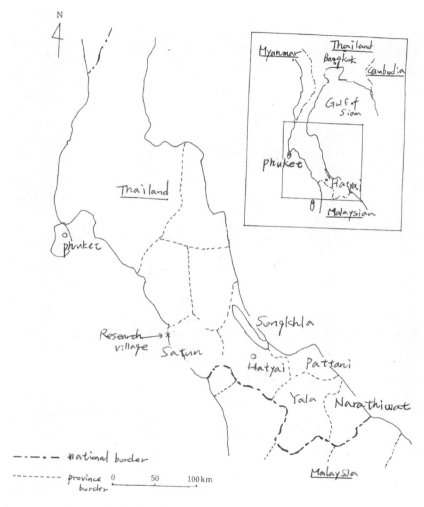

Fig. 6.1 Thai-Malaysian border

village were between Muslims and Buddhists, much higher than in other areas with mixed populations in nearby border provinces. In 1988, 33 of 159 marriages were Muslim–Buddhist and even in 1994 and 2014, respondents in the village reported that the rate of mixed marriages

172 R. NISHII

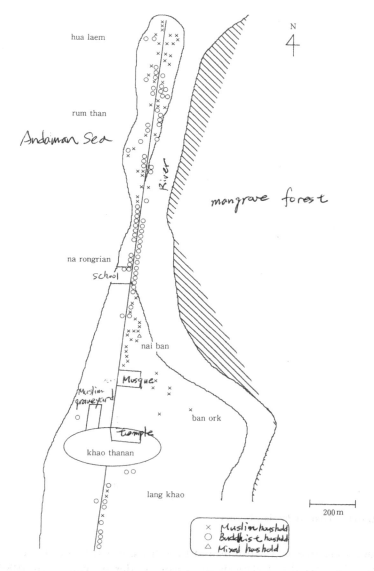

Fig. 6.2 Distribution of Muslim and Buddhist household in a research village (1988)

remained high. The latest research conducted in July 2019 supports these statements. The rate of mixed marriage increased to 30%; 38 of 126 marriages were Muslim–Buddhist. By contrast, in a study of a Malaysian village in the border area, Winzeler reported, that of 161 marriages, only five (3.1%) were inter-faith; Chavivun has also reported that in Pattani, on the east coast of Southern Thailand, intermarriage is rare.[4]

In Satun, it seems that borders between Muslims and Buddhists are easily crossed, that is, the boundary between Muslim and Buddhist identities is more fluid than elsewhere. As we shall see, Muslims and Buddhists convert to the other faith and often convert back.

This flexibility hardens, however, in attitudes and behavior toward corpses. The touching of those who are dead or dying seems critically significant in local Muslim–Buddhist relations. Indeed, religious converts in the villages often cite religious rules surrounding death as a reason for conversion, particularly those stipulating who is allowed to "touch [*torng*]" a deceased person. For example, Buddhists are prohibited from touching a Muslim corpse after it has undergone ritual washing in preparation for burial. Studying how people behave toward dead bodies provides valuable insight into local religious life as it is actually practiced.

To understand how demarcation emerges where there is shifting personal adherence to one faith or another, I will show how focusing on the body at the end of its social trajectory—the period following death, when the corpse may be claimed by either Muslims or Buddhists—can shed light on how religious distinctions can be maintained in an otherwise fluid situation. Consequently, I will examine how relationships demonstrated in daily life motivate decisions connected with death. This approach helps clarify the actual dynamics inherent in Muslim–Buddhist co-existence a Thai village where Muslims and Buddhists speak the same southern Thai language.

---

[4] Robert Winzeler, *Ethnic Relations in Kelantan* (Singapore: Oxford University Press, 1985), 116–117; Chavivun Prachuabmoh, "Ethnic Relations Among Thai, Thai Muslim and Chinese in South Thailand: Ethnicity and Interpersonal Interaction," in *Ethnicity and Interpersonal Integration*, ed. David Y.H. Wu (Maruzen Asia, 1982), 79–80.

EVERYDAY RELATIONSHIPS BETWEEN MUSLIMS AND BUDDHISTS

From the 1980s to the mid-1990s, Muslim villagers often drank alcohol, sometimes with their Buddhist neighbors. From the latter half of the 1990s, however, when Da'wa[5] missionaries started to frequently visit the village, several Muslims adopted the more pious Da'wa lifestyle.[6] This influenced other locally resident Muslims, most of who, moving the activity to the back, out of public view, stopped drinking at the front of their houses.[7]

At that time, religious differences were not an apparent source of tension between Muslims and Buddhists. Villagers of both faiths continued to customarily exchange sweets at religious festivals, and to interact at weddings and funerals. Muslims distribute sweets during the Hari Raya Haji and Buddhists at the Tenth Month Festival—the most important annual festival for southern Thai Buddhists.[8] Villagers of Chinese origin (primarily Buddhist) distribute sweets at the Chinese New Year. These sweets are all similarly based on coconut milk, sugar, and flour. Two or three variations are made for distribution. In 1994, one Buddhist woman told me that after getting sweets from Buddhists, Muslims then began, for the first time, making the same kinds of sweets. A survey I conducted in 1987 showed that 43 households out of 61 Muslim households distributed sweets to Buddhists, each household

---

[5] Numerous Da'wa organizations are currently active, including the Afmadiyya Mission in India, Darul Arqam in Malaysia, Hizbud Da'watil Islamiyya in Iraq, and Jama'at Islami in India and Pakistan. See Muhammad Khalid Masud, "Introduction," in *Travellers in Faith: Studies of the Tablighi Jama'at as a Transnational Movement for Faith Renewal*, ed. Muhamad Khalid Masud (Leiden: Brill, 2000), xxvi. In Thailand, the most widespread Da'wa movement is Tablighi Jama'at and this is the most influential in my research village. Rather than specifying this each time, I prefer to use "Da'wa," the word the villagers commonly use.

[6] I counted 12 of 131 male Muslim villagers over 10 years old to be involved in Da'wa activities in 2007.

[7] I reported Da'wa's transformation of the community in "Is a new community emerging? The futurity of the Da'wa movement in a west coast Southern Thai village," delivered to the panel "Futurity and Practice in Emerging and Transforming Communities," at the 10th International Conference on Thai Studies, Thaikhadi Institute, Thammasat University, January 9–11, 2008.

[8] The celebration occurs twice a year, on the 1st and 15th days of October in the Thai lunar calendar (September in the solar calendar), with the second celebration being larger in scale. On these occasions, villagers prepare a variety of snacks to take to the temple.

distributing, on average, to 16.8 Buddhist households on Muslim holidays. Sweet traffic also goes the other way: 28 Buddhist households distributed sweets at the Tenth Month, and 21 Buddhist households of perceived Chinese ancestry at the Chinese New Year, totaling 39 out of 72 households, each household giving, on average, to 15.7 Muslim households. The maximum number of households that a single household distributed to was 42, the least number was two.

Reciprocal exchange relationships were thus in evidence between two different types of households, Muslim and Buddhist, each giving gifts in turn. If one side failed to reciprocate, the relationship of exchange could be broken, but the expectation of return was not a rigid obligation: the relationship would not end just because a single turn was missed. It seems that three consecutive missed turns were regarded as signaling a lack of motivation to continue the relationship. In 1994, 39 Muslim households distributed to 24 Buddhist households, and 42 Buddhist households distributed to 22 Muslim households. At the end of the subsequent three-year period, while some form of relationship was maintained, six of the 39 formerly participating Muslim households had consistently failed to reciprocate Buddhist gifts of sweets. To maintain a level of intimacy, instead of giving sweets at their own festivals, several households donated ingredients for sweets at other religious festivals. Influenced by the Da'wa missionaries, some Muslims refused to eat Buddhist sweets. Coming into the 2000s, festival exchanges of sweets between Muslims and Buddhists had completely ended.

Muslim and Buddhist villagers still attend each others' funerals and marriages. For Muslim guests at Buddhist wedding feasts, chicken is served. At funerals, Muslims bury their dead within 24 hours and do not provide food to visitors. At Buddhist funerals, Buddhists treat visitors to food for five to ten days. That said, some Muslim families host ritual meals 40 days after the funeral (in the case of deceased males, 44 days later if the deceased was female).

In 1988, I attended a Muslim–Muslim wedding ceremony for a groom and bride who came from my research village. From the signed-in list of guests I ascertained that of 90 guests, 64 were villagers: 27 Muslim (42%), 36 Buddhist (56%), and one of unspecified faith. Meanwhile, in the same year, at a Buddhist–Buddhist wedding ceremony for a couple from the research village, among the 94 guests there were 51 villagers: 23 Muslims (45%), and 28 Buddhists (55%). The religious breakdown for guests from outside the village were, at the Muslim wedding:

20 Muslims (77%) out of 28; and at the Buddhist wedding, 35 Buddhists (81%) out of 43. The majority of non-village guests corresponded with the religious rites of the ceremony.

I also observed a Buddhist funeral in 1994: 223 people attended, including 93 villagers, 40 Muslims (43%), 52 Buddhists (56%), and one non-specified. The proportions almost matched the village Muslim:Buddhist ratio. Attendees from outside the village were only 15% Muslim. Clearly, something sets marriages and funerals apart from other events such as distributing sweets. Villagers have said that attending marriages and funerals is less about religion, and more about social relationships [*sangkhom*]. A Buddhist woman told me, "If they invite us to a funeral, next time they must be invited. We have to spend money at funerals. We have to make merit. We help each other. It is ugly [*na kliat*] if we do not help them, if we do not go while they help us." This shows a reciprocal relationship between households that transcends religion. Subordinating reciprocity to pursuing one's own interests is regarded as "ugly," a social ethic seemingly shared by both Muslims and Buddhists.

INTERMARRIAGES BETWEEN MUSLIMS AND BUDDHISTS

When villagers of different faiths intermarry, one will always convert. Converts still maintain, however, contact with their parents who, subsequent to marriage and conversion, are of a different religion. This contact can be very frequent and of practical convenience. For example, one Muslim–Buddhist convert left her children at her Muslim parents' house almost every day for childcare, showing that conversion did not imply radical changes in family relationships.

About 20% of marriages in the village I studied were between Muslims and Buddhists, as I have already mentioned, much higher than in other areas with mixed Muslim and Buddhist populations on the border provinces of Thailand and Malaysia. This village and adjacent areas on the west coast contrast with other places in the border region, where marriage is rarely accompanied by the conversion of the Muslim partner. Outside of this village, in the few cases I have managed to find conversion connected with intermarriage, the Buddhist partner always converted to Islam. Thus, in the frequency of intermarriage, and in the acceptance of conversion to and from each religion, this village and its neighbors on the west coast area are exceptional.

That said, the high rate of elopement of couples from mixed religious backgrounds can be attributed to barriers that still discourage intermarriage. The rate of marriage by elopement is 39.4% in Muslim–Buddhist marriages, contrasting with only 6.6% in Muslim–Muslim marriages, and 4.6% in Buddhist–Buddhist marriages. In the Thai idiom for elopement, "*ni tam kan pai*," *ni* means "run away," *tam* means "follow," *kan* means "together" and *pai* means "go." So, *ni tam kan pai* may be translated as "to run away together." One of the couples moves in with the other without permission from their parents, or they move and cohabit away from the village. Faced with the *fait accompli* of their child's elopement, most parents eventually accept the marriage.

I found 16 cases of conversion from Buddhism to Islam (5 grooms, 11 brides) and 19 cases from Islam to Buddhism (7 grooms, 12 brides), including two instances of double conversion (Islam to Buddhism, then Buddhism to Islam), among 33 cases of intermarriage in total in 1988 as I mentioned in the previous section. Intermarriage seems to remain frequent from respondents in my several fieldworks after the increasing influence of Da'wa piety on Muslim villagers. I found that one of the most zealous Da'wa activists had married a Buddhist woman, who converted to Islam upon marriage.

When the subject of intermarriage comes up, the stock phrase "*khao khaek*[9] *ao mia*," is often heard. It refers to superficially becoming Muslim for the purposes of taking a wife. It is rooted in the observation that most male converts from Buddhism to Islam do not pray regularly, go to the mosque, or abstain from alcohol and pork. For some reason, this kind of truism only seems to apply to male Buddhism-to-Islam converts. Other conversions—female converts and male-to-Buddhism converts—have not generated judgmental idioms: for example, male-to-Buddhism converts are simply described as, "*pen thai tam mia* [following one's spouse]."

After intermarriage between a Buddhist and a Muslim, the couple is assumed to be Buddhist. By contrast, official conversion to Islam occurs by explicitly declaring the *shahada* [words of faith], a positive act. If the Buddhist partner does not recite the words of faith, the Muslim partner

---

[9] In standard Thai, "khaek" means "guests" or "dark-skinned visitors" and is considered a pejorative label for Muslim (see also Bajunid, "The Muslims in Thailand; A Review," 222). Muslims in Satun, however, use *khaek* to describe themselves without the negative connotations, although they know it is considered insulting outside the village (see also Parks 2009, 12).

178　R. NISHII

is assumed to have converted. In the everyday context, however, villagers regard those who go to the mosque as Muslims and those who go to the temple as Buddhists.

The following cases are provided to illustrate conversion dynamics in more complex situations (Fig. 6.3).

Keeping Up Appearances as a Muslim

The following case concerns Win, a Muslim woman who converted to Buddhism.[10] Win's case spans more than 20 years. Born Muslim, Win married a Buddhist and moved to the same village as her parents-in-law. She was thus unable to attend mosque in her new village and did not feel like attending rituals in the village temple. She behaved like a Muslim, however, when she visited her parents' home in another province. Depending on the context, her identity oscillated between Muslims and Buddhists. Her elder son described his mother as having two minds [*cit*] and two hearts [*cai*]. Her children sometimes also utilized a dual identity. For example, as well as from temple events, they would get sweets from village festivals at the mosque. At school, however, they were required to declare an exclusive religious identity. Every morning, school children must recite sacred words depending on their religion. Muslim children recite Quranic verses with their palms up, while Buddhist children recite their devotion to Buddha, Dharma, and Sanga with their palms together. Win's children were initially undecided on which to recite.[11] Her older sons eventually recited Buddhist phrases, while her younger daughter recited Islamic verses. The daughter confided to me, "I was teased because I was a Muslim with Buddhist brothers". After oscillating between religions during the 20 years of her marriage with a Buddhist man, Win decisively converted to Buddhism only after her elder son married a Buddhist woman.

---

[10] All villager names in this paper are pseudonyms.

[11] Win has six children. The three eldest had already graduated by the time the youngest entered elementary school. Two sons and one daughter were commuting to the same school.

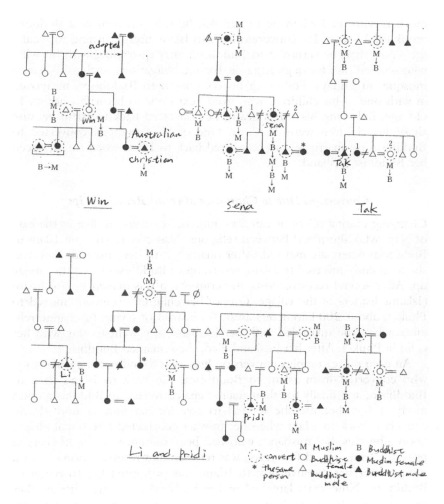

Fig. 6.3 Cases of conversion

Conversion in Order to Make Merit

The next case showcases the importance of merit-making for conversion. Keao was a Buddhist man, who became Muslim, then Buddhist, and who finally turned to Islam again. Keao converted to Islam to follow his wife's religion. Then, to conduct Buddhist ceremonies for his

180   R. NISHII

mother, who died when he turned 43, he was ordained as a Buddhist monk for 14 days. He converted back to Islam after returning to secular life. After that, he returned to Buddhism after quarreling with his wife, who scolded him for neglecting his Islamic obligations, such as to attend mosque on Fridays. Following his conversion to Buddhism, he moved in with one of his children, who lived next door to his wife's house. In old age, following his wife's death, he converted back to Islam because all of his children were Muslims. One of his daughters converted to Buddhism on marriage, but converted back to Islam when she divorced her Buddhist husband.

Conversion Due to Changing Marital Relationships

Changing marital relations can also influence conversion, like in the case of Nap, who alternated between religions. Nap converted from Islam to Buddhism when she married. After quarrels with her husband, however, she frequently reverted to Islam, returning to Buddhism when they made up. After several reconversions, her conversion was denied by the Imam (Islamic leader) of the village. One of her children eventually moved to Phuket, about 200 kilometers away. So instead of trying to change religions when she quarreled with her husband, she went to stay with her child in Phuket. After her husband died, she remained Buddhist.

An even more complex conversion history is found in Sena's life story, who converted from Islam to Buddhism, the back to Islam, then to Buddhism, and finally to Islam again. Sena converted to Buddhism upon marriage but, because she wanted to care for her mother until death, converted back to Islam when her mother contracted a terminal illness. Soon after this, her husband, who had been sentenced to eight years in prison, having served five years, was released and returned home. Just a month after her reconversion to Islam, this prompted her to revert to Buddhism. Nine years later, when her husband ran away with another woman, she returned to Islam.

SATSANA [Religion for Merit-Making] and *Phasa* [Religion as Practice]

Satsana is a religious term that refers to knowledge of *bun* [merit] and *bap* [sin]. Both Muslims and Buddhists believe that humans, unlike beasts, have this knowledge. *Phasa* is a religious term that refers

6 A CORPSE NECESSITATES DISENTANGLED RELATIONSHIPS ...   181

to practices specific to each religion. In standard Thai, *phasa* means "language" or "speech." In Southern Thailand, however, *phasa* is commonly understood as village custom [*prapheni*] or practice [*patibat*]. *Phasa khaek* and *phasa thai* respectively refer to Islamic and Buddhist practices. *Phasa* is used in this way to indicate religious distinction. Differences in *phasa* separate Muslim from Buddhist, excluding each from the other's rituals.

Both Muslims and Buddhists share the crucial terms for religious activities such as *bun* and *bap*. *Bun*, from *puñña* in Pali, means merit, virtue, and good deeds in the religious sense. *Bap* (*papa* in Pali) is the opposite: bad deeds and sin. These are central concepts in Buddhist ethics. Furthermore, both Buddhist and Muslim villagers say that religion [*satsana*] means to know *bun* and *bap* and that it is the "cornerstone of the heart [*yut niao citcai*]." Both also use the phrase "*tham di dai di, tham chua dai chua* [good deeds lead to good rewards or, what goes around, comes around]." As well as informing ideas of reasonable conduct in the village, this karmic reference is a central idea for Buddhists who desire a good rebirth.

Muslim and Buddhist ideas on the consequences of merit and sin may be compatible in the village. In conventional Islamic societies, the expression "*Inshallah* [If God wills it]" is often heard and is said to encapsulate the fatalistic attitudes of Muslims in Malaysia.[12] I do not recall, however, ever hearing these words spoken by the village Muslims, instead, they have adopted the Buddhist phrase, "*Tham di dai di, tham chua dai chua* [what goes around, comes around]" mentioned beforehand. One Muslim woman lost her parents when she was young and was taken in by her sister. When her sister's husband tried to rape her, however, she fled. Talking to her children, she said "I have had so much hardship in this world because I made little merit in a previous life". From my survey in 1994, 60% of village Buddhists and 65% of village Muslims believed that life events were influenced by karma from previous

---

[12] Brien K. Parkinson, "Non-Economic Factors in the Economic Retardation of the Rural Malays," *Modern Asian Studies* 1, no. 1 (1967): 31–40; Masuo Kuchiba, "Keda no Inasaku Noson Padanraran [Rural Village in Kedha]," in *Mare Noson no Kenkyu* [The Study on Malay Villages] (in Japanese), eds. Kuchiba Masuo, Yoshihiro Tsubouchi, and Narifumi Maeda (Sobunsha, 1976), 144.

182   R. NISHII

lives (responses from 48 Buddhists and 54 Muslims). Burr reported a similar tendency for Thai-speaking Muslims Songkhla in the 1970s.[13]

This shared belief of reincarnation is noteworthy because it contradicts Islamic doctrine. Thai-speaking Muslims in Burr and Onozawa's research area in Southern Thailand believed in *bun* and *bap* but rejected reincarnation.[14] Villagers held a diverse set of beliefs, and belief in reincarnation was not uniform in the village. 35% of Muslims said they would be reborn, 33% said they would not and 33% were unsure. Of the Buddhists, 51% said they would be reborn, 20% said they would not and 29% were unclear (1994 responses: Buddhists, 49; Muslims, 55).

Village Muslims are familiar with the Islamic "Day of Judgment." Some, however, combined it with reincarnation, claiming that rebirth was only for those whose merit/*bun* outweighs their sin/*bap*. That said, sins can be atoned for in purgatory, after which rebirth may be possible, with much merit being required for rebirth as a human.

Another interesting aspect relating to notions of rebirth, was the fact that villagers believed in rebirth across religious identification, again allowing for religious flexibility and cultural permeability (see Introduction, this volume). When Sao Dam, a Muslim woman who was very fond of pork died in her 30s, one Buddhist villager said to me, "Sao Dam is reborn as Nam Fon. Kui [Nam Fon's mother, a local Buddhist woman] said that Sao Dam came to her in a dream and said that God was reincarnating her within Kui. After several days, Kui noticed she was pregnant with Nam Fon. Nam Fon cries when Kui gossips about the late Sao Dam, supporting the idea that she is Sao Dam reborn. The point is that Sao Dam loved pork and sinned against no one, and so, as a reward, was able to reincarnate as a Buddhist with no dietary restrictions."

Muslims and Buddhists of the village earn merit for the deceased in different ways: *phasa khaek* [the Islamic way] and *phasa thai* [the Buddhist way]. *Phasa thai* methods include giving alms to monks, and

---

[13] A.M.R. Burr, "Buddhism, Islam and Spirit Beliefs and Practices and Their Social Correlates in Two Southern Thai Coastal Fishing Villages" (PhD dissertation, University of London, 1974), 94.

[14] Burr, "Buddhism, Islam and Spirit Beliefs and Practices and Their Social Correlates," 95; Masaki Onozawa, "Minami Tai Musurimu shakai no tsūka girei to kodomo kan [The Rites of Passage and Perspectives on Children in Southern Thailand]," in *Kodomo bunka no genzō* [Culture of Children] (in Japanese), ed. Iwata Keiji (NHK, 1985), 421.

6 A CORPSE NECESSITATES DISENTANGLED RELATIONSHIPS ...   183

suat nam, a ritual to send merit through water.[15] *Phasa khaek* involves *nuri*, or memorial feasts [Malay: *kenduri*]. The village's *nuri* is not orthodox. In most Islamic communities, it is impossible to send merit to individual deceased persons. While Malaysians do observe *kenduri arwah*, a memorial feast for the dead,[16] it is formally considered to be for all the deceased Muslims of the world.[17] In my research village, *nuri* were held at all religious occasions, including funerals, marriages, and circumcisions, as well as for sending merit to deceased individuals [*tham nuri*]. Burr has also reported that similar ritual feasts, called "*phithi tambun* [merit-making rituals]," took place in her fieldwork area.[18]

One ex-Muslim villager who converted to Buddhism told me that she dreamed of her late grandmother wanting to eat chicken curry, so she bought the ingredients and asked her Muslim mother to conduct a *tham nuri* for her grandmother. Although merit cannot be quantified, it is believed that they can surely make merit by *suat nam* for Buddhists, and *nuri* for Muslims.

Since *phasa* for the dead must correspond with the religion they followed in their lifetime, converts who wish to make merit for deceased of a different faith face a challenge. One solution is to use proxies. When they cannot themselves participate, Muslim converts may give money to their Buddhist parents for merit-making rituals. Following their parents' death, they may give money to relatives to make merit for their parents on their behalf.

Religion, and thus *phasa*, may also be changed right at the last moment, up to when death is impending. This involves "*kham phi* [a deathbed testament by which a dying person converts back to the former religion]" and then is later given the appropriate funeral. In most

---

[15] Keyes emphasized the importance of merit transference to social groups. See Charles F. Keyes, "Merit-Transference in the Kammic Theory of Popular Theravāda Buddhism," in *Karma: An Anthropological Inquiry*, eds. Charles F. Keyes and Errol Valentine Daniel (Berkeley: University of California Press, 1983), 283.

[16] Othman bin Salim, et al., *Kamusu Dewan Edisi Baru* (Kuala Lumpur: Dewan Bahasa dan Pustaka, 1989), 58.

[17] Masaki Nakazawa, who performed fieldwork in Kedah for several years from 1987, suggested this to me on 28 February 1997. Kuchiba's informants said the souls of ancestors came back at *kenduri aruwah* (Kuchiba, "Keda no Inasaku Noson Padanraran [Rural Village in Kedha]," 132).

[18] Burr, "Buddhism, Islam and Spirit Beliefs and Practices and Their Social Correlates," 96.

184 R. NISHII

cases of *kham phi*, seeking absolution for the sin of conversion, former Muslims enact such testaments.[19] This makes practical sense only when they have children who are Muslim and, thus, able to participate in the requisite Islamic rituals, which means that at least one of their children must be a Muslim convert. If all the children have been brought up as Buddhist in a Buddhist household, this can lead to complications for a dying parent who converted from Islam.

THE IMPORTANCE TO THE LIVING OF A CONVERT'S DEAD BODY

Next, I will describe an incident that illustrates the importance of the body for relationships between Muslim relatives and Buddhist relatives of a convert at the critical moment. Considering the incident, we can understand the significance of the corpse for relationships between the living and the dead. It becomes apparent that the central concern is the sometimes complex contention over who has the right, Muslim or Buddhist, to touch the corpse.[20]

Body Snatching

During my fourth short field trip in October 1994, a convert to Islam named Tak died at the age of 29. On the day before he died, he complained of a headache in the evening after playing football. Although he had been prone to headaches, his sudden death shocked everyone. Tak was a medical officer stationed at the public-health center, who had converted from Buddhism to Islam to follow the faith of his wife, a teacher of Islam. His death sparked a religious tussle over his corpse between his wife and his mother.

Tak died at four o'clock in the morning in an official lodging on the second floor of the elementary school where his wife Da was a teacher. When he died, only Da was with him. By the time Tak's relatives arrived, it was nearly nine o'clock, and Da had already begun preparing her

---

[19] Buddhists do not hold that conversion constitutes religious sin.

[20] I have previously analyzed this incident from the perspective of social memory in a Muslim–Buddhist co-resident area. See Ryoko Nishii, "Social Memory as It Emerges: A Consideration of the Death of a Young Convert on the West Coast in Southern Thailand," in *Cultural Crisis and Social Memory*, eds. Shigeharu Tanabe and Charles F. Keyes (London: Routledge Curzon, 2002).

husband's body for a Muslim burial. The first blood relative to get there was Tak's younger brother, Sit. Da told Sit that because she had already bathed the corpse in the Muslim way, non-Muslims could not touch the corpse. Sit persisted against her objections and pulled back the cloth that covered his elder brother's body. When Tak's father came, he asked Da to give Tak's corpse to Tak's mother. Tak's family felt entitled to ask for the body because Da and Tak had only been married for three years and had had no children. Da refused to give up the body. "I could not let them have his corpse," she said, "because he had converted to Islam and died as a Muslim. If I had let them take him away, I would have been committing a sin."

Faced with Da's resistance, Tak's Buddhist relatives resorted to a ruse. They said that a postmortem examination should be carried out at the hospital to determine the cause of death. Da was hesitant, but the relatives quickly removed Tak's corpse into a car. Da followed, bringing 4000 baht (equivalent to one month of her salary) for the examination. On the way to the hospital, however, the car came to an intersection and, instead of turning right toward the hospital, it turned left toward Tak's parents' house, where his body was carried inside. Da's Muslim relatives arrived too late to intervene because they lived further away than Tak's relatives.

For advice, Da consulted the Satun Provincial Islamic Committee, contacted a teacher at the Islamic school from which she had graduated, and phoned her uncle in Pattani. She was told, as a final resort, she could put the case before the Islamic court.[21] The Islamic teacher recommended, however, that she negotiate with the family instead. Members of the Provincial Islamic Committee went to Tak's mother's home to negotiate the return of the corpse, even though the week-long Buddhist funeral had already run half its course. Da's uncle in Pattani also telephoned the crematorium that had been booked for Tak's cremation, warning them that there would be consequences if they cremated the body of a Muslim. Despite these efforts, Tak's body was cremated on October 21, 1994, seven days after the corpse had been forcibly taken to his mother's home. After the cremation, both sets of relatives performed merit-making rites for Tak: his widow in the Islamic way and his mother according to Buddhist practice.

[21] In the four border provinces there are Islamic Courts to which Muslims have the right to petition a *kadi* [judge] concerning marital and property matters.

186   R. NISHII

The story of Tak's corpse highlights how differently the two religions deal with corpses. Generally, Muslims bury their dead and Buddhists cremate bodies. In Thai, this difference is implicit in the terms *tham khaek* [burial as a Muslim] and *tham thai* [cremation as a Buddhist]. Mutual exclusion makes it essential to determine the religious affiliation of the deceased.

In spite of numerous instances of religious appropriation, and boundary transgression, there villagers indicated limits to cultural and religious flexibility. For example, with regard to burial rituals, followers of either faith tend to take a dim view of the other's practices. Tak's mother said that Muslims do not even wait, as Buddhists do, for relatives to pay their last respects. Muslims contend that Buddhists leave the body lying in state until it starts to rot and smell. The differences in funerary practices clearly added volatility to the situation, and determined how those involved, as well as followers of different faiths, interpreted the events.

Nonetheless, more often than not, the bodies of converts are handled in a manner that reconciles competing religious demands. For example, a Muslim convert to Buddhism in his forties who died at about the same time as Tak, rather than undergoing Buddhist cremation, at his parents' request was buried with the consent of his Buddhist in-laws. For corpses that might be claimed by either religious camp, negotiations or consultations between affinal and blood relatives are required to reconcile differences. Tak's funeral, though an exception, shows us that different approaches to handling the dead can be a source of tension.

Official Records of Religious Affiliation

At Tak's death in 1994, no official documents—such as residence record, national ID card, or death certificate—recorded his religion.[22] According to an Islamic court judge in Satun, religious affiliation can only be determined from the death certificate section entry stating how the body is to be treated. In Tak's case, his body was cremated, which implies he was

---

[22]The 1983 act legislating national ID cards, *phraratchabanyat batpracamtua prachachon pho. so. 2526* (1983. *ratchakitcanuneksa lem 100 tornthi 62 long wanthi 20 mesayon 2526, krungthep: samnaklekhathikankhanaratmontri samnaknayokrathamontri.*) was revised in 1999 to require recording religious affiliation (*phraratchabanyat batpracamtua prachachon (chabap thi 2) pho. so. 2542* (1999. *ratchakitcanuneksa lem 116 tornthi 11 long wanthi 2 minakhom 2542, krungthep: samnaklekhathikankhanaratmontri samnaknayokrathamontri*).

not Muslim. The judge had to accept this conclusion even though he knew that Tak had converted to Islam by reciting the shahada. Evidently, funerary rites can settle disputes or uncertainties about a person's religious identity in the same way as a person's religious identity can determine the choice of funerary rites.

The judge suggested that if Tak had in any way certified his conversion to Islam, his true religious affiliation would be clear. Since similar situations seldom arise, few bother with this kind of certification, which does exist. The judge showed me one such certificate of conversion from Kamalun Mosque in Bangkok. It included a will describing how the convert's property and body were to be handled by the heirs.

The Important Relationship for Merit-Making

Tak and Da's childlessness was a factor in the events following his death. Tak's mother said that if they had produced a child who could make merit for Tak, she would not have taken his body away. Since Tak did not have children, and if his wife to remarry, there would be no-one to make merit for him. Both Muslims and Buddhists—even Tak's Buddhist relatives—agreed that the corpse should not have been taken if the couple had had a child. The couple's childlessness was seen as a legitimate reason for snatching the corpse.

After the Tak incident, a villager said, "Tak cannot go either way. His legs are torn in two directions; one toward Islam, the other toward Buddhism. He cannot get into either temple or mosque. We do not know how to make merit for him." Many other villagers, both Muslims and Buddhists, express the same notion using similar phrases.

The principle that husband and wife must be of the same religion is strongly associated with posthumous merit-making. Securing a means for transferring religious merit from the living to the dead requires maintaining relationships, most importantly between the deceased and their children. If parents were to be of different religions, it would cause complications and confusion for their children. This is avoided by insisting that both parents follow the same religion, and that children also follow the religion of their parents. One possible reason for the imperative that husband and wife follow the same religion is to ensure that their children are brought up in a single religion, thus securing a means of posthumous merit-making.

188   R. NISHII

After the critical moment of death, it can be said that touching the body establishes the link for merit transfer. Bearing this in mind, it is easier to understand why there is so much concern over whether a child is qualified to "touch" a deceased parent's body.

TRANSFERRING MERIT (AND SIN) BY TOUCHING THE BODY

As illustrated in the corpse snatching incident, converts frequently express concerns about being able to "touch [*torng*]" the bodies of deceased relatives. Here is another example, from my host family where, as mentioned previously the previously Muslim mother converted to Buddhism.

Win and her family hosted me during my initial fieldwork from 1987 to 1989. Although ostensibly Buddhist, she never cooked pork at home. When other family members wanted to eat pork, they cooked it across the street, at her son's house. One reason that she wavered between Islam and Buddhism for more than 20 years was that her mother was still alive. Win's daughter told me, "If we become Buddhists, we cannot touch grandmother's body. So we have to be Muslims." Win finally decided to be a Buddhist when her son married a Buddhist. He was also worried about not being able to touch his mother's corpse. Their conversation went roughly as follows:

> *Son*: "My mother decided to be a Buddhist because her children were Buddhists."
> *Win*: "Yes, that's right."
> *Son*: "I was worried that if she dies, where would we bury her body?"
> *Win*: "That's a difficult question. I don't want to be a bother."
> *Son*: "She should choose one [*phasa*]."
> *Win*: "If I am a Muslim, they won't be able to touch me when I die. If I am a Buddhist, they can do everything they need to."

Sena, the Muslim woman mentioned previously, explained why she returned to Islam while her husband was in prison by saying, "If I went back to being a Muslim, I could touch the body of my mother if she fell ill and died." In another instance of a woman converting back to Islam, this time after divorcing her Buddhist husband and re-marrying a Muslim, her mother joyfully told me that her daughter could now handle her body upon death. From these cases, we can see that the ability to touch or not touch becomes a rationale for ante mortem conversion and switching religion so as to handle a postmortem body. Those who deal with the dead can make merit by matching the *phasa*—religious way—of the dead with the *phasa* of the living, fulfilling their postmortem duties toward a relative.

For both Muslims and Buddhists in this southern Thai community, the conduit for transferring merit from the living to the dead can also carry sin. Consequently, during the period in which they handle a dead relative's corpse, surviving relatives (commonly the dead person's children) try to avoid sinful deeds and, thus, sin transference.

Such considerations may also motivate the rearrangement of relationships between the living. For example, Chok, a Muslim man, was involved for many years in an extramarital relationship with another Muslim's wife and continued their relationship without a proper religious marriage. Then, the husband of his mistress died in a traffic accident and, when his mother fell seriously ill, saying that he feared that if his mother were to die, through touch, he would transfer his sin to her, Chok decided to marry [*nikka*] his lover and make her his second wife (as permitted by Islam).

Ideally, the living will have only merit to transfer, and the ideal conduit for merit transfer is between children and their parents. These ideals are so ingrained that they galvanize the period surrounding death, and make children and parents very aware of their actions and their circumstances leading up to the moment when they come to touch the other's corpse and open the merit–sin conduit.

Concluding Remarks: Unpacking Entangled Relationships Embodied in a Corpse

The materiality of the body at death aligns surviving relatives in the premortem period. Touching the corpse serves to physically confirm the changed state and the altered materiality of the embodied person. The act of touching also confirms the continuity of relationship between the living and the dead. If the surviving relatives are both Muslim and Buddhist, however, as in the case of converts such as Tak, the materiality of the body may trigger conflict among parties who want to touch the body. And the prospect of diminishing the body's materiality, that is, how to dispose of the corpse, may also be a bone of contention. Li, a male convert from Buddhism to Islam, quarreled with his Buddhist mother about how to treat his body when he died. She insisted on Buddhist cremation because he had Buddhist children with his former Buddhist wife. Li lamented, "My body will vanish. It will be treated neither as a Muslim nor a Buddhist. I shall just disappear." I recorded Li talking to a relative in his mother's presence. He was suggesting that his mother substitute a photo for his body during the Buddhist ceremonies.

Relative: "If you die, do you want to be buried as a Muslim or Buddhist?"[23]

Li: "I want to be buried as a Muslim. She is looking at me. [His mother was indeed glaring at him]. I've had this photo taken to be used in the Buddhist ceremonies. You can bury[24] this photo. That's all right with me."

Li's mother said nothing through the conversation, but she clearly disapproved.

I also observed another convert from Buddhism to Islam, Pridi, discussing with his Muslim wife what he wanted to be done with his body. Like Li, he too proposed using a photo as a substitute for his body.

Pridi: "I want nothing to remain behind. Burn everything and get rid of the evil in the body. I don't want my children and grandchildren to pray for me. I do not want anyone bothered after I die. Forget me."

Author: "Does burning the body mean a Buddhist funeral?"

Wife: "Burning means the Buddhist way."

Pridi: "Not that."

Wife: "It is your own way, isn't it?"

Author: "Not bury, burn, but in neither an Islamic or Buddhist way. Is that what you mean?"

Wife: "Burn."

Pridi: "Just burn."

Wife: "Make everything disappear."

---

[23] Sometimes Buddhists of Chinese descent in this area—like Li—bury their dead, but in the Buddhist manner.

[24] While cremation is most usual for Buddhists in Thailand, burial used to be common among Chinese Buddhists and here, where I did my fieldwork, I did record a few instances of Buddhist burial.

Pridi: "Vanish and disappear."
Wife: "How will the children make merit for you?"

Pridi (after a thoughtful pause) "If you have a photo of me, keep it for the children. If they miss me they can look at it. Isn't that a good idea?"

Both converts suggested substituting photos to avoid conflict over their bodies. The reluctance of others to accept this may be connected with what Walter Benjamin called "aura loss." Through replication, images in photos lose the one-time-only immediacy of "here" and "now." Consequently, photographs are a poor alternative, they are an inadequate substitute for the body.[25] Lacking substantive materiality, since they can only serve as a reminder for relatives after death, photographs cannot enable the transfer of merit between the living and the dead. In the contexts above, however, suggesting a photograph stand-in may just be an expedient distraction, a way of avoiding dispute.

What this ethnographic study shows, is the local social contexts of boundary transgression—but also how religious lines come to be drawn—in the fluid situation of this border area on the periphery of Buddhist and Muslim states. One key to understanding is the actual bodies of converts, a locus of entanglement with affinal and blood relations, Muslim on one side and Buddhist on the other. At death, both sides may have exclusionary claims on the corpse. Here, it is useful to consider Marilyn Strathern's idea that a person actually comprises his or her relationships. After observing that "society" is a Western ethnocentric idea, she suggests that, "instead of trying to find the groups of which a person is a member, one would then consider what modeling of relationships the person him- or herself contain."[26] She notes that Melanesian relationships are intrinsic, not extrinsic to the person. One might say that relations animate the person. If relationships give a person life, then at death, along with life, what is extinguished are the relationships embodied by the deceased. As a singular person, one is an integral part of relations, and conversely, relations appear to be an integral part

---

[25] Walter Benjamin, *Fukusei Gijustu Jidai no Geijustu* [*Das Kunstwerk im Zeitalter seiner technischen Reproduzierbarkeit*] (in Japanese) (Tokyo: Kinokuniya Shoten, 1965), 50.

[26] Marilyn Strathern, "Parts and Wholes: Refiguring Relationship in a Post-plural World," in *Conceptualizing Society*, ed. Adam Kuper (London: Routledge, 1992), 81.

of a person.[27] So, following Strathern, we can assume that person of religious converts comprises relationships with Muslims and Buddhists that are ongoing in their lifetime.

At death, however, the relations comprised in the convert's body reach a crisis owing to differences in *phasa* (the way of merit-making). In his seminal work on anthropology at death, Robert Hertz emphasized the importance of the body at the point of death. He argued that the critical nature of the death transformation revealed the deepest ideals of villagers, which were also immanent in the ordinary course of living. The evolving relationships between dead and living matched the transformative process of decomposition.[28] Hertz only discussed the body after life in terms of the ritualistic process. My discussion shows how the body at the dead–dying transition importantly affects the world of the living.

Religious demarcation emerges owing the effect on relationships during the transformation of a body from living to dead. To the villagers, there is no substitute for the materiality of the body. The body alone enables us to feel this transition from life to death. In life, the body of the active person allows overlapping religious relationships. Passive in death, owing to rules about who may "touch" the body, the corpse does not allow vagueness: it belongs to one side or the other. This strict observance of how the dead body is treated contrasts with the flexibility of Muslim–Buddhist relationships in everyday life. Moreover, the necessity of proper respect for the body's materiality, so as to effectively open a conduit for merit to pass from the living to the dead at the time when life is closest to death, is literally a deadly serious matter. This perspective helps to clarify the actual dynamics inherent in Muslim–Buddhist co-existence in this southern Thai village where Muslims and Buddhists share notions of merit-making.

In closing, I would like to expand on Strathern's observation about relations appearing as an integral part of persons: relations, along with the materiality of the body, are integral parts of persons. Our lives emerge in the intercourse of relations, materials, imagination, and ideas. In the dynamic process of life, by switching affiliation, the Muslim–Buddhist converts described here, in their animated bodies, clearly have intertwined their lives and their imaginations with neighbors of a

---

[27] Strathern, "Parts and Wholes: Refiguring Relationship in a Post-plural World," 83–84.

[28] Robert Hertz, "Contribution à une étude sur la représentation collective de la mort," *L'Année sociologique* 10 (1907): 48–137.

different religion. They may be easygoing about crossing religious borders, but ultimately—in the case of death—they have to draw a line.

REFERENCES

Benjamin, Walter. *Fukusei Gijustu Jidai no Geijustu* [*Das Kunstwerk im Zeitalter seiner technischen Reproduzierbarkeit*] (in Japanese). Tokyo: Kinokuniya Shoten, 1965.

Bourdieu, Pierre. *Outline of a Theory of Practice*. Cambridge: Cambridge University Press, 1977.

Burr, Angela M.R. "Buddhism, Islam and Spirit Beliefs and Practices and Their Social Correlates in Two Southern Thai Coastal Fishing Villages." PhD dissertation, University of London, 1974.

Farouk Bajunid, Omar. "The Muslims in Thailand; A Review." *Southeast Asian Studies* 37, no. 2 (1999): 210–234.

Funston, John. "Governance in the South: Is Decentralization an Option?" In *Divided Over Thaksin: Thailand's Coup and Problematic Transition*, edited by John Funston, 124–134. Singapore: Institute of Southeast Asian Studies, 2009.

Hassarungsee, Ranee, Chittpapat Batphrakhon, and Ekkarin Tuansiri. *Building Peace and People's Security in Southeast Asia: Case Study on the Three Southern Provinces of Thailand*. Social Agenda Working Group, Social Research Institute, Chulalongkorn University, 2008.

Hertz, Robert. "Contribution à une étude sur la représentation collective de la mort." *L'Année sociologique* 10, (1907): 48–137.

Janchitfah, Supara. *Violence in the Mist: Reporting on the Presence of Pain in Southern Thailand*. Bangkok: Kobfai Publishing Project, 2004.

Keyes, Charles F. "Merit-Transference in the Kammic Theory of Popular Theravāda Buddhism." In *Karma: An Anthropological Inquiry*, edited by Charles F. Keys and Errol Valentine Daniel, 261–285. Berkeley: University of California Press, 1983.

Kuchiba, Masuo. "Keda no Inasaku Noson Padanraran [Rural Village in Kedha]." In *Mare Noson no Kenkyu* [The Study on Malay villages] (in Japanese), edited by Kuchiba Masuo, Yoshihiro Tsubouchi, and Narifumi Maeda, 21–160. Tokyo: Sobunsha, 1976.

Masud, Muhammad Khalid. "Introduction." In *Travellers in Faith: Studies of the Tablighi Jama'at as a Transnational Movement for Faith Renewal*, edited by Muhamad Khalid Masud, viii–lx. Leiden: Brill, 2000.

Nishii, Ryoko. *Shi o meguru Jissen Shuukyou* [Death and Practical Religion: Perspectives on Muslim–Buddhist Relationship in Southern Thailand] (in Japanese). Kyoto: Sekai Shisosha, 2001.

194   R. NISHII

————. "Social Memory as it Emerges: A Consideration of the Death of a Young Convert on the West Coast in Southern Thailand." In *Cultural Crisis and Social Memory*, edited by Shigeharu Tanabe and Charles F. Keyes, 231–242. London: Routledge Curzon, 2002.

NRC. *Report of National Reconciliation Commission: Overcoming Violence Through the Power of Reconciliation: Executive Summary*. Bangkok: The National Reconciliation Commission, 2006.

Onozawa, Masaki. "Minami Tai Musurimu shakai no tsūka girei to kodomo kan [The Rites of Passage and Perspectives on Children in Southern Thailand]." In *Kodomo bunka no genzō* [Culture of Children] (in Japanese), edited by Iwata Keiji, 404–422. Tokyo: NHK, 1985.

Parkinson, Brien K. "Non-Economic Factors in the Economic Retardation of the Rural Malays." *Modern Asian Studies* 1, no. 1 (1967): 31–46.

Parks, Thomas I. "Maintaining Peace in a Neighborhood Torn by Separatism: The Case of Satun Province in Southern Thailand." *Small Wars and Insurgencies* 20, no. 1 (2009): 185–202.

Pitsuwan, Surin. *Islam and Malay Nationalism: A Case Study of the Malay-Muslims of Southern Thailand*. Bangkok: Thai Khadi Research Institute, Thammasat University, 1985.

Prachuabmoh, Chavivun. "Ethnic Relations Among Thai, Thai Muslim and Chinese in South Thailand: Ethnicity and Interpersonal Interaction." In *Ethnicity and Interpersonal Integration*, edited by David Y.H. Wu, 63–83. Singapore: Maruzen Asia, 1982.

Saleh, Rattiya. "New Relations: Buddhists and Muslims in the Three Southernmost Provinces." In *Imagined Land? The State and Southern Violence in Thailand*, edited by Chaiwat Satha-Anand, 145–164. Fuchu City, Japan: Research Institute for Languages and Cultures of Asia and Africa, Tokyo University of Foreign Studies, 2009.

Salim, Othman bin, et al. *Kamusu Dewan Edisi Baru*. Kuala Lumpur: Dewan Bahasa dan Pustaka, 1989.

Satha-Anand, Chaiwat. *Islam and Violence: A Case Study of Violent Events in the Four Southern Provinces, Thailand, 1976–1981* (USF Monographs in Religion and Public Policy). Tampa, FL: University of South Florida, 1987.

————. "Introduction: Imagined Land? The State and Southern Violence in Thailand." In *Imagined Land? The State and Southern Violence in Thailand*, edited by Chaiwat Satha-Anand, 1–15. Fuchu City, Japan: Research Institute for Languages and Cultures of Asia and Africa, Tokyo University of Foreign Studies, 2009.

Strathern, Marilyn. "Parts and Wholes: Refiguring Relationship in a Post-plural World." In *Conceptualizing Society*, edited by Adam Kuper, 75–104. London: Routledge, 1992.

Suwannathat-Pian, Kokbua. *Thai-Malay Relations: Traditional Intra-Regional Relations from the Seventeenth to the Early Twentieth Centuries.* Singapore: Oxford University Press, 1988.

Uchibori, Motomitsu. "An Institution Called Death: Toward Its Arche." In *Institutions,* edited by Kaori Kawai Kyoto, 39–58. Melbourne: Kyoto University Press, Trans Pacific Press, 2017.

Uchibori, Motomitsu, and Shinji Yamashita. *Shi no Jinruigaku* [Anthropology of Death] (in Japanese). Tokyo: Kobundo, 1986.

Winzeler, Robert. *Ethnic Relations in Kelantan.* Singapore: Oxford University Press, 1985.

CHAPTER 7

The Role of Myth in Anti-Muslim Buddhist Nationalism in Myanmar

Nyi Nyi Kyaw

INTRODUCTION

This chapter highlights the role of myth in the emergence and re-emergence of the colonial-era myth of deracination that provides a potent scheme of meaning and interpretation to Buddhist nationalism in Myanmar. It contributes to the bourgeoning literature that looks at the contemporary aspects of anti-Muslim violence along the bumpy road of political and social changes in Myanmar since 2010. Taking a historical perspective and engaging with the literature on the myth, this chapter provides a discussion of an often-overlooked role of the myth of deracination that prophesizes a demographic and religious doomsday for the Myanmar Buddhist race. It also shows how the myth that initially targeted Hindu and Muslim Indian migrants to colonial Burma in the

---

I am grateful to Matthew Walton for presenting the previous version of this chapter on my behalf at Asian Studies Association 2016 Annual Conference on March 31–April 3, 2016 in Seattle and providing helpful comments.

N. N. Kyaw (✉)
Myanmar Studies Programme, ISEAS – Yusof Ishak Institute, Singapore

© The Author(s) 2020
I. Frydenlund and M. Jerryson (eds.),
Buddhist-Muslim Relations in a Theravada World,
https://doi.org/10.1007/978-981-32-9884-2_7

nineteenth and twentieth centuries later transformed into a full-blown Islamophobia against Muslims alone especially from the 1990s onwards.

Myanmar is a predominantly Buddhist country whereas Muslims are both a numerical and socio-political minority. The 2014 census only enumerated Muslims in areas outside Rakhine State. The Rohingya together with the Kaman[1] and a few other mixed Muslims reside in Rakhine State. It only recorded 28,731 Muslims in Rakhine State most, if not all, of whom must have been the Kaman estimated between 50,000 and 100,000. 1,090,000 Rohingya almost all of whom are expected to be Muslims were not included but estimated. Therefore, according to the data released on July 21, 2016, it recorded 1,147,495 Muslims who constituted 2.3% of the total population. After including 1,090,000 Rohingya Muslims not counted in the census, the percentage of Muslims stood at 4.3% of the national population. Compared to the percentages reported by the 1973 and 1983 censuses—3.9% in both— that of Muslims in Myanmar nowadays show a negligible increase.[2]

In the aftermath of the much-applauded transition to "democracy"[3] in Myanmar in 2011, this Southeast Asian country faced the most serious communal violence in its history since independence which occurred twice in Rakhine State, in June and October 2012, and then spread to Meiktila (March 2013), Okkan (April 2013), Lashio

---

[1] The Kaman are the *only* predominantly Muslim ethnic group that is recognized by the government as one of 135 national races and also resides in Rakhine State. For the politics of ethnicity surrounding the Kaman, see Nyi Nyi Kyaw, "Myanmar's Other Muslims: The Case of the Kaman," in *Citizenship in Myanmar: Ways of Being In and From Burma*, ed. Ashley South and Marie Lall (Singapore: Institute of Southeast Asian Studies, 2018), 279–300.

[2] Department of Population, Ministry of Labour, Immigration and Population, "The 2014 Myanmar Population and Housing Census. The Union Report: Religion, Census Report Volume 2-C" (Nay Pyi Taw, July 2016).

[3] Given the continued dominance of the military in politics, whether Myanmar transitioned to democracy even according to the minimalist definition of democracy as electoral democracy (Przeworski 1999) is open to question. Several edited volumes have dealt with the nature, content, and extent of Myanmar's so-called transition in its early years. See, for example, Nick Cheesman, Monique Skidmore, and Trevor Wilson, eds., *Myanmar's Transition: Openings, Obstacles, and Opportunities* (Singapore: Institute of Southeast Asian Studies, 2012); Nick Cheesman, Nicholas Farrelly, and Trevor Wilson, eds., *Debating Democratization in Myanmar* (Singapore: Institute of Southeast Asian Studies, 2014); David Steinberg, ed., *Myanmar: The Dynamics of an Evolving Polity* (Boulder, CO: Lynne Rienner, 2014).

(May 2013), Kanbalu (August 2013), Thandwe (September and October 2013), Hlegu (April 2014), and Mandalay (July 2014). It posed a serious challenge to this newly "democratizing" country given its political and social volatility and fragility, now compounded by religious tensions. Hundreds of human lives and thousands of properties were lost or destroyed. Although these conflicts are often depicted as sectarian or inter-communal as they involved both Muslims and Buddhists, it is more commonly understood to be anti-Muslim because Muslims are a demographic minority and possess little or no political representation or leverage in predominantly Buddhist Myanmar. However, Buddhist nationalist monks and their supporters within Myanmar strongly claim that it is Islam and Muslims who posed a grave threat to Buddhism and Buddhists in the first place and that if they are not prevented at all costs, Buddhism and the Buddhist race of Myanmar will vanish sooner or later. They clamoured that Muslims must be further alienated, excluded from political life, discriminated, and securitized.[4]

That neither the Union Solidarity and Development Party (USDP) nor the National League for Democracy party (NLD)—the two largest political parties in Myanmar—chose Muslims as candidates to contest the November 2015 elections proved the unprecedented political exclusion or lack of political representation of Myanmar's Muslims and provided strong evidence of the success of the anti-Muslim narrative of Buddhist nationalists, unlike in the previous elections held in the country.

By tracing that myth of deracination in Myanmar, this chapter argues that one of the underlying causes of anti-Muslim Buddhist nationalism in Myanmar, either violent or non-violent, is that the myth which emerged in response to political, social, and economic pressures under British colonization has persisted into the twenty-first century and contributed to widespread anti-Muslim sentiments and violence.

THE BACKGROUND

Communal conflicts are not new to Myanmar. Indeed, it faced serious anti-Indian riots in 1930 and 1938, with the latter being more anti-Indian Muslim or anti-Muslim by nature. While economic hardships

---

[4] Nyi Nyi Kyaw, "Alienation, Discrimination, and Securitization: Legal Personhood and Cultural Personhood of Muslims in Myanmar," *Review of Faith & International Affairs* 13, no. 4 (2015): 50–59.

due to the Depression and more intense competition for jobs between Burmese and Indians in then Rangoon sparked the 1930 riots, the publication of an anti-Buddhist book by a Muslim author was the trigger or at least one of the key triggers for those in 1938 amidst rising anti-Muslim nationalist sentiments. In other words, the 1930 anti-Indian riots were more communal by nature as they targeted all Indians regardless of their religious orientations whereas the 1938 ones were more religious because they were mainly between Buddhists and Muslims. Also, although equally serious anti-Chinese riots erupted in 1967, no similar disturbances have occurred since. During the period of more than eighty years from the 1930s until today, smaller-scale anti-Muslim riots have taken place, with rather serious ones in Taunggyi and Pyay in 1988, Mandalay in 1997, and Sittwe, Taungoo, Pyay, and Bago in 2001. Political context in which those conflicts broke out is interesting: the Taunggyi and Pyay riots broke out in the midst of anti-socialism protests by students and people; the Mandalay disturbance happened again amidst increasing monastic anger caused by the alleged damage to the belly of the Mahamuni Buddha Image; and the Sittwe, Taungoo, Pyay, and Bago violence was broadly incited by the destruction by the Taliban of the Buddhas of Bamiyan.[5]

As seen above, all the riots, especially those from the 1990s onwards, share the common script of the occurrence of a "perfect" triggering event. Most common alleged triggers include rape, sexual harassment of Buddhist women by Muslim men, forced conversion to Islam of a Buddhist woman after her intermarriage with a Muslim man, and blasphemy of Buddhism by a Muslim man or woman. The triggers are usually followed by an angry Buddhist mob usually joined by monks who would gather and burn Muslim houses and mosques, and often commit murder. All these denote the predominant view of using agency—whether it is focussed upon who triggered the violence or upon who acted upon the trigger against Muslims—in explaining religious or religiously oriented violence in Myanmar over the past thirty years.

On the other hand, commonly highlighted structural causes of the recent anti-Muslim violence in Myanmar include, but are not limited to, Myanmar's nascent democratization, which began in 2011, freer print

---

[5]Images Asia, *Report on the Situation for Muslims in Burma* (Bangkok: Images Asia, 1997); Human Rights Watch, *Crackdown on Burmese Muslims* (Washington, DC: Human Rights Watch, 2002).

media, unbridled social media (mainly Facebook) and the weak or ineffective rule of law. All these structural explanations are undeniably causal to a certain extent, but they largely and effectively omit agency and seemingly absolve the people who engaged in violence and the authorities who failed to proactively prevent or promptly deal with violent episodes and enforce the rule of law.

Unlike structural accounts, the instrumental role of inciters—most prominently Buddhist nationalist monks and lay extremists—as well as that of relevant authorities who failed to manage and contain the outbreak and spread, in provoking and stoking various communal disturbances is often assumed as the sole cause. However, even when a historically rooted argument originating from colonial times which highlights hatred of Muslims is included, this explanation seems insufficient. Although it is undeniable that Indians—particularly Indian Muslims—were widely hated in colonial Burma, we are now in the twenty-first century, approximately seven decades later.

A prominent theory often resorted to explain the occurrence of religious or religiously motivated violence is the theory of scapegoating that claims that Muslims are "used" as scapegoats in politics by those with power.[6] However, this scapegoating theory does not answer why Muslims are—almost always—successfully scapegoated.

Therefore, one is bound to wonder why Muslims are still obviously hated in Myanmar, at least by inciters and angry mobs.[7] Even when inciters are considered the major cause, what has been offered is mainly conspiracy theories pointing to *invisible* masterminds or "hidden hands"[8] behind them whose alleged agenda is to backtrack and revive military dictatorship. Then, one also starts wondering why these masterminds and inciters have been generally successful in inciting mobs to

---

[6] Gerry van Klinken and Su Mon Thazin Aung, "The Contentious Politics of Anti-Muslim Scapegoating in Myanmar," *Journal of Contemporary Asia* 47, no. 3 (2017): 353–375; Gerard McCarthy and Jacqueline Menager, "Gendered Rumours and the Muslim Scapegoat in Myanmar's Transition," *Journal of Contemporary Asia* 47, no. 3 (2017): 396–412.

[7] The term 'angry mobs' or, in Burmese, 'Daw-tha-twet-ne-tè Lu-ôk-kyi', featured prominently in local media's representations of communal violence from 2012 through 2015 in Myanmar, seemingly to condone religiously motivated mobbish vandalism largely targeting Muslim properties and religious buildings.

[8] Justice Trust, *Hidden Hands Behind Communal Violence in Myanmar: Case Study of the Mandalay Riots* (New York: Justice Trust, 2015).

202 N. N. KYAW

engage in riots by constructing an anti-Buddhist narrative out of a single criminal event allegedly committed by a Muslim. We then find ourselves in serious need of understanding the schemas of reference and narrative practices used by those masterminds, inciters and their followers.

Especially during and after the Rakhine violence in 2012, clamorous voices were repeatedly evident on social media sites, mainly Facebook, declaring that the Bamar[9] race and Buddhism were under siege by Rohingya or Bengali[10] infiltrators who, within Myanmar, are largely assumed to be illegal immigrants from neighboring Bangladesh. Interestingly amidst online and offline hate campaigns against the Rohingya and all Myanmar Muslims in general,[11] the well-known anti-Muslim tracts or books also (re)-emerged and widely shared on Burmese-language websites, blogs, and social media.

I will introduce the argument through two sections: the first section discusses the myth and theorizes when myths emerge; and the second traces the emergence of the myth of deracination in the twentieth century and its persistence until today.

MYTH

Once one hears or reads the word "myth," what immediately comes to mind is that it means the opposite to reality, as reflected in both quotidian language and academia. In contemporary understanding, myth constitutes the antithesis of reality[12] whose philosophical root says

[9] "Bamar" is used to refer to the majority ethnic community who are predominantly Buddhist whereas Burmese to the civic identity representing all peoples of Myanmar and to the official language of the country as well. Burma and Myanmar are interchangeably used. However, as the English term "Burman" has usually been used to refer to Bamar, especially in colonial times, it is also used in this chapter in quotations.

[10] The term "Rohingya" is fiercely rejected in Myanmar today. Instead, "Bengali" is used by the Myanmar government and people to refer to the group of people who are predominantly Muslim and concentrated in northern Rakhine State. Both Rohingya and Bengali are interchangeably used because a discussion of the origins of the two terms is beyond the scope of this chapter.

[11] Nyi Nyi Kyaw, "Alienation;" Nyi Nyi Kyaw, "Islamophobia in Buddhist Myanmar: The 969 Movement and Anti-Muslim Violence," in *Islam and the State in Myanmar: Muslim–Buddhist Relations and the Politics of Belonging*, ed. Melissa Crouch (New Delhi: Oxford University Press, 2016), 183–210.

[12] The other common meaning of a myth is its antiquity which is the first thought of the ordinary layperson when he or she hears the word 'myth' and is most probably associated with well-known Greek mythologies.

otherwise. Myth or *mythos* was not conceptualized as such at its entry into vernacular and/or academic vocabulary; *mythos* only meant "word" or "speech" whose meaning was later carried by *logos*.[13]

The view of myth as unrealistic or illogical is even found in anthropology which supposedly studies cultures in depth[14] whereas the view is widely shared among political scientists as well.[15] Even in a widely read paper that highlights the adverse effect of nationalist mythmaking in transitional societies, Snyder and Ballentine define myths as "assertions that would lose credibility if their claim to a basis in fact or logic were exposed to rigorous, disinterested public evaluation" because they obviously aim to pinpoint elites' mythmaking "to mobilize support for nationalist doctrines or to discredit opponents."[16] A Human Rights Watch report[17] that studies communal violence in ten countries or territories including Rwanda, India and Sri Lanka also pinpoints the role of governments and elites in stoking and worsening pre-existing communal tensions. All these view a nationalist myth as some created or constructed script that leaves itself subject to manipulation and misuse by scheming politicians for their own political advantage. In other words, elite agency takes precedence not only over the myth and its content but also over the role of followers who act upon incitation. It simply neglects the fact that a myth—however half-baked, scripted, dubious, fantastic or illogical it is in the eyes of the self-proclaimed *logical* social scientist—holds potent power to incite emotion and stimulate behavior.

Nevertheless, there is an alternative theory of the myth as a story or narrative and its social and political effect. In this view, a myth is "an ideologically marked narrative which purports to give a true account of a set of past, present, or predicted political events and which is *accepted*

[13] Chiara Bottici, *A Philosophy of Political Myth* (New York: Cambridge University Press, 2007), 20.

[14] Joanna Overing, "The Role of Myth: An Anthropological Perspective, or: 'The Reality of the Really Made-Up'," in *Myths and Nationhood*, eds. Geoffrey Hosking and George Schöpflin (New York: Routledge, 1997), 1–18.

[15] Chiara Bottici and Benoit Challand, "Rethinking Political Myth: The Clash of Civilizations as a Self-Fulfilling Prophecy," *European Journal of Social Theory* 9, no. 3 (2006): 315–336.

[16] Jack Snyder and Karen Ballentine, "Nationalism and the Marketplace of Ideas," *International Security* 21, no. 2 (1996): 5–40, 10.

[17] Human Rights Watch, *Playing the "Communal Card": Communal Violence and Human Rights* (New York: Human Rights Watch, 1995).

as valid in its essentials by a social group" (Italics in original).[18] Likewise, Charteris-Black claims that myths provide narratives of "angels" versus "demons" to a *particular* collective community which are "evocative … [of] emotions such as sadness, happiness and fear" (Italics in original).[19] The story or narrative content of a myth furnishes its believers—a collective group—with "an account of the past and the future in light of which the present can be understood."[20] Hence, a myth provides an "explanatory thesis that presupposes a simple causal theory of political events and enjoys wide public support."[21] For a social group, a myth constitutes "*reality postulates* about the world" or "a *moral universe of meaning*" (Italics in original).[22] Some myths, especially nationalist myths, may have some questionable, if not completely falsifiable, content or truth-claims and thus not pass the test of a rigorous, objective fact-check. But, that relative truth quality of myths does not prevent nationalist myths from possessing "cognitive" and "affective" powers for the leader(s) and ordinary members of a nation.[23]

Arguably the most potent type of myth, a nationalist myth is "a story that simplifies, dramatizes and selectively narrates the story of a nation's past and its place in the world, its historical eschatology: a story that elucidates its contemporary meaning through (re)constructing its past."[24] A nationalist myth may therefore be conceptualized as a "national mythscape" or "the discursive realm, constituted by and through temporal and spatial dimensions, in which the myths of the nation are forged, transmitted, reconstructed and negotiated constantly."[25] Nationalist myths are concerned with the past, present, and future on the one hand and

---

[18] Christopher Flood, *Political Myth: A Theoretical Introduction* (New York: Garland, 1996), 44.

[19] Jonathan Charteris-Black, *Politicians and Rhetoric: The Persuasive Power of Metaphor*, 2nd ed. (Houndmills, Basingstoke, Hampshire and New York: Palgrave Macmillan, 2011), 22.

[20] Henry Tudor, *Political Myth* (London: Pall Mall Press, 1972), 13.

[21] Michael Geis, *The Language of Politics* (New York: Springer-Verlag, 1987), 29.

[22] Overing, "The Role of Myth," 12.

[23] David Archard, "Myths, Lies and Historical Truth: A Defence of Nationalism," *Political Studies* 43, no. 3 (1995): 472–481.

[24] Duncan S.A. Bell, "Mythscapes: Memory, Mythology, and National Identity," *British Journal of Sociology* 54, no. 1 (2003): 63–81, 75.

[25] Bell, "Mythscapes," 75.

with territory on the other hand—the latter has become increasingly important for contemporary nationalism.[26] At the beginning of the twenty-first century, late Anthony Smith[27] reminded us that nationalism and religion, both of which are among key components of myths of collective identities, continue to affect how international and local politics play out and are run.

Now we have a working definition: a myth is a simple but powerful causal account that incites a people's emotion and stimulates their collective behavior. Myths die hard; myths withstand the test of time especially when they are concerned with the existence or survival of a group. Myths may also be "institutionalized" and "become a matter of power, resources and ritual."[28] Institutionalization and historical transcendence seem highly probable when myths are carried by groups who have vested "ideal and material interests"—called "carrier groups" by Weber[29]—and may include "elites," "prestigious religious leaders," or "spiritual pariahs."[30] Moreover, not only those leaders but also their members contribute for their own reasons[31] to the cultural reproduction of a myth, resulting in the widespread acceptance of the myth at both group and individual levels.[32] For easier conveyance, myths are often linguistically expressed in metaphor.[33]

---

[26]Jan Penrose, "Nations, States and Homelands: Territory and Territoriality in Nationalist Thought," *Nations and Nationalism* 8, no. 3 (2002): 277–297.

[27]Anthony D. Smith, "The 'Sacred' Dimension of Nationalism," *Millennium* 29, no. 3 (2000): 791–814.

[28]Mary Fulbrook, "Myth-Making and National Identity: The Case of the G.D.R," in *Myths and Nationhood*, eds. Geoffrey Hosking and George Schöpflin (New York: Routledge, 1997), 72–84, 72.

[29]Max Weber, *Economy and Society* (Berkeley: University of California Press, 1968).

[30]Jeffrey C. Alexander, "Toward a Theory of Cultural Trauma," in *Cultural Trauma and Collective Identity*, eds. Jeffrey C. Alexander, Ron Eyerman, Bernard Giesen, Neil J. Smelser, and Piotr Sztompka (Berkeley, CA and London: University of California Press, 2004), 1–27, 11.

[31]John Coakley, "Mobilizing the Past: Nationalist Images of History," *Nationalism and Ethnic Politics* 10, no. 4 (2004): 531–560.

[32]George Schöpflin, "The Functions of Myth and a Taxonomy of Myths," in *Myths and Nationhood*, ed. Geoffrey Hosking and George Schöpflin (New York: Routledge, 1997), 19–35.

[33]Ernst Cassirer, *Language and Myth* (New York: Dover, 1946); Charteris-Black, *Politicians and Rhetoric*.

Despite their sustained carriage, myths may be more widely pronounced and shared at a certain time than other times. Probability of emergence and/or re-emergence of a myth and consequent nationalist conflict seems higher when there are larger macro-social or political changes in a country.[34] Such political changes may include but are not limited to anti-colonization, authoritarianism, and democratization when carrier groups may find it advantageous and effective to formulate, reintroduce, and popularize a myth. Hence, the people will believe, culturally (re)produce and act upon it. A myth then defines who a people are in relation to other peoples and suggests one or more ways to respond to a particular issue or problem that is believed to affect the people's national or collective identity against the backdrops of temporality and spatiality. These discussions of the theory of myth strongly relate to the focus of the chapter on anti-Muslim Buddhist nationalism in Myanmar.

EMERGENCE AND RE-EMERGENCE OF THE MYTH OF DERACINATION

Colonial Burma

For the Bamar majority in Myanmar, to be Bamar is to be Buddhist—a statement usually made in writings on British Burma. British colonization—completed in 1885 after waging three wars—wrought havoc not only on the territoriality and sovereignty of the Burmese kingdom but also on the Buddhist identity of the Bamar nation. Robert Taylor notes that "no event in the history of Myanmar was as complete and as traumatic" as colonization.[35] Hence, "the historiography of colonial Burma is characterized by a singular tragic narrative: colonialism was a deeply traumatic and emasculating experience that left colonized men and women with no choice but to regard foreign people, norms, and practices as oppressive and exploitative."[36]

It led to the dawning of a Buddhist renaissance movement with the emergence of Young Men's Buddhist Association (YMBA) in Rangoon

---

[34] Snyder and Ballentine, "Nationalism and the Marketplace."

[35] Robert H. Taylor, *The State in Myanmar*, 2nd ed. (Singapore: NUS Press, 2009), 15.

[36] Chie Ikeya, *Refiguring Women, Colonialism, and Modernity in Burma* (Honolulu: University of Hawaii Press, 2011), 4.

7 THE ROLE OF MYTH IN ANTI-MUSLIM BUDDHIST NATIONALISM ...   207

in 1906.[37] Its four objectives were "to strengthen the country's sense of race (*amyo*) and national spirit, to enhance national culture and literature (*batha*), to revitalize Buddhism (*thathana* [*sasana*]), and to promote education (*pyinnya*)."[38] For them, Buddhism then had declined since British colonization which they viewed as "as a religious and cosmological threat precipitating the decline of the Buddha's dispensation or *sasana*."[39] It then needed a renaissance or Buddhist response to "save" Buddhism.[40]

Initially, for YMBA deracination was "the fragmentation or loss of a Burman identity."[41] U May Oung—a founder and then President of YMBA—defined the old Bamar as Buddhist and questioned Buddhist identity of the new Bamar on August 9, 1908:

> 'What is a Burman [Bamar]?' 'A Burman is a Buddhist'. For if there was any one thing that may be said to be peculiarly distinctive about the Old Burman it was his intense devotion to his faith, which entered into every thought and word and deed of his ordinary life. ... Was the New Burman a Buddhist?[42]

This seemingly safe fear of deracination or loss of Burman Buddhist identity later carried demographic, racial, and religious connotations. The main cause was Indian migration. Necessitated by high demand for labor in the public, agricultural, and other private sectors, the British brought Indians of all walks of life into Burma. Hundreds of thousands of Indians were seen in Burmese cities and towns; thereby the myth of deracination emerged in two stages. As Tinker notes, "Indians were not few; they

---

[37] Several Buddhist associations existed prior to YMBA but they were religious by nature and provincial or regional in focus.

[38] Juliane Schober, *Modern Buddhist Conjectures in Myanmar: Cultural Narratives, Colonial Legacies, and Civil Society* (Honolulu: University of Hawaii Press, 2011), 68.

[39] Alicia Turner, *Buddhism, Colonialism and the Boundaries of Religion: Theravada Buddhism in Burma, 1885–1920* (PhD dissertation, University of Chicago, 2009), 1.

[40] Alicia Turner, *Saving Buddhism: The Impermanence of Religion in Colonial Burma* (Honolulu: University of Hawaii Press, 2014).

[41] Schober, *Modern Buddhist Conjectures*, 69.

[42] U May Oung, "The Modern Burman," *Journal of the Burma Research Society* XXXIII, no. 1 (April 1950): 1–7, 3–4.

208 N. N. KYAW

were numerous; they were visible; so it was that they became the symbol of colonialism, of foreign exploitation."[43]

It was at the ninth conference of the General Council of Burmese Associations (GCBA)[44] held on October 21, 1921 that Depayin Wunhtauk U Mye—a Bamar elite and state scholar sent to the West by King Mindon (reign: 1853–78)—uttered the metaphorical warning *Mye-myo-ywe Lu-myo-ma-pyôk Lu-chin-myo-hma Lu-myo-pyôk-mi* (A Landslide does not Submerge a Race, but Another Race Does!).[45] In this first stage, the myth targeted migration of Indians—whether Hindu or Muslims—as a potential cause for loss of the Bamar race. Once colonized, Burma was inserted into British India as one of its provinces and nationalists resented it. Although there was disagreement initially between them over whether to stay within or separate from India, the second option became the common position in the late 1920s.

Hence, the felt demographic threat provided nationalists with an expedient ploy. They put Indian immigration in the spotlight "through alarmist discussions of the 'Indian menace', such as the 'menace' posed by the Indo-Burmese marriages and the continued immigration of Indians to Burma."[46] It was a feeding frenzy not only within political circles but also in the indigenous press owned and run by the same nationalists. In debates on the motion for separation at the Legislative Council of the Governor of Burma on 9 and 10 August 1930, U Ba U asserted:

> Burma has all long been classed as a natural part of India and the outside world mistakes the Burmese people as a section of the Indian peoples. All the bad names acquired by the Indian races, by the Indian castes, and intensified by the Indian political complexities, are thought by the outside world to be applicable equally to Burma. Only those who visit India and

---

[43] Hugh Tinker, "Indians in Southeast Asia: Imperial Auxiliaries," in *South Asian Overseas: Migration and Ethnicity*, eds. Colin Clarke, Ceri Peach, and Steven Vertovec (Cambridge and New York: Cambridge University Press, 1990), 39–56, 40.

[44] YMBA became more politically engaged and was renamed GCBA at the eighth YMBA Conference held in Prome (now Pyay) in October 1920.

[45] U Hla Ko, The Law Relating to Foreigners and Immigration = Naing-ngan-cha-tha Nhint Lu-win-hmu Upade (Yangon: Chitsaya Sar Pay, 2003), 153.

[46] Ikeya, *Refiguring Women*, 131.

Burma know that there is a great natural difference between the Indian and the Burman.[47]

Another representative, Mr. Oo Kyaw Khine, echoed:

Burma is the dumping ground for the Indian.[48]

However, racial fears were also highlighted and the myth of deracination referred to. U Ba Pe—representative the Burmese Chamber of Commerce—claimed:

We are sure to be swamped in a few years' time. The peaceful penetration of Indians into Burma is at present not really serious though it is really great. If this state of affairs is allowed to go on forever, the Burmese nation will slowly and surely disappear from the earth.[49]

Another nationalist member, Tharawaddy U Pu, was more assertive by using stronger language:

I don't want the English. I don't want the Kala [contextually referring here to Indians irrespective of religious faith]. Our mothers and sisters are almost all taken. Our Burmese nationals are about to vanish.[50]

Another Council member, U Kun, said:

If we are to remain longer with India, in about a quarter of a century, there will be no Burman worthy of the name of the race. Indians have come into all corners and colonised themselves, have taken Burman wives and the race is impaired.[51]

---

[47] Legislative Council of the Governor of Burma, *Proceedings of the Legislative Council of the Governor of Burma*. Sixth Session (Third Council). XVIII (Rangoon: Government Printing and Stationery, 1932), 282.

[48] Legislative Council of the Governor of Burma, *Proceedings*, 339.

[49] Legislative Council of the Governor of Burma, *Proceedings*, 285.

[50] My translation; Legislative Council of the Governor of Burma, *Proceedings*, 296.

[51] Nalini Chakravarti, *The Indian Minority in Burma: The Rise and Decline of an Immigrant Community* (London: Institute of Race Relations, 1971), 129.

210   N. N. KYAW

Therefore, the Interim Report of the Riot Inquiry Committee formed in the aftermath of anti-Indian Muslim riots in 1938 notes: "It [Indian migration] was continuously represented as a menace to Burma's national life and even to the *Buddhist religion* (emphasis added)."[52] In this way, a racial myth that started out by referring to Indian migration later took on Buddhist–Muslim intermarriage and religious connotations. The popular press was also involved in the debates. As many Burmese farmers were deeply indebted to Indian Chettyar creditors and eventually unable to service and repay their debts due to the Great Depression in the 1930s, they and the Burmese press turned on the Chettyar and their fellow Indians as "Public Enemy No. 1" which was actually "a projection of a people's [the Burmese's] own faults and failings on to a convenient victim [the Chettyar]."[53] In one of the most widely read novels, Thein Pe—who is better known as Thein Pe Myint (1914–1978) after his nom de plume—quoted anti-Muslim arguments by Buddhists during the 1938 riots:

> Which Kala [here contextually referring to Muslim] is good? They take our girls as wives. Our girls must convert to Islam to become their legal wives. How domineering! *We lose our race; we lose our faith.* (emphasis added)
>   Yes, we lose both the race and the faith.[54]

Indeed, such fears of Indian migration that notably did not carry a religious tone were also expressed by largely secular student leaders such as Aung San, Ba Hein, Nu, and Ba Swe who endorsed a compendium composed and published by Thein Pe (the novelist Thein Pe Myint quoted above) in the immediate aftermath of the riots. Interestingly, Thein Pe gave a ratio of 1 Indian to 12 Burmese in the late 1930s and foresaw one of 1 Indian to 8 Burmese if Indian immigration remained unchecked, i.e., gradual deracination.[55] Although Chakravarti[56] and

[52] Riot Inquiry Committee, *Interim Report of the Riot Inquiry Committee* (Rangoon: Government Printing and Stationery, 1939), 23.

[53] Godfrey E. Harvey, *British Rule in Burma, 1824–1942* (London: Faber and Faber, 1946), 55.

[54] My translation; Thein Pe Myint, *A-shae-ka Ne-wun-twet-thi Pa*-ma *(Like the Sun Rises in the East).* 8th Impression (Yangon: Sar Oke Zay, 2001), 45.

[55] Thein Pe, *Kala-Bama Taik Pwe (Indo-Bamar Conflict)* (Rangoon: Nagani, 1938).

[56] Chakravarti, *The Indian Minority.*

Ikeya[57] highlight framing of Indian migrants and Burma's being an Indian province as threats to Burma's political future and social fabric, those discursive practices couched in the language of deracination remained deep-seated in the minds of the people.

Apart from its racial and religious themes, the myth of deracination became infused with geopolitical meaning. Indeed, it was not just the Burmese, but Sir Charles Innes, then the British Governor of Burma, who introduced this geopolitical content of the myth. In his convocation address delivered as Chancellor of the University of Rangoon in 1928, he said:

> Burma is a comparatively small land wedged in between the two great countries of India and China. ... Will the Burmans be able to maintain their individuality as a nation and the distinctive character of their civilization? Or will they, as time rolls on, slowly but *surely be submerged by the teeming millions to the East and to the West?* (emphasis added)[58]

These racial, religious, and geopolitical aspects of the myth were not transported into the mid-1930s and onwards with the fall from grace of early nationalists and their monastic patrons. Burma was separated from India in 1937, a commission to study Indian migration into Burma formed at the suggestion of the Riot Enquiry Committee, an Indo-Burma Immigration Agreement made in 1940, and measures to reduce reliance upon Indian migrants taken. All these new dynamics created an unfavorable political context for hardcore racial (or racist in some ways) nationalists who were replaced by secular nationalists such as Aung San and U Nu. Those young nationalists, most of whom were educated at Rangoon University, found independence the most pressing issue to be dealt with. The myth was not heard again and largely vanished from public discourse.

Independent and Socialist Burma (1948–1988)

Independent Burma was ruled by the U Nu government from 1948 onwards. Nu who was Aung San's close friend was an

---

[57] Ikeya, *Refiguring Women.*

[58] Chakravarti, *The Indian Minority*, 126–127.

internationalist—Burma actively participated in the Non-Aligned Movement. So naturally, he did not share those demographic, racial, and religious fears by which early nationalists were gripped. U Nu even wrote those fears were "groundless."[59] Moreover, his government was occupied with more pressing issues such as communist and ethnic insurgencies since before independence. Despite his personal piety and national promotion of Buddhism both of which were unprecedented compared to his predecessors and contemporaries, he did not use the fear expressed by the myth of deracination to promote Buddhism. He only promoted a peaceful, engaged and practice-based brand of Buddhism. In this context, the myth continued to fade further into the background.

It is of course undeniable that the two-year military Caretaker government (1958–1960) "used" Buddhism in its propaganda campaign against communists in the late 1950s[60] and U Nu in the nationwide campaign for making Buddhism the state religion in 1961.[61] But, in both instances the colonial myth was not provoked. Also, it is true that there were some sporadic Buddhist–Muslim tensions during U Nu's rule, but the myth was not heard either. There are two possible reasons: (1) hundreds of thousands of Indians left Burma for India in the early years of independence that makes a myth of the Indian menace plausible as in colonial Burma[62]; and (2) nation-building in the first two decades after independence was inclusive.[63]

The 1962–1988 rule by the Revolutionary Council (RC)/Burma Socialist Programme Party (BSPP) was a period of military or military-dominated authoritarianism and socialist one-party command. But state ideology was different from the one espoused by the regime that preceded and followed it. Claiming to build socialist Burma, Ne Win's nationalism was more economic than it was racial or religious. Imagining

---

[59] U Nu, *Saturday's Son*. Translated by U Law Yone. Edited by U Kyaw Win (New Haven: Yale University Press, 1975), 314.

[60] Fred von der Mehden, "Burma's Religious Campaign Against Communism," *Pacific Affairs* 33, no. 3 (1960): 290–299.

[61] Donald Eugene Smith, *Religion and Politics in Burma* (Princeton: Princeton University Press, 1965).

[62] Chakravarti, *The Indian Minority*.

[63] Nyi Nyi Kyaw, "Adulteration of the Pure Native Race by Aliens? Kapya and Their Socio-Legal Identity in Colonial Burma and Present-Day Myanmar," *Social Identities* 25, no. 3 (2019): 345–359.

a socialist egalitarian nation, he launched an extensive nationalization project that impoverished the Burmese Indian community. Hundreds of thousands of Indians fled.[64] His disastrous policies gradually led to poverty that reached its zenith in the late 1980s. Then, Ne Win often resorted to discursive attacks upon Chinese and Indian businesspeople by accusing them of selfishness and disloyalty to the nation. He was also accused of diverting public attention when anti-Chinese riots broke out in 1967.[65] Ne Win even framed a project to write a new citizenship law in the late 1970s as a protection against those greedy business people of alien (read Chinese and Indian) ancestry. And due to his anti-Indian (anti-Chinese as well) discourse, informal but very effective barriers were increasingly put on the way to higher public office for government servants who were Muslims.[66]

For Ne Win, what Burma needed was not de-Islamization but de-nationalization of people of alleged alien origin apparent in creation of different citizenship classes with different rights in the 1982 Myanmar Citizenship Law.[67] While he *openly* and *strongly* resented and acted against the fact that many alien citizens were influential in business and *some* in public service, he did not frame it as a religious or racial mythological threat and potential deracination of Buddhism or Buddhists. In short, Ne Win and his socialist military authoritarian regime did not use the myth and its prophecy of demise of the Bamar Buddhist race in a political context defined by isolation, economic nationalism, and mismanagement.[68]

Military Authoritarian Burma/Myanmar (1988–2011)

However, the situation drastically changed when a new military regime—known as the State Law and Order Restoration Council (SLORC) from 1988 through 1997 and the State Peace and Development Council (SPDC) from 1997 through 2011—took power in a coup in 1988

---

[64] Robert A. Holmes, "Burmese Domestic Policy: The Politics of Burmanization," *Asian Survey* 7, no. 3 (1967): 188–197.

[65] Hongwei Fan, "The 1967 Anti-Chinese Riots in Burma and Sino–Burmese Relations," *Journal of Southeast Asian Studies* 43, no. 2 (2012): 234–256.

[66] Nyi Nyi Kyaw, "Adulteration."

[67] Nyi Nyi Kyaw, "Alienation;" Nyi Nyi Kyaw, "Adulteration."

[68] Nyi Nyi Kyaw, "Adulteration."

amidst nationwide protests over poverty and hardship against the BSPP regime. The international community that had been largely uninterested in Burma suddenly and increasingly paid attention to political struggles led by Daw Aung San Suu Kyi, student protesters, and others. The next two decades or so saw Burma or Myanmar become a spotlight of an unprecedented international campaign of democracy and human rights. In this context, the myth re-emerged.

Resenting never-ending international criticisms, the coup regime launched a nationalist propaganda project featured on a daily basis in the state media. Due to lack of a common national identity that was caused by chronic ethnic conflicts between the Bamar majority and several minorities such as the Kachin or Kayin, the SLORC seemed to have resorted to a somewhat radical version of Bamar Buddhist nationalism.

In this anti-West, xenophobic macro-discourse, the myth re-emerged. A series of fourteen articles entitled *Amyo-pyauk-hma So-kyauk-hla-pa-thi* (We Fear Deracination!) were published in February and June 1989[69] in the state-owned Working People's Daily (Burmese version). It traced colonization and xenophobia, discussed various pieces of Myanmar citizenship legislation before and after independence, and concluded that Myanmar is still highly likely to be geopolitically and racially doomed. It constituted official rhetoric, if not official policy. Soon rhetoric became policy when a new Ministry of Immigration and Population (MIP) was established by SLORC on 15 June 1995. As its motto, MIP used *Mye-myo-ywe Lu-myo-ma-pyôk Lu-myo-hma Lu-myo-pyôk-mi*—the same myth uttered by U Mye seven decades ago. It remains MIP's motto until 2019—written on wooden boards and wall-plugged in MIP offices across Myanmar—after a new government led by State Counselor Daw Aung San Suu Kyi came to power in April 2016.

However, an SPDC chronicle[70] states that MIP's motto is *Kamba Ti-tha-ywe Myan-ma-naing-ngan Ti-shi-ya-mi; Kamba Ti-tha-ywe Myan-ma-lu-myo Ti-shi-ya-mi* (As long as the World Exists, There must Exist Myanmar as a Country; As long as the World Exists, There must exist Myanmar as a Race!). This motto is similar in theme to the other and strongly connotes chauvinist longing for Myanmar's *eternal* existence

---

[69] The first seven articles were published daily from the 20th to 26th February and the last seven on 3rd, 5th, 8th, 9th, 13th, 20th, and 28th June.

[70] State Peace and Development Council, *Taing Kyo Pyi Pyu (In Service of Country)* (Yangon: Ministry of Information, 2001), 193.

as both a country and race. Generals echoed this myth as their official mindset. Maj-Gen Ohn Myint, then Commander of the Northern Regional Command, reportedly said at a military quarterly meeting held in October 2005: "We have to understand that the extinction of a race will occur only when it is being swallowed by an alien race, not swallowed by the earth."[71] Thereby, nuanced colonial Indophobia that targeted the Indian race gradually transformed into outright Islamophobia defined in racial, religious, and geopolitical aspects that targeted Rohingya and non-Rohingya Muslims. In this context, *Amyo-pyauk-hma So-kyauk-sa-ya* (In Fear of Deracination)—arguably the second most notorious tract[72] in the Buddhist–Muslim history of Myanmar—appeared and was widely circulated from the 1990s onwards.

Post-transition Myanmar (2011–)

The discourse adopted by monks-led Buddhist nationalist movements of *969* and *Ma Ba Tha* is again found to be strikingly similar to the colonial myth of deracination that re-emerged as a religious oriented one. In a broader narrative context, *Amyo-pyauk-hma So-kyauk-sa-ya* and a newly written sequel *Amyo-ma-pyauk-aung Ka-kwaè-ya-miNi-lan-mya* or *Amyo-pyauk-hma So-kyauk-sa-ya* (2) (Ways to Prevent Deracination or In Fear of Deracination (2)) (re)emerged after the Rakhine riots in 2012. Both tracts are extremist, brimming with hardcore anecdotal anti-Muslim material stories and claims. Several Myanmar e-book websites popular among Myanmar people abroad such as www.shanyoma.org and http://burmeseclassic.com/ created and uploaded newly typeset and high-quality soft copies of the two tracts. Then they were seen to be distributed on social media and other file sharing and digital library sites such as Scribd and Mediafire. Many online conversations were seen to refer to the two tracts. Their title or myth of deracination was repeatedly heard and later carried back into public discourse.

The tracts claim that Muslims now constitute 20% of Myanmar's population and have been waging a secret demographic war funded by

---

[71] Min Zin, "China-Burma Relations: China's Risk, Burma's Dilemma," in *Burma or Myanmar? The Struggle for National Identity,* ed. Lowell Dittmer, 261–294 (Singapore: World Scientific, 2010), 272.

[72] The first tract was U Shwe Phi's *Moulvi-Yogi Awada Sadan,* better known as *Moulvi-Yogi Sadan* and believed to be one of the major causes of the 1938 riots.

216   N. N. KYAW

foreign Muslim countries to Islamize Myanmar by converting as many Buddhist women as possible through intermarriage and then breeding faster than Buddhists and, unless this is checked, Bamar Buddhists as a race and Buddhism as their faith shall vanish. It is strikingly similar to the colonial-era myth although it has carried more religious connotations.

The 969 movement was launched in October 2012 in the immediate aftermath of the second round of interreligious or intercommunal violence between Rakhine Buddhists and Rohingya/non-Rohingya Muslims in Rakhine State. The 969 movement accused Muslims of *only* buying from shops owned by their co-religionists—an accusation that might have been found convincing due to Muslims' dietary practices—and urged Buddhists to retaliate by not transacting with Muslims and buying Buddhist.[73]

All these post-transition dynamics suggest that the myth that has been carried across into the twentieth century recurred amidst Myanmar's political transition from 2010 onwards. In this new context, the myth became more nuanced and began to take up two issues of race and religion laws and Rohingya's citizenship. *Ma Ba Tha*—which literally means the Organization for Protecting and Guarding Race, Religion, and Sāsanā[74] but is officially translated as the Patriotic Association of Myanmar (PAM) or Organization for the Protection of National Race or Religion (OPNRR)—was established in June 2013 and has emerged amidst political changes and consequent sectarian conflicts.

Ma Ba Tha, which is led by Chairman Ywama Sayadaw Ashin Tiloka Biwuntha (better known as Ywama Sayadaw) and Vice Chairman (1) Sitagu Sayadaw Ashin Nyanissara (better known as Sitagu Sayadaw),[75]

---

[73] For details of symbolics, discourses, and activities of the movement, see Nyi Nyi Kyaw, "Islamophobia in Buddhist Myanmar."

[74] However, *Ma Ba Tha* is the best-known name of the organization that is also commonly called the 'Organization/Association for the Protection of Race and Religion' in the international media. So, *Ma Ba Tha* is used throughout this article.

[75] Rather detailed biographies of Ywama Sayadaw and his colleague, Sitagu Sayadaw, can be seen in Kawanami (2009). Although Sitagu Sayadaw was listed as Vice Chairman (1) on *Ma Ba Tha*'s official website, www.pam.org.mm, this organization is generally known as Ywama Sayadaw's brainchild. Moreover, Sitagu Sayadaw has not been actively involved in *Ma Ba Tha*'s campaigns although he joined and gave speeches at its meetings in Yangon and Mandalay in 2012, 2013 and 2015. It seems that he sits on *Ma Ba Tha*'s executive committee to give his blessing to the movement by his paramount influence as the most revered Buddhist preacher in Myanmar. But amidst questions about his involvement in controversial *Ma Ba Tha*, Sitagu Sayadaw later dissociated himself from the organization in

collected millions of signatures from Buddhists, earning the title of the largest signature campaign ever conducted in Myanmar's history until then,[76] and sent them to the government and Hluttaw (parliament). This monastic and popular pressure eventually led then President U Thein Sein to send a message in February 2014 to the Hluttaw regarding this petition, together with its 1,335,600 signatures, calling for the drafting and passing of four bills known as *Myo-saung Upade* (Race Protection Bills). The proposed bills, couched in the language of defense and protection, apparently aimed to prevent the fall or demise of the Bamar or Myanmar Buddhist race.

In the very beginning, *Ma Ba Tha* often referred to the threat to Buddhism and Buddhists of Myanmar posed by a "particular" religion without naming it in public. But gradually, several of its statements and sermons *openly* targeted Islam and Muslims. Moreover, *Ma Ba Tha*'s Islamophobic propaganda is that Islam permits polygamy, Muslim men tend to convert Buddhist women to Islam through interreligious marriage and Muslim families breed more than Buddhist ones—a scheme funded by an international terrorist and Islamization project being implemented by wealthy Muslim countries. All these points create an inevitable demographic apocalypse—if Buddhists do not defend their religion and fellow Buddhists, Buddhism in Myanmar as a faith and Buddhists as a race shall vanish.[77] This grand Islamophobia is furthermore fueled by those narratives widely believed and shared by the general (Buddhist) public which views global Muslims as fundamentalist, extremist, and violent and their local counterparts as introverted, bigoted and potentially violent.[78]

January 2015. Yet he still gave a special speech at the *Ma Ba Tha* rally on 4 October 2015 to commemorate the passage of the four laws.

[76] The anti-Section 436 of the Constitution signature campaign launched by National League for Democracy (NLD) and 88 Generation (Peace & Open Society) in 2014 collected more signatures—around 4 million—than the *Ma Ba Tha* campaign.

[77] Nyi Nyi Kyaw, "Alienation."

[78] Matthew J. Walton, Matt Schissler, and Phyu Phyu Thi, *Threat and Virtuous Defence: Listening to Narratives of Religious Conflict in Six Myanmar Cities* (Oxford and Yangon: Myanmar Media and Society Project, Oxford University and Myanmar ICT for Development Organization, 2015); Matthew J. Walton, Matt Schissler, and Phyu Phyu Thi, *Failed Riots: Successful Conflict Prevention in Four Myanmar Cities* (Oxford and Yangon: Myanmar Media and Society Project, Oxford University and Myanmar ICT for Development Organization, 2017).

Another topic *Ma Ba Tha* addressed is citizenship of Rohingya Muslims, most of whom do not possess any proper Myanmar citizenship documents.[79] Amidst the Rakhine conflicts involving Rakhine Buddhists and Rohingya and non-Rohingya Muslims, feverish claims that northern Rakhine was being swamped by hyper-fertile Bengali Muslims, and the whole Rakhine State and other parts of Myanmar were on the verge of Islamization, started to be widely seen on Facebook and in local media. Buddhist sermons given by *Ma Ba Tha* monks, most prominently Ashin Wirathu[80] of Mandalay and leaders of the 969 movement, which often used religious maps to show how Buddhism was a shrinking demographic and geopolitical minority in the world, and was under threat from Muslim Southeast Asia and South Asia added fuel to the fire. The most common examples of such countries used by those monks to support their claims were Indonesia, Malaysia, Afghanistan, India,[81] Pakistan, and Bangladesh which, they claim, were once majority Buddhist or Hindu but are now Muslim. The southern Thailand conflict has often been used because, for many Myanmar Buddhists, the Malay Muslims there are just soldiers of Islam seeking to Islamize Buddhist Thailand.

Amidst international calls for the revision or repeal of the 1982 citizenship law, which in fact includes several provisions for Rohingya citizenship,[82] statements issued by the *Ma Ba Tha* headquarters in Yangon and its Mandalay chapter representing Upper Myanmar assert that it shall oppose any such moves and call for respect of Myanmar's sovereignty. Like most Myanmar people, *Ma Ba Tha* seems to take it for granted that most, if not all, Rohingya are *illegal* immigrants and ineligible for any form of permanent Myanmar citizenship under the 1982 law,

---

[79] Most Rohingya held temporary identity cards known as White Cards which were revoked by a Presidential order in February 2015 and expired in end of March. For details of this lack of documentation and presumed statelessness of the Rohingya, see Nyi Nyi Kyaw, "Unpacking the Presumed Statelessness of Rohingyas," *Journal of Immigrant and Refugee Studies* 15, no. 3 (2017): 269–296.

[80] As the most vocal advocate of the 969 slogan to shun Muslim businesses, Ashin Wirathu is believed to be the de facto leader of the 969 movement although he is not officially affiliated with the *Tha-tha-na Pa-la-ka Gana-wasaka Sangha Apwè* based in Mawlamyine which formed the 969 movement in October 2012.

[81] India is an interesting example since, although it is largely Hindu, it has a large Muslim minority. Probably, monks just want to point out that India, the birthplace of Buddhism, is not Buddhist now.

[82] Nyi Nyi Kyaw, "Unpacking."

and believes that the amendment or repeal of that law would naturalize the Rohingya. Moreover, almost indoctrinated by the allegations of the Rohingya as illegal Bengali migrants, the people of Myanmar are simply unaware of the fact that that the Rohingya have been arbitrarily deprived of their citizenship documentation and denationalized.[83] Besides, another barrier that now seems almost impenetrable has been erected from 2012 onwards against unconditional acceptance of the Rohingya as fellow citizens. It is emergence of the notion of indigeneity of so-called national races among which the Rohingya are not one. According to this notion, since the Rohingya are not recognized as one of the races, their *legal* citizenship shall never be on par with that of Rakhine Buddhists who are a national race. Indigenous citizens are legally, socially, and politically superior to non-indigenous citizens who mostly constitute Indians, Chinese, and Rohingya (or Bengalis).[84]

In particular, the *Ma Ba Tha* campaign against the Rohingya's right to citizenship and for the four laws to make polygamy illegal and control population growth can be said to target the Rohingya who are widely assumed to be polygamous and hyper-fertile. For *Ma Ba Tha*, 969 and their believers and followers, Muslims in Myanmar—that now includes *both* Rohingya and non-Rohingya Muslims—have been engaged in a "wombfare."[85] Ashin Wirathu and other 969 leaders also promote the myth of deracination in their sermons against Buddhists' patronization of Muslim shops while 969's rhetoric can be summarized as: if Buddhists buy from Muslim shops, Muslims will become increasingly prosperous and be in a better position to take poor Buddhist women as wives and convert them to Islam. Then, as Muslims will breed more quickly

---

[83] Nyi Nyi Kyaw, "Unpacking."

[84] Nyi Nyi Kyaw, "Alienation;" Nick Cheesman, "How in Myanmar 'National Races' Came to Surpass Citizenship and Exclude Rohingya," *Journal of Contemporary Asia* 47, no. 3 (2017): 461–483.

[85] Christian Leuprecht, "Deter or Engage? The Demographic Structure of Ethno-Nationalist Mobilization," in *Political Demography: How Population Changes Are Reshaping International Security and National Politics*, eds. J.A. Goldstone, E.P. Kaufmann, and Monica D. Toft (New York: Oxford University Press, 2012), 226–237; Monica D. Toft, "Wombfare: The Religious Basis of Fertility Politics," in *Political Demography: How Population Changes Are Reshaping International Security and National Politics*, eds. J.A. Goldstone, E.P. Kaufmann, and Monica D. Toft (New York: Oxford University Press, 2012), 213–225.

than Buddhists, the latter are doomed as a race. The 969 leader, Ashin Wimala Biwuntha, claims:

> We Buddhists are like people in a boat that is sinking. If this does not change, our race and religion will soon vanish.[86]

Similarly, Ashin Wirathu echoes:

> With money, they become rich and marry Buddhist Burmese woman who convert to Islam, spreading their religion. Their businesses become bigger and they buy more land and houses.[87]
> Because the Burmese people and the Buddhists are devoured every day, the national religion needs to be protected.[88]

It all suggests that re-emergence of the nationwide Buddhist nationalist movement led by *Ma Ba Tha* and 969[89] stems from an historical Buddhist-inspired myth that originated in colonial times and carried across time. Notably, the myth re-emerged at a time of political change or transition where identities were in flux. So, common Buddhist identity alleged to be under threat by Islamization was promoted by *Ma Ba Tha* by hijacking by the colonial-era myth to which the people of Burma/Myanmar has been accustomed to. The *Ma Ba Tha* campaign was apparently found convincing by millions of its supporters and supported by the U Thein Sein administration. It became fruitful in 2015 when the Heal Care Law Relating to Adjustment of Population Growth, Law Relating to Religious Conversion, Special Law relating to Marriage of

---

[86] Kyaw Zaw Moe, "A Radically Different Dhamma," *The Irrawaddy*, June 22, 2013, https://www.irrawaddy.com/news/a-radically-different-dhamma.html, accessed July 1, 2019.

[87] JasonSzep, "Special Report: Buddhist Monks Incite Muslim Killings in Myanmar," *Reuters*, April 8, 2013, https://www.reuters.com/article/us-myanmar-violence-specialreport/special-report-buddhist-monks-incite-muslim-killings-in-myanmar-idUS-BRE9370AP20130408, accessed July 1, 2019.

[88] Tin Aung Kyaw, "Buddhist Monk Wirathu Leads Violent National Campaign Against Myanmar's Muslims," *Global Post*, June 21, 2013, https://www.pri.org/stories/2013-06-21/buddhist-monk-wirathu-leads-violent-national-campaign-against-myanmars-muslims, accessed July 1, 2019.

[89] Although neither 969 nor *Ma Ba Tha* has officially stated that the former is part of the latter, the fact that two of the five 969 leaders and its de facto leader Ashin Wirathu are executive members of PAM suggests that they overlap.

Myanmar Buddhist Women, and Law Relating to Practice of Monogamy became law on 19 May, 26 August, and 31 August, respectively.

CONCLUSION

This chapter has argued that anti-Muslim-cum-Buddhist arguments made by anti-Muslim tracts, *Ma Ba Tha*, 969 and Myanmar authorities should be understood to stem from the myth of deracination which originated in colonial Burma. Through its trajectory spanning over a century, the myth gradually changed its content from Bamar versus Indian to Buddhist versus Muslim.[90] It is also contended that Myanmar Buddhist nationalism, in both its old and new versions,[91] has been chronically fixated on this colonial-era myth, which emerged in a different time and context, to make sense of, and respond to, new changes and contexts. This persistence has led to chronic anti-Muslim sentiments which remain widely shared among Buddhists and play the role of fuel whenever there is a spark.

The racial, religious and geopolitical content of the myth have evidently played out in the country-wide rejection of the Rohingya as fellow Myanmar citizens, the citizenship and various other rights of whom must be protected by Myanmar authorities and people. In rejecting the Rohingya, the commonly heard argument is this: since Myanmar, with a population of around 51.4 million, shares its borders with Bangladesh which has 150 million people and an allegedly explosive population growth, unless the alleged immigration of over-breeding Bengalis (the more common name for Rohingya within Myanmar) is curtailed, first Rakhine and then other parts of Buddhist Myanmar will eventually find themselves at the behest of Islamization. This anti-Rohingya rhetoric was introduced mainly by Rakhine nationalist politicians in the aftermath of the Rakhine riots in 2012 to de-legitimize the legal and political identity of Rohingya, and was readily accepted by a large section of the Buddhist public elsewhere in Myanmar partly due to the sheer continuity

---

[90] Renaud Egreteau, "Burmese Indians in Contemporary Burma: Heritage, Influence, and Perceptions Since 1988," *Asian Ethnicity* 12, no. 1 (2011): 33–54; Nyi Nyi Kyaw, "Alienation."

[91] Tharaphi Than, "Nationalism, Religion, and Violence: Old and New *Wunthanu* Movements in Myanmar," *Review of Faith & International Affairs* 13, no. 4 (2015): 12–24.

of the colonial-era myth of deracination transported through time and space. To reinforce its travel, important institutions such as Buddhist monks and military have carried the myth across history by adding more nuances along the way.

It first emerged as a demographic and racial response by Burmese nationalists to British colonization and Indian migration. Then, it was almost forgotten for several decades until the late 1990s when the military authoritarian regime re-used and invigorated it in its response to criticisms by the West of its repression of the people. History has repeated from 2010 onwards when the time was ripe for re-emergence of thick cultural myths such as the myth of deracination because Myanmar underwent a transition from 2011 onwards. Actors have changed and content has been modified but the essential content of the myth that constructs the Buddhist race of Myanmar as presently or potentially threatened by deracination due to alien races remains unchanged. Even after the democratic government led by Daw Aung San Suu Kyi came to power, the Ministry of Labour, Immigration and Population has continued to use the myth as its motto. All say that the myth has been part and parcel of different forms of nationalism in the history of the country and is highly expected to remain into the near future, if not longer. Because the myth is all about the survival of Buddhism and Buddhists in Myanmar, it will also justify whatever actions the leaders and people of Myanmar undertake against alleged aliens and potential deracination the latter may cause. The myth shall continue to tell the leaders and people of Myanmar how to define who they are in relation to alien peoples such as the Rohingya and Bengalis and pressure them to stop an imminent deracination by all means.

REFERENCES

Alexander, Jeffrey C. "Toward a Theory of Cultural Trauma." In *Cultural Trauma and Collective Identity*, edited by Jeffrey C. Alexander, Ron Eyerman, Bernard Giesen, Neil J. Smelser, and Piotr Sztompka, 1–27. Berkeley, CA and London: University of California Press, 2004.

Archard, David. "Myths, Lies and Historical Truth: A Defence of Nationalism." *Political Studies* 43, no. 3 (1995): 472–481.

Bell, Duncan S.A. "Mythscapes: Memory, Mythology, and National Identity." *British Journal of Sociology* 54, no. 1 (2003): 63–81.

Bottici, Chiara. *A Philosophy of Political Myth*. New York: Cambridge University Press, 2007.

Bottici, Chiara, and Benoit Challand. "Rethinking Political Myth: The Clash of Civilizations as a Self-Fulfilling Prophecy." *European Journal of Social Theory* 9, no. 3 (2006): 315–336.

Cassirer, Ernst. *Language and Myth.* New York: Dover, 1946.

Chakravarti, Nalini. *The Indian Minority in Burma: The Rise and Decline of an Immigrant Community.* London: Institute of Race Relations, 1971.

Charteris-Black, Jonathan. 2011. *Politicians and Rhetoric: The Persuasive Power of Metaphor.* 2nd ed. Houndmills, Basingstoke, Hampshire and New York: Palgrave Macmillan.

Cheesman, Nick, Monique Skidmore, and Trevor Wilson, eds. *Myanmar's Transition: Openings, Obstacles, and Opportunities.* Singapore: Institute of Southeast Asian Studies, 2012.

Cheesman, Nick, Nicholas Farrelly, and Trevor Wilson, eds. *Debating Democratization in Myanmar.* Singapore: Institute of Southeast Asian Studies, 2014.

Cheesman, Nick. "How in Myanmar 'National Races' Came to Surpass Citizenship and Exclude Rohingya." *Journal of Contemporary Asia* 47, no. 3 (2017): 461–483.

Coakley, John. "Mobilizing the Past: Nationalist Images of History." *Nationalism and Ethnic Politics* 10, no. 4 (2004): 531–560.

Egreteau, Renaud. "Burmese Indians in Contemporary Burma: Heritage, Influence, and Perceptions since 1988." *Asian Ethnicity* 12, no. 1 (2011): 33–54.

Fan, Hongwei. "The 1967 Anti-Chinese Riots in Burma and Sino–Burmese Relations." *Journal of Southeast Asian Studies* 43, no. 2 (2012): 234–256.

Flood, Christopher. *Political Myth: A Theoretical Introduction.* New York: Garland, 1996.

Fulbrook, Mary. "Myth-Making and National Identity: The Case of the G.D.R." In *Myths and Nationhood,* edited by Geoffrey Hosking and George Schöpflin, 72–84. New York: Routledge, 1997.

Geis, Michael. *The Language of Politics.* New York: Springer-Verlag, 1987.

Gravers, Mikael. ed. *Burma/Myanmar: Where Now?* Copenhagen: NIAS Press, 2014.

Harvey, Godfrey E. *British Rule in Burma, 1824–1942.* London: Faber and Faber, 1946.

Holmes, Robert A. "Burmese Domestic Policy: The Politics of Burmanization." *Asian Survey* 7, no. 3 (1967): 188–197.

Human Rights Watch. *Playing the "Communal Card": Communal Violence and Human Rights.* New York: Human Rights Watch, 1995.

———. *Crackdown on Burmese Muslims.* Washington, DC: Human Rights Watch, 2002.

Ikeya, Chie. *Refiguring Women, Colonialism, and Modernity in Burma.* Honolulu: University of Hawaii Press, 2011.

Images Asia. 1997. *Report on the Situation for Muslims in Burma*. Bangkok: Images Asia.

Justice Trust. *Hidden Hands Behind Communal Violence in Myanmar: Case Study of the Mandalay Riots*. New York: Justice Trust, 2015.

Klinken, Gerry van, and Su Mon Thazin Aung. "The Contentious Politics of Anti-Muslim Scapegoating in Myanmar." *Journal of Contemporary Asia* 47, no. 3 (2017): 353–375.

Kyaw Zaw Moe. 2013. "A Radically Different Dhamma." *The Irrawaddy*, June 22.

Legislative Council of the Governor of Burma. *Proceedings of the Legislative Council of the Governor of Burma*. Sixth Session (Third Council). XVIII. Rangoon: Government Printing and Stationery, 1932.

Leuprecht, Christian. "Deter or Engage? The Demographic Structure of Ethno-Nationalist Mobilization." In *Political Demography: How Population Changes Are Reshaping International Security and National Politics*, edited by J.A. Goldstone, E.P. Kaufmann, and M.D. Toft, 226–237. New York: Oxford University Press, 2012.

McCarthy, Gerard, and Jacqueline Menager. "Gendered Rumours and the Muslim Scapegoat in Myanmar's Transition." *Journal of Contemporary Asia* 47, no. 3 (2017): 396–412.

Mehden, Fred von der. "Burma's Religious Campaign Against Communism." *Pacific Affairs* 33, no. 3 (1960): 290–299.

Min Zin. 2010. "China-Burma Relations: China's Risk, Burma's Dilemma." In *Burma or Myanmar? The Struggle for National Identity*, edited by Lowell Dittmer, 261–294. Singapore: World Scientific.

Myanmar Media and Society Project, Oxford University & Myanmar ICT for Development Organization.

Nyi Nyi Kyaw. "Alienation, Discrimination, and Securitization: Legal Personhood and Cultural Personhood of Muslims in Myanmar." *Review of Faith & International Affairs* 13, no. 4 (2015): 50–59.

———. "Islamophobia in Buddhist Myanmar: The 969 Movement and Anti-Muslim Violence". In *Islam and the State in Myanmar: Muslim–Buddhist Relations and the Politics of Belonging*, edited by Melissa Crouch, 183–210. New Delhi: Oxford University Press India, 2016.

———. "Unpacking the Presumed Statelessness of Rohingyas." *Journal of Immigrant and Refugee Studies* 15, no. 3 (2017): 269–296.

———. "Myanmar's Other Muslims: The Case of the Kaman." In *Citizenship in Myanmar: Ways of Being In and From Burma*, edited by Ashley South and Marie Lall, 279–300. Singapore: Institute of Southeast Asian Studies, 2018.

———. "Adulteration of the Pure Native Race by Aliens? Kapya and Their Socio-Legal Identity in Colonial Burma and Present-Day Myanmar." *Social Identities* 25, no. 3 (2019): 345–359.

Overing, Joanna. "The Role of Myth: An Anthropological Perspective, or: 'The Reality of the Really Made-Up'." In *Myths and Nationhood*, edited by Geoffrey Hosking and George Schöpflin, 1–18. New York: Routledge, 1997.

Penrose, Jan. "Nations, States and Homelands: Territory and Territoriality in Nationalist Thought." *Nations and Nationalism* 8, no. 3 (2002): 277–297.

Przeworski, Adam. "Minimalist Conception of Democracy: A Defense." In *Democracy's Value*, edited by Ian Shapiro and Casiano Hacker-Cordón, 23–55. Cambridge: Cambridge University Press, 1999.

Riot Inquiry Committee. *Interim Report of the Riot Inquiry Committee*. Rangoon: Government Printing and Stationery, 1939.

Schober, Juliane. *Modern Buddhist Conjectures in Myanmar: Cultural Narratives, Colonial Legacies, and Civil Society*. Honolulu: University of Hawaii Press, 2011.

Schöpflin, George. "The Functions of Myth and a Taxonomy of Myths." In *Myths and Nationhood*, edited by Geoffrey Hosking and George Schöpflin, 19–35. New York: Routledge, 1997.

Smith, Anthony D. "The 'Sacred' Dimension of Nationalism." *Millennium* 29, no. 3 (2000): 791–814.

Smith, Donald E. *Religion and Politics in Burma*. Princeton: Princeton University Press, 1965.

Snyder, Jack, and Karen Ballentine. "Nationalism and the Marketplace of Ideas." *International Security* 21, no. 2 (1996): 5–40.

State Peace and Development Council. *Taing Kyo Pyi Pyu* (In Service of Country). Yangon: Ministry of Information, 2001.

Steinberg, David. ed. *Myanmar: The Dynamics of an Evolving Polity*. Boulder, CO: Lynne Rienner, 2014.

Szep, Jason. 2013. "Special Report: Buddhist Monks Incite Muslim Killings in Myanmar." *Reuters*, April 8.

Taylor, Robert H. *The State in Myanmar*, 2nd ed. Singapore: NUS Press, 2009.

Tharaphi Than. "Nationalism, Religion, and Violence: Old and New *Wunthanu* Movements in Myanmar." *Review of Faith & International Affairs* 13, no. 4 (2015): 12–24.

Thein Pe. *Kala-Bama Taik Pwe* (Indo-Bamar Conflict). Rangoon: Nagani, 1938.

Thein Pe Myint. *A-shae-ka Ne-wun-twet-thi Pa-ma* (Like the Sun Rises in the East). 8th Impression. Yangon: Sar Oke Zay, 2001.

Tin Aung Kyaw. 2013. "Buddhist Monk Wirathu Leads Violent National Campaign against Myanmar's Muslims." *Global Post*, June 21.

Tinker, Hugh. "Indians in Southeast Asia: Imperial Auxiliaries." In *South Asian Overseas: Migration and Ethnicity*, edited by Colin Clarke, Ceri Peach, and Steven Vertovec, 39–56. Cambridge and New York: Cambridge University Press, 1990.

Toft, Monica D. "Wombfare: The Religious Basis of Fertility Politics." In *Political Demography: How Population Changes Are Reshaping International*

Security and National Politics, edited by J.A. Goldstone, E.P. Kaufmann, and M.D. Toft, 213–225. New York: Oxford University Press, 2012.

Tudor, Henry. *Political Myth.* London: Pall Mall Press, 1972.

Turner, Alicia. "Buddhism, Colonialism and the Boundaries of Religion: Theravada Buddhism in Burma, 1885–1920." PhD dissertation, University of Chicago, 2009.

Turner, Alicia. *Saving Buddhism: The Impermanence of Religion in Colonial Burma.* Honolulu: University of Hawaii Press, 2014.

U Hla Ko. *The Law Relating to Foreigners and Immigration= Naing-ngan-cha-tha Nhint Lu-win-hmu Upade.* Yangon: Chitsaya Sar Pay, 2003.

U May Oung. "The Modern Burman." *Journal of the Burma Research Society* XXXIII, no. 1 (April 1950): 1–7.

U Nu. 1975. *Saturday's Son.* Translated by U Law Yone. Edited by U Kyaw Win. New Haven: Yale University Press.

Walton, Matthew J., Matt Schissler, and Phyu Phyu Thi. 2015. *Threat and Virtuous Defence: Listening to Narratives of Religious Conflict in Six Myanmar Cities.* Oxford and Yangon: Myanmar Media and Society Project, Oxford University and Myanmar ICT for Development Organization.

———. 2017. *Failed Riots: Successful Conflict Prevention in Four Myanmar Cities.* Oxford and Yangon: Myanmar Media and Society Project, Oxford University and Myanmar ICT for Development Organization.

Weber, Max. *Economy and Society.* Berkeley: University of California Press, 1968.

CHAPTER 8

Arakanese Chittagong Became Mughal Islamabad: Buddhist–Muslim Relationship in Chittagong (Chottrogram), Bangladesh

D. Mitra Barua

> The Emperor [Aurangzeb] ordered Chatgaon to be renamed Islamabad [Residence of the Faithful] (*Alamgirnamah* in Sarkar 1989: 148).

At the end of September 2012, Bengali Buddhists witnessed the worst atrocity against them. Muslims with anti-Buddhist slogans looted Buddhist villages, set fire on many ancient Buddhist temples and threatened Buddhist monks, men, women and children. Thousands of Buddhists became homeless overnight, and more than twenty ancient Buddhist temples were attacked, vandalized and some of them burnt down to ashes. The whole Bengali Buddhist community across the Chittagong region and beyond were spellbound, shaken and scared.

Violence against religious minorities including Buddhists in Bangladesh has been a recurring theme since the 1947 religion-based India-Pakistan formation. Previous communal anti-Buddhist attacks were on non-Bengali Buddhists with political tension with the Bangladeshi state and the Muslim settlement in the Chittagong Hill Tracts (CHT).

D. M. Barua (✉)
Rice University, Houston, TX, USA

© The Author(s) 2020
I. Frydenlund and M. Jerryson (eds.),
Buddhist-Muslim Relations in a Theravada World,
https://doi.org/10.1007/978-981-32-9884-2_8

227

228   D. M. BARUA

The 2012 attack was on Bengali Buddhists who share the same language and culture and live in small clusters among Bengali Muslims in the Chittagong plains. Bengali Buddhists have been careful in mitigating potential violence against them by ethnically distancing themselves from the CHT fellow Buddhists and by not engaging in party politics. Their minimal socio-economic position does not seem to pose noticeable threat or challenge to the ambient Muslim majority society. More importantly, Bengali Buddhists have complied with the Muslim majority cultural ethos so that their behaviors neither cause cultural provocation and nor hurt majority sentiment. With such cautionary behaviors, Bengali Buddhists have avoided communal attacks on them until the 2012 violence. The pretext for that violence was an image of the Islamic holy book Qur'an on fire tagged onto a Facebook account with a Buddhist name. The investigation on the issue revealed that the pretext was fabricated for the sole purpose of instigating violence against this tiny Buddhist community.[1] The timing of the attack suggests that the 2012 anti-Muslim violence in Chittagong's neighboring region, Myanmar's Rakhine state, triggered the anti-Buddhist violence in Chittagong.

As the Buddhist–Muslim conflict in Rakhine (Arakan), Myanmar increasingly overshadows the Buddhist–Muslim peaceful coexistence in the Chittagong plains, this chapter seeks to layout the latter's history. It does so by highlighting an interpretation and historical application of the term Maga/Mog that is often cried out by contemporary Bengali Muslims who protest against the Burmese/Myanmar government and Rakhine (Arakanese) Buddhists. In order to give a comprehensive picture of the Buddhist–Muslim relationship in Chittagong, I also discuss about Buddhists in CHT, who along with their counterparts in the plains provide us with an ideal case study on the topic in question. The 2012 Muslim rhetoric and violence against Buddhists in Chittagong have revived anti-Buddhist sentiments predicated upon the historical nomenclature of Buddhists—Maga/Mog—since the Mughal invasion of Arakanese ruled Chittagong in 1666 CE. I argue that the Mughals' disapproval of Buddhism coupled with their anti-Arakanese prejudices has shaped the Muslim–Buddhist relationship in four successive states: the Mughal Empire, colonial India, Muslim Pakistan and Bangladesh.

---

[1]Meghna Guhathakurta, "Religious Minorities," in *Routledge Handbook of Contemporary Bangladesh*, eds. Ali Riaz and Mohammad Sajjadur Rahman (London and New York: Routledge, 2016), 323.

The foregoing argument unfolds in four main sections below, starting with a description of Chittagong to contextualize the discussion to follow. Chittagong has become cosmopolitan with its centuries-long trade connections and historical presence of multilingual and multireligious population. The second section explains how the term Maga/Mog came to be associated with the Mughal negative portrayals of Buddhism and Buddhists as the Mughal-Arakanese political rivalry intensified in the seventeenth century. The third section details how the Mughal religious and racial bigotries inadvertently continued in colonial and postcolonial policies related to the Buddhist majority CHT. The last section narrates how Buddhists in the Chittagong hills and plains have variously responded to the centuries long ethno-religious bigotries against them. These four core sections with a few sub-sections in between lay out an interesting and comprehensive picture of the Buddhist–Muslim relationship in cosmopolitan Chittagong.

Cosmopolitan Chittagong

Chittagong (Chottrogram in Bengali) is Bangladesh's second largest city with a 157 km^2 land area. Its busy seaport made the city the economic hub of Bangladesh. The city's name also extends to the coastline area (Chittagong and Cox's Bazar Districts) and the upland area to the east (the CHT) as well as the entire surrounding region (Chittagong Division). Being located at the north tip of the Bay of Bengal, Chittagong city has been a nodal point with access to both riverine and seaborne networks.[2] Historically the major rivers like the Brahmaputra, the Padma, the Meghna, the Karnaphuli, the Songu and the Matamuri brought commodities to Chittagong from the expansive inlands of east India, the Himalayas and beyond. Then the seaborne networks in the Bay of Bengal made the commodities accessible to the far and wide market across Asia, Africa and beyond. Commodities flowed in both ways. Inland resources such as spices, cotton, timber, cane, etc., flowed from north to south and from hilly lands to sea lands. Commodities like salt, dried fish, chinaware, wax, etc., went other direction from south to north and from sea to lands and hills. People from far and wide gathered

[2]Willem Van Schendel, "Spatial Moments: Chittagong in Four Scenes," in *Asia Inside Out: Connected Places*, eds. Eric Tagliacozzo, Helen F. Siu, and Peter C. Perdue (New York: Harvard University Press, 2015), 102.

230 D. M. BARUA

at entrepôt Chittagong to exchange profitable commodities. Similar to contemporary Bangladesh's textile industries, Chittagong's natural harbor channeled through many Bengali textiles throughout the medieval time.[3]

Chittagong's trade strategic position made the city metropolitan early on. Chatgaia, the colloquial vernacular of Chittagong, is considered to be a dialect of Bengali as it now closely relates to the latter. Historically, however, it has also adopted loanwords from Asian Middle Eastern and European languages. Willem van Schendel states "the Chittagonian language...is an Indo-Aryan language related to Bengali, peppered with Arabic, Persian, and Portuguese expressions."[4] Others also notice considerable influences of Urdu[5] Assamese[6] and Arakanese/Burmese.[7] In the 1600s, a mint in Chittagong produced coins with Arabic, Arakanese and Bengali expressions.[8] These trilingual coins remind us that Chittagong housed multilingual speakers who engaged in local and long-distance trades. Buddhism, Hinduism, and Islam inspired multilingual (Arakanese, Bengali, Pali and Persian) literary tradition also characterized the region throughout the seventeenth and eighteenth centuries.[9]

Similar to linguistic diversity, Chittagong has also been known for religious diversity. Historical evidence indicates that Chittagong has been controlled at one point or another by political powers inspired and influenced by four major world religions since early medieval time: Buddhism, Christianity, Hinduism and Islam. The Buddhist Chandras (ca. 825–1035 CE) ruled the medieval Samatata-Harikela region including the Chittagong seaport.[10] Sultan Fakhr al-Din Mubarak Shah of

[3] Richard M. Eaton, *The Rise of Islam and the Bengal Frontier (1204–1760)* (Oxford: Oxford University Press, 1993), 11, 97.

[4] Van Schendel, "Spatial Moments," 104.

[5] Samuel Berthet, "Boat Technology and Culture in Chittagong," *Water History* 7 (2015): 181.

[6] Md Aslam Mia, et al., "Chittagong, Bangladesh," *Cities* 48 (2015): 32.

[7] Charles P. Caspersz, "Memorandum on the Revenue History of Chittagong," *Calcutta Review* 71, no. 141 (1880): 170.

[8] Van Schendel, "Spatial Moments," 105.

[9] Thibaut d'Hubert, *In the Shade of the Golden Palace: Alaol and Middle Bengali Poetics in Arakan* (New York: Oxford University Press, 2018); Christian Lammerts, "The Murray Manuscripts and Buddhist Dhammasattha Transmitted in Chittagong and Arakan," *The Journal of Burma Studies* 19, no. 2 (2015).

[10] Eaton, *The Rise of Islam and the Bengal Frontier*, 11.

Sonargaon (r. 1338–1349 CE) invaded Chittagong and established the Muslim rule.[11] In subsequent centuries, the Chittagong port became the epicenter of political rivalry among three medieval kingdoms, i.e., Muslim sultanate in Bengal, Hindu kingdom in Tripura (now India's Tripura state) and Buddhist kingdom in Arakan (now Rakhine state of Myanmar).[12] This three-way contest for supremacy made Chittagong more open to religious tolerance that generally characterized medieval Bengal.[13] Since early 1500s Europeans, traders added another dimension of religio-cultural and linguistic diversity to Chittagong. While the Portuguese brought Catholicism to Chittagong,[14] the Dutch and the English, particularly the latter's colonial administration (since 1760s) added an influential Protestant presence in Chittagong. This historical multireligious presence still remains visible but in an increasingly diminishing form. Contemporary Chittagong city houses 885 mosques, 178 Hindu temples, 10 Churches, and 6 Buddhist temples.[15] Out of its 25, 82401 population, 10.6% are Hindus, 1.5% are Buddhists, and 0.2% are Christians.[16]

Bangladesh is still a multireligious country with one of the largest Muslim populations in the world. Nearly 90% of its 163 million people are Muslims; the rest 10% constitute Hindus, Buddhists, Christians and Animists. According to the 2011 Bangladesh census, nearly one million Buddhists from diverse ethnic backgrounds currently live in Bangladesh. The majority of them reside in the CHT, and they uphold various ethnic identities such as Chakma, Marma, Tanchanya, Mrung, etc. Nearly one-third of the total Buddhists in Bangladesh live in the Chittagong plains,

---

[11] Mohammed Ali Chowdhury, "The Arrival of Islam in Chittagong Before Muslim Conquest," *Journal of the Pakistan Historical Society* 47, no. 1 (1999): 49.

[12] Jorn Deyell, "Monetary and Financial Webs: The Regional and International Influence of Pre-Modern Bengali Coinage," in *Pelagic Passageways: The Northern Bay of Bengal of Before Colonialism*, ed. Rila Mukherjee (Delhi: Primus Books, 2011), 295.

[13] Swapna Bhattacharya, *The Rakhine State (Arakan) of Myanmar: Interrogating History, Culture and Conflict* (Kolkata: Maulana Abul Kalam Azad Institute of Asian Studies, 2015), 69. "Neither orthodox Buddhism, nor the conservative Islam, or pure Hinduism could set its foot upon Bengal mainly owing to political, topographical, social and economic reasons."

[14] Van Schendel, "Spatial Moments," 104.

[15] Chittagong City Corporation, "Media Brief of Chittagong City Corporation," available at http://www.ccc.org.bd/media_brief, accessed on November 8, 2016.

[16] Mia et al., "Chittagong, Bangladesh," 35.

232 D. M. BARUA

and they ethnically identify themselves as Bengali. There is also a small Arakanese speaking Rakhine Buddhist community along the southern coastal area closer to the Myanmar border. They mostly live in Patuakhali but also in Cox's Bazar, the direct west and south of Chittagong respectively.[17] Despite of their ethnic differences, they all practice the same form of Theravada Buddhism. Bengali Muslims and Hindus derogatively call them as "Maga/Mog" with a sense of disapproval of Buddhist beliefs and practices.

THE TERM "MAGA/MOG" AND MUGHALS' NEGATIVE PERCEPTIONS OF BUDDHISTS

The social origin of the term "Maga/Mog" yet to be academically established; the oral history of Buddhists in the Chittagong plains suggests that the term derives from their ancestral land medieval Magadha (the Bihar State of India).[18] The oral tradition narrates that Buddhists in the Chittagong plains have descended from a group of Buddhist immigrants who had arrived in Chittagong after leaving medieval Magadha region via Assam. Syed Jamil Ahmed (2008) succinctly records:

> Their [Chittagong plain Buddhists'] ancestors were forced to migrate from Magadha (west-central Bihar in north-eastern India) during Brahmanical resurgence in the 13th-14th centuries. Undertaking a long and arduous journey through Assam, they finally arrived in the plains of Chittagong where they found a safe haven to settle in.[19]

According to this oral tradition, the term Maga/Mog derives from "Magadha," and therefore, it referred to those Buddhist immigrants and their descendants.

---

[17] Abdul Mabud Khan, *The Maghs: A Buddhist Community in Bangladesh* (Dhaka: University Press, 1999).

[18] Lewis Sydney Steward O'Malley, *Eastern Bengal District Gazetteers: Chittagong* (Calcutta: The Bengal Secretariat Book Depot, 1908), 67.

[19] Syed Jamil Ahmed, "Halfway 'Becoming' on the Interface of Trsna and Desire: Examining Bauddha Kirtan as a Minor Performance in Bangladesh," in *Reading Against the Oriental Grain: Performance and Politics Entwined with a Buddhist Strain*, ed. Syed Jamil Ahmed (Kolkata: Anderson House, 2008), 306.

8 ARAKANESE CHITTAGONG BECAME MUGHAL ISLAMABAD ...   233

This geo-specific reference eventually became ethno-religious designation. Syed Hasan Askari states that Maga/Mog is "a term applied to a people of Buddhist persuasion and of the Mongloid race closely akin to those from whom sprang the Burmans of the Lower Irrawadi."[20] With the same ethno-religious connotations, early seventeenth-century Christian missionaries also used the term.[21] The early seventeenth-century use of the term had not conveyed the negative connotations that the term later came to be associated with. Recording the late eighteenth-century connotation of the term, Francis Buchanan notes,

> I find, that the appellation of Mug is given by the people of this province [=Bengal] to all the Tribes, and nations, east from Bengal, who as differing from the Hindoos, and Mussulmans, are considered as having no Cast [Caste?] and as therefore being highly contemptible.[22]

How and why did the Maga/Mog become "highly contemptible" in the eyes of majority Bengalis in the late eighteenth-century Bengal? Answering that important question directly helps us understand the Buddhist–Muslim relationship in Chittagong. Buchanan explains that the Maga/Mog's denial of caste system made them undesirable. His reference to "differing from the Hindoos, and Mussulmans" resonates with the Mughal characterization of Buddhism and Buddhists.

In Mughal vast territory, only Chittagong had a living Buddhist tradition. Even then it joined the empire too late in 1666 CE with too little influence. Therefore, Buddhism remains mute in the Mughal court history. The available few Mughal references to Buddhism and Buddhists were made in relation to their travel experience in neighboring Buddhist

---

[20] Syed Hasan Askari, "The Mughal-Magh Relations Down to the Time of Islam Khan Mashhadi," in *Indian History Congress: Proceedings of the Twenty-Second Session 1959, Gauhati*, eds. George Moraes, V.G. Hatalkar, and V.D. Rao, 201–213 (Bombay: Indian History Congress, 1960), 202.

[21] Jacques Leider, "On Arakanese Territorial Expansion: Origins, Context, Means and Practices," in *The Maritime Frontier of Burma: Exploring Political, Cultural and Commercial Interaction in the Indian Ocean World, 1200–1800*, eds. Jos J.L. Gommans and Jacques Leider (Amsterdam: Amsterdam KITLV Press, 2002), 127–149.

[22] Willem Van Schendel, "The Invention of the 'Jummas': State Formation and Ethnicity in Southeastern Bangladesh," *Modern Asian Studies* 26, no. 1 (1992): 100ff21.

234   D. M. BARUA

societies.[23] As the discussion on a Mughal text below indicates that the Mughals in fact lacked cultural frameworks to comprehend Buddhist beliefs and practices.

Tahir Muhammad's five-volume *Rauzat ut-Tàhirïn*, "The Immaculate Garden" (written during 1602–1607) was a well-circulated Persian work in Mughal India during the seventeenth and eighteenth centuries. It details Tahir Muhammad's (Moghul chronicler and emissary) visits to Buddhist Pegu and Arakan kingdoms (both are in contemporary Myanmar) while making passing comments on Buddhists in Sri Lanka. For Tahir Muhammad, Sinhalese were under Hindustan, by that he perhaps meant they were Hindus, and the Arakanese were a sort of Hindus.[24] In relation to the Buddhists in Pegu, Tahir Muhammad comments, "their way of life is different from both Muslim and Hindu (*az tariqa-i Musalmdndn-o-Hindu 'an alahida asi*)."[25] As Buchanan observed that the same non-affirmative description of Maga/Mog Buddhists (as neither Hindus nor Muslims) was in place in Chittagong during the late eighteenth century. Buchanan's echoing of Tahir Muhammad's description of Buddhists nearly after two centuries indicates the influence of the Mughal work, *Rauzat ut-Tàhirïn*, in shaping how general population in Bengal perceived Buddhists and Buddhism. This influential Mughal text also helps us discern why the Maga/Mog Buddhists in Chittagong were held "highly contemptible" by the people of Bengal in the late eighteenth century.

Tahir Muhammad passes on negative perceptions of Buddhists in Arakan and Pegu. In relation to the non-restrictive food consumption of the Buddhists, he records, "They ate all kinds of creatures, and had no restrictions on the kinds of food that were legitimate, not distinguishing *haram* from *halal*."[26] In fact, the Maga/Mogs were known for unrestricted food preparation that eventually provided them with new employment opportunities to serve as cooks in European households in colonial India.[27] It was not necessarily Buddhists' relaxed dietary habits

---

[23] Muzaffar Alam and Sanjay Subrahmanyam, "Southeast Asia as Seen from Mughal India Tahir Muhammad's 'Immaculate Garden' (Ca. 1600)," *Archipel* 70 (2005): 209–237.

[24] Alam and Subrahmanyam, "Southeast Asia," 219, 223.

[25] Alam and Subrahmanyam, "Southeast Asia," 220.

[26] Alam and Subrahmanyam, "Southeast Asia," 221.

[27] Francis Buchanan (Hamilton), "An Account of the Frontier Between Ava the Part of Bengal Adjacent to the Karnaphuli River," *Edinburgh Journal of Science* 3 (April–October 1825): 34.

or unconstrained food preparation made them undesirable; rather, Tahir Muhammad's judgments of them based on Islamic dietary restrictions made Maga/Mog Buddhists "highly contemptible." Interestingly, Tahir Muhammad in the same book expresses no distaste for the cannibalism found in Muslim Aceh (Indonesia)! As such Muzaffar Alam and Sanjay Subrahmanyam comment that the lack of Islam in Arakan and Pegu created a barrier for the Mughal writer to see the inhabitants of Arakan and Pegu as fully human beings. The people of those Buddhist societies were "rather peculiar creatures from Tahir Muhammad's viewpoint."[28] Alam and Subrahmanyam observe that the Mughal text *Rauzat ut-Tàhirïn* was quite well known and widely circulated. Its copies were found in Lucknow, Hyderabad, Calcutta, Mysore as well as in London and Oxford.[29] Its negative sentiments of Buddhists that derived from travel experiences in Arakan and Pegu later paved the way the Mughals perceived the Arakanese, particularly when both political forces faced each other as arch-rivals over the control of the Southeast Bengal region.

In early seventeenth century (approx. in 1612 CE), the Mughals defeated the local Hindu and Afghan *zamindars* and made East Bengal a Mughal territory. By then, the Arakanese had already made Chittagong an Arakanese territory since 1578 CE.[30] Until the Mughal conquest of Chittagong in 1666 CE, the Pheni River marked the boundary between two territories. For over five decades between 1612 and 1666 CE, the Arakanese and Mughals who respectively made Chittagong and Dhaka as their regional fortresses tried to invade each other's territories more than once; each time they defended their territories viciously. For example, the Mughal forces attacked Arakanese Chittagong twice.[31] Similarly, the Arakanese, with the help of the Portuguese naval forces, raided the Mughal powerhouse Dhaka twice: once in 1625 and then again in 1664.[32] They were rare contestants who challenged the expanding Mughal Empire in the seventeenth century with swift maritime raids.

Commenting on the Arakanese attacks on the Mughals, Shihabuddin Talish, a seventeenth-century Mughal historian who wrote under the name of *Fathiyyah-i-ibriyyah*, details:

[28] Alam and Subrahmanyam, "Southeast Asia," 223–234.

[29] Alam and Subrahmanyam, "Southeast Asia," 217.

[30] Leider, "On Arakanese Territorial Expansion," 133.

[31] Leider, "On Arakanese Territorial Expansion," 136.

[32] Leider, "On Arakanese Territorial Expansion," 141.

236 D. M. BARUA

Arracan pirates, both Magh and Feringi [the Portuguese], used constantly to [come] by the water-route and plunder Bengal. They carried off the Hindus and Muslims, male and female, great and small, few and many, that they could seize, pierced the palms of their hands, passed thin canes through the holes, and threw them on above another under the deck of their ships.... On their return to their homes, they employed the few hard lived captives that survived [this treatment] in tillage and other hard tasks, according to their power, with great disgrace and insult. Others were sold to the Dutch, English and French merchants at the ports of the Deccan.[33]

Such description not only justifies the Mughal takeover of Chittagong, but it also paves the way to demonize their political rivals, the Arakanese. In 1665, a year before the Mughals' final attack over Chittagong, Talish further humiliates, "The people of the country are called Maghs—which is an abbreviation of *Muhamil-i-sag* (despicable dog)...The inhabitants have no definite faith or religion, but incline rather to the Hindu creed."[34] If we read the above Mughal definition of the Arakanese with Edward Said's[35] insight on labeling "others," the term "Maga/Mog" itself articulates the Mughal "self" as the opposite of their "uncivilized other"—the Arakanese with no religion. In fact, the Mughal court records on its assemblies and dialogues with Asiatic others demonstrate that "the Mughals conceived of themselves as civilizing heroes."[36]

These demonizing portrayals of the Arakanese, as Jacques Leider calls them "Talish's emotive account[s]"[37] eventually influenced the Muslim perception of the Arakanese as well as Buddhists in Chittagong. Two examples, one from Muslim folk literature and the other from the Mughal political history of Chittagong, shed some light on the ways in which Muslims perceived Arakanese Buddhist Chittagong. According to the Muslim populous belief, "Chatigaon" is the Muslim rendition for the name Chittagong. Many Muslims in Chittagong believe that the name derived from an Islamic purifying ritual performed by Pir Badar with a

---

[33] Jadunath Sarkar, *Studies in Aurangzib's Reign* (London: Sangam Books, 1989), 127–128.

[34] Sarkar, *Studies in Auranzgzib's Reign* (1989), 124.

[35] Edward W. Said, *Orientalism* (New York: Vintage Books, 2003).

[36] Corinne Lefèvre, "The Majālis-I Jahāngīrī (1608–11): Dialogue and Asiatic Otherness at the Mughal Court," *Journal of the Economic and Social History of the Orient* 55 (2012): 27.

[37] Leider, "On Arakanese Territorial Expansion," 141.

8 ARAKANESE CHITTAGONG BECAME MUGHAL ISLAMABAD ... 237

chati (earthen lamp) to dispel, disperse and ultimately destroy "the evil spirits infesting the place."[38] If we read this popular narrative within the overlapping and interchanging religious history of Chittagong, then the ritual conveys a Muslim inhabitation of a non-Muslim space. Perhaps a more convincing example appears within Mughal court historical records. Mirza Muhammad Kazim's *Alamgirnamah*, the court history of Emperor Aurangzeb, records that "the Emperor ordered Chatgaon to be renamed Islamabad" after the Mughal's conquest of Chittagong in 1666.[39] The new name means "the Residence of the Faithful."[40] If we contextualize these two examples to the seventeenth century Mughal portrayals of Buddhists in Arakan and Pegu as "peculiar creatures" with "no definite faith or religion," the Muslim purifying ritual and the Mughal name for Chittagong make sense. They meant Islam and Muslim conquest brought civilization to Chittagong; that goes without saying that Buddhist Chittagong under the Arkanese rule (1589–1666 CE) was uncivilized and culturally backward. That is what exactly the term "Maga/Mog" came to mean in the subsequent periods when the Arakanese and Buddhist identities perceived to be one and the same.

The inclusion of the Arakanese under the name of Maga/Mog has added a racial dimension of negativity to already existing religio-cultural prejudice attached to the term. As we have noticed above, in Mughal Bengal, the Arakanese rule (1589–1666 CE) in Chittagong was portrayed to be an epitome of anarchy. Consequently, the Mughal anti-Arakanese racial prejudice gets subsumed in the term Maga/Mog with a new definition:

> The term *Mogh* derives from Sanskrit word *Moghdu* meaning *pirate*. The Moghs (the Rakhines) were engaged in abduction, looting and killings in Patuakhali together with the Portuguese pirates using the local *Bharai* canal as the main hub during the 16th century.[41]

---

[38] Lewis Sydney Steward O'Malley, *Eastern Bengal District Gazetteers: Chittagong* (Calcutta: The Bengal Secretariat Book Depot, 1908), 1.

[39] Jadunath Sarkar, *Studies in Aurangzib's Reign* (London: Sangam Books, 1989), 146.

[40] William Wilson Hunter, *A Statistical Account of Bengal (Chittagong Hill Tracts, Chittagong, Noakhali, Tipperah, Hill Tipperah, 1876)* (1876): 113–114.

[41] Sattendra Ghosal, *Bangladesh District Gazetteers: Patuakhali* (Dhaka: BG Press, 1982), 1.

238 D. M. BARUA

Notice that the preceding quotation historicizes the term Maga/Mog. Elaborating the term, Gayen racializes it below:

> *Mogher Muluk*, an adage (state of anarchy), came into common use in Bengal as referring to the time when these pirates held sway over the poor Bengalis. This is one reason the Rakhines [Arakanese] are still termed as *Mogh* in Bangladesh.[42]

Adding a voice of reason, Abdul Mabud Khan states,

> The history and tradition of Arakan manifestly proofs that Arakanese had largely been a civilized nation and no one from this race has taken to water piracy as a profession before the fourteenth century. The whole Rakhine populace should not be termed as Mogh or pirate for a handful of their ancestors were engaged in piracy several centuries earlier.[43]

These repeated examples illustrate that a racial bigotry derived from political rivalry has been added to what appears (according to the oral history of Bengali Buddhists) to be a religio-place oriented term Maga/Mog. With that development, the term became racialized. That is why all Buddhists in Chittagong regardless of their ethnic background are still called Maga/Mog, and it still means the Arakanese "other" who are perceived to be culturally backward, uncivilized and less progressive.

The preceding discussion indicates how the term Maga/Mog evolved from a neutral geo-religious reference to a racialized negative ethno-religious resignation. Such semantic evolution of the term demonstrates the cultural and religious hegemony of the Mughals shaping the Buddhist–Muslim relationship in the Bengal region. Buddhists in Chittagong have responded to this majority-cultural hegemony variously depending on where they have lived but also how they have been governed by the states since the Mughals.

---

[42] Audity Falguni Gayen, *The Rakhaines of Patuakhali and Barguna Region, in Quest for a Distance Homeland* (Chittagong: Codec Publication, 2007), 24.

[43] Abdul Mabud Khan, "Patuakhali Zillar Bauddha Sampraday," *CLIO: A Journal of History Department, Jahangirnagar University, Dhaka* 1 (June 1983): 8.

State Policies and the Muslim–Buddhist Relationship in the CHT

Due to geo-political policies and cultural (ethno-religious and linguistic) differences, Chittagong Buddhists' experiences with Muslims have been diverse. The CHT Buddhist–Muslim relationship has been closely tied with the politics of Chittagong; therefore, this section exclusively focuses on the Buddhist–Muslim relationship in CHT by discussing the state policies in detail. Since the mid-seventeenth century Mughal rule in the Chittagong plains, Buddhists in CHT had to come to terms with the powerful rulers of Chittagong district. With subordinate position, their political autonomy has gradually diminished. In this section, we will see that the Mughals did not interfere that much in the CHT. The British however imposed "indirect rule" by officially separating the CHT from the directly ruled plains. This CHT-plains separation was dismantled by the successive postcolonial states deteriorating the Buddhist–Muslim relationship. The colonial and postcolonial developments will be discussed in two separate sub-sections after a brief reference to the legend that illustrates the Mughal-CHT connection.

The Mughal's military might that ousted the powerful Arakanese rule of Chittagong must have overwhelmed the people of the CHT. Out of that subordination, an interesting legend emerged that suggests that Chakmas, the dominant ethnic group of the CHT, descend from the inter-marriages between Mughal soldiers and Arakanese women. With seven Chakma kings with the Afghan Muslim Khan name (from 1715 to 1830 CE),[44] the legend pretends to bear a historical truth. Taking the Muslim name Khan does not mean conversion to Islam[45]; it rather indicates political co-operation, negotiation and subordination to the Mughals. The Chakmas paid yearly tributes to the Mughal to convey their submission; some of them in fact resisted it. With less economic incentive and no challenging military power, the Mughals left the Chakmas and other ethnic groups in the CHT more or less alone. They were more concerned about the Arakanese in the south whom they displaced and the looming British power who would eventually replace them in Chittagong.

[44] Captain Thomas Herbert Lewin, *The Hill Tracts of Chittagong and the Dwellers Therein* (Calcutta: Bengal Printing Company, 1869), 63–64.

[45] Van Schendel, "The Invention of the 'Jummas'," 107.

240   D. M. BARUA

British Colonial Policies on the CHT

With the political power shift from the Mughals to the British, the people of the Chittagong hills became more integrated with political power of the Chittagong plains. Although the British East India Company took control of Chittagong district as early as 1760, it did not bother imposing political, economic or judicial intervention over the CHT until 1860. During the century in between, the people of the CHT were considered "tributaries" rather than "subjects."[46] The leaders of Chittagong hills continued to pay the yearly contribution to the British via a third party resident in Chittagong plain "to purchase the privilege of free-trade between the inhabitants of the hills and men of the plains."[47] This suggests that the initial contacts between the CHT Buddhists and Bengalis in the Chittagong plains were purely trade oriented and regulated by the British. The people in the hills exchanged their produce (cotton, timber, cane, umbrella leaves, etc.) with the people down the hills for dried fish and salt. Moreover, people from the plains including Bengali Muslims and Hindus were employed to serve the chiefs as well.[48] These trade arrangements continued throughout the colonial period with some supervision of the British officers.

In 1860, the British made the hill people colonial subjects by annexing the Chittagong hills with some governing measurements. The office named "Hill Superintendent," was introduced for "supervision of the independent tribes."[49] The hill region was renamed as the CHT and divided into three circles: Khagrachari with the Mong chief, Rangamati with the Chakma chief and Bandarban with the Bohmong chief. These three circles remained as a single district until they became three separate hill districts in the 1980s.[50] According to the CHT Regulation 1900 (the Hill Tracts Manual), the chiefs were expected to look after the productivity in their respective territory and share the proportionate tribute to the colonial officer. In addition to that, they were responsible for

---

[46] Lewin, *The Hill Tracts of Chittagong*, 22.

[47] Lewin, *The Hill Tracts of Chittagong*, 22.

[48] Van Schendel, "The Invention of the 'Jummas': State Formation and Ethnicity in Southeastern Bangladesh," *Modern Asian Studies* 26, no. 1 (1992): 99.

[49] Lewin, *The Hill Tracts of Chittagong*, 23.

[50] Bhumitra Chakma, "The Post-Colonial State and Minorities: Ethnocide in the Chittagong Hill Tracts, Bangladesh," *Commonwealth and Comparative Politics* 48, no. 3 (2010): 283.

8 ARAKANESE CHITTAGONG BECAME MUGHAL ISLAMABAD ...   241

maintaining peace and order within their groups.[51] These administrative measurements were introduced not only for effective revenue collection but also for military subjugation of the hill frontiers.

The 1860 annexation of the CHT was a direct colonial response to a murderous raid against some colonial subjects committed earlier that year by Kukies, an independent tribe in Tripura hills further north of the CHT. In 1860 a colonial expedition punished the members of Kukies who were responsible for the raid.[52] The annexation brought a sense of power balance between the hill people and people in the plains. Van Schendel explains, "before annexation the hill people were free agents who were feared by the plains people for their independence and military prowess."[53]

More importantly, the colonial annexation of the CHT and the subsequent plain-hill division demonstrate the quintessential colonial policy of "divide and rule." The nineteenth-century colonial records indicate that the plain-hill division was not merely topographical; it was also an ethno-cultural division. The 1860 hill-plain division in fact imposed the colonial perception of Bengali vs. non-Bengali population in the Chittagong region.[54] With the annexation, the colonial administration became the intermediary power that oversaw and regulated the hill-plain relationship. In order to regulate the growing encroachment of people from the plains to the CHT, the Manual was revised in 1920 and 1935. Both revisions declared the CHT as an "excluded area" and a "totally excluded area," respectively. Within these revisions, one had to receive permission from colonial and local authorities for resettlement. Bhumitra Chakma says that revisions were intended "to protect the hill people from the massive influx of Bengalis from the plains."[55] These colonial policies seem to have provided two ammunitions that hardened the Buddhist–Muslim relationship in the postcolonial period: territorial claim and perpetuation of Maga/Mog being culturally backward.

---

[51] Chakma, "The Post-Colonial State and Minorities," 284.

[52] Lewin, *The Hill Tracts of Chittagong*, 23.

[53] Van Schendel, "The Invention of the 'Jummas'," 108.

[54] D. Mitra Barua, "Thrice Honored Sangharaja Saramedha (1801–1882): Arakan-Chittagong Buddhism Across Colonial and Counter-Colonial Power," *The Journal of Burma Studies* 23, no. 1 (2019).

[55] Chakma, "The Post-Colonial State and Minorities," 184.

242   D. M. BARUA

The idea of territory-based governance and claims were new to the hill people who were historically nomads and organized around the idea of kinship. The power, authority and legitimacy of leadership derived from owning and mobilizing the manpower for cultivation and also for group defense by preemptive raids against perceived enemies. The mode of livelihood was *Jhum* or swidden cultivation: cleaning up a piece of the jungle, setting fire on the cutting to fertilize the ground, and then planting the seeds after a rainfall. After collecting the harvests, cultivators move on to a new piece of the jungle. This agriculture type is appropriately called shifting cultivation. In relation to the CHT people, Van Schendel observes, "all groups were continually on the move, not only because of their style of agriculture but also because of raids and warfare."[56]

The British administration considered *Jhum* cultivation to be antithetical to effective revenue generation and stationary livelihood. It therefore repeatedly tried to introduce plough cultivation to supplant *Jhum* cultivation, and the hill people time and time again resisted it.[57] Consequently, colonial legacy in economic fronts in the CHT has been minimal, but the most enduring colonial legacy has been rather in the ways in which the hill people have perceived and expressed their collective claim to the CHT. The British introduced the hill-plain division, and the hill people's territorial claim for the hill tracts have persisted by deteriorating the Buddhist–Muslim relationship in postcolonial setting. The postcolonial Pakistan and Bangladesh states have not quelled the territorial claims of the hill people; they rather inflamed them with aggressive policies.

Postcolonial State Policies in Relation to the Buddhist Majority CHT

The Buddhist majority CHT remains an anomaly in the formation of Hindu India and Muslim Pakistan in 1947. As religion was the determining factor in the postcolonial India-Pakistan state formation, theoretically the Buddhist CHT belonged neither to Pakistan nor to India. Due to its Buddhist majority and ethno-linguistic affinity, it would have been a better fit to integrate into Burma/Myanmar. But that option was

[56] Van Schendel, "The Invention of the 'Jummas'," 99–100.

[57] Van Schendel, "The Invention of the 'Jummas'," 112, 116.

not available. Due to religio-cultural affinity, the next best choice would have been to join Hindu India; that indeed was the wish of the CHT Buddhists. That wish was negotiated for the wish of Punjabis to join India rather than Pakistan.[58]

Postcolonial Pakistan and Bangladesh have used majority religion and language to unify their territories. Early on the Lahore-based postcolonial Pakistan government envisioned a unified Pakistan along with its east and west wings. It used Islam and Urdu as nation-unifying forces. With only 5% Urdu speakers in East Pakistan,[59] the Pakistan government imposed Urdu on the Bengali-speaking majority. Bengali resistance to the Urdu language policy eventually led to the 1971 independence of Bangladesh. The Bangladeshi government replaced the Urdu language policy with the Bangla language. Similarly, Islam has continued to define Bangladesh after a few years of secular state experiment. Neither Islam nor the national language Urdu/Bangla has resonated with the majority people of the CHT, who consequently have felt disintegrated first from Urdu-speaking Muslim Pakistan and then from Bangla-speaking Muslim Bangladesh. The national language and religion have become the media to express the tensions between the CHT and the rest of the country.

The postcolonial national territory of East Pakistan/Bangladesh has subsumed the colonial CHT regional territory. Although the Pakistan government started governing the CHT according to the colonial regulations in place, it soon replaced the colonial CHT designation "Excluded Area" with "Tribal Area."[60] This change in constitutional wording marks a turning point in the Bengali-CHT people relationship. It enabled the postcolonial state to access the resources in the CHT resulting in an economic exploitation of the area. Particularly the Kaptai Dam (1957–1962) construction on the Karnaphuli River in Rangamati district cost the Chakmas fortune. Over 100,000 people were displaced as they lost homes and cultivable land.[61] They received neither the benefit of the project nor the compensation for the property loss.

---

[58] Lailufar Yasmin, "The Tyranny of the Majority in Bangladesh: The Case of the Chittagong Hill Tracts," *Nationalism and Ethnic Politics* 20, no. 1 (2014): 122.

[59] Chakma, "The Post-Colonial State and Minorities," 285.

[60] Yasmin, "The Tyranny of the Majority," 122.

[61] Chakma, "The Post-Colonial State and Minorities," 286.

244   D. M. BARUA

More importantly, the hydraulic project also brought Bengali people into the CHT area in the 1960s[62] increasing the Buddhist–Muslim tension. This Bengali encroachment intensified in the early 1970s with newly found Bangladesh's Bengali nationalism. The CHT people have felt disempowered and disappointed; the privileges that they had enjoyed under the British administration were taken away. The political indifference to the legitimate concerns of the CHT people led to an armed struggle starting in the late 1970s and ending with the 1997 peace accord. At the core in this struggle were two types of territories: the colonial CHT territories and the postcolonial national territories. Chakma summarizes how an arm conflict developed between the Bangladeshi government and the CHT people:

> The post-colonial states' military, bureaucratic, political and economic encroachment into *the territories of the indigenous peoples* produce strong reaction from them, which is perceived by state elites as a threat to national security and *[the nation's]territorial integrity* and in turn generates militarized security policies which lead to the systematic destruction of the cultures and identities of indigenous communities. [emphasis added][63]

Thus, we see that the colonial separate governance of the CHT has influenced to form the CHT peoples' territorial claim in postcolonial setting. Similarly, the Bengalis too have found the counter-ammunition to dominate the CHT people in colonial description of the latter.

Scholars have observed that the impact of the nineteenth-century colonial ethnological literature in shaping the plain-hill people relationship in the postcolonial period. On the one hand, the hill people were often described as "primitives" "savages" and "wild hill tribes" with no civilization, and the term "tribe" has persisted and even got enshrined in postcolonial Pakistan constitution.[64] On the other hand, there was already the ancient village-forest distinction in South Asia that associates civilization with the village camp. Van Schendel argues that these emit and colonial etic perspectives have paved the way to form the following dominant Bengali view in the 1970s:

---

[62] Yasmin, "The Tyranny of the Majority," 122.

[63] Chakma, "The Post-Colonial State and Minorities," 282.

[64] Yasmin, "The Tyranny of the Majority," 122.

8 ARAKANESE CHITTAGONG BECAME MUGHAL ISLAMABAD ... 245

They [the hill people] are backward and childlike, and therefore need to be protected, educated and disciplined by those who are more advanced socially. The relationship between Bengalis and hill people is seen as one of guardianship, and Bengalis assume the responsibility to 'uplift' their charges, to bring them into contact with the modern world.[65]

This patronizing view was certainly to be blamed for deteriorating the Bengali-CHT people relationship at the formation of Bangladesh.

In 1972, a CHT delegation came to Dhaka to share their concerns including the influx of Bengali people into the CHT. It had a meeting with Sheikh Mujib Rahaman, the founder of Bangladesh. Instead of sympathizing the CHT concerns, the founder instructed the delegation "to forget their ethnic identities"[66] and "go home and become Bengalis."[67] These demoralizing instructions imply that the non-Bengali ethnic identities are not worthy of remembering and maintaining; instead, they deserve to be replaced with Bengali identities. With that state ideology, state-sponsored systemic Bengali settlement was introduced in 1972; that made the hill people almost a minority by the time the government agreed to stop it in 1997. In 1951 Bengali people in CHT constituted only 9.9%; that number increased to 48.57% in 1991. With this development, Islamization of the CHT has surged[68] resulting in frequent Buddhist–Muslim confrontations. Commenting on the religions of CHT people who are mainly Buddhists, the Bengali writer Abdus Sattar states, "their religious beliefs and practices completely insulates [*sic*] them against the demands of modernism."[69] The terms like insulation, isolation and exclusion have been used to suggest that the CHT people have lacked civilization, progress, development and modernity. This is a continuation of the anti-Buddhist and anti-Arakanese Bengali sentiments imbued in the term "Maga/Mog" that we discussed earlier. As we will notice in the next section, the multiethnic Buddhists in Chittagong have responded to these religio-cultural and racial bigotries variously.

[65] Van Schendel, "The Invention of the 'Jummas'," 103.

[66] Chakma, "The Post-Colonial State and Minorities," 288.

[67] Yasmin, "The Tyranny of the Majority," 123.

[68] Chakma, "The Post-Colonial State and Minorities," 291, 294.

[69] Abdus Sattar, *Tribal Culture in Bangladesh* (Dacca: Muktadhara, 1975), 7.

246   D. M. BARUA

BUDDHIST RESPONSES TO THE MUSLIM MAJORITY HEGEMONY

Bangladesh is a predominantly Muslim country with tolerance of religious minorities. This tolerant image is increasingly under attack with politicization of majority religion, a phenomenon characterizes the whole region including neighboring India and Myanmar. Although religion has been deeply entrenched in the region's politics throughout the twentieth century, politicization of religion in Bangladesh has never been so minority-unfriendly until the last decade of the twentieth century. Perhaps, the Islamization of the Bangladesh constitution is to be blamed for the change. In 1977 the constitution replaced its spirit of secularism with the invocation of absolute trust in Allah and then making Islam as the state religion in 1988. These Islamicist seizes of the country's constitution, for some Muslim fundamentalists, meant that religious minorities like Hindus, Buddhists and Christians do not have the constitutional right to live in Bangladesh unless they convert to Islam. The same constitution with the Islamic overtone, however, guarantees the practice of non-Islamic religions.

All religious minorities who constitute only 10% or so of the country's total population formed the Hindu Bouddho Christian Oikyo Parishad (the Hindu Buddhist Christian Unity Council) to collectively raise awareness and demand justice for the anti-minority atrocities.[70] One could expect a similar collective response from Buddhists who constitutes less than 1% of nearly 163 million Bangladesh populations. But they have been diverse in responding to Muslim aggression due to their living arrangement with majority Muslims. In the two sub-sections below, I separately discuss how Buddhist responses to majority Muslims in the CHT differ from their counterparts in the Chittagong plains.

The CHT Buddhists' Responses to the Muslim Majority

The CHT Buddhists historically have been majority. As this religious majority status has been challenged with systematic Bengali resettlement, the CHT Buddhists' main concern has been to mitigate growing Muslim aggression. They responded variously with one main goal: limiting the Muslim encroachment into the CHT area. As the Pakistan government dismantled the special status of the CHT, which was effective from the

---

[70]Guhathakurta, "Religious Minorities," 320.

early nineteenth century, the CHT Buddhists resisted it with forming the "Pahari Chattra Samity" (Hill Students Society)[71] to stop the state economic exploitation of the CHT with the Kaptai Dam. As their concerns received no attention, they secretly formed the "Chittagong Hill Tracts Welfare Association" in 1966 to politically resist the state. This organization later renamed as the "Parbotyo Chottrogram Jono Shonghoti Shomiti" (Chittagong Hill Tracts People's Solidarity Association), which has represented the political voice of the CHT people.

With the Pakistan-backed military government coming to power in 1975, the CHT people formed the armed group "Shanti Bahini" (Peace Troops) to resist the state and state-sponsored Bengali in-migration.[72] The Indian government was behind the formation of the armed resistance as well as its end with the Peace Accord signed in 1997.[73] Although almost all members of the "Shanti Bahini" came from Buddhist families, they never defined their struggle as Buddhist. For them it was an inter-ethnic conflict from beginning to the end. Therefore, Buddhists in the Chittagong plains were not directly affected by the civil war that lasted over 20 years. The government, in addition to the state's armed forces, equipped the Muslim migrants with arms who not only fought against the Shanti Bahini but also killed Buddhist monks and attacked Buddhist institutions in the CHT. In hindsight, the armed struggle was deadly. It cost many lives from both parties and made many CHT people refugees in India. More importantly, if the conflict accelerated the Bengali settlement in the CHT, which it seems to have, then the armed resistance was counterproductive. With the 1997 Peace Accord signed, at least the state assisted Bengali settlement in the CHT has been terminated.

In addition to the political and military responses, the CHT Buddhists also responded culturally and socially to the Muslim majority encroachment into their home region. The CHT people are multiethnic and multireligious. The majority of them practice Buddhism, although many Christians, Animists and some Hindus do exist among them. Despite of all these differences, what binds them together is their experience as a hill people who have relied on *Jhum* or swidden cultivation. This

---

[71] Chakma, "The Post-Colonial State and Minorities," 286.

[72] Van Schendel, "The Invention of the 'Jummas'," 120.

[73] Yasmin, "The Tyranny of the Majority," 124.

248   D. M. BARUA

common experience has become the basis for the creation of the *Jumma* people. Van Schendel notes,

> A remarkable cultural innovation occurred which was reflected in the emergence of a new term to designate the people of the Chittagong hills. They were now called 'Jumma'. An old *pejorative term for 'swidden cultivator'* in the Chittagongian dialect of Bengali... It is remarkable that this term came up at a time when many hill people had been *forced to give up swidden cultivation*. [emphasis added][74]

Interestingly, the *Jumma* identity encapsulates all the derogatory attitudes of the Mughals, the British, the Pakistanis and Bengalis against the ethno-religious minority in Chittagong: wild, hilly, uncivilized and unprogressive. Historically the term Maga/Mog seems more fitting than *Jumma*. The latter enabled the CHT people to deemphasize the ethno-religious (Arakanese Buddhist) connotation of the former. By doing so, the *Jumma* designation includes non-Buddhists (i.e., Christian and Animists, but not Muslim settlers from plains) in the CHT. This newly adopted self-identity does not signal the CHT people's internalization of the hegemonic attitudes; it rather signifies their resistance to them.

In addition to the *Jhum* experience, the hill people also share the common experience of resistance to the Bengalis from the plains. By embracing a derogative term used by their cultural outsiders (Bengalis), the hill people refuse to yield to the cultural pressure and aggression of Bengali settlers. Nile Green and Mary Searle-Chatterjee observe, "the use of stereotyped and derogatory labeling for distancing other people is a two-way process that may be employed by those who resist power as much as by those who possess it."[75] Thus *Jumma* is a reactionary identity that draws upon not only on what identity holders have common but also what they are up against collectively: the Bengali Muslim aggression in the CHT. Due to a more pervasive Muslim presence, we see a different Buddhist response in the plains.

---

[74] Van Schendel, "The Invention of the 'Jummas'," 120–121.

[75] Nile Green and Mary Searle-Chatterjee, "Religion, Language, and Power: An Introductory Essay," in *Religion, Language and Power*, eds. Nile Green and Mary Searle-Chatterjee (New York: Routledge, 2008), 13.

The Buddhist–Muslim Relationship in the Plains

Unlike their fellow Buddhists in the CHT, Buddhists in the Chittagong plains share the same ethnicity and language with Bengali Muslims. Since early twentieth century, they have identified themselves as Bengali Buddhists; that seems to have led them to be excluded from the growing scholarship on Bangladesh's non-Bengali population.[76] That absence itself indicates their integration into the Bengali ethnicity.[77] Bengali Buddhists' relationship with Muslims characterizes an inter-religious coexistence. Historically, they have been living in rural villages dotted across the Chittagong division, mainly in the districts of Chittagong and Cox's Bazar, but also in Noakhali and Comilla districts. In my recent survey, I have noticed that there are over 250 Buddhist villages, and their sizes vary from 30 families to 800 families.

As these villages are surrounded by those of Muslims, Bengali Buddhists' everyday socio-economic interaction with fellow Bengali Muslims is inevitable. Although Bengali Buddhists live in major cities like Dhaka and Chittagong; one can hardly find Buddhist urban neighborhoods. As such, active Buddhist life either in village or town with no contact with Muslims is unthinkable. The Buddhist–Muslim interaction extends from labor sharing in farming or working together in factories or offices, to land leasing and to children's schooling. Friendly Muslim–Buddhist relationship is pervasive at all age groups; the adjective "friendly," however, does not convey a sense of equality.

As the term majority-minority suggests, the Muslim–Buddhist relationship is asymmetrical. Paradoxically, friendliness and inequality characterize the Muslim–Buddhist coexistence in the Chittagong plains. The preceding Muslim–Buddhist description significantly differs from its counterpart in the CHT. This striking difference, perhaps, stems

---

[76] Philip Gain, ed., *Indigenous Peoples of Bangladesh* (Dhaka: Society for Environment and Human Development, 1993); Philip Gain, ed., *Culture of Adivasis in Bangladesh* (Dhaka: Society for Environment and Human Development, 2008); Abul Barkat, et al., *Life and Land of Adibashis: Land Dispossession and Alienation of Adibashis in the Plain Districts of Bangladesh* (Dhaka: Pathak Shamabesh, 2009); Sanjeeb Drong, ed., *Ādibāsīdera Arthanaitika O Sāmājika Adhikāra, Saṃhati, 2008 (Economic and Social Rights of Indigenous Peoples, Solidarity 2008)* (Ḍhākā: Bāṃlādeśa Ādibāsī Phorāma, 2008); Āiẏuba Hosena, et al., *Baṃlādeśar Kshudra Jātigoṣṭhī*, 1st ed. (Ḍhākā: Hākkānī Pābaliśārsa, 2009).

[77] Despite of this ethnic integration, Bengali Buddhists are not free from religious connotation of Maga/Mog. One can still hear Muslims call them as "Bengali Maga/Mog."

from the fact that Bengali Buddhists in Chittagong plains do not have a geo-political territory to claim or to defend for. No single publication to my knowledge thus far has talked about how Buddhists in the plains have maintained a relative peaceful coexistence with majority Muslims. The dearth of scholarship on the issue does not mean that Buddhists in the plains are free from Muslim majority aggression; it rather suggests that inter-religious conflicts are louder than inter-religious coexistence. Bengali Buddhist minority's responses to the Muslim majority aggression significantly differ from those of the CHT Buddhists.

Rather than highlighting the cultural differences, Buddhists in Chittagong plains have emphasized the cultural similarities with Bengalis to fend off the anti-Buddhist sentiments expressed in the term Maga/Mog. As the majority Bengali equated the term with the Arakanese ethnic/racial identity, Buddhists in the Chittagong plains dropped the term altogether from self-reference, although the term might have derived from Magadha—their oral tradition based ancestral home. Perhaps, they found the racialized term's associated connotations like piracy, abduction and slavery to be too negative that would jeopardize their coexistence with Bengalis.

During the late nineteenth and early twentieth centuries, Buddhists in the Chittagong plains variously strived to reintroduce themselves anew. First, a few written efforts were made in the Bengali language to trace back to the history of the community.[78] Second, Buddhists in the Chittagong plains decoupled themselves from the Arakanese. Some family history and genealogy documents of Buddhists in the Chittagong plains indicate gradual decline and eventual termination of Arakanese surnames such as Manfru, Satangfru-and Nonditafru (derived from the Chittagong Plain Buddhists-Arkanese inter-Buddhist marriages). Third, various Arakanese surnames (noted above) as well as those Mughal origin such as Talukdar and Mutsuddi were replaced with the "Barua" common surname. For instance, the internationally acclaimed Indologist and Buddhologist Beni Madhab Barua (1888–1948) gave up his paternal last name Mutsuddi for Barua as he moved from Chittagong to Calcutta in the early twentieth century. He believed that Barua surname represents the ancestral history of the Buddhists in the Chittagong plains.

---

[78] Ram Chandra Barua, *Moger Itihas (History of Mogs)* (Calcutta: Katan Press, 1905); Kalikinkar, *Adi Purush (Early Ancestors)* (Rangoon, 1915).

Since the early twentieth century, Barua surname became popular creating a sense of communal homogeneity. An overwhelming majority of Bengali-speaking Buddhists living in Chittagong and Dhaka identify themselves with Barua surname. A similar phenomenon is also noticeable in Calcutta and Siliguri of India's West Bengal as well as in a few other cities across India's northeast region. Bengali-speaking Buddhists with Barua surnames in these places mentioned above trace their history to the Chittagong plains itself. Currently, Barua has become an exclusive Buddhist surname in Bangladesh; however, that is not the case in India where Buddhism and Hinduism tend to overlap among the Bengali-speaking Buddhists. Moreover, there is an influential Assamese Hindu community with the same last name (spelled as Baruah) in Assam. Assamese history suggests that Baruah title predates the early seventeenth-century socio-political origin of the higher administrative office namely "Barbarua" by Ahom King Pratab Singh (r. 163–143).[79] In Chittagong, the ubiquitous Buddhist family name is often associated with the oral tradition of the Magadha-Chittagong Buddhist migration via Assam discussed above. This suggests that although Barua was collectively adopted or revived by Bengali-speaking Buddhists in the Chittagong plains, the underlying oral narrative of Magadha-Chittagong Buddhist migration implied in the Maga/Mog identity has remained the same. The adoption also indicates Bengali Buddhists' resistance to the Maga/Mog identity and preference for alternative identities.

In the late nineteenth century, Buddhists in Chittagong plains gravitated toward regional identities, i.e., Chittagong and Bengal Buddhists. They went out of Chittagong in search of employment in colonial cities like Calcutta (Kolkata), Akyab (Sittwe) and Rangoon (Yangon). These outward movements increasingly put them in contact with other Buddhists such as the Sinhalese and the Burmese. Such repeated inter-Buddhist interactions very likely have heightened their need for distinct and positive self-identification. They presented themselves as "Chittagong Buddhists" at the inter-Buddhist gathering organized by Henry Steel Olcott in the 1880s.[80] They formed "Chittagong Buddhist Association" in Chittagong (1887) and Rangoon (1902). Those who

---

[79] Swarna Lata Baruah, *A Comprehensive History of Assam* (New Delhi: Munishiram Manoharlal Publishers, 1985), 673.

[80] Henry Steel Olcott, *A Buddhist Catechism, According to the Canon of the Southern Church. The Biogen Series, no. 3* (Boston: Estes and Lauriat, 1885).

252   D. M. BARUA

ended up being in colonial Calcutta and Akyab however preferred a broader self-identification, i.e., Bengal Buddhists. As such, the "Bengal Buddhist Association" in Calcutta (1892) and the "Bengal Buddhist Temple" in Akyab (1910s) were established. Dr. Beni Madhab Barua, the Professor of Indology at the University of Calcutta wrote "Bongiya Bauddha Samaj" (The Bengal Buddhist Society) in *Jagajjyoti*[81] and that refers to five Buddhist ethnic groups with historical roots to the greater Chittagong area.

The inclusive and regional reference "Bengal" has served as a springboard to emerge an exclusive and ethnic identity: Bengali Buddhist. In 1937, Sri Umesh Chandra Chowdhury, a Chittagong lay Buddhist leader living in colonial Burma addressed his fellow Buddhists as the "Bengali Buddhists, the descendants of Indian Buddhists" (*Hey hatabhagya Bharatiya Bauddader Bonshodor Bangali Bauddhagan*). He encouraged fellow Chittagong Buddhists in Burma to learn the Burmese language to strengthen connections with the Burmese and to better understand Buddhist scriptures to translate them in Bengali.[82] He however warned not to get into inter-ethnic marriages with the Burmese. He admits that such marriages may not hurt their Buddhist identity, but he worries that such inter-ethnic marriages may eventually lead to lose "Bengali identity."[83] How and why did a regional designation become an ethnic designation? In other words, in what socio-political conditions in the 1930s did "Bengal Buddhists" become "Bengali Buddhists"?

The contents of three community periodicals (*Bauddhabandhu, Jogojjyoti*, and *Sangha Shakti*) of the time suggest that the 1930s anti-foreign/Indian sentiment in Colonial Burma and anti-colonial movements in Chittagong and Bengal were crucial for the emergence of Buddhist affiliation to the Bengali ethnic identity. Chittagong plain Buddhist migrants in Rangoon and Akyab found cultural and linguistic affinities with wider Indian migrants there. Therefore, they too became the subject of the 1930s Burmese revolt against non-Burmese individuals. Chowdhury who identified Chittagong plain Buddhists as "Bengali

---

[81] Benimadhab Barua, "Bongiya Bauddha Samaj," *Jagajjyoti: A Buddhist Monthly in Bengali* 4, no. 5 (1912).

[82] Sri Umesh Chandra Chowdhury, "Brahma-Prabashi Bangali Bauddhagoner Kartavya (The Duties of Bengali Buddhist Expatriates in Burma)," *Snagha Shakti*, no. Mahasanghadan Ashari Purnima (1937): 230.

[83] Chowdhury, "Brahma-Prabashi Bangali Bauddhagoner Kartavya," 233.

Buddhists" expresses ethnic and cultural pride that separates them from the Burmese despite of their shared Buddhist identity with the latter.[84]

Similarly, a shared Bengali affinity has overshadowed the Buddhist–Muslim religious difference in Mongdaw in Rakhine state, one of the epicenters of the contemporary Buddhist–Muslim violence. The 9th and 10th issue of the *Sangha Shakti* (Vol. 12) in 1941, reports that Dhirendra Lal Chowdhury, the son of Chittagong Buddhist leader Krishna Chandra Chowdhury, became a wealthy landlord in Wailadong, Mongdaw in northern Arakan (Rakhine). Many people worked for him; majority of them were Muslims although Arakanese and Chittagong plain Buddhists also were there. They all lived on his land, and Chowdhury sponsored a hospital, a registry office, a temple (Bodhiratna) and, more importantly, a mosque and Urdu education for Muslims in Arakan. The *Sangha Shakti* notes,

> For the religious practices of his Muslim workers, he [Dhirendra Lal Chowdhury] donated 13 acres of his land [to build] mosque in the area. He also made 60 acres of his land tax-free for the benefit of mosque. He also financially supported for the Urdu education.[85]

These reports in the community periodical speak aloud about the Buddhist–Muslim harmony and coexistence. Moreover, Buddhists in the Chittagong plains worked shoulder to shoulder with other Bengalis in anti-colonial activities, particularly in the Chittagong Uprising (1930–1941).[86] Working with other Bengali Hindus and Muslims to form a united Bengali front against the British colonial administration and to face the 1930s anti-Indian/Bengali sentiments led to crystalize their affinity with ethnic Bengali identity. This identity has been expressed through Bengali language, dress, food, music, etc., as a result of the coexistence with other Bengali Hindus and Muslims for centuries.

Bengali Buddhist identity suggests that ethnicity evolves over-time. Not all ethnic identities are genetic or inherited. Some are in fact learned and ascribed. Historically, Bengali has been primarily a linguistic

---

[84] Chowdhury, "Brahma-Prabashi Bangali Bauddhagoner Kartavya."

[85] Sangha Shakti, Vol. 12, 1941: 338.

[86] Bongopadyaya, 2011: 61–65; Ajay Singh Badua, "Inspector of Faridpur Killed," in *Easter Rebellion in India: The Chittagong Uprising*, ed. Mallikarjuna Sharma (Hyderabad: Marxist Study Forum, 1993), 305.

identity[87] although it has been used to express ethnicity. Replacing Maga/Mog with Bengal/Bengali identity over a century ago foreshadows a scholar's advice to the Muslim minority hoping for peaceful coexistence with the Buddhist majority in Sri Lanka: "assert a more distinctively Sri Lankan cultural identity."[88] The articulation of Bengali identity has thus far helped Buddhists in the Chittagong plains to secure peaceful coexistence with Muslim majority, but the 2012 anti-Buddhist violence has challenged such co-ethnicity based coexistence.

As the 2012 Ramu violence indicates that Buddhists in Chittagong have become the victims of Myanmar's Rohingya crisis. The wide-spread and simplistic characterization of the crisis as simply being a Buddhist majority's violence against a Muslim minority has further exacerbated Chittagong Buddhists' predicament of being a tiny religious minority (less than one percent of Bangladesh's total population) in a predominantly Muslim majority country. What is warranted is a nuanced understanding of the Rohingya crisis as a conflict over a contested notion of indigeneity predicated upon the Rohingya identity. Debunking the reductionist and black-and-white interpretations of the crisis, Anthony Ware and Coast as Laoutides argue that the Rohingya crisis is neither a "merely oppression of a minority" nor "about a denial of citizenship or statelessness"; it is rather "a multi-polar conflict with complex social-political dynamics … in which at least three groups [the Rohingya hardliners, the Rakhine nationalists, the Burmese military] react defensively, out of deeply compelling existential fears."[89] At this conflicts' core, as Ware and Laoutides discern, is the Rohingya identity, particularly non-Rohingya Myanmar population's perception of it: "the term 'Rohingya' is widely perceived by most people inside Myanmar … to be a gambit by a recent mixed-origin migrant group for greater political rights by claiming indigeneity under Myanmar law—through that, to claim territory and self-governance."[90] This suggests that the Rohingya crisis is

---

[87] M.H. Klaiman, "Bengali," in *The Major Languages of South Asia, the Middle East and Africa*, ed. Bernard Comrie (London: Routledge, 2005), 55.

[88] Dennis B. McGilvray, "Rethinking Muslim Identity in Sri Lanka," in *Buddhist Extremists and Muslim Minorities: Religious Conflict in Contemporary Sri Lanka*, ed. John Clifford Holt (New York: Oxford University Press, 2016), 76.

[89] Anthony Ware and Coastas Laoutides, *Myanmar's 'Rohingya' Conflict* (London: Hurst & Co., 2018), 18, 21.

[90] Ware and Laoutides, *Myanmar's 'Rohingya' Conflict*, xvi.

fundamentally a political one: an autonomous territorial claim for the Muslim minority within Myanmar's Rakhine state. This political claim itself was initially inspired by the idea of Pakistan as a separate state for Muslim minority within Hindu majority India.[91] Such politicization of religion has victimized Hindu and Muslim minorities across the political borders in the region; Buddhist minority in Bangladesh have become the latest victims of it. As Myanmar's Rohingya conflict intensified in 2012, the centuries-long Buddhist–Muslim peaceful coexistence in the Chittagong plains has been lost. That interreligious harmony in the Chittagong plains had been strong enough to endure the two-decade-long (1975–1997) conflict between the Bangladeshi government and Buddhist majority Chakmas in its own backyard: the CHT. Nevertheless, the Chittagong plains uncharacteristically became vulnerable to religious intolerance resulting from the unprecedented Rohingya exodus into its domain.

As repeated bilateral and multilateral repatriation talks failed, over one million Rohingya refugees have taken shelters in Bangladesh's Ukhiya-Teknaf area. They have almost tripled the region's local population that amounts to only four-hundred thousands. The environmental, social, and economic impacts of the Rohingya exodus on the local community yet to be sufficiently assessed. It has already eroded Buddhists' trust in fellow Muslim majority neighbors. Since the anti-Buddhist attack in 2012, some of the Buddhist temples have been under security surveillance and the Bangladeshi police force is employed for 24/7 to deter and avoid possible attacks on these temples. During my fieldwork in the region in December 2017, I witnessed police personnel are on duty at Buddhist temple premises. Buddhist laity expressed that they have taken the responsibility of feeding the policemen three times a day so that the personnel do not leave the temples unprotected during the meal hours. It seems that feeding the policemen has become their religious obligation, similar to feeding temple monks twice a day. In my interview with the head monk of the Ramu Central Sima Vihar, Ven. Satraypriya Mahathera who survived the 2012 violence, expressed "Thanks to the government's forces/guards we are still alive. Without the security personnel constant presence, we could have been dead now." As long as the Rohingya crisis remains unresolved and Rohingyas are camped in

---

[91] Swapna Bhattacharya, *The Rakhine State (Arakan) of Myanmar: Interrogating History, Culture, and Conflict* (Kolkata: Manuhar, 2015), 33.

256   D. M. BARUA

Bangladesh, Buddhist minority in Bangladesh continue to live in fear and insecurity hoping for the return of the historical Buddhist–Muslim peaceful coexistence.

Conclusion

In the preceding discussion, I have laid out how an ethnically diverse Buddhist community in the greater Chittagong area displays a unique Buddhist–Muslim relationship. By focusing on the derogative term Maga/Mog, a designation referred to all multiethnic Buddhists in the region, I have discussed the shifting Buddhist–Muslim relationship in four successive states from the Mughal Empire to contemporary Bangladesh. The term might have had invoked a generic Buddhist identity due to its etymological connection to Magadha, the Buddhist stronghold in medieval India. In seventeenth century, the term absorbed Mughals' religio-cultural and moral judgment on the Southeast Asian Buddhists as "peculiar creatures" with no faith, no religion and no ethics. In Mughal India, Buddhism sustained as a living tradition only in Arakanese Chittagong. Therefore, it was exclusively associated with Mughals' arch political rival—the Arakanese. In this context, Maga/Mog carried racial and religious bigotries. Accordingly, Maga/Mog has conveyed the meaning of anarchy, piracy and more explicitly lack of civilization.

The Mughal religio-racial bigotry against Buddhists continued with the British colonial exclusion policy that governed the CHT, a Buddhist majority region. In postcolonial setting the territories of the CHT were violently contested that deteriorated the Bengali Muslim-CHT Buddhist relationship. Bengali Muslims charged the CHT Buddhists being anti-civilized, unprogressive and anti-modern. In a reactionary response, the CHT people invented the *Jumma* identity, another derogative term associated with *Jhum* or swidden cultivation. They did so to highlight their cultural difference with Bengali Muslims. On the other hand, Buddhists in the Chittagong plains responded to the charge of being uncivilized by rejecting the Maga/Mog identity altogether by embracing the Bengali identity in the early twentieth century. They, as Bengali Buddhists, have highlighted cultural similarity with Bengali Muslims.

These two opposite responses from a Buddhist minority to the Muslim majority partly derive from two distinct historical Muslim–Buddhist existences: separate governance of the CHT that limited the

8 ARAKANESE CHITTAGONG BECAME MUGHAL ISLAMABAD ...   257

Buddhist–Muslim interaction and inter-religious coexistence in the Chittagong plains. The latter also stems from Bengali Buddhists' localization and articulation of their ethnic identity to resonate with that of the Muslim majority. The 2012 Ramu violence against Bengali Buddhists reminds us that religious difference overtrumps ethnic similarity; that itself is a new troubling turning point in the Muslim–Buddhist relationship in Bangladesh. Since 2012, Bengali Buddhists in the Chittagong plains have been living in fear of being victimized for the armed conflict between the Arakanese Rohingya Salvation Army and the Burmese National Army in Myanmar's Rakhine state that has made over one million Arakanese Muslims to seek refuge in Chittagong. In December 2017, I witnessed a few government security personnel were on duty at main temples in Cox's Bazar and Chittagong for 24/7. The recently developed religio-nationalism and religio-terrorism in the region have kept challenging the strength of the Buddhist–Muslim coexistence and relationship in Chittagong cultivated for many centuries.

Acknowledgements I am grateful to the Robert H.N. Ho Family Foundation Postdoctoral Fellowship in Buddhist Studies (administered by the American Council of Learned Societies) for its generous funding that enabled me to conduct the research. I also would like to thank the esteem editors of this volume Michael Jerryson and Iselin Frydenlund for their thoughtful comments that enriched the chapter in many ways.

References

Ahmed, Syed Jamil. "Halfway 'Becoming' on the Interface of Trsna and Desire: Examining Bauddha Kirtan as a Minor Performance in Bangladesh." In *Reading Against the Oriental Grain: Performance and Politics Entwined with a Buddhist Strain*, edited by Syed Jamil Ahmed, 232–323. Kolkata: Anderson House, 2008.

Alam, Muzaffar, and Sanjay Subrahmanyam. "Southeast Asia as Seen from Mughal India: Tahir Muhammad's 'Immaculate Garden' (Ca. 1600)." *Archipel* 70 (2005): 209–237.

Askari, Syed Hasan. 1960. "The Mughal-Magh Relations Down to the Time of Islam Khan Mashhadi." In *Indian History Congress: Proceedings of the Twenty-Second Session 1959, Gauhati*, edited by George Moraes, V.G. Hatalkar, and V.D. Rao, 201–213. Bombay: Indian History Congress.

258 D. M. BARUA

Badua, Ajay Singh. "Inspector of Faridpur Killed." In *Easter Rebellion in India: The Chittagong Uprising*, edited by Mallikarjuna Sharma, 304–305. Hyderabad: Marxist Study Forum, 1993.

Bandyopadhyay, Biswanath. *Chttagram Abhyuthane (1930–1941) Musulman, Bauddhya Eban Samagra Mahila Samaj*. Kolkata: Rupali, 2011.

Barkat, Abul, Mozammel Hoque, and Sadeka Halim. *Life and Land of Adibashis: Land Dispossession and Alienation of Adibashis in the Plain Districts of Bangladesh*. Dhaka: Pathak Shamabesh, 2009.

Barua, Benimadhab. "Bongiya Bauddha Samaj." *Jagajjyoti: A Buddhist Monthly in Bengali* 4, no. 5 (1912): 35–38.

Barua, D. Mitra. "Thrice Honored Sangharaja Saramedha (1801–1882): Arakan-Chittagong Buddhism Across Colonial and Counter-Colonial Power." *The Journal of Burma Studies* 23, no. 1 (2019): 37–85.

Barua, Ram Chandra. *Moger Itihas (History of Mogs)*. Calcutta: Katan Press, 1905.

Barua, Swarna Lata. *A Comprehensive History of Assam*. New Delhi: Munishiram Manoharlal Publishers, 1985.

Berthet, Samuel. "Boat Technology and Culture in Chittagong." *Water History* 7 (2015): 179–197.

Bhattacharya (Chakraborti), Swapna. "Contributions of Kripasaran Mahasthavir to the World of Buddhist Reform and Buddhist Scholarship of the 19th Century India and Beyond." In *Karmayogi Kripasaran Mahasthavir Commemorative Volume*, edited by Shimul Barua, 368–376. Chittagong: Chittagong Buddhist Monastery, 2015.

———. *The Rakhine State (Arakan) of Myanmar: Interrogating History, Culture and Conflict*. Kolkata: Maulana Abul Kalam Azad Institute of Asian Studies, Kolkata, 2015.

Buchanan (Hamilton), Francis. 1825. "An Account of the Frontier Between Ava the Part of Bengal Adjacent to the Karnaphuli River." *Edinburgh Journal of Science* 3 (April–October): 32–44.

Caspersz, Charles P. "Memorandum on the Revenue History of Chittagong." *Calcutta Review* 71, no. 141 (1880): 169–175.

Chakma, Bhumitra. "The Post-Colonial State and Minorities: Ethnocide in the Chittagong Hill Tracts, Bangladesh." *Commonwealth and Comparative Politics* 48, no. 3 (2010): 281–300.

Chittagong City Corporation. "Media Brief of Chittagong City Corporation." 2016. Available at http://www.ccc.org.bd/media_brief. Accessed on November 11, 2016.

Chowdhury, Mohammed Ali. "The Arrival of Islam in Chittagong Before Muslim Conquest." *Journal of the Pakistan Historical Society* 47, no. 1 (1999): 49–54.

8 ARAKANESE CHITTAGONG BECAME MUGHAL ISLAMABAD ... 259

Chowdhury, Sri Umesh Chandra. "Brahma-Prabashi Bangali Bauddhagoner Kartavya (The Duties of Bengali Buddhist Expatriates in Burma)." *Snagha Shakti*, no. Mahasanghadan Ashari Purnima (1937): 229–33.

d'Hubert, Thibaut. *In the Shade of the Golden Palace: Alaol and Middle Bengali Poetics in Arakan*. New York: Oxford University Press, 2018.

Drong, Sanjeeb, ed. *Ādibāsīdera Arthanaitika O Sāmājika Adhikāra, Saṃhati, 2008* (Economic and Social Rights of Indigenous Peoples, Solidarity 2008). Ḍhākā: Bāṃlādeśa Ādibāsī Phorāma, 2008.

Eaton, Richard M. *The Rise of Islam and the Bengal Frontier (1204–1760)*. Oxford: Oxford University Press, 1993.

Gain, Philip, ed. *Indigenous Peoples of Bangladesh*. Dhaka: Society for Environment and Human Development, 1993.

———. ed. *Culture of Adivasis in Bangladesh*. Dhaka: Society for Environment and Human Development, 2008.

Gayen, Audity Falguni. *The Rakhaines of Patuakhali and Barguna Region, in Quest for a Distance Homeland*. Chittagong: Codec Publication, 2007.

Ghosal, Sattendra. *Bangladesh District Gazetteers: Patuakhali*. Dhaka: BG Press, 1982.

Green, Nile, and Mary Searle-Chatterjee. "Religion, Language, and Power: An Introductory Essay." In *Religion, Language and Power*, edited by Nile Green and Mary Searle-Chatterjee, 1–23. New York: Routledge, 2008.

Guhathakurta, Meghna. "Religious Minorities." In *Routledge Handbook of Contemporary Bangladesh*, edited by Ali Riaz and Mohammad Sajjadur Rahman, 316–324. London and New York: Routledge, 2016.

Hosena, Āiẏuba, Charu Haq, and Rijuyana Rinti. *Baṃlādeśar Kshudra Jātigoṣṭhī*. 1st ed. Ḍhākā: Hākkānī Pābaliśārsa, 2009.

Hunter, William Wilson. *A Statistical Account of Bengal (Chittagong Hill Tracts, Chittagong, Noakhali, Tipperah, Hill Tipperah)*. Vol. 6 (of 20). Delhi and London: D. K. Pub. House and Trubner, 1973.

Kalikinkar. *Adi Purush (Early Ancestors)*. Rangoon: [Buddhist Mission Press?] 1915.

Khan, Abdul Mabud. "Patuakhali Zillar Bauddha Sampraday." *CLIO: A Journal of History Department, Jahangirnagar University, Dhaka* 1 (June 1983): 6–27.

———. *The Maghs: A Buddhist Community in Bangladesh*. Dhaka: University Press, 1999.

Klaiman, M.H. "Bengali." In *The Major Languages of South Asia, the Middle East and Africa*, edited by Bernard Comrie, 54–72. London: Routledge, 2005.

Lammerts, Christian. "The Murray Manuscripts and Buddhist Dhammasattha Literature Transmitted in Chittagong and Arakan." *The Journal of Burma Studies* 19, no. 2 (2015): 407–444.

Lefèvre, Corinne. "The Majālis-I Jahāngīrī (1608–11): Dialogue and Asiatic Otherness at the Mughal Court." *Journal of the Economic and Social History of the Orient* 55 (2012): 255–286.

Leider, Jacques. "On Arakanese Territorial Expansion: Origins, Context, Means and Practices." In *The Maritime Frontier of Burma: Exploring Political, Cultural and Commercial Interaction in the Indian Ocean World, 1200–1800*, edited by Jos J.L. Gommans and Jacques Leider, 127–149. Amsterdam: Amsterdam KITLV Press, 2002.

Lewin, Captain Thomas Herbert. *The Hill Tracts of Chittagong and the Dwellers Therein*. Calcutta: Bengal Printing Company, 1869.

McGilvray, Dennis B. "Rethinking Muslim Identity in Sri Lanka." In *Buddhist Extremists and Muslim Minorities: Religious Conflict in Contemporary Sri Lanka*, edited by John Clifford Holt, 54–77. New York: Oxford University Press, 2016.

Mia, Md Aslam, Shamima Nasrin, Miao Zhang, and Rajah Rasiah. "Chittagong, Bangladesh." *Cities* 48 (2015): 31–41.

Olcott, Henry Steel. *A Buddhist Catechism, According to the Canon of the Southern Church. The Biogen Series, no. 3*. Boston: Estes and Lauriat, 1885.

O'Malley, Lewis Sydney Steward. *Eastern Bengal District Gazetteers: Chittagong*. Calcutta: The Bengal Secretariat Book Depot, 1908.

Sarkar, Jadunath. *Studies in Aurangzib's Reign*. London: Sangam Books, 1989.

Sattar, Abdus. *Tribal Culture in Bangladesh*. Dacca: Muktadhara, 1975.

Said, Edward W. *Orientalism*. 25th Anniversary ed. New York: Vintage Books, 2003.

Van Schendel, Willem. "The Invention of the 'Jummas': State Formation and Ethnicity in Southeastern Bangladesh." *Modern Asian Studies* 26, no. 1 (1992): 95–128.

———. "Spatial Moments: Chittagong in Four Scenes." In *Asia Inside Out: Connected Places*, edited by Eric Tagliacozzo, Helen F. Siu, and Peter C. Perdue, 98–127. New York: Harvard University Press, 2015.

Ware, Anthony, and Coastas Laoutides. *Myanmar's 'Rohingya' Conflict*. London: Hurst & Co., 2018.

Yasmin, Lailufar. "The Tyranny of the Majority in Bangladesh: The Case of the Chittagong Hill Tracts." *Nationalism and Ethnic Politics* 20, no. 1 (2014): 116–132.

PART III

Concluding Thoughts

CHAPTER 9

Buddhists, Muslims and the Construction of Difference

Michael Jerryson and Iselin Frydenlund

On October 30, 2017, one of Myanmar's most prominent Buddhist monks Sitagu Sayadaw delivered a sermon to Burmese soldiers at the Bayintnaung garrison and military training school in the Karen state. His sermon took place amidst the Burmese military atrocities against Rohingya civilians. Sitagu Sayadaw chose in the sermon to draw upon sections from the Lankan fifth century chronicle the *Mahavamsa*, specifically the victory by the Buddhist king Duttugemunu (Dutthagamani). Sitagu Sayadaw provided the soldiers with reasons for the Sri Lankan Buddhist king's victory, explaining:

> We are talking about the powers of the Dhamma. The victory of this battle is due to the power/quality of the Dhamma over King Duttagamani. The battle was won because of the effects of the power of the Dhamma. And as a result of the unity of the monks in fighting the battle together,

---

M. Jerryson
Department of Philosophy and Religious Studies,
Youngstown State University, Youngstown, OH, USA

I. Frydenlund (✉)
MF Norwegian School of Theology, Religion and Society, Oslo, Norway

© The Author(s) 2020
I. Frydenlund and M. Jerryson (eds.),
Buddhist-Muslim Relations in a Theravada World,
https://doi.org/10.1007/978-981-32-9884-2_9

the battle was over. That was how they had a landslide victory in beating the invaders.[1]

His sermon uses the *Mahavamsa* to condone the killings of non-Buddhists. Beyond the scriptural implications, there is the context for this sermon. During the Burmese Buddhist military attacks on Rohingya Muslims, one of Myanmar's most famous monks gave the Burmese military a justification for killing non-Buddhists. Upon doing this, high-ranking monks did not publicly voice their opinion about this direct sanction of killing of non-Buddhists. In fact, with only a few exceptions, Buddhist monks in Myanmar have not spoken out against the violence committed against Rohingya Muslim civilians.

This rhetoric is not new. In many ways, it resembles the rhetoric of others, like the Thai monk Kittiwuttho. In his anti-communist campaign in the 1970s, Kittiwuttho explained that communists were a danger to the country. He argued that killing communists did not constitute killing a person, "because whoever destroys the nation, the religion, or the monarchy, such *bestial* types (man) are not complete persons. Thus, we must intend not to kill people but to kill the Devil (Mara); this is the duty of all Thai" (italics added).[2] As in the case of Buddhist adversaries in the Sri Lankan *Mahavamsa* or in contemporary Burmese Buddhist depictions of Rohingya Muslims, we find another group, communists, who are perceived as non-Buddhist and thus not fully human. Through such Buddhist rhetoric, people, cultures, and histories become the Other.

On June 29, 1976, Kittiwuttho expounds on his view of communists in an interview with *Caturat*, "It is just like when we kill a fish to make a stew to place in the alms bowl for a monk. There is certainly demerit in killing the fish, but we place it in the alms bowl of a monk and gain much greater merit."[3] Over forty years later on July 17, 2014, the high-ranking Burmese Buddhist monk U Wirathu used similar rhetoric in his interview with Global Post about Muslims: "Muslims are like the African carp. They breed quickly and they are very violent and they eat

---

[1] Sithagu Sayadaw, Youtube, October 10, 2017, https://www.youtube.com/watch?v=GAukEq-GzMs, last accessed March 20, 2018.

[2] Charles Keyes, "Political Crisis and Militant Buddhism," in *Religion and Legitimation of Power in Thailand, Laos, and Burma*, ed. Bardwell L. Smith (Chambersburg, PA: ANIMA Books, 1978), 147–164.

[3] Keyes, "Political Crisis and Militant Buddhism," 147–164.

their own kind. Even though they are minorities here, we are suffering under the burden they bring us...."[4]

There is a destructive pattern connected to Othering a community or group of people. The philosopher Sam Keen argues that in order to create an enemy, one must "stain the strangers with the sinister hue of the shadow."[5] We frame those who are not "us" with negative traits that are widespread—and uniform for the whole group. Othering does not simply marginalize groups of people. It is the justification and catalyst for violence. Reflecting on the field of psychology, James W. Jones finds that religious rhetoric is especially instrumental in "Satanizing the Other." He writes, "The over idealization of one's own tribe, tradition, or gender in the name of religion provides a ready rational for violence against the 'other,' who is now seen as demonic and impure and thus having been dehumanized and having died a social death can now be slaughtered with impunity."[6] Once a group is Othered, the moral significance of murder exponentially diminishes. The examples of U Wirathu and Kittiwutho are examples within Buddhist traditions to create the Other.

Often, Buddhists present their religion with the claim that their religion retains a particular tolerance. For evidence, they cite early Buddhist scriptural sources. This positive evaluation of interreligious hermeneutics identified in canonical texts largely has been unquestioned in the academic study of Buddhism. Yet this Buddhist perspective raises two important questions: first, who counts as "Buddhist" and "non-Buddhist"? Second, what does tolerance toward the defined "non-Buddhist Other" mean? Recent scholarship has begun the important task of un-packing constructions of religious "Self" and "Others" in early Buddhist texts, and what tolerance could actually mean in this context.[7]

---

[4] Tin Aung Kyaw, "Buddhist Monk Wirathu Leads Violent National Campaign Against Myanmar's Muslims," *GlobalPost*, June 21, 2013, https://www.pri.org/stories/2013-06-21/buddhist-monk-wirathu-leads-violent-national-campaign-against-myanmars-muslims, last accessed March 25, 2018.

[5] Sam Keen, *Faces of the Enemy: Reflections of the Hostile Imagination* (New York: HarperCollins, 1986), 9.

[6] James W. Jones, *Blood That Cries Out from the Earth: The Psychology of Religious Terrorism* (New York: Oxford University Press, 2008), 44.

[7] Oliver Freiberger, "How the Buddha Dealt with Non-Buddhists," in *Religion and Identity in South Asia and Beyond: Essays in Honor of Patrick Olivelle*, eds. P. Olivelle and S.E. Lindquist (London: Anthem Press, 2011).

266   M. JERRYSON AND I. FRYDENLUND

All religious systems have historical patterns of "Othering". In this vein, religious traditions have imagined Buddhists as the Other. Historically, the most notable cases are the Brahmanical traditions in India, the Chinese Tang Dynasty, Shinto practitioners in Meiji Japan, and communist promoters in Mongolia and Cambodia.[8] However, the reverse is also true: Buddhists have cast people of other religions (or traditions) as the Other as well. This Buddhist "Othering" is identifiable across Buddhist traditions. As this volume examines Buddhist traditions, with particular reference to those traditions that self-identify as "Theravada,"[9] our aim in this chapter is to identify Buddhist strategies and patterns of Othering. While there are philosophical approaches to Buddhist alterity there is a dearth of scholarship on historical and sociological approaches to Buddhist otherness.[10] In pursuit of this latter direction, this chapter analyzes the ways in which Theravada Buddhists have constructed their religious identity vis-à-vis non-Buddhists, and how they, particularly in our current times, have made Muslims the Other.

As our primary concern is hostility and marginalization of religious others, this chapter draws upon the work of the historian of religion Jonathan Z. Smith, who provides an instructive structure to religion and Othering.[11] In doing so, we also make use of previous research that identify patterns in Buddhism's relations to other religions.[12] Following with

[8] For examples of European and Islamic ways to Other Buddhism and Buddhists, see Donald S. Lopez, *From Stone to Flesh: A Short History of the Buddha* (Chicago: University of Chicago Press, 2013). For Islamic caricatures of Buddhists and Buddhism, see Johan Elverskog, *Buddhism and Islam on the Silk Road* (Philadelphia: University of Pennsylvania Press, 2010).

[9] By "Theravada" we refer to those traditions who today self-identify as "Theravada Buddhist"—as a particular type of Buddhism. See "Introduction" for further clarification of the term.

[10] One of the notable contributions to this underdeveloped discourse is Perry Schmidt-Leukel's expansive edited volume that predominantly draws on philosophical reflections, *Buddhism and Religious Diversity* (London: Routledge, 2012).

[11] The differentiation and Othering per se is not necessarily hostile and violent. For example, as Ronald Inden reminds us, Orientalism (as a form of Othering) can be both negative and positive, see Ronald Inden, "Orientalist Constructions of India," *Modern Asia Studies* 20, no. 3: 401–446.

[12] David, W. Chappell, "Buddhist Responses to Religious Pluralism: What Are the Ethical Issues?" in *Buddhist Ethics and Modern Society: An International Symposium*, eds. Charles Wei-hsun Fu and Sandra A. Wawrytko (Oxford and New York: Greenwood Press, 1990), 443–444; Oliver Freiberger, "Negative Campaigning: Polemics Against Brahmins in a Buddhist Sutta," *Religions of South Asia* 3, no. 1 (2009): 61–76; Freiberger,

Smith's analysis of alterity, we apply his theoretical framing to the ways in which Theravada Buddhists make Muslims the Other.

Previous Work on Buddhism and Exclusivism

Conceptions of superiority are at odds with internalized models of Buddhist tolerance. Drawing upon insights from the field of interreligious hermeneutics, Oliver Freiberger argues that pluralism—by John Hick defined as the view that all religious paths will lead to one Ultimate Truth—is yet to be identified in the Pali canon.[13] On the contrary, Freiberger shows, there are numerous examples of strict repudiation and exclusivism. When talking to his monks, the Buddha often speaks about the inferiority of non-Buddhist ascetics, even portraying their practices useless or even harmful. Freiberger suggests a five-model Buddhist strategy for interaction with the "Other":

1. Strictly rejecting other beliefs and practices;
2. Re-interpreting terms;
3. Internalizing and ethicizing practices;
4. Using polemics to disparage others;
5. Employing concessions of several sorts.

These are all rhetorical instruments used by the early Buddhist communities to "sell" the Buddha's teachings in a diverse religious market in which the Buddhists comprised just one among many ascetic groups. In a slightly different direction, David Chappell draws upon examples from the Pali Canon as well as other sources to show the variety of ways in which Buddhists regard non-Buddhists. He lists six methods in which Buddhists interpret and respond to religious differences. Buddhists either see themselves as:

1. separate and superior to other religions;
2. compassionately engaged with other religions;

"How the Buddha Dealt with Non-Buddhists"; Elizabeth Harris, "Buddhism and the Religious Other," in *Understanding Interreligious Relations,* eds. David Cheetham, Douglas Pratt, and David Thomas (Oxford and New York: Oxford University Press, 2013).

[13] Freiberger, "How the Buddha Dealt with Non-Buddhists," 189.

268 M. JERRYSON AND I. FRYDENLUND

3. latter stages of development from other religions;
4. complementary to other religions;
5. historically relative and limited like other religions; or,
6. sharing the same essence as other religions.[14]

While the majority of these methods provide space for conceptions of diversity, the first and third methods exemplify Buddhist constructions of superiority.

Elizabeth Harris also identifies six attitudes toward non-Buddhists. Similar to Chappell, she finds that some of these attitudes allow for views of pluralism. Importantly, she stresses that the attitudes that dominate a particular era are due to socio-economic factors and power relations.[15] Along similar lines, we evince in this chapter that particular periods and locations provide the socio-economic factors and power relations to create Buddhist attitudes of superiority over non-Buddhists. That Buddhism makes claims of spiritual superiority should come as no surprise as most religions would make such claims. Hence, the question is *how* Buddhists have constructed difference between the Self and Other.

To explore this question, we turn to the work of Jonathan Z. Smith. In his chapter "Differential Equations on Constructing the Other" of *Relating Religion*, Smith provides three basic models in which people make the Other. The first model has the Other represented metonymically as the presence or absence of one or more traits. His second model is when the Other stands topographically as the periphery compared to the center. In this model, the Other is often mapped as the wild anomie as opposed to the urban nomos. While both the first and second models assert levels of superiority over the Other, Smith finds the third model the most pernicious and mischievous form of Othering. This is where the Other represents deficient linguistic or intellectual abilities—the bar-bar-bar that becomes the nomenclature for barbarians.[16] This type of Other becomes depicted as subhuman. The people or communities

[14]Chappell, "Buddhist Responses to Religious Pluralism: What Are the Ethical Issues?," 443–444.

[15]Harris, "Buddhism and the Religious Other," 89.

[16]Jonathan Z. Smith, *Relating Religion: Essays in the Study of Religion* (Chicago: University of Chicago Press, 2004), 231.

9 BUDDHISTS, MUSLIMS AND THE CONSTRUCTION OF DIFFERENCE   269

become—to use a term by the eminent historian of religion Charles Long—*signified*.[17]

In addressing the Buddhist approach and application of the Other, we map out Smith's models in the Buddhist context and examine the third model and its manifestations in the contemporary period. We aim to identify patterns of differentiation, that is, the processes by which difference is made. "Otherness" may be a static category, but the differentiation that creates the Other is a process. Looking at Buddhists and the "Others" in this way, allows for change over the course of time. As the following analysis will show, Buddhist differentiation is there from the very beginning and integral to the Buddha's message. Yet, the process changes over time, and how the Other is constructed is contingent upon historical realities as well as upon cultural particularities of the "Other" in question. For example, constructions of the "Muslim Other" differs from constructions of the "Brahmanical Other" in canonical sources in that Muslims are portrayed as invading and foreign, while Brahmins are portrayed as inferior, or as backwards.[18]

LOCATING SMITH'S MODELS IN A THERAVADA WORLD

Buddhism was absent from Jonathan Z. Smith's description of the three models, but this absence does not mean that Buddhism is exempt from such social patterns of exclusion. Obviously, the processes of religious boundary-making are also present in Buddhist traditions. For example, Buddhist authors have held a long tradition of labeling their opponents as "non-Buddhist," and in early Buddhist texts, there are multiple examples of polemics and negative campaigning of the Buddha's opponents.[19] While Buddhist traditions provide examples that fit the first two models, the more prevalent examples come from the third model's Othering of Muslims.

---

[17] See Charles H. Long, *Significations: Signs, Symbols, and Images in the Interpretation of Religion* (Aurora, CO: The Davies Group, 1995), 1–10.

[18] Freiberger, "Negative Campaigning: Polemics Against Brahmins in a Buddhist Sutta," 61–76.

[19] Freiberger, "How the Buddha Dealt with Non-Buddhists."

I. The Metonymical Other

The metonymical model, Smith says, occurs most frequently in connection with naming, in which "one group distinguishes itself from another by lifting up some cultural feature."[20] In this model, Smith also includes the characterization of difference by naming the others as a nonhuman species. There are various metonymical Others within Buddhist traditions. For instance, Theravada Buddhist practitioners have been Othered by their rivals. In Mahayana and Vajrayana Buddhist scriptures and societies there are references to Theravada Buddhist practitioners who follow "Hinayana." The term derives from the combination of *hina*, which means vile, defunct, or to put it more kindly, "lesser", and *yana*, vehicle—namely, the means or way to become enlightened.

Those who utilize this appellation within the Mahayana schools call themselves part of the "Greater" vehicle. In doing so, they acknowledge the "Buddhist" component to their competitors, but only as a means of displaying their superiority. As Jonathan Silk notes in his analysis of categories within Mahayana Buddhism, "Thus portrayed Mahayana Buddhism is at once both a timeless, universal truth, a path to liberation for all, monk and layperson (man or woman) alike, and a replacement for the older, limited, indeed inferior, Hinayana path."[21] This derogatory term has been applied to various Buddhist traditions, particularly those who adhere to the Theravada traditions. This means of Othering devalues a community, but does not necessarily lead to violence.

II. The Topographical Other

Smith's second category is for those others who are topographically distant or remote from the core. He explains that this model focuses on the geographical dislocation of the Other and that "it characteristically takes the form of an imperial model with replication."[22] Geography becomes a powerful means of subordinating peoples and places. The historian

---

[20] Jonathan Z. Smith, *Relating Religion: Essays in the Study of Religion* (Chicago: University of Chicago Press, 2004), 232.

[21] Jonathan A. Silk, "What, if Anything, Is Mahāyāna Buddhism? Problems of Definitions and Classifications," *Numen* 49, no. 2 (2002): 355–405.

[22] Jonathan Z. Smith, *Relating Religion: Essays in the Study of Religion* (Chicago: University of Chicago Press, 2004), 234.

9 BUDDHISTS, MUSLIMS AND THE CONSTRUCTION OF DIFFERENCE 271

Marshall Hodgson reminds us that everyone wants to place themselves in the center of the map.[23] This form of Othering inhabits various conceptualizations in Buddhist traditions.

Perhaps the boldest assertion of a center (and classifying others on the periphery) in Buddhism is the cosmological depiction of six domains of rebirth. In this framework, the realms of humans and animals are the only visible; conversely, the realms of gods, the titans (*asuras*) and hell-beings are not. On the borderline to the human realm are the ghosts, who occasionally can be caught a sight of. The *bhavacakra*, or "Wheel of Life," is a circular diagram that visualizes six realms depicting the realms of human, titans, and gods as superior to the other three. The cosmos is hierarchically mapped and organized. One's actions (*karma/kamma*) determine where one goes. It does not depend on ascribed religious or other cultural categories. Beings find their place along an ascending scale of perfection according to their relative degree of moral, mental, and physical purity. Therefore, following the teachings on impermanence and karmic retribution, no being is condemned to reside eternally in any of these realms. Buddhist "Others," then, might well be condemned to hell, or opponents might be called non-Buddhists, but in Buddhist cosmology this is never a permanent state.

The Othering takes place in the geographical mapping within the human realm, particularly the depiction of the South Asian subcontinent as Jambudvipa (Pali: Jambudipa). In Buddhist traditions, humans reside in the realm of desire (*kamadhatu*). The center of this realm is Mount Meru, which is surrounded by four continents. Of the four continents, only Jambudvipa is ruled by ideal Buddhist rulers (often referred to as wheel-turning kings, (*cakravartin/cakkavatti*) and *buddhas*. Steven Collins notes that scriptures underscore that the continent provides a suitable environment to practice a religious life of celibacy (*brahmacariya*). Through such provisions, people in Jambudvipa can choose lifestyles more suited to reaching enlightenment or better rebirths.[24]

---

[23] Marshall G.S. Hodgson, *Rethinking World History: Essays on Europe, Islam and World History* (Cambridge: Cambridge University Press, 1993), 29–34.

[24] Steven Collins points out that Buddhist scriptures praise the continent Uttarakuru for the naturally selfless white-skinned people who abstain from killing animals or eating meat. They are wealthy and life is good, but because life is good this makes enlightenment untenable, "On the contrary, nirvana cannot be attained when life is so good that beings have few desires unfulfilled, as in the heavens or in Uttarakuru: one must wait for rebirth as a human

Jambudvipa and its inhabitants are in the center. However, the other continents and their people are along the periphery, fitting Jonathan Z. Smith's second category. In this manner, Buddhist authors identify Others based upon their remote geography to their prescriptive "Center," Jambudvipa. There are other applications of this mapping throughout Buddhist traditions.[25]

The model of center and periphery, Smith notes, is "in the form of a contrast between the inhabitants of cities and the hinterlands."[26] As Buddhism spread to other parts of Asia, it adopted various localization strategies, including specific forms of territorialization. These strategies included the spread of relics, the planting of the sacred Bodhi tree and the incorporation of local deities in the "hinterland" into the Buddhist nomos. The deities were often converted to protectors of the Buddhist teachings, one of the most famous examples being Saman, the god of Sri Pada (or Adam's Peak) in Sri Lanka who, according to the *Mahavamsa*, subdued to the Buddha and was then turned into one of the guardian gods of Buddhism in the island.

Because the Buddha himself visited and meditated at these places, they belong to the special category of "relics of use" (*paribhogikadhatu*), and are sites of pilgrimage. Hence, according to the "*vamsa*" tradition, the whole island is sacred Buddhist land. Moreover, the *Mahavamsa* presents Buddhism as a civilizational force to "uncivilized" hinterlands, only inhabited by demons. The cosmopolitics of center-periphery can take on several forms: one centripetal that establishes the center and one centrifugal that maintains order at the periphery, the latter being the one that "displays spatial 'otherness' most frequently."[27] In the traditional "galactic kingdoms" of South and Southeast Asia, political and religious

---

being in Jambudipa." Steven Collins, *Nirvana and Other Buddhist Felicities* (Cambridge: Cambridge University Press, 1998), 553.

[25] In his examination of eighteenth century Tibetan cosmology and geography, Matthew Kapstein notes that in the third chapter of the *Treasury of Abhidharma* (*Abhidharmakośa*) India is identified as Jambudvīpa. He identifies that places "like Tibet, China, and Mongolia, which ordinary humans could in principle reach by traveling from India, were assumed to be part of Jambudvīpa....The three remaining continents, though present in the imagination, were for all practical purposes off the map."

[26] Smith, *Relating Religion*, 234.

[27] Smith, *Relating Religion*, 234.

authorities were more concerned with order at the center, and less so with the periphery. This play of center and periphery builds into the third model, which places those along the periphery into an intellectual diminutive or subordinate role. This second model displays the ways that Othering justifies the conquering and subordinating of communities. However, the most pernicious means of Othering—and one that directly links to violence—is in the third model.

III. The Linguistic and Intellectual Other

Smith notes that the first two models have an us-versus-them dichotomy with implicit superiority; however, these models can provide complex reciprocal relationships. In contrast to these two models, he deems the third model substantively different: "The third model, where the 'other' is represented linguistically and/or intellectually in terms of intelligibility, admits no such ambivalence."[28] It is due to the third model's historic links to violence that we devote the remainder of this chapter to its exploration.

Classification of the world in which we live is a basic human enterprise, and self-identities are constructed by distinguishing ourselves from what we are not. Being "civilized" and not "uncivilized" is thus a specific conception of self. Throughout history, it has been an important part of religious self-understanding to represent "civility" and "civilization" and others as "uncivil," "barbarians," "subhuman," or possibly infants yet to be civilized. Examples of such ideas abound in world history, but it is perhaps less well known that such ideas also flourish in Buddhism, a religion often perceived to be tolerant and inclusive.

In his classic study, the anthropologist Stanley Tambiah notes that Buddhist institution building by forest monks often interconnected with state formation. Tambiah writes:

> Starting as little-endowed fraternities, and locating themselves on forest edges on the frontiers of advancing settlements, the forest monks could act as elite carriers of literate civilization and could serve as foci for the collective religious activities and moral sentiments of frontier settlements. It is an alliance of this sort, a paired relationship between founding kings... with expansionist ambitions and the ascetically vigorous forest monks at

[28] Smith, *Relating Religion*, 237.

the moving edge of human habitation...that domesticated the local cults and incorporated them within a Buddhist hierarchy and cosmos.[29]

The idea of "civilizing" the non-Buddhist Other is clearly expressed in early Buddhist texts. For example, the early Buddhist sources from Sri Lanka, the *Dipavamsa* (fourth century CE) and the *Mahavamsa* (fifth century CE) portray the island's inhabitants prior to the advent of Buddhism in terms of demons and beasts that the Buddha tamed, pacified, and civilized through his extraordinary powers.[30] Furthermore, in the so-called *vamsa* literature, the Buddha is said to *conquer* the island through harsh means, and the island is seen as belonging to him.[31] There are various versions of the account of the Buddha's first visit to the island. The most dramatic narration of the encounter of the Buddha with the island's nonhuman inhabitants (demons called *yakkhas*) is found in the *Vamsatthappakasini* (sometimes called the *Mahavamsatika*), where the Buddha harasses the nonhuman beings with eleven different types of afflictions. After the Buddha has assailed them with, among other things, thunderstorms, drought and hot ashes, the *yakkhas* promise the Buddha the right over the island.[32]

The sociologist James Aho argues that in order for us to identify as a hero, we need to make an enemy. In his book *This Thing of Darkness*, Aho writes, "The warrior needs an enemy. Without one there is nothing against which to fight, nothing from which to save the world, nothing to give his life meaning. What this means, of course, is that if an enemy is not ontologically present in the nature of things, one must be

---

[29] Stanley Tambiah, *The Buddhist Saints of the Forest and the Cult of Amulets: A Study in Charisma, Hagiography, Sectarianism, and Millennial Buddhism* (Cambridge: Cambridge University Press, 1984), 69.

[30] *Mahāvamsa* (*Mhv.*), verses 3–4, in Mahānāma, *Mahāvamsa*, trans. W. Geiger (London: Pali Text Society, 1912). *Mvh.* builds upon the earlier *Dipavamsa*, which builds on the now lost *Sīhalatthakathā-Mahāvamsa*, which was part of the Mahāvihāra Canon, written down in the first century BCE, see Jonathan S. Walters, "Buddhist History: The Sri Lankan Pāli Vamsas and Their Community," in *Querying the Medieval: Texts and the History of Practices in South Asia*, eds. J.S. Walters, R. Inden, and D. Ali (Oxford: Oxford University Press, 2000), 107.

[31] See R.A.L.H. Gunawardana, "The Kinsmen of the Buddha," in *Religion and Legitimation of Power in Sri Lanka*, ed. B.L. Smith (Chambersburg: Anima, 1978), 98–101, for further discussion.

[32] Gunawardana, "The Kinsmen of the Buddha," 98.

9 BUDDHISTS, MUSLIMS AND THE CONSTRUCTION OF DIFFERENCE 275

manufactured."[33] The *Mahavamsa*'s glorifying narrative of its hero, the Buddhist king Dutthagamani (161–137 BCE), is a prime example of this process. The *Mahavamsa* provides one of the most controversial and radical examples of Buddhist Othering. The text tells of king Dutthagamani, who in order "to bring glory to the doctrine"[34] killed the (Tamil) king Elara together with thousands of men in the battlefield.[35] As he was feeling remorse for the slaughter, eight *arahants* come to comfort him, but the king asks: "How shall there be any comfort for me, O venerable sirs, since by me was caused the slaughter of a great host numbering millions?"[36] The *arahants* reply that

> From this deed arises no hindrance in thy way to heaven. Only one and a half human beings have been slain here by thee, O lord of men. The one had come unto the (three) refuges, the other had taken on himself the five precepts. Unbelievers and men of evil life were the rest, not more to be esteemed than beasts. But as for thee, thou wilt bring glory to the doctrine of the Buddha in manifold ways; therefore cast away care from thy heart, O ruler of men![37]

The text states that non-Buddhists are subhuman, and through a strategy of dehumanizing the opponent, killing for the sake of the *dhamma* is justified. At the onset of this chapter, we discussed how the prominent Burmese monk Sitagu Sayadaw drew from the *Mahavamsa* in a late 2017 sermon. The direct reference to a text that condones the killing of non-Buddhists, was perceived with sorrow and disbelief among Myanmar's many religious minority groups.

Steven Jenkins points out the ways in which Buddhist texts are concerned with the moral standing of the victim for the karmic repercussion of the perpetrator.[38] If the victim is of low moral, the killing is less bad than if the victim had been of high moral status. One of the vilest

---

[33] James A. Aho, *This Thing of Darkness: A Sociology of the Enemy* (Seattle: University of Washington Press, 1994), 26.

[34] Mahānāma, *Mhv.*, XXV 3.

[35] Although the king in fact is portrayed as just.

[36] Mahānāma, *Mhv.*, XXV 108.

[37] Mahānāma, *Mhv.*, XXV 109–111.

[38] Stephen Jenkins, "On the Auspiciousness of Compassionate Violence," *Journal of the International Association of Buddhist Studies* 33, no. 1–2 (2010): 299–331.

acts one could do is spill the blood of a Buddha. Conversely, one of the least morally objectionable acts is to hurt or kill someone with no moral worth. In the middle of absolute morality and no morality lies the gray area of animals and beasts.

This slight turn of phrase, "not more to be esteemed than beasts," has important connotations, both within the taxonomy of alterity and in Buddhist doctrine. Throughout the centuries, people have dehumanized their opposition as a means to legitimate substandard and harmful treatment. Sam Keen explains in his seminal work *Faces of the Enemy* that part of the process of creating an enemy is to obscure the person's face and to not think about their humanity.[39] Dehumanization interrupts our cognitive process of feeling affinity toward another or our capacity to relate to her/him. Turning to the Pali canon, we find that negative campaigning against non-Buddhist Others are frequent, and some texts even portray *brahmins* as *inferior* to dogs.[40] Finally, it should be noted that in Buddhist ethics there is the consistent admonishment that one should not harm or injure (*ahimsa*) a sentient being. There are categories within this admonishment that Other sentient life from others. The harming of a human is the worst crime; slightly less is to harm a supranatural being. The least offensive is to harm an animal.[41] When the *arahants* tell the righteous Buddhist king of the *Mahavamsa* that millions are not more esteemed than beasts, this is not merely a process of dehumanization. It is this process of Othering that devalues people's lives and justifies violence.

EARLY BUDDHIST CONSTRUCTIONS OF THE MUSLIM OTHER

As Islam is a thousand years younger than Buddhism, Buddhist scriptures explicitly discussing Islam and Muslims are "late" texts. The social and political circumstances for the Buddhist–Muslim encounter vary, but it is clear that some of these Buddhist texts construct negative and sometimes

[39] Sam Keen, *Faces of the Enemy: Reflections of the Hostile Imagination* (New York: HarperCollins, 1986), 24.

[40] Freiberger 2009, 65.

[41] *The Book of the Discipline (Vinaya-Pitaka): Vol. I (Suttavibhanga)*, trans. Isaline Blew Horner, 1938 (Oxford, UK: Pali Text Society, 1992), 146–147; *The Book of the Discipline (Vinaya-Pitaka): Vol. III (Suttavibhanga)*, trans. Isaline Blew Horner, 1942 (Oxford, UK: Pali Text Society, 1983), 1.

dehumanizing images of Muslims, labeling Muslims as the "intellectual Other," by calling them barbarians and also animals.[42]

When exactly was the "Muslim Other" constructed as an object and in need of Buddhist theorizing? As we point out in the Introduction, as Islamic trade networks—and later empires—spread into Asia, Muslims and Buddhists came into contact. This was especially evident throughout the Mongol Empire in Central Asia (thirteenth to fourteenth centuries), and, later, the Mughal Empire in South Asia (1526–1857). The Mongols for centuries recognized multiple religious practices, and Kublai Khan's Buddhist government interacted regularly with representatives of the Mongol's Il Khanate, which had converted its religious affiliation to Islam (1256–1335). But when this open policy shifted, tensions between the Buddhist eastern parts and Muslim western parts, grew.

As the Muslim Mughal emperors extended their reach though much of South Asia, they had interactions with both Buddhists and Hindus. As we remember from Barua's contribution to this volume, the Mughals held very negative views about their Buddhist neighbors to the East, particularly the Arakanese.

Smith points out that difference is constructed as "alien" when the Other is perceived as challenging "a complex and intact world-view." As these empires began to spread and thrive, they offered complex and intact worldviews that held religious connotations. Often, these empires either incorporated foreign worldviews, such as the Islamic empires' use of the nomenclature "people of the book," in which Islamic states recognized and respected Jewish, Christian, and Zoroastrian adherents, or negotiated with communities whose worldviews were not assimilative. This lack of assimilative properties produced complex responses. Among the less complementary responses was the Buddhist characterization of Muslims as the Other. In his review of the *Kalacakra Tantra*, Johan Elverskog explains how Buddhist author/s identify the Muslim as uncivilized and in need of the Buddhist doctrine: "The barbarians observe the

---

[42] The Sanskrit term *barbara*, is synonymous with a fool or loon and relates to the Greek *barbaros*. Both the Sanskrit and Greek terms derive from the imbecilic stammering of those who cannot speak the in-group's language; those who stumble with their words, resulting in a "buh, buh, buh." In this passage, barbarian is the translation of the Sanskrit term *mleccha*. The term *mleccha* derives from the verbal root *mlech*, which means to speak indistinctly. Similar to *barbara*, the nominal case refers to a person who cannot speak Sanskrit. This person is a foreigner and outcaste Other.

278   M. JERRYSON AND I. FRYDENLUND

demonic dharma; they are proponents of a Creator, a soul, and are free of casteism." Much of this negative depiction occurs through articulations of Islamic dietary preferences, which Buddhist scriptures depict as both primitive and inane: "[The barbarians] kill camels, horses, and cattle, and briefly cook their flesh together with blood. They cook beef and amniotic fluid with butter and spice, rice mixed together with vegetables, and forest fruit, all at once on the fire. Men eat that, O king, and drink bird eggs, in the place of the demon [barbarians]." For the author/s of the *Kalacakra Tantra*, Muslims are the barbarians, their diet primitive and unfit for civilized society.[43]

Turning to precolonial Sri Lanka we see in popular Buddhist folk tales and myths that Muslims (as well as other minorities such as Hindus or the indigenous Veddas) are included in Sinhala Buddhist cosmologies, but as Bastin and de Silva show (this volume), they are equaled to demons, thus representing a threat to the ideal order of the Sinhala Buddhist polity.

Yet, it should be remembered, "Muslim Otherness" is *not* the result of an inherent or fixed Buddhist theory of Otherness or of Islam, but is rather contingent upon political and social realities. It is not a constant religious syntax of violent radical difference.

ANTI-COLONIAL CONSTRUCTIONS OF THE MUSLIM OTHER

The British and French colonization of South and Southeast Asia and their colonial perspective on religion had dramatic impacts on the conquered countries, including Siam, which resisted direct European colonial rule. Across the region—as several of the chapters in this volume testify—the colonial period inflamed ethno-religious tensions, highlighting a particular point in time marked by radical Othering of Muslims in Buddhist majority societies.

In Siam, seizing upon the colonial view of religion, King Mongkut (r. 1851–1868) argued that the Siamese territory extended further south into the British controlled Malay Muslim region because of a historic Buddhist monastery (*wat*).[44] His son and successor to the throne, King Chulalongkorn (r. 1868–1910), saw Buddhist monks as integral

---

[43] Elverskog, *Buddhism and Islam on the Silk Road*, 252.

[44] Mongkut used *wat* as cultural perimeter posts to demarcate the borders of Siam from the Malay Muslim regions of Kedah, Kelantan, Terenganu, and other southern Malay

9 BUDDHISTS, MUSLIMS AND THE CONSTRUCTION OF DIFFERENCE   279

to nation-building and securing the newly crafted nation-state. These and other political efforts during Siam's nation-building phases elevated Buddhism to national importance. One example was in King Vajiravudh's (r. 1910–1926) creation of the national flag in which the three colors symbolized Religion, King, and Nation (a slight derivation from the British flag's God, King, and Country). But just as in the case of England, in which God was not the Islamic or Jewish God, the Siamese regarded "religion" (*sasana*) not as Islam or Christianity, but as Buddhism. Vajiravudh makes this very clear in his speech to the Wild Tiger Corps on May 26, 1911, in which suggested "that those members of Thai society who abandoned the Buddhist faith were not really Thai."[45] Thus, as discussed in detail by Scupin and Joll (this chapter), Muslims were placed outside of "Thai" identity from the very inchoation of the modern Thai state.

Colonial codification of ethnic and religious identities, the creation of new states and borders, as well as British colonial policies of moving workers from one colony to another—as Walton clearly demonstrates with regard to Burma—all contributed to new conditions for Muslim–Buddhist relations. Resistance to demographic changes, Indian and/or Muslim dominance in the colonial economy, as well as an "open religious market" where Buddhism lost its state privilege, produced conducive conditions for large-scale anti-Muslim sentiments. In this period of struggle for independence from British India, antipathy and distrust of Muslims became widespread, and several severe anti-Muslim riots took place. Nyi Nyi Kyaw shows how Muslim Othering was mediated through popular culture. In one of the most widely read novels, Thein Pe Myint quoted anti-Muslim arguments by Buddhists during the 1938 riots: "Which Kala [here contextually referring to Muslim] is good? They take our girls as wives. Our girls must convert to Islam to become their legal wives. How domineering! We lose our race; we lose our faith" (quoted in Nyi Nyi Kyaw, this volume). Furthermore, lullabies scaring Buddhist children with the *kalar* (derogative term for dark-skinned/

---

principalities. Michael Jerryson's personal conversation with Irving Johnson at National University of Singapore, February 20, 2006.

[45] Scot Barmé, *Luang Wichit Wathakan and the Creation of a Thai Identity* (Singapore: Institute of Southeast Asian Studies, 1993), 30.

Muslims) stems from this period.[46] On a comparative note, of the three Theravada-dominated states under scrutiny in this volume, it would be fair to state that Muslim Othering in colonial Burma exceeds what we find of exclusionary nationalist practices in both Thailand and Sri Lanka.

Another aspect of British colonial activities that informed Buddhist–Muslim relations was the colonial rediscovery of India's Buddhist past. Knowledge of South Asia's past became accessible to colonial subjects throughout the British Empire, including colonial Ceylon and Burma. In the late nineteenth and early twentieth century, Buddhist revivalists and modernist reformers such as Anagarika Dharmapala applied the history of India to champion the Sinhala Buddhist cause. At times, they advanced Buddhist issues by contrasting Islam as intellectually or linguistically inferior. For example, in a letter written in 1922, Dharmapala positions Islam as the cause of Buddhism's decline in India. He states, "The vestiges of Buddhism were destroyed by this inhuman, barbarous race. Thousands of Bhikkhus were killed, temples were destroyed, libraries were burned and Buddhism dies in India." For Dharmapala, the decline of Buddhism in India, then, is no less the result of Islamic expansionism. Furthermore, he argues, "The Mohammaden, an alien people by Shylockian method, became prosperous like the Jews."[47] It is noteworthy that the point of reference for Dharmapala's anti-Muslim sentiments is not local Buddhist–Muslim interactions, but in fact European (Shakespeare and the Jews). Thus, one aspect of Buddhist anti-Muslim sentiments can be traced back to European anti-Semitism; European anti-Semitic ideas about the greedy and prosperous Jew were transferred onto local Muslims in Ceylon.[48]

As research of Buddhist revivalism has shown, the dark side of Buddhist anti-colonial revivalism was the exclusion of not only Christianity (as the colonial religion), but also other non-Buddhist religions, such as Hinduism and Islam.

[46] Frydenlund, Interviews and fieldwork, Mandalay 2015.

[47] Dharmapala, quoted in Guruge 1965, 207.

[48] Anagarika Dharmapala was under strong European and North American influence, particularly through contact with the Theosophical Society.

Contemporary Buddhist Othering of Muslims

As evidenced by examples provided by the contributors to this volume, Buddhist constructions of an intellectual Other spawn from conceptions of existential threats. This matches Smith's third model. Examining instances in the postcolonial era, we see that communism's widespread regional influence throughout Southeast Asia was seen as a potential—or even real threat like in the case of Cambodia—to many Buddhist communities. As communism receded in Southeast Asia, another perceived existential threat loomed: Islam. The largest populated Muslim country in the world is Indonesia, and neighboring Thailand's border is Malaysia, an Islamic state. Perhaps with the exception of Burma under military rule, in our contemporary times Buddhists have generally not perceived Islam or Muslims as a threat until there were global examples that connected Muslim identity with violence to non-Muslims. One of the more vivid events was the Afghan Taliban's bombing of the Bamiyan statues in 2001, which they made sure to record and broadcast over the Internet. This destruction and its symbolism remain strong in Buddhists' minds, and anti-Muslim violence took place in various places in Myanmar. In Sri Lanka, Buddhist monks in the Eastern province who were engaged in local land disputes, made reference to this event so as to strengthen their own claims to "Buddhist land."[49]

Furthermore, following the Al Qaeda attack on the United States on 9/11 and the subsequent wars in Iraq and Afghanistan, there has been an escalation in transnational Islamophobic discourses. These influences, coupled with the rise of ISIS, have caused many South and Southeast Asian Buddhists to see Islam as a threat.

Across the region, we find that most—if not all—Buddhist fears of Islam and Muslims ultimately evolve around two key themes: the destruction of Buddhism and the triumph of Islam. Thus, anti-Muslim discourses are connected to larger concerns about "Islamization" of Buddhist majority societies and subsequent eradication of Buddhism, expressed in what Nyi Nyi Kyaw in this volume calls a "myth of deracination." As previously discussed, Buddhists often invoke Buddhism's extinction from India in the twelfth century CE as proof for their fear of Islam today. Such fears of violent Islamic expansionism were "confirmed" with the destruction of the Bamiyan statues.

[49] Frydenlund, fieldwork notes, Eastern Sri Lanka 2005–2006.

Thailand

Although, as the contributions of Nishii, and Scupin and Joll in this volume demonstrate, conviviality and the level of tolerance between Buddhists and Muslims is greater in Thailand compared to Myanmar and Sri Lanka, contemporary Thailand has its shares of anti-Muslim sentiments as well. Such sentiments are often (though not exclusively) connected to the conflict in the three southernmost provinces (Pattani, Yala, and Narathiwat, along with some parts of Songkhla), collectively called the Deep South.

As discussed earlier, the British colonized Malaysia and carved out a border between their territory and the remaining land governed by Siam (Thailand). In response, the Siamese created provinces out of the Islamic kingdom of Patani; ever since then, there has been conflict in the region between Buddhists and Muslims. What makes this region especially significant is that it is considered by many Southeast Asian Muslims as one of the early pilgrimage locations for Islamic civilization. Likewise, the region is considered by Thai Buddhists the birthplace of the Buddhist kingdoms; this primarily refers to Langkasuka (second-eighth century C.E.) and the Srivijaya thalassocracy (eighth-twelfth century C.E.), which existed prior to the spread of Islam.

Since the early 1900s, Thai Malay Muslims have fought against the Thai government, which they see as a vehicle for Thai Buddhist imperialism. The Thai government sees the southern provinces as a region of instability that needs to be preserved for national unity. Their policies, such as forcing Thai Malay Muslims to bow to Buddhist statues, take Thai surnames, and not speak their Malay language, have energized the Thai Malay Muslim insurgency.[50]

The most recent surge in this conflict began in 2004, when Thai Malay Muslims targeted multiple police headquarters and stole munitions located in the Deep South. Shortly after these coordinated attacks, Thai Malay Muslim insurgents killed Buddhist monks. The Thai government saw the attack on the Buddhist monks as an attack on national identity. In response, the Thai government declared martial law over

---

[50]For a background on the Thai government's racial and religious discrimination of Malay Muslims, See Surin Pitsuwan's seminal dissertation on this subject, *Islam and Malay Nationalism: A Case Study of Malay-Muslims of Southern Thailand* (Bangkok: Thai Khadi Research Institute, Thammasat University, 1985).

9 BUDDHISTS, MUSLIMS AND THE CONSTRUCTION OF DIFFERENCE 283

the area, a status that remains in effect leading into 2019. Throughout this period, the Barisan Revolusi Nasional-Koordinasi (BRN-C) became the leading Muslim insurgent group fighting for Muslim regional independence. They spearheaded random bombings, arson attacks, and murders, providing a demonstration of military control over the Deep South. Conversely, the Thai government transformed southern Buddhist monasteries (*wat*) into military headquarters and employed Buddhist soldiers as secret military monks.[51] They issued armed guards to insure the Buddhist monks could go on their morning alms, and tortured suspected insurgents, sometimes within Buddhist monastic grounds like Wat Chang Hai.[52] These military actions have curbed the historical practice of Thai Malay Muslim and Thai Buddhist social collaborations, which historically took place in Thai Buddhist monasteries and public facilities.

As the violence persists in the Deep South, some Buddhist monks advocated for Buddhist-inspired retributions. In October 2015, the Thai monk Phra Maha Apichat took to Facebook and posted a mosque should be burnt to the ground for each Buddhist monk killed in the conflict. He also cited his support for U Wirathu and the 969 Movement and Ma Ba Tha. In response to this, the Thai monastic council did what the Burmese and Sri Lankan councils did not do: they expelled him for these words and actions. This has not quelled the Buddhist nationalist waves that have brought about national discussions over making Buddhism the official state religion.[53]

These efforts reach a new level when the radical anti-Muslim Othering reached national-level Thai politics: during the 2019 elections a new political party emerged, the Pandin Dharma Party ("Land of Buddhist Teachings"). Party members claim that Buddhism needs stronger state protection against what they see as a threat from Islam (Scupin and Joll, this volume). Some of its members, in line with Phra Maha Apichat's views, have expressed sympathy with U Wirathu, the nationalist firebrand

---

[51] For information on military monks, see Michael Jerryson, *Buddhist Fury: Religion and Violence in Southern Thailand* (New York: Oxford University Press, 2011), 114–142.

[52] Amnesty International, *Thailand: Torture in the Southern Counter-Insurgency* (London: Amnesty International Publications, 2009), accessed at https://www.amnesty.org/download/Documents/48000/asa390012009eng.pdf on July 1, 2019.

[53] Rodion Ebbighausen, "Islamophobia in Asia: What Drives Buddhist Anti-Muslim Feeling?" *Quantara.de*, September 4, 2018, https://en.qantara.de/content/islamophobia-in-asia-what-drives-buddhist-anti-muslim-feeling, accessed on July 1, 2019.

284   M. JERRYSON AND I. FRYDENLUND

monk of Myanmar. While anti-Muslim views have affected the Thai military's actions and many of the national conversations about Muslims in the Deep South, many southern Thais continue to practice interfaith communal living.

Sri Lanka

Since the end of the war in 2009, attacks on religious minorities have grown in number and intensity in Sri Lanka. While the civil war had strong religious overtones—with the majority of Buddhist monks strongly opposing Tamil nationalist demands for a separate state—religion was never at the heart of the conflict. There certainly was on overlap between ethnic and religious identities, but the fault lines followed ethnic rather than religious lines. Muslims in Sri Lanka self-identify as a distinct ethno-religious group, but has generally been loyal to the Sinhala-dominated state. With this in mind, the strong antipathy toward Islam from 2012 onwards came as a surprise to many, but has to be understood within a specific political setting of postwar Sinhala triumphalism and increased authoritarianism of the Rajapaksa regime, as pointed out by Haniffa (in this volume).

Studies of Buddhist anti-Islamic discourses point to the importance of rumor in creating a moral panic against the Other. Such rumors range from claims that *halal*-certification organizations fund terrorist networks, to Muslim cooks putting sterilization pills in the food served to Buddhist guests, or that mosques store weapons. Furthermore, following the "*vamsa*-ideology," Sri Lanka is sacred Buddhist land, only providing non-Buddhist groups with the status of "guests." This trope of "host" and "guest" is a recurrent theme in current anti-Muslim discourse across Buddhist-majority states analyzed in this volume. Buddhists often use the derogatory term "*khaek*" for Muslims of southern Thailand. While the term means "guest," it connotes a person who does not fit with normative Thai society. In Sri Lanka, the Bodu Bala Sena (BBS) has argued that they maintain a global principle that minorities must reside in a country in a way that does not threaten the majority race and its identity, and, moreover, that the Muslims have been ungrateful to their Sinhala Buddhist hosts. In an interview in 2014, BBS Chief Executive Officer Dilanthe Withanage claimed that "It is the Sinhala Buddhists who are in danger. We are the ones who live in fear. Our Sinhala Buddhist leaders are helpless due to the vast powers of these so-called minorities."[54] During his interview with Michael Jerryson the same year, Dilanthe explained that the Muslim scholarly community (*ulama*) is engaged in a conspiracy to take over the country and that part of this takeover is their dietary restrictions through *halal* certification;

> The *ulama*'s interest is to spread Islam in the country. What we were saying is: why should Buddhists pay for *halal* certifications? We don't need certification, but ultimately the money goes to them, and at the same time, the *halal* affects the culture of the society....We went to the texts and found that this was a part of Islamification. This is the first step of Islamification. Therefore, we thought we should fight against it.[55]

During BBS sermons, they claim Muslims in Sri Lanka are like "greedy ghosts" threatening the majority race and its identity. BBS Secretary General, the Buddhist monk Galagoda Gnanasara, echoed Dilanthe's remarks in a subsequent interview. He wove the defense of Buddhism from Islam to the longer legacy of protecting Buddhism in Sri Lanka, "According to Buddhism, there is no extremism, no fundamentalism. So if you kill someone you will go to hell for that. But for Muslims, killing someone for the benefit of Islam will be rewarded spiritually. For the last 2,300 years people were fighting for the protection of Buddhism in Sri Lanka. Now, we don't have much; I think we have to practice this [protection]."[56] For the Bodu Bala Sena, Buddhists have survived many threats in the past; the most recent and pressing threat comes from the Sri Lankan Muslims.

The horrific 2019 Easter attacks on churches and hotels in Sri Lanka—which left 250 dead and more than 500 people injured—fit into the Buddhist anti-Muslim narrative (predating the attacks) of local Muslims as representatives of global jihadism, thereby "confirming" the fear of the Muslim Other. Soon after the attacks, Muslim clothing such as *abaya*, *burqa* and *niqab* was prohibited. Also, Ven. Rathana,

---

[54]"Our Fight Is for All Sri Lankans. BBS CEO," at http://www.ft.lk/columns/our-fight-is-for-all-sri-lankans-bbs-ceo/4-286624, last accessed February 20, 2018.

[55]Michael Jerryson's personal communication with Dilanthe Withanage, Bodu Bala Sena headquarters, Colombo, June 25, 2014.

[56]Michael Jerryson's personal communication with Galagoda Gnanasara, Bodu Bala Sena headquarters, Colombo, June 25, 2014.

a prominent Buddhist monk of the monastic political party, the Jathinka Hela Urumaya, went on a hunger strike in early June 2019 to sack senior Muslim officials,[57] and the chief abbot of one of the leading monastic orders in Kandy claimed that he would not condemn the stoning of Muslims.[58] Finally, pre-2019 Easter attack rumors about secret Muslim plans for sterilization of Buddhist women (for example through the distribution of sweets) increased to unprecedented heights. In the wake of massive anti-Muslim moral panic after the attacks, rumors were spread that Muslim doctors carry out forced sterilization of Buddhist women in hospitals.[59]

Myanmar

After a tough interview on the violence in Rakhine in 2013, Aung San Suu Kyi was recorded as saying: "Why didn't anyone tell me I was going to be interviewed by a Muslim?" This outburst, as well as the controversy following the publication of the quote in 2016, is telling of the renewed sensibilities when it comes to Muslim–Buddhist relations in Myanmar. Why would the religious identity of the reporter matter to the Nobel Peace Laureate? The 2012 communal violence in Rakhine drew the world's attention to the lack of state protection of certain Muslim minority communities in Buddhist majority states today. Violence spread from Rakhine to other parts of Myanmar in 2013 and 2014, mostly affecting Muslim communities. These waves of violence culminated with the ethnic cleansing of the Rohingya community in 2017, in which Buddhist Rakhine civilians in certain villages took part together with the Burmese

[57] The government obeyed his demands of removing two governors and one minister from government. In solidarity with the sacked Muslim officials, eight Muslim ministers left the government, leaving the Muslim communities without representation in the government, see https://www.nytimes.com/2019/06/03/world/asia/sri-lanka-muslim-ministers-resign.html.

[58] "Sri Lanka: Buddhist Prelate Invites Sinhalese to Join Anti Muslim Hate Campaign," film clip on YouTube, https://www.youtube.com/watch?time_continue=9&v=P7AVLS m2I_A.

[59] https://www.reuters.com/article/us-sri-lanka-doctor-insight/unsubstantiated-claims-muslim-doctor-sterilized-women-raise-tensions-in-sri-lanka-idUSKCN1T71HS, last accessed June 6, 2019.

military.[60] In addition, anti-Muslim hate speech has been prominent on social media throughout such violent campaigns.

The Buddhist fearful sentiments against Muslims became widespread, as shown by the interviews with "ordinary people" below. In 2014 the journalist Nicholas Kristof met with young Buddhists and asked them about their perspectives. In one powerful interaction, Kristof asked a young Burmese Buddhist what he would do if he met a Muslim. As boys kicked the ball around, the boy replied with a shy smile, "I'd kill him."[61] This sentiment is shared more broadly than expected, and is based upon a well-nurtured fear of Burmese Muslims dating back to the British colonial period. In 2015 and 2016, Matt Schissler and colleagues conducted 78 interviews in six Burmese cities. They found a reoccurring narrative that Islam and Muslims were a general threat to Myanmar. In the northern Shan State city Lashio, they interviewed a 38-year-old Buddhist woman who seemed to be on verge of tears. She explained, "They [Muslims] are swallowing our religion... I am so worried about it for our future generations, our grandchildren and so on. In our time, horrible things like this happen to our children. For the future of our children, I am so worried that our religion will disappear."[62]

In another interview carried out by Schissler and his team, a 36-year-old Buddhist man expressed great fear over communicating with Muslims. He explained, "I can give many examples of worldwide incidents. For example, they attacked the World Trade Center in America and you can also see [examples] in Myanmar. They are the sources of these incidents. Nowadays, we are more and more afraid of them and also you can see the situation of ISIS. I don't trust Islam in Myanmar because of this ISIS."[63] Global attention to ISIS and, even earlier, the

---

[60] Wa Lone, Kyaw Soe Oo, Simon Lewis and Antoni Slodkowski, "Massacre in Myanmar. A Special Reuter's Report," *Reuters*, February 8, 2018, https://www.reuters.com/investigates/special-report/myanmar-rakhine-events/, last accessed December 15, 2019.

[61] Nicholas Kristof, "21st Century Concentration Camps," *New York Times*, June 16, 2014.

[62] Matt Schissler, Matthew Walton, and Phyu Phyu Thi, "Reconciling Contradictions: Buddhist-Muslim Violence, Narrative Making and Memory in Myanmar," *Journal of Contemporary Asia* 47, no. 3 (2017): 376–395, 383.

[63] Matt Schissler, Matthew Walton, and Phyu Phyu Thi, "Reconciling Contradictions: Buddhist-Muslim Violence, Narrative Making and Memory in Myanmar," *Journal of Contemporary Asia* 47, no. 3 (2017): 376–395, 384–385.

Fig. 9.1 Posters from U Wirathu's temple wall in Mandalay. Before elections in 2015 U Wirathu had supported Aung San Suu Kyi and NLD's call for democratic reform. However, during the 2015 elections he became her most ardent critic for her refusal to support the "race and religion laws" and claimed that she was becoming too Muslim-friendly (Photo: Iselin Frydenlund)

Taliban and the US war in Iraq, catalyze and inflame Burmese Buddhist fears of their Muslim neighbors.

Another aspect of contemporary Buddhist concerns over Islam relates to the female body and sexual reproduction, particularly Buddhist women in Buddhist–Muslim marriages. The popular Buddhist perspective is that Muslim males force their Buddhist spouses to become Muslim. From this perspective, mixed marriages conceptualize conversion and thus represent a danger to the very survival of Buddhism. Such fears—and the political use of them, created the political space necessary to pass four laws to "protect race and religion." Buddhist monks helped create these laws in order to stop the "Islamization" of Myanmar.[64] Buddhist organizations such as the Ma Ba Tha intended to use the laws to trump Buddhist family law over Islamic family law.[65] The ratification of these four race and religion laws sent a strong signal to Myanmar citizens that inter-religious marriages (particularly between Buddhist women and Muslim males) were regarded with suspicion, and moreover, that (Buddhist) conversion (to Islam) had to be under strict state supervision (Fig. 9.1).[66]

Glocal Properties

Scholars have given scant attention to Buddhist anti-Muslim sentiments as a discursive field that is glocal—a term Roland Robertson gave to describe phenomena that is both local and global. Old and new, local and global concerns and issues are interwoven into one, coherent narrative of Islamic expansionism. A close look at anti-Muslim conspiracies reveals that such discourses operate at different levels, serving various interests and concerns: some discourses relate to local business competition, while others portray Muslims and Islam as a security threat to the state. Furthermore, Buddhist activists in South and Southeast Asia use discourses, signs and symbols that first came into use in European, Indian or North-American settings, indicating global flows of Islamophobic ideas and objects.[67]

Fueled by new forms of communication such as Twitter and Facebook, worldwide concerns over the rise of global jihadism, and the subsequent securitization of Islam, local Muslims in Buddhist societies

---

[64] Iselin Frydenlund, "The Birth of Buddhist Politics of Religious Freedom in Myanmar," *Journal of Religious and Political Practice* 4 (2018): 107–121.

[65] Melissa Crouch, *Islam and the State in Myanmar: Muslim-Buddhist Relations and the Politics of Belonging* (New York: Oxford University Press, 2016).

[66] The laws themselves only mention "religion" in the generic, but it was explicitly stated by Buddhist monks that the laws intention was to stop alleged islamization of Myanmar (see Frydenlund 2018) for further detail.

[67] For further details on this, see Iselin Frydenlund, "Buddhist Islamophobia. Tropes. Themes. Actors," in *Handbook of Conspiracy Theory and Contemporary Religion*, eds. Dyrendal, D.G. Robertson, and Asprem (Leiden: E.J. Brill, 2019).

are increasingly portrayed as a threat to national security. Buddhists see Muslim associations as representatives of international terrorist networks and local agents of Islamic global imperialism. Leading monks have called mosques "enemy bases," and they have identified the *niqab* as a direct threat to the state and its territory. The BBS, for example, has published posters that show Sri Lanka as a *niqab*-dressed woman with evil-red eyes, symbolically identifying the *niqab* as a direct security threat to the state and its territory.

In Burmese Buddhist discourse, but increasingly also in BBS understanding, the Rakhine state in Myanmar, which borders the populous Muslim state of Bangladesh, is glossed as a "frontier state" between what is seen as two distinguishable and separate worlds of Buddhism and Islam. This is the home of the Muslim Rohingya population, which is denied citizenship in Myanmar and for those who have fled to Bangladesh, also face dire living conditions there. In contemporary anti-Muslim discourse, the Rohingyas are seen as filthy, as hyperfertile, underdeveloped, and—according to the Rakhine Buddhist nationalist Aye Chan—as "virus."[68]

A Brief Addendum: The Distant and Beastly Other

Smith challenges the reader to question how different difference has to be in order to constitute "Otherness." Under what circumstances and to whom are such distinctions of interest?[69] The point Smith wishes to make is that distinctions are made sharpest between close neighbors—the proximate Other. While this point seems to fit well with Muslims and other Abrahamic traditions or early Buddhism and its competition with *brahmins* or Jain groups, it does not fit with Buddhist–Muslim relations. On the one hand, it is plausible to argue that internal discipline and intra-Buddhist distinctions are more important to the state than "Distant Others;" traditionally, Theravada Buddhist states have not been concerned with regulation of Muslim religious practice. Thus, it is the discipline of the Buddhist Self, and not the distant Other that is of primary concern. On the other hand, as we shall discuss in detail below, there is a

[68] See Aye Chan and U Shwe Zan, *Influx Viruses: The Illegal Muslims in Arakan* (New York: Arakanes in United States, 2005).

[69] Smith, *Relating Religion*, 252.

perception that the "Muslim Distant Other" is coming closer, constituting an existential threat to Buddhism.

In contemporary Chiang Mai, Thailand, Brooke Schedneck observes Buddhist monks engaged in a program called Monk Chat at popular tourist temples. Drawing on Pattana Kitiarsa's taxonomy of Siamese Occidentalism,[70] she finds that these monks describe Westerners, Chinese, and Muslims in very distinctive ways. White Westerners are the "beneficial" Other. Schedneck explains that monks see their Western presence as "possibilities of English conversational practice, but also prestige to a temple community in which foreigners would travel to and be interested to visit."[71] The monks see Chinese tourists as the "familiar" Other. As opposed to the Westerners, who might have little to know familiarity with Buddhism and Thailand, Chinese tourists generally have some knowledge.[72] Yet, the monks treat Muslims as the most "distant" Other. According to the monks, Muslims display less interest in Buddhism than the Christian Westerners. Some of these monks and other Thai Buddhists see Muslims as a threat to their country and Buddhism.[73] Also, in the contemporary period, there is a perception among Buddhists in Thailand, as well as in Myanmar, that Buddhist monks are not allowed into mosques.[74]

It is not just Muslim tourists who are the "distant" Other. Even Thai Muslims endure the perception of being "distant." In southern Thailand, Thai Malay Muslims are doubly displaced from normative identity due to their Malay ethnicity and Muslim identity.[75] When this displacement couples with perceived threats to normativity, the caricature becomes more pronounced. It gravitates from the "distant" other to the beastly other.

---

[70] Pattana Kitiarsa, "An Ambiguous Intimacy: *Farang as Siamese Occidentalism*," in *The Ambiguous Allure of the West: Traces of the Colonial in Thailand*, eds. Rachel V. Harrison and Peter A. Jackson (Hong Kong: Hong Kong University Press, 2010), 57–74.

[71] Brooke Schedneck, "Religious Others, Tourism, and Missionization: Buddhist 'Monks Chats' in Northern Thailand," *Modern Asian Studies* 52, no. 6 (2018): 1888–1916.

[72] Schedneck, "Religious Others."

[73] Schedneck, "Religious Others."

[74] Iselin Frydenlund, interviews, Bangkok, Yangon and Mandalay 2015. Certain neo-conservative mosques in Myanmar do not allow non-Muslims to enter their premises.

[75] See Michael Jerryson, *Buddhist Fury: Religion and Violence in Southern Thailand* (New York: Oxford University Press, 2011), 143–177.

CONCLUSION

Theravada Buddhists have lived alongside their Muslim neighbors for centuries. Periodically, political and social strife awaken Buddhist fear-based narratives about Muslims. While unsubstantiated, these narratives work to mobilize Buddhist communities into angry respondents.

In her monograph *The Curse of Cain*, Regina Schwartz argues that the origin of violence is a person's identity formation. She locates the origin of violence in identity formation and finds that "imagining identity as an act of distinguishing and separating from others, of boundary making and line drawing, is the most frequent and fundamental act of violence we commit."[76] For Schwartz, the making of the Other is, in itself, an act of violence. Religion can be a forceful tool in the construction of exclusivist identities in violent conflict because religious teachings and practices create and maintain boundaries between the community and the outside world and may contribute to the separation between communities. The discourse of inclusion and exclusion creates a distinction between friends and enemies. This allows little room for uncertainties or ambiguous identities: unity requires strict boundaries between "self" and "other."

Buddhists have imagined their neighbors as the Other metonymically, topographically, and most insidious of all, intellectually. Often, the Buddhist depiction of the Muslim as the intellectual Other occurs in the wake of particular socio-political upheavals. In reviewing the negative Buddhist rhetoric about Muslims, Buddhists consistently depict Muslims as the barbaric Other. Or, as U Wirathu put it, Muslims are African carp that breeds quickly, are very violent, and eat their own kind. The framing of Muslims as barbaric and fearful Others triggers Buddhist communities into violence.

However, any exploration of Buddhist Othering of Muslims needs also to take into account violence committed in the name of Islam against Buddhist symbols, or in Buddhist majority societies. The 2019 terror attacks in Sri Lanka, albeit not directed at Buddhist symbols or institutions, represent a new chapter in Buddhist–Muslim relations in Asia, one which affects not only Buddhist–Muslim affairs in Sri Lanka, but in Myanmar and in the wider region as well.

---

[76] Regina Schwartz, *The Curse of Cain: The Violent Legacy of Monotheism* (Chicago: University of Chicago Press, 1997), 5.

Nonetheless, in the midst of terror, fear and moral panics, it is also important to remember that islands of civility are to be found in nearly all conflict settings, or even war zones. One particular form of Buddhist–Muslim interaction is in interreligious dialogue initiatives. Interreligious dialogue here is understood as covering a wide range of initiatives, ranging from informal encounters at the local level to intentional and more formal types of interreligious interaction. Since 2012 numerous Buddhist–Muslim dialogues have been facilitated across South and Southeast Asia, including local, regional and international actors. The most famous dialogue was the so-called "Yogakarta Statement" where high-level Muslim and Buddhist leaders affirmed that both religions were religions of compassion and mercy, rejecting "the use of our religions for the purpose of discrimination and violence."[77] The notion of "critical civility" might be useful in capturing ideas and practices in which members of one group transcend the boundaries of their community to show empathy for human suffering in defined out-groups, including a broad sense of community.[78] Although certain Buddhist monks like U Wirathu, U Wimala Bhiwunta or Sitagu Sayadaw have been particularly vocal in articulating anti-Muslim sentiments—or even conveying support to military operations in Rakhine during the Rohingya exodus—other monks have challenged such exclusionism and violence.

For example, when anti-Muslim violence in Meiktila in 2013 left hundreds dead, the Buddhist monk U Withudda, the abbot of the Yadanar Oo Monastery, opened his monastery for 800 Muslims (in addition to 300 Buddhists) who took refuge in his temple premises. Amidst anti-Muslim hate speech and violence, the Buddhist monks of the Yadanar Oo monastery took great personal risk in saving hundreds of Muslim lives.[79] Together with U Seindita and U Zawtikka, U Withudda was awarded the World Harmony Awards, presented by the Parliament

---

[77] "Yogakarta Statement", or the "Final Statement: Shared Values and Commitments" from "The High-Level Summit of Buddhist and Muslim Leaders. Overcoming Extremism and Advancing Peace with Justice" (Indonesia, March 3–4, 2015), 2.

[78] Iselin Frydenlund, "Religion, Civility and Conflict—Towards a Concept of 'Critical Civility'," *Studies in Interreligious Dialogue* 23, no. 1 (2013): 109–124.

[79] Iselin Frydenlund, interviews, Mandalay 2014 and Meiktila 2015.

of the World's Religions, at the Nobel Institute in Norway.[80] In Sri Lanka, civil society groups, Buddhist, Christian and Muslim religious leaders, as well as people in culturally diverse neighborhoods, have united across religious divisions after the Easter bombings.[81] Importantly, other voices challenge destructive forms of alterity—be they Muslim or Buddhist—by emphasizing dialogue, co-operation, and efforts for the common good.

REFERENCES

Aho, James A. *This Thing of Darkness: A Sociology of the Enemy.* Seattle: University of Washington Press, 1994.

Amnesty International. *Thailand: Torture in the Southern Counter-Insurgency.* London: Amnesty International Publications, 2009. Accessed at https://www.amnesty.org/download/Documents/48000/asa390012009eng.pdf, July 1, 2019.

Barmé, Scot. *Luang Wichit Wathakan and the Creation of a Thai Identity.* Singapore: Institute of Southeast Asian Studies, 1993.

Chan, Aye, and U Shwe Zan. *Influx Viruses: The Illegal Muslims in Arakan.* New York: Arakanes in United States, 2005.

Chappell, David, W. "Buddhist Responses to Religious Pluralism: What Are the Ethical Issues?" In *Buddhist Ethics and Modern Society: An International Symposium,* edited by Charles Weihsun Fu and Sandra A. Wawrytko, 443–444. Oxford and New York: Greenwood Press, 1990.

Collins, Steven. *Nirvana and Other Buddhist Felicities.* Cambridge: Cambridge University Press, 1998.

Crouch, Melissa, ed. *Islam and the State in Myanmar: Muslim-Buddhist Relations and the Politics of Belonging.* New York: Oxford University Press, 2016.

Daily FT. "Our Fight Is for All Sri Lankans. BBS CEO." http://www.ft.lk/columns/our-fight-is-for-all-sri-lankans-bbs-ceo/4-286624. Last accessed February 20, 2018.

Dharmapala, Anagarika. *Return to Righteousness: A Collection of Speeches, Essays and Letters of the Anagarika Dharmapala,* edited by A. Guruge. Colombo:

---

[80] Parliament of Religions, "The Parliament of the World's Religions Awards Three of Burma's Leading Monks at Norway's Nobel Institute," *Parliament Blog,* January 7, 2015, https://parliamentofreligions.org/content/parliament-world%E2%80%99s-religions-awards-three-burma%E2%80%99s-leading-monks-norway%E2%80%99s-nobel-institute, last accessed February 19, 2018.

[81] https://www.bbc.com/news/av/world-asia-48068793/sri-lanka-attacks-fighting-back-with-peace?fbclid=IwAR3Kv33cul3mwSi6PIVCuEHCpFptY3rxf6uYjNoqdY-DZNYCZos8iUf3WxKk.

Anagarika Dharmapala Birth Centenary Committee, Ministry of Education and Cultural Affairs, Ceylon, 1965.

Elverskog, Johan. *Buddhism and Islam on the Silk Road*. Philadelphia: University of Pennsylvania Press, 2010.

Freiberger, Oliver. "How the Buddha Dealt with Non-Buddhists." In *Religion and Identity in South Asia and Beyond: Essays in Honor of Patrick Olivelle*, edited by Olivelle P. Lindquist. London: Anthem Press, 2011.

———. "Negative Campaigning: Polemics Against Brahmins in a Buddhist Sutta." *Religions of South Asia* 3, no. 1 (2009): 61–76.

Frydenlund, Iselin. "The Birth of Buddhist Politics of Religious Freedom in Myanmar." *Journal of Religious and Political Practice* 4 (2018): 107–121.

———. "Buddhist Islamophobia. Tropes. Themes. Actors." In *Handbook of Conspiracy Theory and Contemporary Religion*, edited by Asbjørn Dyrendal, David Robertson, and Egil Asprem. Leiden: E.J. Brill, 2019.

———. "Religion, Civility and Conflict—Towards a Concept of 'Critical Civility'." *Studies in Interreligious Dialogue* 23, no. 1 (2013): 109–124.

Gunawardana, R.A.L.H. "The Kinsmen of the Buddha." In *Religion and Legitimation of Power in Sri Lanka*, edited by B.L. Smith. Chambersburg: Anima, 1978.

———. *Robe and Plough: Monasticism and Economic Interest in Early Medieval Sri Lanka*. Tucson: University of Arizona Press, 1979.

Harris, Elizabeth. "Buddhism and the Religious Other." In *Understanding Interreligious Relations*, edited by David Cheetham, Douglas Pratt, and David Thomas. Oxford and New York: Oxford University Press, 2013.

Hodgson, Marshall G. S. *Rethinking World History: Essays on Europe, Islam and World History*. Cambridge: Cambridge University Press, 1993.

Holt, John, ed. *Buddhist Extremists and Muslim Minorities: Religious Conflict in Contemporary Sri Lanka*. New York: Oxford University Press, 2016.

Inden, Ronald. "Orientalist Constructions of India." *Modern Asia Studies* 20, no. 3 (July 1986): 401–446.

Jenkins, Stephen. "On the Auspiciousness of Compassionate Violence." *Journal of the International Association of Buddhist Studies* 33, no. 1–2 (2010): 299–331.

Jerryson, Michael. *Buddhist Fury: Religion and Violence in southern Thailand*. New York: Oxford University Press, 2011.

Jones, James W. *Blood That Cries Out from the Earth: The Psychology of Religious Terrorism*. New York: Oxford University Press, 2008.

Kapstein, Matthew T. "*Just Where on Jambudvipa Are We?* New Geographical Knowledge and Old Cosmological Schemes in Eighteenth Century Tibet." In *Forms of Knowledge in Early Modern Asia: Explorations in the Intellectual History of India and Tibet, 1500–1800*, edited by Sheldon Pollock, 336–364. Durham: Duke University Press, 2011.

Keen, Sam. *Faces of the Enemy: Reflections of the Hostile Imagination.* New York: HarperCollins, 1986.

Keyes, Charles. "Political Crisis and Militant Buddhism." In *Religion and Legitimation of Power in Thailand, Laos, and Burma*, edited by Bardwell L. Smith, 147–164. Chambersburg, PA: ANIMA Books, 1978.

Kitiarsa, Pattana. "An Ambiguous Intimacy: *Farang as Siamese Occidentalism.*" In *The Ambiguous Allure of the West: Traces of the Colonial in Thailand*, edited by Rachel V. Harrison and Peter A. Jackson, 57–74. Hong Kong: Hong Kong University Press, 2010.

Kristof, Nicholas. "21st Century Concentration Camps." *New York Times*, June 16, 2014.

Lone, Wa, Kyaw Soe Oo, Simon Lewis, and Antoni Slodkowski. "Massacre in Myanmar: A Special Reuter's Report." *Reuters*, February 8, 2018. https://www.reuters.com/investigates/special-report/myanmar-rakhine-events/.

Long, Charles H. *Significations: Signs, Symbols, and Images in the Interpretation of Religion.* Aurora, CO: The Davies Group, 1995.

Lopez, Donald S. *From Stone to Flesh: A Short History of the Buddha.* Chicago: University of Chicago Press, 2013.

Mahānāma. *Mahāvaṃsa.* Translated by W. Geiger. London: Pali Text Society, 1912.

Parliament of Religions. "The Parliament of the World's Religions Awards Three of Burma's Leading Monks at Norway's Nobel Institute." *Parliament Blog*, January 7, 2015. https://parliamentofreligions.org/content/parliament-world%E2%80%99s-religions-awards-three-burma%E2%80%99s-leading-monks-norway%E2%80%99s-nobel-institute. Last accessed February 19, 2018.

Pitsuwan, Surin. *Islam and Malay Nationalism: A Case Study of Malay-Muslims of Southern Thailand.* Bangkok: Thai Khadi Research Institute, Thammasat University, 1985.

Schedneck, Brooke. "Religious Others, Tourism, and Missionization: Buddhist 'Monks Chats' in Northern Thailand." *Modern Asian Studies* 52, no. 6 (2018): 1888–1916.

Schmidt-Leukel, Perry. *Buddhism and Religious Diversity.* London: Routledge, 2012.

Schissler, Matt, Matthew Walton, and Phyu Phyu Thi, "Reconciling Contradictions: Buddhist-Muslim Violence, Narrative Making and Memory in Myanmar." *Journal of Contemporary Asia* 47, no. 3 (2017): 376–395.

Schwartz, Regina. *The Curse of Cain: The Violent Legacy of Monotheism.* Chicago: University of Chicago Press, 1997.

Silk, Jonathan A. "What, if Anything, Is Mahāyāna Buddhism? Problems of Definitions and Classifications." *Numen* 49, no. 2 (2002): 355–405.

9 BUDDHISTS, MUSLIMS AND THE CONSTRUCTION OF DIFFERENCE 297

Smith, Jonathan Z. *Relating Religion: Essays in the Study of Religion*. Chicago: University of Chicago Press, 2004.

Tambiah, Stanley J. *The Buddhist Saints of the Forest and the Cult of Amulets: A Study in Charisma, Hagiography, Sectarianism, and Millennial Buddhism*. Cambridge: Cambridge University Press, 1984.

The Book of the Discipline (Vinaya-Pitaka): Vol. I (Suttavibhanga). Translated by Isaline Blew Horner, 1938. Oxford, UK: Pali Text Society, 1992.

The Book of the Discipline (Vinaya-Pitaka): Vol. III (Suttavibhanga). Translated by Isaline Blew Horner, 1942. Oxford, UK: Pali Text Society, 1983.

Tin Aung Kyaw. "Buddhist Monk Wirathu Leads Violent National Campaign Against Myanmar's Muslims." *GlobalPost*, June 21, 2013. https://www.pri.org/stories/2013-06-21/buddhist-monk-wirathu-leads-violent-national-campaign-against-myanmars-muslims. Accessed March 25, 2018.

Walters, Jonathan S. "Buddhist History: The Sri Lankan PāliVaṃsas and Their Community." In *Querying the Medieval: Texts and the History of Practices in South Asia*, edited by J. S. Walters, R. Inden, and D. Ali. Oxford: Oxford University Press, 2000.

Walton, M., M. McKay, and Ma Khin Mar Mar Kyi. "Women and Myanmar's 'Religious Protection Laws.'" *Review of Faith and International Affairs* 13, no. 4 (2015): 36–49.

"Yogakarta Statement" or the "Final Statement: Shared Values and Commitments" from "The High-Level Summit of Buddhist and Muslim Leaders. Overcoming Extremism and Advancing Peace with Justice." Indonesia, March 3–4, 2015.

INDEX

A

Abhyankaron, Ramachandra B., vii
Afghanistan, vi, 92, 115, 117, 218, 281
agriculture, 27–28, 33–36, 40, 43, 45–46, 48, 50, 55–57, 115, 242
  aquaculture, 44
  gama (agrarian village), 35, 45, 46. *See also* plantation economy
  Jhum, 242, 247, 248
  Sri Lanka, 25–56
ahimsa, 276
Ahmed, Akbar, 129–130
Aho, James, 274
Allen, Charles, x
alterity, 311–312, 322, 344. *See also* Jonathan Z. Smith
animals, 271, 276
  killing of, 276
  sacrifice, 6
  realm of, 271
Animism, 231, 247
ancestor, 183
  worship, 64
annexation

Chittagong Hill Tracts, 241
  Pakistan, 88–89
Anti-Fascist People's Freedom League (AFPFL), 86–89
Association of Southeast Asian Nations (ASEAN), 4
asura, 271

B

Balkanization, 130
Bamar Buddhists, v, 202, 206–208, 213–217, 221
Bamar Muslim Conference, 86–87
Bangkok, 105, 106, 111–116, 118, 119, 120, 124, 127, 187. *See also* Thailand
  Arab quarter, 116
Bangladesh, 2–4, 8, 10–13, 18, 89, 92, 115, 117, 162, 202, 218, 221, 227–257, 290. *See also* Chittagong
  1971 independence, 243
  1977 Constitution, 11, 243–246; Islamization, 246

© The Editor(s) (if applicable) and The Author(s), 299
under exclusive license to Springer Nature Singapore Pte Ltd. 2020
I. Frydenlund and M. Jerryson (eds.), *Buddhist-Muslim Relations in a Theravada World*, https://doi.org/10.1007/978-981-32-9884-2

300 INDEX

anti-Buddhist/anti-CHT; 2012 attacks, 228; "Maga/Mog", 228, 232–238, 245, 248, 250, 254, 256; violence, 227, 254–255

Buddhist presence, 249–252. *See also* Chittagong Hill Tracts (CHT)

Hindu Bouddho Christian Oikyo Parishad, 246

peace, 253–254

population, 245–246

Barua, Mitra, 8, 18, 227–257, 277

Bastin, Rohan, 7, 16, 25–58, 278

Battuta, Ibn, 31–32

Benjamin, Walter, 191

bhikkhu/s, 103, 280

Buddhadasa, 121

Bodu Bala Sena (BBS), 26, 55, 140–145, 1458–151, 153, 154–155, 160, 161–162, 164, 284–285, 290. *See also* Sri Lanka

British East India Company, 240

Buchanan, Francis, 233–234

Buddha, x, 9, 35, 37, 178, 207, 267, 269, 272, 247–276

Bamiyan statues, vi, vii, 92, 200, 281

footprint, 9

Mahamuni, 200

tree of wisdom, x

Buddhism

bandāra deity, 38–40

Bodhi tree, 272

reformism, 121–122, 280

Buddhist constitutionalism, 11–13, 127–128, 146

Buddhist-Muslim relations

peace, 3, 78, 25–254, 293–294; inter-faith projects, 78, 94; inter-religious dialogue, 120, 127, 293, 294

Burma, 10, 63–94. *See also* Myanmar

1857 Panthay Rebellion, 68

anti-Indian, 209–210, 212–213. *See also* riots

boycotts, 79, 84–85, 91

colonial period, 82–88, 197

precolonial period, 78–81

Riot Inquiry Committee, 210, 211

Burmese politics

1982 Citizenship Law, 12, 69, 93, 213, 218

Burma Laws Act of 1898, 73

Burma Socialist Programme Party (BSPP), 91, 212–213

Indo-Burma Immigration Agreement, 211

Ne Win, 114, 212–213

Revolutionary Council (RC), 212

State Law and Order Restoration Council (SLORC), 213–214

State Peace and Development Council (SPDC), 213–214

U Nu, 88–91, 212

Young Monks' Association, 85, 89

C

Cambodia, 7, 108, 169, 266, 281

capitalism, 118, 121, 124, 129–130

petro-capitalism, 53

plantation, 45–50. *See also* plantation economy

caste system, 33, 37, 208, 233

goyigama, 36, 55

Sinhalese, 7, 36–38, 43–45, 46–47, 55, 57; feudalism, 44

Thai, 109

Ceylon, 10, 47, 280. *See also* Sri Lanka

Ceylon Legislative Council, 48–49

Ceylon Moors, 47, 49

Chakma, 231, 239–240, 243, 255

Chakma, Bhumitra, 241, 244

Chan, Aye, 290

Chappell, David, 267–268

INDEX 301

Charney, Michael, 8, 70
Charteris-Black, Jonathan, 204
Cheesman, Nick, 69, 93
China, 5–6, 29, 31, 74, 103, 105,
110, 116, 211, 266, 291
  Buddhists, 174
  Chinese New Year, 174
  Muslims, 116–117
  Yunnan, 9, 68, 116
Chittagong, 229. *See also* Bangladesh
  Arakan region, 82, 87–89, 228,
  227–257
  Chittagong Uprising, 253
Chittagong Hill Tracts (CHT), 10, 15,
227, 239–248
  1997 Peace Accord, 247
  Buddhist presence, 246–251; associations, 251–252
  Hill Students Society, 247
  labeling of, 244; ethnic designation,
  252–254, 256–257; *Jumma*,
  248–249, 256
  People's Solidarity Association, 247
  resettlement, 246; "Shanti Bahini",
  245
  religious diversity, 230–231, 248,
  256
Christianity, 26, 30, 32–33, 41–46,
48, 57, 79, 83, 86, 88, 126, 127,
156, 231, 233, 246, 247, 277,
279, 280, 291, 294
  Anglican, 44–45
  Roman Catholicism, 33, 41,
  51, 58
circumcision, 6, 183
civility, 3, 273, 293
Collins, Steven, 271
colonialism, 6–13, 16, 118, 278–279
  British, 9–10, 32, 44–45, 76,
  81, 222; Burma, 10, 79–88,
  206–207, 279–280; Ceylon,
  10, 49, 280; Chittagong Hill

Tract, 239–242, 256; India, 10,
81, 83, 207, 234
  Portuguese, 42
communism, 266, 281
  Burma, 88, 211–212
  violence against, 264
conversion, 5, 15, 17, 42, 45, 81, 173,
176–180, 184, 186–189, 200,
239, 288
  kham phi, 184
  laws, 26, 220–221
corvée labor, 108
Cox's Bazar, 229, 232, 249, 257. *See
also* Bangladesh
Crouch, Melissa, 66, 72

D
dakwah (dawah), 120, 123. *See also
salafi*
Dalrymple, William, x
Dambadeni Asna text, 7, 38
Day of Judgment, 182. *See also* Islam
death, 173, 183, 188, 189, 191–193.
  See also Satun
  rituals, 18
democracy, 129
  democratization, 48, 49
  Myanmar, 198, 200, 213–214
  Sri Lankan, 152–153
demons, 204, 272, 274, 277–278
  deity-demon, 38–40
deracination, myth of, 18, 83, 93,
197–222, 281
  969 Movement, 92, 215–221, 283.
  See also Islamophobia
  Ma Ba Tha Movement, 215–221,
  283, 289
de Silva, K.M., 34–36
de Silva, Premakumara, 7, 16, 25–58,
278
dhamma, 35, 121, 263, 275

302 INDEX

Dharmapala, Anagarika, 146, 280
dietary restrictions
  Buddhism, 121, 182, 234
  Islam, 117, 119, 216, 235, 277–278
Dobama Asiayone, 84. *See also* Burma,
  nationalism
Dutch
  colonialism, 9, 43–46, 57, 231
  Dutch East India Company (VOC),
    44, 46
  Dutch Reformed Church, 44, 46

E

economy, 14, 44, 146, 162, 279
  plantation economy, 46, 50, 52
  "religious", 86
  spice, 39, 43, 45, 57
education, 14, 55, 78, 87, 110–112,
  117–118, 128, 159, 163, 207,
  253
Egypt, vii, 116
Elverskog, Johan, v–xi, 6, 16, 277
Eriksen, Thomas Hylland, 123
essentialism, 122–130
ethnicity, 7, 9–12, 17. *See also*
  Chakma, Chittagong Hill Tracts
  (CHT), race/racism, Rohingya,
  Sinhala, Tamils
  Bangladesh, 227, 231, 238–239,
    245, 247–249, 250, 2252–253,
    256–257
  Myanmar/Burma, 63–68, 70–71,
    72, 75, 82–83, 87–88, 93, 286
  purity, 15, 16
  Sri Lanka, 26–28, 31–38, 43,
    47–51, 54–58, 145, 147, 150,
    162, 164–165, 284
  Thailand/Siam, 102–107, 109–111,
    114–115, 116–117, 122–125,
    128–131, 212, 214, 279, 291
exclusivism, 267–268, 292. *See also*
  Oliver Freiberger

F

Farook, Latheef, 159–160
fascism, 86, 110, 112
federalism, 90
feminism
  solidarity, 161
  Sri Lanka, 143, 150, 161–165; Al
    Muslimaath, 163; mistrust of
    address, 150, 163
festivals, 33, 175, 178
  Eid, 79
  Tenth Month Festival, 174
feudalism, 44, 53. *See also* caste system
forest monks, 273–274
Freiberger, Oliver, 267–268
Friedman, Jonathan, 129
Frydenlund, Iselin, 1–19, 93, 263–294
fundamentalism, 54, 129–130, 164,
  217, 246, 285. *See also* Islam,
  Islamophobia

G

gender, 13, 17, 36, 123, 139–165,
  265, 288–289
  femininity, 140
  Global Gender gap index, 162
  hierarchies, 159, 162
  masculinity, 140, 142, 150; preda-
    tory, 155–159
  sexual violence, 149–151, 156–158,
    160
  treatment of women, 77, 143;
    Muslim women, 148–151,
    158–165; Sinhalese women, 154
genocide, v, viii, xi, 71
ghosts, 271, 285
Gilquin, Michel, 125
globalization, 13, 53, 121, 124,
  129–130
  glocal, 289
gonibilla, 148–149, 153. *See also* Sri
  Lanka

INDEX   303

Great Depression, 210
Green, Nile, 86, 248
Grottanelli, Cristiano, 13

H
Haniffa, Farzana, 13, 17, 55, 139–165, 284
Harris, Elizabeth, 268
Hatch, Rodney, vii
headscarf, 145, 159. *See also* Islam
  burqa, vii, 161, 285
  hijab, 120, 148, 159–161, 163
  niqab, 120, 145, 148–150, 152–153, 155–157, 159, 163, 285, 290
Hertz, Robert, 192
Hindu Bouddho Christian Oikyo Parishad (Unity Council), 246
Hinduism, x, 28, 44, 46, 75, 76, 83, 84, 86, 103, 106, 197, 208, 218, 277–278, 280
  Bangladesh, 230–232, 234–236, 240, 243, 246, 248, 253
  Hindu-Buddhist, 31–32, 35, 57, 106
  India, 251, 255
  Tamil, 34, 35, 44–46
Hodgson, Marshall, x, 271
Horstmann, Alexander, 119
Human Rights Watch, 203

I
Ibrahim, Azeem, 71
Ibrahim, Muhammad, 108
Ikeya, Chie, 74, 77, 83, 211
impermanence, 271
India, 6, 8, 10, 18, 26, 32, 42, 53, 110, 203, 218, 246, 247, 266
  Bengali identity, 250–254
  Bihar state, 232

Brahmanical traditions, 266
Buddhist presence, 280
end of the Dharma, 6, 8
Hindu presence, 255
independence, 72, 83, 117, 279
Modi, Narendra, xi
Muslim presence, x, 2, 5; in
    Myanmar, 64, 67–69, 71–77,
    80–86, 198, 199, 201, 207–215, 221; in Thailand, 114
Punjabi state, 243
Tripura state, 231
India-Pakistan formation, 227, 242
Indophobia, 84, 215. *See also* India
Indonesia, 104, 114–115, 120, 124, 169, 218, 281
  Aceh, 235
  cannibalism, 235
  Muslims, 104, 115
Iran, 5
  Iranian Revolution, 124
  Qum, 124
Iraq, 281, 288
Islam, 27, 86, 89, 90, 111, 113–115, 116–117, 124, 230, 276, 279–282
  dhimmi status, 6
  dress. *See also* headscarf; *abhaya*, 145, 148, 149, 285
  Islamification/Islamization, 2, 11, 16, 122, 217, 218, 220, 221, 245, 246, 281, 289
  law, 73, 103, 186–187, 289
  Mawlid al-Nabi, 124
  movements, 120, 170; piety, 163–165
  reformists, 118–120. *See also salafi*, Wahhabism
  rituals, 112, 127, 181, 184, 236; Shia Muharram rite, 9, 108
  Shia, 7, 9, 108, 114, 124
  Sufi, 16, 79, 120–121

304 INDEX

Islamophobia, vii–viii, x, 77, 94,
  125–126, 148–152, 198, 215,
  217, 281, 289
  Muslim Kluen Phut, 126. *See also*
    Thailand
  Myanmar/Burma, 197, 287
Ismail, Qadri, 162

J
Jainism, 290
Japakiya, Ismail Lutfi, 119
Japan, 72, 87, 110, 112
  Shintoism, 266
Jenkins, Steven, 275
Jerryson, Michael, 1–18, 263–294
jihadism, 143, 285, 289
  conspiracy theories, 140, 147,
    152–153, 217–218, 285–286,
    289
Joll, Chris, 9, 17, 101–131, 279, 282,
  283
Judaism, 32, 156, 277, 279
  anti-Semitism, 280
justification of violence, 2, 264, 265,
  274–276. *See also* othering

K
Kachin, 214. *See also* Myanmar
Kalacakra Tantra text, 6, 277–278
karma, 181–182, 271, 275
Kayin, 214. *See also* Myanmar
Keck, Stephen, 68, 76–77, 81–82, 85
Keen, Sam, 265, 276. *See also* othering
kenduri arwah, 183
Keyes, Charles, 125–127
kingdom/s, China
  Qing, 68
  Yunnan, 9, 68, 116
kingdom/s, India, 28

Chola, 28–30, 34
Mughal, 6, 8–9, 18, 227–257, 277;
  Magadha, 232, 250–251, 256
Pegu, 234–235, 237
Tripura, 231
kingdom/s, Mongol, 68, 277
kingdom/s, Myanmar/Burma, 7, 206
  Arakan, 8, 18, 67–68, 80–82,
    227–257
  Ava, 80
  Mrauk-U, 8
  Pagan/Bagan, 8, 68
kingdom/s, Sri Lanka/Ceylon, 34
  Dambadeniya, 7–8, 37–39, 43
  Kandy, 42–51
  Kotte, 32, 40–42
  Lanka, 7
  Rājaraṭṭa, 28–29, 34–35
  Sītavāka, 42
kingdom/s, Thailand. *See also* state
    formation
  Ayutthayan, 9, 105–108, 114–115
  Patani, 101, 103, 106–107, 282
  Siamese, 7, 101–130, 278–279
  Sukhothai, 105, 107
king/s, Myanmar/Burma
  Anawrahta, 64, 78
  Bayinnaung, 79
  Bodawpaya, 79
  Mindon, 75, 79, 208
  Naramithla, 80
  Thibaw, 80, 251, 256
king/s, Sri Lanka, 30
  Bhuvanekabāhu VII, 42
  Dharmapala IX, 42
  Duṭṭhagamaṇi, 263, 275. *See also*
    vamsa literature
  Jaffna, 31–32
  Māgha, 28
  Parākaramabāhu I, 30
  Vijayabāhu VI, 41

INDEX 305

Vīra Alakeśvara, 32
Wattimi (Galē) Baṇḍāra, 38–41, 43
king/s, Thailand
Bhumiphol, 127
Maha Vajiralongkorn (Rama X), 128
Mongkut (Rama IV), 121, 278
Narai (Ramathibodi III), 107–108
Rama I, 105, 115
Rama V (Chulalongkorn), 115, 278
Ramkhamhaeng, 107
Vajiravudh, 279
Kitiarsa, Pattana, 291
Ko, Taw Sein, 76
Kodikara, Chulani, 144, 162
Kristof, Nicholas, 287
Kyaw, Nyi Nyi, 10, 18, 84, 93,
197–222, 279, 281
Kyi, Daw Aung San Suu, v, 214, 222,
286

L
language, 17, 30, 74, 80
Bengali, 11, 115, 227, 230,
243–244, 248, 250, 253–254;
Chittagong, 229
Burmese, 81, 202, 252
Gujerati, 115
Malay, 282
Pashto, 115
Persian, 31–32, 33–35, 230
Rohingya, 69
Sinhala, 10, 33–35, 40
Tamil, 7, 27, 30–32, 34–35, 144
Thai, 103, 111, 117–118, 170, 173,
181, 282
Urdu, 11, 86, 243
Laoutides, Costas, 71, 254
Lebanon, 116
Liberation Tigers of Tamil Ealam
(LTTE), 139, 144–145, 161

Libya, 113
Lincoln, Bruce, 13
Long, Charles, 269

M
magic, 39, 65–66
Mahayana, 270
Malaysia, 3–4, 101, 106, 115,
120–121, 169, 176, 181, 183,
218, 281
colonialization, 282
marriage, 170
marriage, 31, 250, 252
inter-faith, 13–16, 83–85, 154, 170,
239, 250, 252, 288
Myanmar/Burma, 12, 83–85, 200,
208–209, 216–217; Special
Law relating to Marriage of
Myanmar Buddhist Women,
220–221, 288–289
polygamy, 37, 217, 219
Sri Lanka, 144
Thailand, 117–118, 173, 175–178,
183. *See also* Satun
McCargo, Duncan, 125–127
meditation, 15
merit-making, 15
Thailand, 179–184, 187–190, 192;
phasa khaek, 181, 182; *phasa
khaek, nuri*, 183; *phasa thai*,
181, 182; *phasa thai, suat nam*,
183; *satsana*, 180–181
migration, labor, 48, 54, 55, 207
misogyny, 145, 150–151, 164. *See also*
gender, othering
modernization, 10, 17, 56, 118, 121,
123, 125
monastery, 13, 278, 283. *See also* wat
as military headquarters, 283. *See
also* Thailand

Bodh Gaya, x
Nalanda, vi–viii
Yadanar Oo, 293–294
Mongolia, 266
monk/s, Myanmar/Burma
  Sayadaw, Sitagu, 216, 263, 265, 275, 293
  U Seindita, 293
  U Wimala Bhiwunta, 293
  U Wirathu, 92, 218, 219, 264–265, 283–284, 292–293
  U Withudda, 293–294
  U Zawtikka, 293
monk/s, Sri Lankan. *See also bhikkhu/s*, Bodu Bala Sena (BBS), Sinhala
  Abhayatissa, Madegoda Thero, 149, 151, 153–154
  Gnanasara, Galebodathe, 141–143, 149, 154, 285
  Rathana, Athuraliye, 285
monk/s, Thai, 346. *See also bhikkhu/s*
  Apichat, Phra Maha, 283–284
  Kittiwuttho, 264
  Payutto, Prayudh, 126
  Medee, Korn, 129
  Thammayut order, 121
morality, 12, 122, 276
  moral panic, 284, 286, 293
mosque, 33, 47, 51–52, 58, 77, 91–92, 290, 291
  Bangladesh, 231, 253
  conspiracy theory of weaponization, 284, 290
  Myanmar, 200
  Sri Lanka, 150, 284
  Thailand, 107, 112, 115–116, 117, 121, 177, 180, 187, 283
Muhammad, Tahir, 234–235. *See also* Bangladesh
Muslim. *See also* Islam, Rohingya, Zerbadee
  Cham, 108, 114, 124–125

ethnification, 122–125
"indigenous", 68–72
Kaman, 67, 198
Malay, 3, 10, 122–125, 218
Myanmar, v–xi, 1–4, 8–9, 63–94, 197–222, 286–290. *See also* Burma
  anti-Muslim, 281, 287–288; boycotts, 91, 216
  Burman Konbaung dynasty, 75
  population, 198, 215, 220, 289
  post-independence; Parliamentary Period, 88–91
  Rangoon, 69, 77, 82, 85, 91, 200, 206, 251, 252; University, 211
Myanmar politics
  2015 Myanmar elections, 12, 16, 77, 199
  Burma Moslem Society, 71
  General Council of Burmese Associations (GCBA), 83, 208
  Ministry of Immigration and Population (MIP), 214, 222
  National League for Democracy party (NLD), 77
  Race Protection Bills, 217, 288. *See also* race and religion laws
  State Law and Order Restoration Council (SLORC), 213–214
  State Peace and Development Council (SPDC), 213–214
  Union Solidarity and Development Party (USDP), 77, 199
  Young Men's Buddhist Association (YMBA), 206–207
Myint, Thein Pe, 210, 279
Myint-U, Thant, 75, 79
Myth, 18, 37–41, 197–222, 278, 281

N
nationalism, 9–11, 204
  Bangladesh, 244, 245, 257

Myanmar, 10, 84, 197–222
Sri Lankan, 36, 51–53, 151, 162;
　bhumiputra, 26; Sinhalese, 10,
　146
Thailand, 10, 109–110, 114
Nishii, Ryoko, 14, 17–18, 169–193,
　282

O

Occidentalism
Siamese, 291
Orientalism, viii, 36
othering, 74–78, 148, 265–281, 283,
　290–292
anti-colonial constructions,
　278–279
barbaric other, 292
distant other, 290–291
Hinayana, 270
kalar, 72, 74, 210–211, 279
khaek, 284
"Maga/Mog", 236, 256
models; linguistic/intellectual,
　273–277, 281, 292; metonym-
　ical, 270, 292; topographical,
　270–273, 292
of Rohingya, 264
of women, 143–144, 149–151,
　153–165
proximate other, 290
yakkhas, 274. *See also* demons
Oung, U May, 207. *See also* Myanmar

P

Pali Canon, 103, 267–268, 276
Pakistan, 10–11, 87–88, 115, 117,
　126, 227, 228, 255
postcolonial, 242–248
East, 88, 117, 243. *See also*
　Bangladesh
photography

aura loss, 228. *See also* Walter
　Benjamin
pilgrimage, 9, 89, 272, 282
Mecca, 113
piracy
Moghs, 236, 237–238, 250, 256
Kotte Period, 40–41, 44
plantation economy, 44–50, 52, 146,
　162
pluralism, 6, 125, 127, 129, 131,
　267–268
president, Sri Lanka
Rajapaksa, Mahinda, 55, 142–144,
　150, 164, 284
Sirisena, Maithripala, 142
prime minister, Thailand
Chan-o-cha, Prayut, 127

Q

qadi, 111
Qadriyyah, 120. *See also* Islam,
　Thailand
turuq, 121
queen/s, Thailand
Sirikit, 114
Quran, 13, 111, 127, 159, 178, 228

R

race/racism, 10. *See also* fascism
Myanmar/Bamar, 12, 16, 75,
　84–85, 197–198, 202, 206,
　207–211, 213, 215–221, 222,
　280, 289
Sri Lanka, 25–26, 29, 144, 149,
　164, 284–295
Thailand, 109–110
race and religion laws, 16, 216, 288,
　289
radial polity, 105, 109
Rakhine State, 8, 65, 67, 70–71, 82,
　92, 93, 198, 218, 231, 253, 255,

308 INDEX

257, 290, 293. *See also* Myanmar, Rohingya
Buddhists, v, 71, 216, 218–219, 228, 232, 237
violence, 216, 228, 286
regicide, 42
reincarnation/rebirth, 181–183, 271
bhavacakra, 271
realms, 217
reproduction, 13, 27, 149–154, 161–162, 288. *See also* gender, sexuality
abortion, 155
conspiracy theory of sterilization, 284, 286
family planning, 152, 155
reproductive health, 144
wombfare, 219
riots. *See also* race and religion laws
Myanmar/Burma, 200–202; anti-Chinese, 163, 200, 213; anti-Indian, 210–211; anti-Indian, 1930, 10, 199; anti-Muslim, 33, 211; anti-Muslim, 1938, 10, 200
Rakhine, 215, 221
Sri Lanka; anti-Muslim, 33; Catholic-Buddhist Kotahena, 49; Chilaw grain riots, 50–52
Rohingya Muslims, v, 2, 4, 8, 12, 14, 65–94, 215, 218, 221, 264, 290. *See also* Myanmar
citizenship, 12, 216, 218–219, 221, 290
population, 198, 288
Bangladesh, 255, 290, 293; Arakanese Rohingya Salvation Army, 257
violence against, 198, 202, 254–256, 264; ethnic "cleansing", v, 2, 26, 286
Rwanda, 203

S
Said, Edward, 236
salafi, 118–120, 122, 129–130, 145. *See also* Islam, Wahhabism
Sangha, 35, 36, 55, 111, 164
sasana, 12, 109, 127, 207, 279
Satun, 120, 169–193. *See also* Thailand
conversion, 179–180
Da'wa missionaries, 174–175, 177
food, 175
funerals, 175–176, 183–186
treatment of corpses, 173, 184–192
marriage, 175–178; elopement, 177
Schedneck, Brooke, 291
Schissler, Matt, 287. *See also* Myanmar
Schwartz, Regina, 292
Scupin, Ray, 9, 17, 101–131, 279, 282, 283
Searle-Chatterjee, Mary, 248
secularism, 52, 57
Bangladesh, 243, 246
Buddhism, 112, 121
Myanmar, 211
Thai, 129, 131
sexuality, 13, 139–165, 288
Silk Road, vi–vii, 5–6
sin, 180–185, 188–189
Sinhala, 9–10, 16–17, 25–58, 139–165, 278, 280, 284–285. *See also* Sri Lanka
Dharmapala, Anagarika, 146, 280
People's Revolutionary Front (JVP), 26, 55
population concerns, 152–154, 155–156
Sinhala Ravaya, 26
Smith, Anthony, 205. *See also* nationalism
Smith, Donald, 91
Smith, Jonathan Z., 266–277, 281 290

INDEX   309

models, 268–277. *See also* othering
social media, 4, 13, 140, 158, 161,
    201, 202, 215, 287
  Bangladesh, 13, 228
  Facebook, 13, 152, 154, 201, 202,
    218, 228, 283, 289
  Myanmar, 200, 202, 215
  Sri Lanka, 152, 154–155
  Thailand, 283
  Twitter, 289
spirit propitiation rituals, 64, 66
Sri Lanka, vi, xi, 1–5, 7–11, 12,
    14–17, 18, 25–58, 139–165, 203,
    234, 254, 263–264, 272, 274,
    278, 280, 281, 283–286, 290,
    292, 294
  2004 Sri Lanka tsunami, 54
  2019 Easter attacks, 58, 285–286,
    292, 294
  anti-Muslim, 140–142, 145–146,
    152–162, 284–285; boycotts,
    147, 154; Fashion Bug, 142,
    146, 154; halal suspension,
    140–141, 147, 284–285
  Colombo, 33–34, 42, 46–48, 58,
    145–146, 160
  hydraulic civilization, 28–30, 34–35,
    53, 57
  independence, 32, 145. *See also*
    democracy
  Muslim presence; All Ceylon
    Jamiathul Ulema (ACJU),
    147, 155; Sri Lanka Muslim
    Congress (SLMC), 146
  population, 155
Sri Lankan politics
  Ceylon Legislative Council, 48, 49
  Colombo Municipal Council, 48
  Chilaw Planter's Association, 48
  Jathika Hela Urumaya, 25, 55, 286
  Orient Club, 49

state formation, 4, 9, 13–14, 27, 242,
    273–274, 279
  contemporary, 11–13
  galactic state, 7, 9, 35, 105, 111
  pre-colonial, 7
  Sri Lanka, 49, 52, 56
Strathern, Marilyn, 191–192
Sulong, Haji, 119. *See also* Islam, *salafi*
Swearer, Donald, 125
syncretism, 64, 70, 118
Syria, 30, 113

T
Tablighi Jamaat, 119, 145, 148. *See
    also* India, Islam, *salafi*
Tagliacozzo, Eric, 73, 76, 79
tajwid, 127
Tambiah, Stanley, 7, 102, 105, 123,
    273
Tamils, 7, 9, 25–58, 139–165,
    144–145. *See also* Sri Lanka
  pogrom, 54, 145
  separatist movement, 53, 284
  Thailand, 122
tariqa, 120–121
Taylor, Robert, 206
terrorism, 58, 257, 282. *See also*
    jihadism
  9/11 attack, 281
  Al Qaeda, 281
  Bhishana samaya, 153. *See also* Sri
    Lanka
  ISIS, 281, 287
  Taliban, vi, 92, 200, 281, 337
Thai constitutions
  1997 constitution, 127–128
  2007 constitution, 127–128
  2017 constitution, 127–128
Thaification, 102, 282

310 INDEX

Thailand, vi, 2–4, 7, 10–11, 14–15,
   17–18, 74, 101–131, 169–193,
   218, 280–282, 284. *See also* Satun
   2004 south Thailand; insurgency,
   102, 114, 125, 126, 130
   2006 coup d'etat, 127
   Ayutthaya period, 102, 107–109,
   114
   Bangkok period, 102, 105, 111–115
   Buddhist-Muslim; interactions.
   See also Satun, 16, 17–18,
   101–131; education, 111–112,
   178, 250; peace, 117–118,
   250, 253; violence, 14, 114,
   282–283
   Chiang Mai, ix, 117, 291
   middle class, 121
   Narathiwat province, 101, 103, 113,
   120, 170, 282
   Patani, 10, 106–107, 111, 113,
   116, 119, 282
   Pattani province, 101, 103, 118–
   119, 120, 170–171, 282
   population, 169
   Siamese state, 10, 107–108
   Southern Thailand, 169–193
   Yala province, 101, 103, 113, 119,
   120, 170, 282; Yala Islamic
   University, 119
Thai politics
   Barisan Revolusi Nasional (BRN),
   113
   Barison Revolusi Nasional-
   Coordinate (BRN-C), 113, 283
   National Liberation Front of Patani
   (LFRP), 113
   Pandin Dharma Party, 128–129,
   283
   Patani United Liberation
   Organization (PULO), 113
   Patronage Act of 1945, 112–113

Theravada, xi, 1–2, 11–12, 63–64,
   86, 101–130, 169–193, 232,
   266–267, 270, 280, 290–291
Three Pillars, 109, 111, 127. *See also*
   Thailand
   chat, 109
   phramahaksat, 109
Tibet, 6
trade, 8, 34–36, 38–40, 81
   Arab, 5–9, 25, 32, 56–57, 116, 144.
   See also Silk Road
   Bangladesh, 230
   Burma, 68, 78
   European, 9, 231, 236
   India, 29, 30, 37, 44, 50
   Muslim, 6, 8, 27, 36–56, 64, 78–
   80, 105, 116, 146–147, 276
   Tamil, 27–36
transculturation, 15
Triple Gem, 35. *See also* Buddha,
   dhamma, Sangha

U
United Nations Population Fund
   (UNFPA), 65
United States of America, 281
   US Navy, 53
urban spaces, 14, 46, 118, 147
U Seindita, 293
U Withudda, 293
U Zawtikka, 293

V
Vajrayana, 270
vamsa literature, 274, 284
   Dipavamsa, 274
   Mahavamsa, 263–264, 272,
   274–276
   Vamsatthappakasini, 274

INDEX 311

Van Schendel, Willem, 241–242, 244, 248
vegetarianism, 122
Vietnam, 108
vihāra, 35. *See also* monk/s, Sri Lanka
violence, theories of, 17, 58, 158, 201, 265, 270, 278, 292–293
  ethnicity, v, 2
village defense volunteer system, 114.
  See also Thailand

W
wage labor, 44, 47, 48
Wahhabism, 51, 119, 122
Walton, Matthew, 8–9, 17, 63–97, 279
Ware, Anthony, 71, 254
wat, 111, 114, 278, 283
Wathakan, Luang Wichit, 110. *See also* Thailand
Weber, Max, 105, 205
Westernism, viii, 118, 191, 291
Westernization, 160
women's suffrage
  Sri Lanka, 32

World Harmony Awards, 293
World War I, 51
World War II, 10, 70, 72, 87, 110, 112

X
xenophobia, 10, 52, 214. *See also* nationalism

Y
Yangon, 14, 77, 89, 91, 218, 251
Yegar, Moshe, 66–69, 79, 81, 86–88
Yemen, 116
Yi, Khin, 84
"Yogakarta Statement", 293
Yusuf, Imtiyaz, 122

Z
Zakaria, Rafia, v
Zarni, Maung, 74
Zerbadee, 69. *See also* Burma
Zheng, Admiral, 31–32
Zoroastrianism, 6, 277

9789813298866